Archival Science

ARCHIVAL SCIENCE

Education and Training In India

An All-India Perspective

DR MEENA
GAUTAM

Vitasta

Published by
Renu Kaul Verma
Vitasta Publishing Pvt Ltd
4348/4C, Ansari Road, Daryaganj
New Delhi-110 002
info@vitastapublishing.com

ISBN: 978-81-991712-7-5

First Edition 2025
MRP ₹950

The Publication of this book has been supported by the Indian Council of Historical Research. The responsibility for the facts stated or opinions expressed is entirely of the author and not of the council.

Edited by Vichitra Goel & Reena Singh
Layout by Rohit Gautam
Cover Design by Smriti Maheswari
Printed by Vikas Computer and Printers, New Delhi

वी. श्रीनिवास, आई.ए.एस.
V. Srinivas, IAS
सचिव
SECRETARY

सत्यमेव जयते

भारत सरकार,
कार्मिक, लोक शिकायत तथा पेंशन मंत्रालय,
प्रशासनिक सुधार और लोक शिकायत विभाग,
सरदार पटेल भवन, संसद मार्ग,
नई दिल्ली-110001
GOVERNMENT OF INDIA
MINISTRY OF PERSONNEL, PUBLIC GRIEVANCES & PENSIONS,
DEPARTMENT OF ADMINISTRATIVE REFORMS & PUBLIC GRIEVANCES
SARDAR PATEL BHAWAN, SANSAD MARG,
NEW DELHI-110001

MESSAGE

Dr. Meena Gautam's book– 'Archival Science: Education and Training In India" presents a comprehensive analysis on addressing the challenges of increasing volume of paper along with a boom in machine-readable records. It is imperative that archival science education and training in India are given necessary encouragement and the publication of a comprehensive research work on Archival Science is indeed very timely. While teaching history or another subject at undergraduate and post-graduate level in the colleges and universities, there is already a hidden academic linkage with archives and what we need in today's digital environment is to promote integrated studies in archival science education to meet the challenges of digital archiving in today's time. I am very confident that this project study will be a valuable source to mitigate and address these issues and will be a reference book for students of archival science in universities and colleges across the country.

(V. Srinivas)

Please Visit our Website : http://darpg.gov.in, http://goicharters.nic.in

Ph. : 91-11-23742133, Fax : 91-11-23742546 Email : vsrinivas@nic.in, secy-arpg@nic.in

Prof Rajaneesh Kumar Shukla

Former VC

Mahatama Gandhi
Antararashtriya Hindi
Vishwavidyalay
Wardha,
Maharashtra,India

Former MS
Indian Council of
Philosophical Research
New Delhi, India
&
Indian Council of
Historical Research
New Delhi. India

Professor & Head

Deptt of Comparative
Philisophy & Religion,
SSVV Varanasi. India

President
Afro-Asian Philosophy Congress.

+919415201031

rksphilosophy@gmail.com

rkshukla@ssvv.ac.in

About the book and author

It is eloquently asserted that "there can be no history without archives." In our contemporary era, the fifth revolution of information and communication technology (ICT) has ushered in a remarkable diversification of primary sources for historiography. The advancement of digital archives, however, cannot be realized without a robust foundation in archival science education, which is essential for imparting theoretical knowledge and cultivating the skills necessary for archival professionals to navigate the complexities of the 21st century's digital landscape.

This book arrives at a pivotal moment, illuminating the stark reality that the majority of universities are yet to offer dedicated courses in archival science. It tackles this pressing issue, providing a comprehensive examination that is both timely and necessary. Immense effort has been devoted to this scholarly work, and I am confident it will serve as an invaluable resource for archival professionals, fostering the growth of archival education. Moreover, it will stand as a reference for students of archival science across our universities and colleges.

I extend my heartfelt congratulations to the author for this commendable achievement and wish her every success in her future endeavors.

Prof Rajaneesh Kumar Shukla

This timely publication arrives as a significant contribution, aligning well with the earlier collaborative study by IGNCA and UNESCO on Mapping of Archives in India. In today's rapidly evolving information landscape, it compels a critical re-examination of archival theory and practice in the context of emerging technologies and their growing application in Indian archival processes. I am confident this work will serve as a valuable reference for archival professionals and students of Archival Science across the country.

— Dr Jagdish Arora
Advisor, National Board of Accreditation (NBA)
Former Director, INFLIBNET Centre

Contents

Preface

Under the subject study on Archival Science Education and Training in India, an effort has been made to study very briefly the emergence of modern archives and archival training schools in India and the impact of Western Archival training Schools on Indian Archives. Studies on archival science have been a neglected field of education in the country; hence the work was taken up in project mode for conducting research and field surveys to study and analyse the current status. In India, archival training is still evolving, as our survey widely establishes these facts.

The main objectives and scope of the research project study have been:

- To advocate and promote formal study of Archival Science Education in our schools, colleges and universities.
- To popularise the course so as to increase its demand as a discipline in view of emerging new institutional archives both in public, corporate and in the private sector, considering that there is immense scope for promotion and development of Archives as a profession.
- To help students understand that the subject offers a promising

and challenging career of an Archivist, which is both professionally and financially rewarding.

- To project the scope of the discipline as a career option to students.
- To help in preserving and understanding the value of documenting the heritage of the country as Archives that are authentic and valuable sources of information.
- To draw the attention of the government, Indian Universities and other heritage Educational Institutions to explore and take up teaching of archival science education and popularise the studies as in other western and Asian countries like China, Japan, and Singapore.

Historically, Archival education and training in India was never a subject of discussion of the British Colonial Government, despite the establishment of the UK Public Record Office in1838 by passing the Public Record Office Act. The Act was not extended to administer the archives of its Colonial Governments for upkeep of their records. The establishment of the Imperial Record Department (now the National Archives of India-NAI) in 1891 was only administrative, seeking to preserve some useful records for administrative purposes and clearing space by removing them from public offices. Instead of giving access to Indian historians and research scholars and appointing archivists, they chose the publication of selected documents and for advice, preferred to seek help from the British Historical Records Commission, thereby acting on the advice of the Royal Commission in its second report in 1914. Eventually, the Indian Historical Records Commission was established in 1919 as a government body with government officials as members. Despite demand from Indian historians, researchers and IHRC, Indian natives were not given access to these archives formally before 1939.

Archival education and training was not given due attention before Independence. It's only NAI, which provides some in-service training in Repair and Conservation of Records, but does not train future professional archivists from outside the Archives. A formal beginning was made in 1952 when NAI started a one-year Diploma Course in Archives Keeping after a number of experiments since 1942. The Archival Legislation Committee in its 1960 Report stressed on Archival Training and eventually, the School of Archival Studies was established. However, the school still looks to western practices for archival education, training and course curriculum and textbooks. Publications of the NAI are mostly selections from its record holdings, Introduction to Archives, Guide to various series of Records, and Growth of Secretariat, with less focus on preparing text books. Some books and articles have been sporadically written on archival training and published in Indian Archives or individually presented at Indian Historical Records Commission (IHRC) academic sessions, thematic conferences and seminars. Some textbooks were penned during the late 1980s by Senior and Junior Fellows, affiliated with the School of Archival Studies (SAS), but this was discontinued by 1990. Some of the archivists' attempted Ph D works on Archival subjects such as Evolution of Archives, Archives Administration, Archival Legislation, but never on Archival Science Education and Training as a full-fledged subject of study.

Even Prof Sabyasachi Bhattacharya has not touched the issue of archival education in India either during colonial rule or after Independence according to his Project Study as a Tagore Fellow with NAI on 'Colonial Archiving Policy, 1858-1947–Early Modern Historiography in India'. *(Published with the title Archiving the British Raj, by Oxford.)*

No work has been done so far on the subject of Archival

Science Education in India. The project study is simply an attempt to make a comprehensive study of the system of Archival Education in India, its beginning, evolution, growth and development and likely future trends.

The study is in two parts:

- I. Origin and development of archival science education, and training in India in historical perspective, its evolution and how it's still evolving.
- II. Its Current Status as it has been a neglected field of education during the twentieth and twenty-first centuries. The report is a narrative of the difficulties in the growth and development of archival education and training in India besides archival institutions both in the Centre and States. It doesn't delve into the historical developments or events. Rather, the objective and focus of the study has been on Archival Science Education and Training viz a viz the growth and development of archival institutions in the public sector based on Archival records.

  An attempt has been made to piece together data from archival sources since the beginning of archival education and training in India, before and after Independence. The growth and development of archival science education and training and evolution of archives and archival institutions in India complement each other. Had this not been the case, I would not have succeeded in dealing with the subject, simultaneously.

Part I of the study (Chapters 1-5) has been conducted, based on archival sources available in NAI and some important states archives.

Part II (Chapters 6-7) of the study is based on a survey conducted through a Questionnaire and field study conducted under the project. Finally, the findings of the project study are based on the survey and the field study as elaborated in chapter 7 (Conclusion). The chapterisation was based on this strategy.

The report is a narrative of the difficulties in growth and development of archival education and training in India. Chapters 1 to 5 are in Part I. Chapters 1-4 deal with the evolution, growth and development of archival education in India based on the British Colonial Government model. Chapter 5 is on relations with International bodies, important from both national and international perspectives, as the Indian archival community had played a very significant role from the 1970s to the 1990s, when India emerged as a hub centre of archival science education and training in India as the School of Archival Studies at NAI, the only institution giving education in the discipline, had been recognised by UNESCO as a regional centre for the Afro-Asia region in1980. Every year, ten to fifteen foreign students were enrolling from African and Asian countries.

For Part II of the study, two questionnaires were developed, the first for archival repositories in the public and private sector, and the second for the University Departments of History that taught the subject in some form, besides University Libraries and Archives. Field visits, personal interaction with State Archives, University Archives, Professors and students of the Department of History were conducted and appended with Chapter 6. An analytical study was then done on the basis of the replies to the questionnaires and of the field visits to various State and University Archives, Departments of History and personal discussions with archival professionals, Professors and students.

The concluding chapter gives the findings and recommendations of the research project study.

The study reveals that we need to promote and support teaching of Archival Science education as a regular degree or diploma course in our educational institutes. Besides National Archives of India, Osmania University and State Institute of Archaeology, Art, History, Conservation, and Museology are already conducting post-graduate diploma courses in Archives. The Archives of the National Centre of Biological Studies, (NCBS) Bangalore, School of Cultural Texts and Records (SCTR) Jadavpur University, and the Indira Gandhi National Centre for the Arts, besides NAI is also actively conducting courses.

The system has to keep pace with the new challenges of digital archiving and accessibility in digital environments, so that records are accessible virtually and also, online. Other basic issues also need to be addressed.

The focus earlier was on care of archival material, but now it is on the newer, digital age. With new technology, new dimensions of digitisation have been added to Archival Science Education and training, such as Metadata capturing, Ontology, Semantic Web of Libraries and archives, and tools and techniques.

Future archivists must learn and know how digitisation and digital archiving is to be done to preserve archival resources. But even these digital materials cannot survive beyond a particular time span. How one migrates the information in digital form is therefore, key to the task. Blockchain Technology is widely used as a record creating technology, and is designed so that it is impossible to hack the system or forge the data stored on it. Distributed ledger technology (DLT), a digital system for recording transactions and related data in multiple places at the same time is being used. (Lemieux, 2018, pp. 34-42)

In the process, we are moving away from professionalism to standardisation. The challenge is to maintain and keep the

Archivist relevant to Archival services by providing the narrative, yet keeping the context in the storytelling, by adding human element to the automation and at the same time, emphasising the importance of the authenticity of the material. The new breed of Archivists or information professionals need an understanding of technology, and be skilled enough to develop tools to help users in identifying records, evaluate their reliability and trace contexts.

Archivists' works are being taken over by technology firms, but they cannot substitute real Archivists who are needed as only they can preserve and provide access to contextualised evidence. It is the Archivist professional's skills and knowledge which forms the basis of our importance to society. Despite automation, Archivists will always be needed for their specific knowledge and skills. Archives will continue to be curated and Archivists will select information, apply Metadata to ensure that it is properly accessed and provide effective storage and preservation while maintaining authenticity and integrity of the material for future generations. These activities will require human intervention besides technological inputs. Sadly, there is no coordination in this piecemeal approach and all that everyone is concentrating upon is in converting from print to digital or non-print to digital or audio to digital mode without any systematic, long-term approach to planning and storing the data and the digital archiving system to be used. How are we going to make it a good information retrieval system?

Many web resources exist today for individual queries tackling archival arrangement, description and conservation practices. But the Indian archival community tends to work separately. The community would greatly benefit from sharing of resources and ideas. An archives association or common mailing groups and lists will help.

The current research work and methodology in Archival Science Education and training in India is the same as that followed in archival research, collecting data from primary and secondary source materials in NAI Records Repository and Library. Since source material is limited, oral interaction was often held with the existing faculty and students in universities. Data was also collected through online questionnaires and surveys sent to the faculty and students of University Departments of History teaching Archival Science as a subject, and to institutes offering a Diploma or Degree course.

The different archives in the country are in a bad state because of lack of trained archivists to look after them. Archives lie in store rooms and more than 500 archives have no trained Archivist to look after them. IGNCA undertook a UNESCO project on Mapping of Archival Institutions and Libraries in the country to arrive at this figure. Even Delhi University, which has Archives, does not have a trained Archivist on its rolls. But, even if DU had created a position, would suitable trained candidates have been available?

- A very pertinent question in this regard has been raised by Godrej Archives highlighting the difference between Indian Archival courses vis a vis those available abroad that train Archivists to work in the corporate, personal, business or government sectors.

First, there is no uniformity in the curriculum being followed by the Archival Training Schools and in other Institutes in India. No degree course in the subject is conducted by any Indian University as in other western and Asian countries like China, Japan and Singapore. Neither is there any uniformity in the recruitment of Archivists, except in Government Repositories like National Archives of India and the State/Union Territory archives in the country. This is also true of archives in the private, corporate and business sectors including in the new emerging Archives of Scientific and Medical Institutions in both the public and private sector. Unlike other countries like USA, there is no certification authority or regulatory body for authorising one to work as an Archivist as in Medical and other fields.

Archives and records professionals have to make the transition into new record keeping modes. Given the rise of networks in human mental models, in social relations and in the material world, it is hard to imagine a future of archives that is not networked. However, the specific form this may take is still uncertain. But it is safe to assume that records and archives professionals will likely see a networked, decentralised and autonomous future manifest in the material form of a blockchain record keeping system in which Archives and Records professionals will engage deeply with technology.

What will transpire for the future of Indian Archives in the next few decades is still unknown as humanity seems to be on the verge of a major shift in human thought. The basis of this study is to give some ideas, a kind of road map for understanding the current status and to take stock of some new ideas to move ahead.

This study will be helpful in implementing in the Heritage Institute and the NAI Archival School, taking a modern approach to Archival Science Education. Summary of the findings of the project study are analysed in Chapter VII. Archives are important and without archives one cannot visualise history. Recording history is not possible without archives as they are the only primary documented sources of information of events of the past.

So far studies in archival science have been neglected in the country, even though it has increasing potential for employment.

This study increases understanding of the subject and

analyses the future scope of the discipline as a viable career option for students looking for scope as archivists, conservators, and social scientists.

The study promotes Archival Science Education and Training in the country to produce competent professionals in the field of Archives Administration, Records Management, Conservation, Reprography, ICT and other related fields of Archival Science besides history. And the history can only be written more objectively on the basis of archival source material. To preserve archives as valuable sources of information for posterity, we need to teach Archival Science not as an optional subject but formally as a regular degree course in our Universities and Institutions.

These degree-holders, in turn, will ensure conservation and preservation of Archival documentary heritage of the country for posterity and facilitate the work of historians and research scholars to know their history while providing access to past information through modern technology.

Dr Meena Gautam

Senior Academic Fellow (ICHR) and formerly Dy Director of Archives (NAI) and Director, National Mission of Monuments, and Antiquities (NMMA), (ASI)

Foreword

In a country as historically and culturally rich as India, archives are far more than mere storehouses of memory—they are the foundational infrastructure of accountability, identity, and knowledge. Yet, despite their profound significance, the professional and academic recognition of archival science has remained marginal in our educational policy and institutional practice. This is not simply an oversight; it is a structural gap with deep implications for heritage preservation, public administration, and scholarly inquiry.

It is in this critical context that *Archival Science Education and Training in India: An All-India Perspective*, authored by Dr. Meena Gautam—former Deputy Director of the National Archives of India—emerges as a landmark study. With a practitioner's authority and a scholar's rigour, Dr. Gautam undertakes the first comprehensive national review of archival education in India. The work traces its colonial antecedents, surveys its post-Independence evolution, and critically assesses its present state through empirical fieldwork, institutional analysis, and national-level surveys.

The study is structured in two parts. The first examines the historical emergence of archival education, spotlighting its fragmented growth and lack of formal recognition. The second presents field-based insights and institutional surveys across public, private, scientific, and corporate archives. The findings are urgent: India lacks a standard curriculum, formal academic programs, or a national certification framework for archivists. Most archives—over 500 institutions, according to the IGNCA's *Mapping of Archives in India* project led by Prof. Ramesh Chandra Gaur—operate without a single trained archivist. Even major institutions, including universities, often lack the human infrastructure to care for or curate their collections adequately.

The implications are sobering. Without trained professionals, archives risk becoming inaccessible, disorganized, and disconnected from their users—whether scholars, government departments, or the public. Furthermore, as archival functions increasingly shift to digital environments, the need for archivists trained in metadata, digital preservation, ontology, and blockchain-based records management is more pressing than ever.

Dr. Gautam argues persuasively that archival science must be recognized as a specialized and interdisciplinary academic discipline in India, one that is distinct from history or library science but closely allied to both. She calls for the establishment of degree-granting programs, standardized curricula, certification mechanisms, and faculty development. Drawing on international examples—from China, Japan, the USA, and the UK—she urges Indian institutions to reimagine archival science as a profession with technological, ethical, and scholarly dimensions.

The study also offers a forward-looking vision. It emphasizes the need to integrate digital technologies into archival training—covering areas such as blockchain, semantic web, and digital conservation—while maintaining the irreplaceable human role of archivists in contextualizing records and preserving authenticity. It advocates for the adoption of the GLAM (Galleries, Libraries, Archives, Museums) model not only as a policy framework but as an educational and institutional strategy.

Perhaps most importantly, the report provides a roadmap for action. It recommends steps for the University Grants Commission, Ministry of Culture, and academic institutions to introduce and support formal education in archival science at both undergraduate and postgraduate levels. It highlights successful initiatives at institutions like the NCBS Archives, IGNCA, SCTR–Jadavpur University, and Jamia Millia Islamia, showing that innovation is possible within existing structures.

Dr. Gautam's work is more than a research study—it is a national resource. For university administrators, it offers a curriculum blueprint. For policymakers, it presents the data and analysis necessary for structural reform. For heritage professionals, it is a mirror and a manual. And for the next generation of archivists, it lays the foundation for a career that is not only essential but increasingly future-facing.

It is my sincere hope that this study receives the institutional and academic attention it deserves. The time to recognize archival science as a vital, independent discipline is now. Without archives, history is mute. Without archivists, archives are inert. The preservation of India's documentary heritage depends on our willingness to invest in both.

Ramesh C Gaur

Dean (Admin), HoD Kala Nidhi, IGNCA

Acknowledgements

I am deeply obliged to ICHR for the financial grant, in particular Dr Rajneesh Shukla, the then Member Secretary, for his support and wisdom for allowing me to take up the project and completing it in time. I am deeply grateful to Dr BR Mani, Vice Chancellor, National Museum Institute (Deemed University), for his support and in extending affiliation to the project. I would like to thank Dr Praduman K Sharma, the then Registrar and other officers of NMI and in particular, Dr Kalyani, Assistant Registrar for her moral support and encouragement. I am equally indebted to my colleagues in National Archives of India, particularly Pranav Khullar, Jt Secretary, and the then Director General, NAI for all his support and permission to access records in their Departmental Record Room, Syed Farid Ahmad, Head of School and Deputy Director, NAI and other officers in the NAI Research Room Library, particularly Ravinder in DRR, and Dhaneshwar, in Library for all their support and timely supply of records.

I would also like to thank Chandan Sinha, Director General, NAI for his kind cooperation and support in supply of Xerox copies besides the staff in the Reprography Division, JK Luthra, and Jain Micro-photographists. Without their support, it would have been difficult to complete the study in time. I cannot forget the support of the faculty and students of the School of Archival Studies, particularly Ms Kalpana Shukla, ADA, SAS, to have allowed me to use the School Library and interact with the students from time to time, extending support and help in every manner, without which I would not have completed the project study.

I am deeply indebted to Prof (Dr) RC Gaur, Head, Kalanidhi Division, IGNCA and Director, National School of Drama for his guidance and moral support from time to time while reviewing the manuscript for publication and for sharing my findings during International Archives Weeks' celebrations in June 2021, organised by IGNCA.

Last, but not the least, I owe all obligations to my family as without their support, day and night, I would not have completed the study.

Dr Meena Gautam

Archival Science Education and Training
A Modest Beginning

Introduction, Archival Training: A Beginning

The National Archives of India was established in 1891 as the Imperial Records Department (IRD) and after Independence in 1947, was renamed as the National Archives of India (NAI). Archives also existed back then in many of the Princely States in the country. There was lack of trained professional archivists and archival training institutions in the country and general ignorance about modern archival principles and practices as had evolved in western European nations in the nineteenth and early twentieth Century. The Government and the Indian Historical Records Commission (IHRC established in 1919)[1] were aware of these weaknesses of the archival profession in India.

1. IHRC Resolution dated19 March 1919;Indian Historical Records Commission: A Retrospect 1919-1948, Calcutta, 1948, pp-52-23. IHRC was set up by the GOI in 1919 as an advisory body on matters connected with proper management of Records and their use for historical research. So far it has held more than 65 sessions and has contributed significantly to the growth of Public and Government interests in the scientific management and use of Archives.

Professional training in archives in India can be traced to the year 1920. Mr Scholfield, the then Keeper of Records at IRD, had reorganised the Preservation Branch and trained menders in-house in repair techniques. State repositories turned to IRD for technical advice, support and training. In 1920, one assistant and two attendants were deputed by the Madras Records Office to IRD for training in the newly introduced methods of repair and preservation of records. The next call for help came from the princely state of Jaipur with its medieval records being the richest source of information in Mughal history, followed by Punjab in 1927. CV Joshi from the princely state of Baroda also underwent training at the Imperial Records Department followed by BN Raleraskar (after two years), and then by Assam (1930), Bombay Secretariat (1935) and Deccan College, Pune, who deputed DV Gokhale to undergo a three-month training in all branches of Archives keeping in 1941.[2]

The Government of India had been contemplating to start a training course in archival science for professionals. A beginning was made in 1941[3] necessitated by the records at IRD/NAI and in Provincial State Archives. These records needed to preserved scientific lines based on Indian archival practices in the past and modern practices found in the administration of the British colonial Government and in western countries like UK, Portugal, France, and those developed by the Dutch. Some of the notes on development of Archives in Europe in this project study are based on articles published in journals like American Archivist, Indian Archives and other journals on the subject available in the

2. F.No. August, B, 1941, No.22.IRD.
3. F.N. 49-1/42-P, Dept Edu. Health and Lands, F. No. 92-9/40-E, Resolution dated16 September 1941.

Library of National Archives of India.** The practices followed in India are those the nation inherited as a legacy of the British colonial rulers from their time in India from 1600 to 1947.

Growth of Modern Archival Practices, Education and Training in the West

Michael Duchein writes that the practice of archival administration grew in Europe as a natural 'organic' phenomenon as soon as the practice of writing on perishable materials was invented. Each European country followed its own system of archival development, linked narrowly to its governmental and bureaucratic system. He observes that despite Europe achieving some kind of cultural homogeneity since the Middle Ages, it did not see a unifying political or legal unity, between countries whose language, religion, and other cultural factors have much in common. (Duchein, 1993, p. 14)

Certain rules of keeping incoming and registering outgoing letters had been observed in the Roman and Byzantine empires. The system was adopted by the bishoprics and monasteries in Greece and Italy. Archives of the Vatican date back to the third or fourth century and practices similar to those used in Rome must have been adopted in some countries of Western Europe. This was recorded by Posner in 1940, p 159.[4] Characteristic features of the early mediaeval archives; ecclesiastical as well as secular, as pointed out by Posner were restricted to incoming materials and chiefly to instruments that had financial or legal bearing. Kings

4. Posner, 1940. P-159.

** Most of the issues are available in National Archives of India and online as well, as digitised by the Society of American Archivists. Many historians, scholars and students of history of colonialism and colonial history have widely made use of this archival material from time to time and are rereading those archives to comment on colonial narratives from their perspectives.

and princes who had no permanent residence would preserve these documents, together with the treasury and precious relics of saints, in a safe place or deposit them with the institutions of the church, and they were the first to develop a system for keeping records. Those early documents usually not connected with the chanceries or the sole or main administrative agencies during the Middle Ages, were usually independent units. Posner says that gradually; the practice of retaining copies of outgoing materials began in Europe. Ancient Greece and the Roman Empire had archival repositories, a tradition of record-keeping that survived, as stated by Duchein, 1992, p 15). These archives were later destroyed, with only a very few documents prior to 1000 AD surviving in Europe.

European archives revived only in the eleventh and twelfth centuries when the new political and religious order of the continent gradually emerged from the chaos. From that point onward, Michel Duchein observes:

> It is no longer possible to speak of 'European archives except in a purely geographical sense. All the new monarchies (German, French, English, and later Spanish), the great feudal powers, the Church, and the towns organised their own records-keeping independently so that little by little local or national traditions and methods were created, giving birth in modern times to the various archival systems which now exist.

Gradually with the emergence of local and national administration out of feudal practices, archival repositories too began to function. Silvestre in 2016 reports:

> Nearly all the Italian and Flemish towns organised the conservation and management of their archives within the framework of their municipal institutions. The archives of the

kingdom of Aragon were created in 1346. The recent 'archival turn' in the humanities has indicated the early modern age as the turning point for the establishment of central governmental archives across Europe, as a result of the explosion in record-keeping.

However, the Crown of Aragon was at the forefront of this innovative process from the fourteenth century, during which time its kings developed a number of documentary stores across the Mediterranean. The archival network was connected to the history of the state and its structure, adds Silvestre, Another description by Duchein is reproduced below:

> Two kinds of archives emerged during this period; maintaining the original documents, received in the course of transaction, preserved in a safe place as being considered precious possessions; and the registers or similar types of copied outgoing materials kept by the agency that had issued the originals. Occasionally a combination of the two sets was brought about when the chancery deemed it necessary to acquire copies of the documents received in order to have them at hand in the dispatch of its business. Official archives were consolidated towards the end of Middle Age, especially in Italy, as they began establishing archival depositories. The scope of administration expanded due to imperialistic expansions. During the 16-17th centuries Archives were concentrated; National Archives of Spain was created in 1542 and similarly records of the councils, courts, chanceries, secretaries, treasuries etc., of the Castilian Crown came together until they were concentrated by 1567.[5]

5. Duchein, 16.

In England, the foundation of the Public Record Office of the United Kingdom in 1610 was laid when James I appointed Levinus Monk and Thomas Wilson as 'Keepers and Registers of Papers and Records', creating the series of State Papers, which formed the core of the Archives. With the emergence of these 'administrative monarchies' described by Duchein in Europe, the production of records and their importance grew. It then became necessary to develop systems for their conservation, arrangement, description, and general management. The authorities now recognised the Archivist as offering a distinct activity, and this led to a demand for the development of 'Archival Science' as a subject of study by the seventeenth century.

Duchein adds that after the first-known treatise on the management of archives by Baldassare Bonifacioin 1632, several treatises and manuals appeared on the subject in Italy, France, Germany, and Spain with conflicting theories on the best methods for the arrangement and description of archives. In France, J Godefroy and J de Chevrieres recommended a chronological order while others preferred a methodical arrangement of documents by place names or according to the juridical nature of the documents.[6]

It is believed that professional growth of modern archives began after the French Revolution in 1789. Archives were declared people's property by a decree in 1794, with the responsibility of the State to maintain them for protection of people's rights and property, with their right to access public records, that had been hitherto denied. Earnest Posner notes in 1940:[7]

> Thus the French Revolution marks the beginning of new developments in the field of archives administration. First

6. Ibid
7. Posner, 1940, p.161-162.

of all, the framework of a nation-wide public archives administration was established. The Archives Nationales, was established in 1789, initially as a parliamentary archives office of the Assemble Nationale, developed under the decree of June 24, 1794 (Messidor II), into a central archives establishment of the state, to which the then existing depositories in the provinces were subordinated. Although during the first years of the Revolution the possibility of an actual centralisation of all records in the one national archive was considered, under a law of October 26, 1796, sectional and local depositories were finally organised as Archives Departmentales. The result was that for the first time an organic administration of archives covering the whole extent of existent depositories of older materials and of record-producing public agencies was established. The second main effect of the revolutionary legislation seems to have been that the state acknowledged its responsibility respecting the care of the documentary heritage of the past, after destruction of many such historical records in the early years of the revolution as monuments of the feudal regime of the country.

The third outstanding contribution of the archives legislation of the French Revolution was the principle of the accessibility of archives to the public, proclaimed by Article 37 of the Messidor decree: 'Every citizen is entitled to ask in every depository...for the production of the documents it contains.' It was not so much the desire to create opportunities for scholarly research that caused this regulation as the wish to provide for the needs of persons who had acquired part of the national property.

Scholars have mixed opinions on handling of public records during the French Revolution. Posner writes in 1940 of Minister

Garat gave to the archivist of Lille this significant advice: 'All the old documents with gothic script are presumably there as elsewhere only legal titles of feudalism, of the subjection of the feeble to the strong'; they could, therefore, be burned without hesitation.[8]

Critics of the Revolution denounced the wholesale destruction of records under the law. Archivists found fault with the system of selecting records for retention. According to Professor Judith M Panitch, the French Revolution has been widely considered as a turning point in archival history, and scholars have explored the complexities and contradictions of this crucial and critical period of history of France and how it influenced archival theory and practices, having world–wide implications.[9] Another author, Panitch observed that the Revolution fostered two divergent tendencies. Records and documents from the Old Regime were reviled and frequently destroyed, even as archival structures were developed to care for new records of the Republic, and some selected records from the past. The article treats archival institutions as cultural institutions. Panitch concludes by quoting Charles Keeskemeti, who also affirms that 'history of modern archives starts with the French Revolution'.[10]

The French Revolution and the Napoleonic wars had impacted the political, administrative and legal structure in Europe and archival theory and practices were reviewed in Europe, except in UK and Russia. By 1815, archival repositories too underwent a radical change in the Netherlands, Italy, Germany, and Spain. All archives now came under the control of new forms of government, and lost their practical and immediate relevance since they were

8. Ibid.

9. Panitch, 1966, pp.30-47.

10. Ibid,31.

associated with defunct institutions. This transition in the role of the archives had important consequences for the future, a point validated by Duchein in 1992.[11]

With these sweeping changes, new training schools to train persons in administration, management and preparation of catalogues had to be established in different European countries. One such school was established at Naples in 1811 and at Munich in 1821. The Paris Institute of Ecole des Chartes came up in 1821.[12]

Spain has a number of such archives and archival schools. The decrees governing the Archivo General de Indias (Seville) were formulated in 1792.[13] While the study of archival history and practices were evolving in the nineteenth century, the functions of an Archivist, Librarian and Museum Curator were fully recognised by the establishment of the Escuela de Diplomatica (School of Diplomatics) in 1856. The first faculty was appointed in 1858. These archivists later joined government administrative and historic archives.[14]

Madrid University started teaching archival education formally from 1900 onwards. The Teaching programme covered 350 themes, common to the intellectual and organisational skills of archivists, librarians and museum curators. Archivists

---

11. Duchein, 1992, p.17.
12. Michael Duchein, 'The History of European Archives and the Development of Archival Profession in Europe', American Archivist, Winter 1992, p.17.and Earnest Posner 'Some aspects of Archival Development since the French Revolution', American Archivist, Vol .III, No.3, July 1940 pp.160-161. Please also see 'Liberty, Equality, Posterity,': Some Archival Lessons from the Case of French Revolution' ,Judith M. Panitch, American Archivist/ Vol 59, No. / Winter 1996, pp. 30-47, Robert Bahmer,' Archives,' in Encyclopedia of Library and Information Science, vol 1(New York: Marcel Dekker, 1968), 516;James M. O'Toole, Understanding Archives and Manuscripts (Chicago; Society of American Archivists,1990), 29; Charles Keeskemeti, 'The Professional Culture of the Archivist' American Archivist, 50 (Summer 1987): 412.
13. Vicenta Cortes Alonso, 'Archival Education in Spain', American Archivist, Vol 51/Summer 1988, pp.330-331.
14. Ibid, p.331

studied Paleography, Diplomatics, Epigraphy (study of ancient inscriptions), and archival theory, History of Archives, Legislation, Philology, and Institutions. These courses were designed to produce archivists capable of selecting, organising and describing documents from any time and period or institution. Archivists were also trained to help researchers.[15] The Dutch National Archives School established in 1919, was closed in 1925 due to low enrolment, but reopened in 1955.[16]

The University of London had a School of Librarianship at University College, London since 1919 and offered a diploma in Librarianship which included teaching of English Paleography. But it did not provide specialised training for archivists till 1947, when the university introduced a one-year Diploma Course in Archives at the instance of the Deputy Keeper at the Public Record Office, London. The first session began with 15 students in October 1947.[17]

The subjects of study included Paleography, Archives Administration, Administrative History, Medieval Latin, and Anglo-Norman French. The course was open to graduates with an honours degree in arts and could be taken up, part-time. Practical work was carried out during the course, both at Public Records Office and certain County Record Offices.[18] Subsequently, more universities started under-graduate and Master's Programmes like University of Liverpool, which established the Liverpool Centre for Archive Studies and now offers a Certificate, Diploma and Master's Programme in Archives and Records Management.

15. Ibid. p. 331
16. Ibid, Archival Training in the Land of Muller, Feith and Fruin: The Dutch National School, p. 337.
17. The Indian Archives, Vol I, October 1947, No. 4, pp.353-354, the News Notes.
18. Ibid.

The curriculum was divided into three parts: Professional, Historical and International. Professional included teaching of archival theory and practices, Records Management, Information Technology and Dissertations, was taught in the historical group including modern and paleography, medieval and modern diplomatic, archives and history. International covered subjects like conservation, information and organisation, business records and environment, information management and source-based studies.

In Germany, Prussian State Archives had a one-year course of special training at the State Archives, followed by a one year's apprenticeship in a Provincial Archive. In 1930, an Institute for Archival Science and Historical Training was established by the Prussian State Archives in Berlin. But training of the 18-month course did not guarantee a job, although it was a pre-requisite for appointment as an archivist.[19]

In the Soviet Union most archives were centralised by the government in the twentieth century. The Moscow State Historico-Archival Institute (MGIAI) was established in 1931. Now there are many more, but MGIAI remains the most unique in scope, size and breadth. The Institute is administered by the State Committee for Public Education. Day classes in 1987 had 1,250 students; the evening sessions were attended by 1,800 and 2,200 took correspondence courses. This was stated in a report by Francis X Blowing Jr, during his visit to the then USSR under the US-USSR Commission on Archival Cooperation of the American Council of Learned Societies and the main Archival Administration of the then USSR Council of Ministers,

19. S.Flagg Bemis, the Training of Archivists in the USA, American Archivist, (July, 1939), Vol II. p.156.

administered in the USA by the International Research and Exchanges Board (IREX).[20]

In Austria, the Institute for Historical Research, a Department in the University of Vienna had been training archivists as it was made mandatory in 1927 by an ordinance by the Austrian Government to appoint candidates trained here in Austrian State Archives.[21]

During this time, some dedicated archivists were also making efforts to provide similar education in the United States of America. A Committee on the Training of Archivists was formed in 1936, by Samual Flagg Bemis to bring in a report with recommendations for the training of Archivists in America.[22]

After a review of foreign practices, American archives were divided into two groups; federal, state and local government archives; and archives of business houses, churches, universities, colleges, hospitals and other public and private institutions. The first group seeking education and training for the position of responsible archival direction in major municipal, state and national archives, were designated archivists of the first class and required training as Doctor of Philosophy in American history, at par with a PhD degree, in preparation of a career in Archives. The second group included archivists of small municipal divisions, county states, and special commissions and other groups of lesser significance seeking a Master's level in Social Sciences with support in Library techniques.[23]

Group one had comprehensive courses at Graduate and Masters Level in American History, Diplomatics, History of

20. Report of the visit of Francis X Blowing Jr. published in American Archivist/Fall 1988, pp. 501-511.
21. Ibid, Bemis, pp.154-61.
22. Ibid, p.156
23. Ibid, pp. 58-60.

archives, archival practices, and special literature relating to archives, knowledge of languages like German, French, and Spanish, as indispensable for adequate study of archival practices abroad. The course qualified them both as archivists and as teachers of American history. The Universities with this curriculum offered apprenticeship as part of the course, in collaboration with National Archives at Washington or with State archives. Later, University of Washington started a course with NARA. Archives Administration was another option. For archivists of Group two, the Committee recommended a two-year course at Masters Level with social sciences and other subjects from the Class I Group.[24]

Back in 1948, Solon J Buck described the archival profession in the US as a 'recent one.' The first course for Archivists had been given by him at Columbia University ten years earlier. Buck records that the Instructor did not know much more about his subject than his students. From 1939, such a course was given annually in Washington, under the auspices of the American University and the National Archives, and several hundred students opted for it. Dr Ernst Posner, formerly a professional archivist in Germany was teaching in the USA since1939, and after citizenship in 1941, had the full responsibility for these training courses.'[25]

When Buck started teaching Archives Administration, there was barely any literature available in English, on the subject, unlike now. The establishment of the Society of American Archivists in1936 and its quarterly journal, the American Archivist, soon after, accomplished a great deal in promoting the archival profession in the USA. The Institutions and Repositories of manuscripts were able to establish themselves as agencies

24. Ibid.
25. Indian Archives, p. 28

necessary to society.[26] The Society of American Archivists has since offered several basic and advanced courses in the subject.

In Canada, the National Archives provided in-service training for archivists and Records Managers while University of British Columbia, University of Toronto and Montreal have been offering courses at pre- and post-graduate levels in history and Library Science encompassing Archival Sciences. In Italy, the archives movement started seriously only after Unification of Italy in 1860, though the first School of Archivists was created in Bologna in 1765, followed by schools at Milan (1770), Naples (1777), Padua (1806), Palermo (1843), Venice (1854), and Florence (1856). But it was only in 1975, with the creation of the Ministry of Cultural and Environmental Properties that State Archives came under its jurisdiction and became the official responsibility of the State.[27]

Let us now review Indian archival practices and the concept of Modern Archives and archival science education. The concept of Modern Archives keeping came to India through European Trading Companies when we inherited the official archives of India from the British Colonial Rulers. Indians had, however, tried to solve the problem of record-keeping long before the coming of the Europeans.

In ancient times, information and wisdom was passed from one generation to another by oral traditions. There is evidence to substantiate the existence of Archives in ancient times having regional, provincial and central units. But information on how the ancients executed management, maintenance and preservation of records is missing. Still, excavations and available treatise tell us about our past history and of traditional methods used

26. Ibid.
27. L.Duranti, Education and Role of the Archivist in Italy, American Archivist, Vol 51/Summer1988, pp.346-355.

for documentation and preservation of information. Paper was invented in China in first or second century A.D. and is believed to have been introduced in India some five to six centuries later.

Till the nineteenth century, birch and palm leaf was used as writing material. Record offices existed in India during Buddhist times, giving us a good idea about India's great Heritage. Chinese Travelers to India between the third and seventh centuries AD refers to record offices in India. European and Arab travellers who visited India during the Muslim Rule (1000-1600AD) like Peter Mundi, Razaak and others wrote about record offices during the period.[28]

The idea of Archives administration travelled from Italy to England and to India during the nineteenth century. The British Government of India did not inherit any records in the name of Archives from the Mughals barring those seized by the British troops when they occupied Delhi in September after the 1857 Mutiny. These were seized from the Red Fort Palace of Bahadur Shah Zafar, the last Mughal Emperor.

There are references to Maratha Records, though. Chatrapati Shivaji and the Peshwas followed many of the Mughal practices and maintained their records as Bastas that are still available in Peshwa Daftar, Pune.

S Ghose adds that the British inherited the Mughal legacy of records management (particularly land records), known as the Kaghazi Raj. Akbarnama gives a fair description of how Emperor Akbar established a Record Office in 1574 AD, known as Daftar Khana by issue of an order stating that what happens at the court should be recorded and preserved.

The British system of Record Keeping and Archives

28. S Ghose in 1963, p. 5-7

Administration was an amalgam of Indian, Persian, Portuguese, Dutch and English systems, but was mainly influenced by the Dutch pattern. The transition of the East India Company from a trading Company to a territorial power resulted in rapid expansion of its administrative activities and secretariat. Intense correspondence was generated on account of the distance between Britain and their trading stations and settlements in India and elsewhere, explaining their actions.

The British Government in India was not keen to give access to Indians or 'natives' to public records. Neither was there any talk of an archival training programme. Since 1920, IHRC sessions[29] provided a platform for discussions to historians, archivists and officials to discuss theoretical and practical training related to access, arrangement, and description of archives. IRD had already begun practical training through working in archives management in accessioning, arrangement, classification and cataloguing of records. But stress was largely on preservation training and methods, as an Archival Research Laboratory was established in 1940, even before starting any regular training. However, a formal training programme following international archival methods on scientific lines was needed. The scholars and historian community in India had been clamouring for access to records for reference and historical studies. IHRC had been emphasising the need for archival training for accession and arrangement of records with IRD, so as to make them accessible to people. Finally in 1939; access was given to bona-fide research scholars to IRD records up to 1880.

29. Dept of Edn (Genl.), Resolution No77, dated21 March 1919. IHRC established in 1919 is a national organisation, an advisory body, constituted by Government of India, by nomination of individuals and Institutions, engaged in the study, upkeep and preservation of records and historical manuscripts.

The British Government of India adopted Resolution, No. F. 92-9/40-E on 16 September 1941 for training some record office employees on the lines of archival education in England, from the Provinces, Residencies, Indian States, including private students in Archives administration and rehabilitation and preservation of records[30] Research and Publication Committee (R&P) of IHRC resolved at its sixth session in March 1942, New Delhi, that a two-year full training scheme be approved. The training would be open to candidates for even one year's training in any two subjects. Special training course in preservation were to be offered to members and students interested in that subject. The Government of India approved the scheme after endorsement by IHRC, and it was circulated to all provincial Governments, Indian States, Universities and learned institutions in India.[31]

The IRD introduced a regular system of training in Archives Keeping with long and short courses of Instructions in Indexing, Calendaring and Preservation of Records, and Historical Researches among Records and Library Science, to a limited number of outsiders with requisite qualifications. Detailed syllabuses were drawn up and diplomas were to be granted to the successful trainees. The first session commenced on 1 July 1942. By 1943, thirteen candidates had applied from provinces and Indian States. Five of the applicants were selected for different courses based on their qualifications. An examination was held in 1944 and two candidates, Dr Saletore and Mr Damodaran Nambiar were successful. Seven candidates were enrolled as trainees during the year from Bombay University; Cochin State; Nizam's Government, Hyderabad; Commercial

30. Dept Edu Health and Lands, F. No. 92-9/E, Resolution dated16 September 1941
31 IHRC Resolutions – 1919-1948, p.139.

College, Delhi; Calcutta University; Orissa Government, Cuttack; and Commercial Higher Secondary School. IRD had sent out pamphlets on training in archival theory and practice to offices and institutes, seeking their guidance in repairing their own records and by training men deputed by the Provincial and State Records offices, universities and Institutions. Classes were held in the Department in theory and practice of archives. Some twenty candidates applied for various courses but only seven were selected. In 1945, eight candidates did the training.[32]

By 1946, the course was fully reorganised and the syllabus revised to follow developments in archival training in foreign countries. A leaflet on the course was circulated among the provincial Governments, Indian States, universities and archival Institutions and in other learned societies in India and abroad. The remodeled scheme was appreciated by foreign authorities on archival training such as Prof Galbraith, Hilary Jenkinson, and others. Women candidates had also applied, but none could be admitted as there was no hostel arrangements for them. By 1946, there were 11 candidates, two from Alwar, Jaipur Government, Gwalior, Harding Library, Delhi, Kolhapur Government, Baroda Government, Western India States Agencies, Bombay Government and Central India Agency, Indore.[33]

A Records Keeper's job was now regarded as a very special job, requiring skill, training and natural aptitude. Archival Science Education was now an established discipline and subject

---

32. NAI Annual Reports for the year 1942, pp.3-4; 1943, p. 4; 1944, pp. 2-4; 1945, pp. 2-4; 1946, pp 11-12 and Proceedings of the first meeting of IHRC, held in Shimla in June 1919, Resolution VI, pp. 10-11, inviting information from all Record offices to submit annual report regarding new accessions, records catalogued, listed, published, preservation, number of search cases, storing and housing of records as Government of India was deeply interested in all these developments.
33. For details of Schedule of Courses and Curriculum as introduced in 1946, please see Appendices, Annexure - I

of study in the west. The Imperial Records Department was doing valuable work, although much still had to be done under the guidance of this Indian Historical Records Commission. The work being done in Delhi would soon become a model for other important centres in India and other Asiatic countries. The Commission now proposed a fulltime School of *'Archivism'* to be run in conjunction with IRD. Three courses were being conducted simultaneously now and IRD invited applications for two-year, one-year and six-month courses, respectively. Diploma Courses in Archives Keeping were as under:

1. **Two-years course:** All candidates for this course had to possess an MA Degree in History of an Indian University.
2. **One-year course:** All candidates for this course were to be at least a graduate in History from an Indian University. The short course was on any of the two subjects, but if Librarianship was selected, Preservation was compulsory.
3. **Six-months course:** This short course was on Preservation. Graduates in Science were given preference as trainees had to do laboratory work and also learn microfilming and other highly scientific methods of preservation. But other students could also be admitted and given lessons in all other methods, excepting those requiring knowledge of Chemistry and Physics. This course was also open to menders, records personnel of Offices and Institutions. Certificates were given on completion. No fee was charged for any of the courses, but candidates were to meet their personal expenses. For Diploma students, written tests/exams were held after completion of the course and successful candidates were awarded a Diploma by the Government of India.[34]

34. F.no.14/1950-C, p.39, and IHRC Prods., 23rd Session. 20 Dec.1946, Appx. G. Pt. I, Indore, pp. 150-152. Curriculum of 3 Courses, introduced in 1946.

In the beginning, the department was unsure whether to hold examinations or stress on hands-on practical training besides theory classes. It was initially submitted that students on completion of training would be certified by the Branch concerned if the work was satisfactory. Then, the Director of Archives was to hold a Viva-Voce Examination and a diploma to be awarded if the candidate passed. But Dr SN Sen, Director of Archives, ordered on 4 April 1944 that '...a written examination should be held before the Diploma is granted'.[35] So, examinations were scheduled after training was completed. We have already mentioned the names of the first two successful candidates, Dr GN Saletore and Damodar Nambiar.[36] The results could not be notified in the Gazette, due to the ongoing World War, so a Press Note was released on 23 November 1944.[37]

Students continued to be trained in the diploma courses in Archives Keeping, sponsored by Provincial and Princely State Governments and Universities from various states as mentioned. Other Institutions like Imperial Library Calcutta and Provincial Library Training Centres were also conducting training courses in Librarianship. The Director of Archives, IRD (NAI) maintained uniformity in aggregate marks of 600 like the Imperial Library, Calcutta. To enhance the importance and status of the Library Training, Director of Archives had invited experts from Messrs Dasgupta, Gopalan and Guha Ray as instructors and examiners of some of the papers.[38]

A perusal of the file on conducting of exams reveals that

35. F.No 14-1/44-C, IRD, pp.1-2/notes.
36. Ibid, pattern of Examination and Award of Diploma.
37. Ibid, p.2 and 5/notes and pp.3-4/Corr.
38. Ibid. p.15/notes.

though examinations were being held, more emphasis was still given to hands-on practical training, besides theory classes. Laxity on the part of a trainee was not taken lightly and such students were not allowed to sit for exams subject to their performances.[39] It was a period of trials and experiments by IRD/NAI before they could formalise the one-year Diploma Course in 1952. Besides providing training to students sponsored by other Institutions, NAI, itself, deputed its own officers for advanced training abroad as had been recommended in the Report of the Committee on Post-war re-organisation of Archives offices in India.[40]

Due to World War II, nothing much could be done for expansion of the training scheme. In 1946, suggestions and opinions were invited from well-known Archivists in India and abroad and the Scheme accordingly revised in 1946 by the Government of India in consultation with international authorities. Two stipends of Rupees 100 each were introduced. The revised scheme of training was put in operation in 1947. Sixteen students were on the rolls in this year from across the country. A sum of Rs 3,600 was provided for award of three stipends to the interns receiving training in the Department, but the funds could not be utilised as it was not sanctioned by the Government.[41]

On the recommendation of the IHRC, a plan for the post-War reorganisation of the Archives Offices and Historical Researches in India was submitted to the Government of India in 1944, according to John Sargent in his report.[42] This plan

39. Ibid, pp.17-18/notes.
40. F.No. 101/1947-G. IRD/NAI.
41. NAI Annual Report for the year 1947, p.5. For details of the Curriculum please see Appendix 1 to the report.
42. John Sargeant, Report of Post War Reorganisation of Archives Offices in India, Indian Historical Records Commission, A Retrospect, 1919-1948, Appendix G, pp.111-123.

was considered by the Standing Committee of Legislature in March 1945.[43] All post-War plans would be taken up from 1947 onwards and all the preliminary data collected by annual reports, was fundamental for implementation of the plan.

At the 12th meeting of the Local Records Sub-Committee in February 1946, at IRD, New Delhi, the Committee considered and recommended that the Government of India should authorise the Director of Archives to collect data and to correspond with Provincial Governments and Indian States to find out how the new Plan would affect them. Members of this Committee were Dr Sir John Sergeant, Chairman, Captain PJ Keen, and MBE-Member-in-Chair, Dr IH Qureshi, and Dr SN Sen, as Member Secretary. Recommendations were also sought on the normal publication and printing programme of IRD, amendments to Historical Research Rules, Storage and Preservation of Documentary Motion Picture Films of the Information and Broadcasting and the War Department by IRD, provision of air-conditioning plants to the IRD Microfilming Laboratory and responsibility of the IRD in respect of the Records of such Government Agencies that had not transferred their archives to its custody.

The proposals if accepted and embodied in a Statute Book would have enabled the Centre to enforce a uniform policy throughout the country regarding accessibility, repair, renovation and publication of historical records and to coordinate the activities of the Provincial Records Offices. The Committee visited IRD and made an assessment of required trained manpower after the war.[44] The Committee observed that many more trained archivists would be needed when all eleven Governor's Provinces

43. F.N. 3-3/46-C, p.13, and 31-33 report/recommendations of the committee.

44 F.No. 13/45-C, vide para III 4, pp.80-81/Corr., extracts Appendix F.

in British India and leading Indian States would put their Records Offices in order after the War. Anticipating this demand, the IRD had already formulated a training Scheme and with the approval of the Government of India and had been preparing for the future. Though only a few students had so far come for the complete course, the Committee decided that the new training classes should form a permanent feature of IRD activities and in due course, these should be developed into a regular School. To encourage students, the Government stepped up stipends and scholarships for the course. The Committee recommended that (i) early steps be taken to air-condition the Muniment Rooms of the IRD to secure uniformity of temperature and relative humidity. (ii) That Vacuum Fumigation and Laminating Machines be installed in IRD at an early date. (iii) That imparting Instructions in theory and practice in Archives Keeping be recognised as part of the normal duties of IRD.[45] These developments and shortage of trained manpower necessitated the need for creating a suitable training programme by the Imperial Records Department, to ensure availability of trained manpower to archival institutions and to those wanting to take up Archives Keeping as a profession.

Training Scheme after WW II and Independence[46]

Altogether, only 23 students could be trained since 1942 and it was expected that this number would increase with the growth in demand for trained archivists in the States as well as in Provinces.

According to statistics in 1948, out of one hundred applications, only thirteen were selected for the two-year course;

45. F.No. 13/45-C, para 5, p.32 and p.34 of the report.
46. F.No. 13/46-C, pp.96-97/corr.

and in 1949, only six were selected out of sixty. Five students out of thirteen had completed their two-year course in 1948; seven in 1949, and none in 1950. The six-month course was successfully completed by 5 candidates during these years.[47] Training continued normally after Independence, in Archives Administration and Preservation of Records, with candidates deputed by Provincial and State Governments and Private Institutions interested in the maintenance of manuscripts and records. The stipend of Rs 100/month helped two of the candidates to continue their training. IHRC wanted this amount enhanced to meet the high cost of living in Delhi. It was also submitted to the Standing Committee of IHRC for approval, but due to financial stringency, the request was put on hold.[48]

NAI, itself, had deputed its own officers for advanced training abroad under the Scheme of Overseas Scholarship of the Central Government in1947-48. Scientific Officer RC Gupta and Dr P Basu were selected for Education in General Archives Keeping and Archives Preservation-Microphotography and Documentary Reproduction in the School of Library Service, Columbia University, New York, USA and at National Archives, Washington, respectively. Dr Basu worked for ten months as an intern, and then enrolled in the Graduate Division of School of Social Sciences and Public Affairs, Washington University, studying history and administration of archives in Europe and America, management and control of current Government Records, historiography and principles and evolution of public administration.[49] S Chakravarty, Archival Chemist, also completed

47. The Quinquennial Review, NAI, 1948-1952, pp. 24-25.# (has been discussed in detail in Chapter IV)
48. F.No. 101/1947-G, IRD/NAI
49. F.No. 101/1947-G, IRD/NAI

his training in Archives Preservation and Microfilming, and was deputed to National Archives, Washington in 1947.[50]

After Independence, there were many archival problems being faced by Independent India. One major challenge was fear of destruction of records in the absence of any rules for the administration and disposal of Central Government archives. The ministries were also full of an untrained working force. Ministries as well as agencies subordinate to them, therefore, considered themselves entitled to dispose of the records created, owned or inherited by them in any way they liked. Accordingly, as requested by Department of Education, NAI drafted and forwarded a Note on Dispersal of Records' of the Government of India on 24 May 1948.[51]

The Weeding Rules were circulated by the Ministry of Education, to all the Provincial Governments and Chief Commissioners besides Ministries, Government Departments and their offices.[52] This further necessitated immediate training of officials handling the records and at the same time to meet the challenges faced by the Division of Archives due to Partition.

The Supreme Partition Council and NAI followed international practices that directed that original archives of undivided India should remain with the Government of India and Pakistan would get duplicate copies of papers which might be of interest to them.

Another big problem to be addressed was because of the merger of a large number of States with neighbouring provinces or with bigger Unions. No clear-cut policy had yet been formulated about the future of the records of the now defunct states. IHRC and

50. The Indian Archives, Vol I, July 1947, No. 3, News Notes, pp.246-47.
51. F.N. 33-16/48-Rec. p.1-13/Corr.
52. Ibid, p. 22/Corr.

National Archives of India addressed these issues and prevented records from dismemberment, just as it had prevented its own records from dismemberment after the Partition of India; much also depended on the reorganised provinces, to follow the directions and guidelines for establishing or reorganising their own record offices.

At the Indian Historical Records Commission (IHRC) Indore Session held in 1946, members pressed for fundamental and urgent reforms for preservation of historical records. Many of the resolutions of the Commission and Research and Publication Committee could not be implemented by the Provincial Government and Indian States, because of the ongoing war and financial reasons.[53] This led the Government to make general arrangements for the preservation and maintenance of public records in India. A questionnaire was circulated by the Central Government to ascertain conditions prevailing in the provinces. The result was not satisfactory and therefore, IHRC was brought in to advise the Government on the treatment of archives, facilities for research and archival training in particular, and on expenditure on publication and other related questions. IHRC had adopted approximately 250 resolutions in the course of over twenty meetings on problems relating to archives.

Since the Commission was an Advisory Body, its recommendations were not mandatory and consequently its resolutions had little influence on the archives policy and on Provincial Governments and States. As for setting up of a Records Office in UP, five resolutions had been adopted by IHRC, but they were yet to be implemented. Provincial Governments had only responded twice citing financial reasons. States like Assam and

53. F.No. 3/1946-C.p.113-115.

the North East Frontier Province had not complied because of the War. IHRC was aware that unless Records Offices were established, no reorganisation of records offices and preservation of historical manuscripts could be possible for historical research. IHRC insisted on appointment of a fulltime trained Officer in-Charge.[54]

Hence coordination and central control was necessary for preservation, servicing and re-conditioning of old and damaged documents by trained archivists. The Director of Archives on invitation or deputation had inspected records at Poona, Madras, Calcutta, Assam, Baroda, Mysore, Trivandrum, Hyderabad, Jaipur, Alwar, and Abu (Rajputana Agency). Except in a few cases, scientific methods were not in use. The Director's experience showed that there were reasons for alarm. At least IHRC could thus prevent destruction of records by North West Frontier Province and Bombay. The case of the North East Frontier Province highlights as to how records came to IRD/NAI, and were returned later on. Even training was provided to the Archives Keeping officer later.[55] The Central government had treated IHRC recommendations and framed their archival policy on more liberal lines. But it was for the Central Legislature to take up the question of formulating legislative measures towards co-ordination and unification of activities regarding preservation and utilisation of archives in India.

The following proposals were thus, made:

1. All Provincial Governments should throw open their records in conformity with the practices at the Centre (up to 1880 for the present) for bonafide research.

54. F.No.1-1/1946-C. pp.210-213.
55. F.No.15-2/46-C,

2. These open records should be declared as 'historical' records. Historical records in the custody of provincial Governments, District and High Court Authorities should be brought under the Central Government and be concentrated at provincial capitals in properly constituted records offices managed by trained personnel.
3. The control of all historical records in the Provinces should be vested in the Central Records Office of the Government of India.
4. The Provincial Records Offices should be in the charge of the Central Revenue.

The above proposals if accepted and embodied in the Statute Book would have enabled the Centre to enforce a uniform policy on the accessibility, repair, and activities of the Provincial Records Offices besides archival training. But, the Provincial Governments did not favour control by the Central Government.

The Records Survey Committees in Provinces had been working since 1944 under the guidance of the Research and Publication Committee of IHRC. It embraced a comprehensive survey of all records and manuscripts of historical value in possession of private individuals, educational and learned Institutions, religious establishments, municipal offices, banks, insurance offices—wherever they may be located.[56]

In a letter dated 25 July 1947, the Director of Archives wrote to a Deputy Secretary in the Government of India, Department of Education, stating that since 1942, 10 Regional Survey Committees had been set up in the Provinces and 17 in the States under the auspices of the Commission and that the secretary had to direct and supervise their work. Important suggestions

56. F.No.1-1(a)/46-C, pp.42-43/c.

in the letter included:

- A legal status and recognition for a body like IHRC, with suitable powers of control and initiative.
- Recognition of the Diploma of Archivism as instituted at IRD; and its development into a regular School of Archivism, provision of scholarship for further training of Archivists in foreign countries like USA.
- Historical records to be immediately placed in the charge of trained, expert Archivists; preference being always given to recognised chemists, diploma holders who must also be well versed in Indian History, both modern and medieval.[57]

By 1946, only two provinces, Madras and Bengal had got fully organised Records Offices. Some Provincial and Indian States Governments had also decided to establish Central Records Offices with qualified whole time trained Officers. These included:

- Bombay, which decided to establish a Centralised Records Office with qualified, full-time officers.
- NWFP had established a Central Records Office at Peshawar with Mr Jaffar, the nominee of the Provincial Government on the Research and Publication Committee of IHRC as its first Keeper of Records and Director of Historical Research.
- Rajputana States Agency, Mount Abu, appointed Dr GN Saletore, a diploma holder, to reorganise the Historical Record Department at Mount Abu.
- Kolhapur State, Historical Records Department was created in July 1946, with Dr AG Pawar (an associate member of IHRC). He

57. F.No.1-4/46-C, pp.1-6/c

was also the Chief Archivist of the State and an IHRC member. He organised Records Office on scientific lines, prepared and published guide books, hand list, catalogues, and a calendar of state records, revision of state gazetteer and to collect materials for authoritative history of Kolhapur State.[58]

- Mewar State appointed Motilal Menaria as superintendent to the Saraswati Bhandar. Historical records of the State whether at the centre or in various departments were to be collected and centralised. He also collected documents of historical importance in the possession of non-officials.[59]

UP was yet to establish a proper Records room as per the IHRC resolution back in 1922.[60] Finally, fresh resolutions were adopted in 1933 and 1938 to centralise pre-mutiny records. Records were in possession of district or divisional officers and were closed for historical research. This was part of the post-War plan for reorganising archives of India. Centralisation and administration would bring in economy and efficiency, better servicing and supervision. After several reminders, the UP Government said that they had two Records Rooms at Allahabad and Lucknow. But the one at Allahabad was in a state of neglect.[61]

Partition and events thereafter affected implementation of the schemes. There were four main items: Contribution to regional survey committees, subvention of societies, acquisition of documents by purchase and stipends for trainees seeking a

58. Ref.F.No.3-3/44-C. IRD.
59. Ibid.pp.119-20. Vide Agenda 10.
60. IHRC Proceedings, Vol IV, Bombay, 7th January, 1922, p. 55.
61. Ref.F.No.3-3/44-C. p.121/c. (IHRC Proceedings Vol XXI, part iii, p.17 and appendix F, p.29, para 8, and F.N.81/47-G

diploma in Archives Keeping.[62] Rs 3,600 had been sanctioned as stipends for such trainees for the year 1947-48. Dr Sen, Director of Archives wrote to Ministry of Education, that it would be difficult for NAI to utilise the budgeted sum under various new items in the remaining months of 1947-48, if not taken up immediately. The Diploma courses had commenced from 15 July 1947, and applications from existing trainees were invited and three stipends, one for the one-year course and two for the two-year course were awarded to deserving candidates with retrospective effect.

The Ministry of Education now agreed to suggestions of the Director of Archives to invite applications next year from deserving candidates for the grant of stipends to trainees and to formulate and submit definite proposals and submit to the Government of India for expenditure sanction for the year 1947-48.[63]

The Secretary, Ministry of Education, vide letter dated 4 March 1948, gave expenditure sanction for four items including stipends during 1947-48 and conveyed the sanction of the Governor General for the grant of stipends of Rs 100/month to two trainees in Archives Keeping at NAI for one year wef 1 January 1948.[64] The Standing Committee of the Central Legislature on Education in a meeting at Shimla on 19-21 May 1947 approved the proposal of the IRD on the report submitted on further development of the IRD in 1946-47, forwarded by Director of Archives to Department of Education on 21 April 1947.[65]

62. F.N.42-33/47-E.I, pp. 20-21/Corr.
63. Vide Letter dt 15.11.1947, F.N. 1-4/46-c. to Dr. D.M. Sen, Dy. Secretary, p.22/C
64. F.N. 42-33/47-E-I, p. 24/c
65. F.No. 13/47-C, pp. 10-31/corr.

The Committee at its last meeting had recommended that the Training Scheme sponsored by the Department should be taken up and financial assistance be accorded to encourage students to take the courses. The IRD had reorganised the training system and revised the syllabus. The remodelled syllabus was commended by authorities from abroad, such as VH Galbraith, Director, Institute of Historical Research, London and Hilary Jenkinson, Secretary to British Records Association and by the American Archivist, the journal of the Society of American Archivists.

The Department also expected that Rs 3,600 would be provided in the budget for creation of three studentships of Rs 100 each. The Department also recommended that this amount be enhanced to Rs 150/month for each student.[66] In a meeting at Shimla in May 1946, the Standing Committee of Parliament considered the training Scheme and recommended that financial assistance also be given. Subsequently three stipends at the old rate of Rs 100/month were sanctioned, with no enhancement.[67]

The Department had consistently since 1941corresponded with professional archivists and archival Institutions of the world including National Archives, Washington, the Huntington Library, the Colorado Archives, the Library of Congress, the Archives of Illinois State, the Society of American Archivists, the British Records Association, the Institute of Historical Research and many others and had exchanged pamphlets, publications and technical information, and information on nominations of world-renowned archivists as corresponding members of IHRC.

66. F.N.2/1948-C. p. 5/n, P. 155. IHRC proceedings, 24th Session, Jaipur, 21st February, 1948.

67. F.N. 3/47-C. p. 67 /c, and F. No. 2/1948-C, p.5/notes and p.7 of the printed Proceedings of the Standing Committee of Central Legislature on Education.

The Department derived immense benefit from this cooperation and advice from sister Institutions. It was gratifying that the Department's activities had attracted appreciation from foreign archival authorities. The Notes on Preservation of Records compiled by NAI was acclaimed in USA as "one of the best comparisons between silking and lamination that had ever been made.'The Department's physical protection of records against insects and fungus growth aroused interest among archivists like Dr SJ Buck, Margaret Norton, Dr Hiller and JJ Barrow.[68]

The Post-War Construction Plan of the Imperial Records Department was acclaimed by Archivists in USA as a most significant document and was published in the American Archivist. These appreciations now saddled the Department with additional responsibilities of fulfilling expectations aroused by these activities. Appointment of suitably trained staff in the latest methods of preservation and archival storage was necessary.[69]

The Department had deputed one of its senior officers for training to the National Archives, Washington for nine months. Three more were sent to USA and elsewhere for training in various branches of archival science. The policy of sending out candidates to foreign countries for training had become a regular feature according to the Memorandum on Development in the Imperial Records Department submitted to the Standing Committee of the Indian Legislature on Education in May 1946.[70]

While considering the Memorandum of the Post-War Reorganisation of the Archives Offices and Historical Research

68. F.No. 13/46-C. pp. 13-14/c
69. Ibid. p. 101
70. F. No. 101/47-C, pp.100-101corr

in India IRD/NAI (Imperial Record Department/National Archives of India)[71]# was requested to submit a proposal for the development of the Imperial Record Department after Independence, and accordingly, it submitted on 27 June 1946, a five-year Archival Development Plan from 1947-48 to 1951-52 costing Rs 5,57,000, with a yearly detail of expenditure. Dr S Sen says that his motive was to bring IRD in line with the leading archival Institutions of the world.[72] Some grants were sanctioned

71. IRD. F.No. 13/45-C

The Post-War Reorganisation of the Archives Offices and Historical Research in India-The Report begins highlighting problems of access to records and identifying the availability of information on Indian history in foreign repositories in view of the gaps in the official records of IRD beginning from 1748. The post-war reconstruction plan of archives in India with particular reference to IRD made recommendations broadly under three categories.

- **Manuscripts Records** i.e. supplement gaps in official record series from British Museum and Public Record office London besides non-official sources from servants of East India Company who had played significant role in shaping history of India apart from repositories of Dutch, Portuguese, and France to help Indian students of history in their research as all of them could not afford to go out of India for their historical research. Discusses important issues and concerns of IRD/NAI in their endeavors for exploring and acquiring the manuscripts in private custody within India through Regional Record Survey Committees.
- **Library Facilities**– The report also highlights the need of developing archival libraries and need and importance of information in print for the research students. Recommended to acquire reprints/microfilms of important rare books and publications on Indian history and develop IRD/NAI library as a good reference library as no such facilities exists anywhere in India.
- **Technical equipment and training**- State of records in India was another problem as had been neglected due to lack of organised record offices barring few provinces. District Record Rooms often furnish models of what they should not be. Equally it was true regarding the status of records and manuscripts in the custody of private people due to ignorance and lack of care particularly in rural India and how to make technical services of Government records offices available to private owners for the repair and preservation of old manuscripts in their provinces as per resolutions of IHRC and Research and publication Committee. It also recommends how to go for costly scientific apparatus and equipment for IRD and other record offices. For IRD to function efficiently and to serve the cause of records in India, recommends to mechanise its technical services by using latest scientific equipment for repair and conservation of records. Recommended for air-conditioning of IRD/NAI repositories and acquisition of laminating machines.
- After reviewing complete status of archives and record offices in India the committee observed that a large number of trained archivists will be needed when each of the eleven Governor's provinces in British India and the leading Indian Princely States will put their record offices on a proper basis as they are expected to do after the Second World War. In anticipation of this demand the Imperial Records Department has already formulated a training scheme and with the approval of the Government of India has been imparting instructions in the theory and practice of archives-keeping to suitable persons deputed by the provincial governments, universities and Indian States. Though only a few students have so far come for the complete course, the Committee felt that the newly offered training facilities should not be restricted but, if possible, the training classes should form a permanent feature of the normal activities of the Imperial Records Department and in due course be developed into a regular school. Meanwhile the Government of India will be well advised to encourage students to come in larger number for the full course of training by awarding suitable stipends and scholarships. Also recommended that imparting instructions in theory and practice of archive-keeping should be recognised as one of the normal duties of the Imperial Records Department.
- The committee briefly indicates the financial implications of its recommendations; the expansion of the activities of IRD will demand a corresponding addition to the Imperial Records Department staff and the installations of machines like microstate, vacuum fumigation and laminating machine, etc. thereby need of additional Capital and recurring expenditure for IRD, including expenses for deputing Archivists to European countries and USA for education, training and to secure microphotographs of records and other relevant manuscripts. In conclusion the Committee observes that besides a capital grant of Rs. 7,00,000 and a recurring grant of Rs. 10,000 the Government will have to meet further expenditure for expanded accommodation and additional staff an estimate for which should be called for from the Department concerned.

72. F.No, 100/1946-G, p. 1/corr

and the success of NAI's Development Scheme tabulated at IHRC's 26th Session at Nagpur in December 1950.[73]The Plan included plans for office accommodation, technical sections, stacks and stack equipment, and more for the next 50 years expansion scheme under the IRD plan. For archival training, the Government sanctioned for 1950-51, only two stipends of Rs 100 each per month ignoring the demand for the enhanced amount. It also resolved that a contract be signed with the stipend holder. If there was no deserving candidate, no stipend was to be awarded. It establishes the fact that a stipend was given to deserving candidates only through a selection process of written test after one month of joining the course.[74]For the proposed Diploma Course in Archives Keeping, the Secretary gave a brief account on the subject at the Nagpur IHRC session. The following Resolution was passed:

- All State Governments in India should fall in line with the Government of India in recognising Records Administration as Technical Work;
- Ultimately all appointments to records Repositories in India should be made from among Diploma holders in Archives Science from recognised institutions (for the time being the NAI is the only Institution which offers on a limited scale a Diploma course in Archives Science);
- All Ministries of the Government of India and State Governments who have to retain large bodies of 'current records' in their custody should employ full-time Records Officers who should be Diploma holders in archives science, if such a person is available, or the

73. IHRC Proceedings, Part I, 26th Nagpur Session, December 1950, pp. 48-52, the details of the progress report of IRD are on pp. 51-56 of the proceedings
74. Ibid.

Officer should after appointment be sent up to the NAI or to an organised State Records Office for training; and for the next five years, four annual stipends of the value of Rs 150/month should be awarded by the Government of India to good candidates who come for training at NAI.

It was further resolved that in awarding the scholarship, a contract should be entered into with the stipend-holders to the effect that they would be expected to serve the Government of India or a State Government for a specified period after completion of training in NAI.[75]

The Resolution was subsequently circulated by NAI to Ministries/Departments of Government of India, State Governments, Universities and some learned institutions. Andhra Pradesh, Assam, Jammu and Kashmir, Bhopal, Bilaspur, and Madhya Bharat in Madhya Pradesh, Maharashtra, former PEPSU States, former Saurashtra, Tamil Nadu, Tripura, and Uttar Pradesh accepted the resolution. Himachal Pradesh and Punjab noted the Resolution. Andaman and Nicobar and Manipur did not consider it necessary to implement in view of their relatively small number of records. Calcutta, Madras, Nagpur, Travancore and Utkal Universities accepted the resolution. Agra, Bombay, Gujarat and Poona took note of it, while Baroda and Karnataka said they would consider it. Allahabad, Jammu and Kashmir and Lucknow were not in favour of accepting the resolution. Bhandarkar Oriental Research Institute, Poona already had a specialist in Archives Administration.[76]

Later, the Inter-University Board at its twenty-fifth annual

75. IHRC Proceedings, Pt.I. 26th Session, Nagpur, December 1950, p. 57.
76. IHRC proceedings, 29th Session, Bhopal, December 1953, ATR, pp. 68-70.

meeting at Banaras on 28 February 1949 considered the proposal from Ministry of Education, for inclusion of the Study of Archives and historical Manuscripts in the University History syllabus.

The Ministry of Education had taken an initiative earlier, too. The explanatory note submitted then stated that 'both the postgraduate worker in history as well as undergraduate students doing an honours degree in history cannot do without knowledge of and a facility in the use of Archives.' It added that Archives and Historical Manuscripts are raw materials for students and the tools of the craft in the same sense as elements, compounds, fossils and asteroids, test tubes and balances, microscopes and spectrometers are tools for scientists.

Students of all ages accept uncritically whatever they see in print. This is not only about facts, but also questions of the interpretation of the fact, upon cause and effect. This defect could be cured by instilling in students a spirit of doubt. It was believed that access to archival material would result in strengthening in students, a proper and wholesome skepticism of the views of others.[77] The Board deliberated on the Memorandum and resolved that 'these matters be referred to individual universities.'This decision of the Inter-University Board was communicated by S Mathai, Secretary of the Board to Secretary, Education, Ministry of Education in the letter dated18 April 1950.[78] It was left to the universities to consider and implement voluntarily, but it never happened as no university took the matter seriously.

At the IHRC session at Bhopal, Prof SS Bhatnagar spoke about the responsibility NAI had undertaken for imparting training to Record Keepers and Record Rooms staff with a

77. F. No. 3-4/49-C. NAI,

78. Ibid. p. 5/ notes and p. 17-18/corr.

three-month course. The syllabus of the course included general methods of Records Keeping, preservation and repair of records.

The training helped not only in proper maintenance of records but how these records were to be received in NAI.[79]

IHRC had been promoting teaching of Archival Science through various resolutions and to establish University and College archives. Inclusion of research among University and college archives as part of the post-graduate history curriculum was also being promoted by IHRC.[80] The Commission observed that post-graduate study of history in Universities is usually based on secondary sources. To make history more realistic and more effective, it was considered essential that students be encouraged in fairly early stages to handle original documentary materials. A paper on the study and criticism of unpublished documents was proposed in History Schools as part of their post-graduate history curriculum, something that university and college archives could very well provide. But such material in universities was scanty. Professors such as Dr Bisheshwar Prasad favoured research among original records, but university archives would not be adequate for producing a good thesis. Moreover, no university in India was old enough to have any such archives.

The Secretary suggested that it was not necessary to produce a good thesis based on University Archives but that a first-hand opportunity to study archival material and gain practice of handling, studying and appraising unpublished documents be given to students. Further, he believed universities were old enough to have their archives and that all organised institutions by

79. Ibid.
80. Ibid.,p. 60

virtue of transaction of their official business produced documents automatically and generated its archives even if they were only a few days old. Accordingly, IHRC adopted a resolution stating that 'The Commission recommends that Curriculum for the Master's degree in History and Commerce in Indian universities should include the handling of archives and the study and criticism of unpublished documents with a view to giving the students early training and practice in original research.'[81]

Training after WW II and Independence

The Training Scheme was closely interlined with the technical service provided by the Department with the definitive syllabus of studies. It catered to candidates deputed by Provincial and State Governments besides learning Institutions. Altogether, twenty-three students could be trained since 1942 and this number was expected to grow, these courses were very popular, judged by the numerous applications for admission to them as previously stated.[82]

But the IRD (NAI after Independence) was facing acute problems and several changes were proposed.

- The Department had neither special staff, nor adequate staff for imparting the training. With staff shortage, multiplicity of courses was another challenge. This confusion permeated down to the students who found it difficult to make the right choice. Continuing with the Librarianship paper in the NAI was equally puzzling when more specialised agencies such as National Library, Calcutta, were already conducting a full-

81 Ibid. p. 63 of the proceedings, National Archives of India, 1948-1952, A Quinquennial Review, p.24.
82 F.No. 13/46-C. pp. 96-97/corr.

fledged Librarian's Diploma course.

- Another issue was the preference being given to Science graduates over Arts graduates in History or other subjects in these courses. Perhaps this was because, from the very beginning, more emphasis was being given by IHRC members and the IRD on the preservation of records and in specialised training in preservation. But there was no justification in over-emphasising the subject at the cost of study of other aspects of archival science. Hence, the course, itself, required a thorough revision to incorporate knowledge of modern archival practices, and in improving understanding of modern and contemporary period of Indian history. Moreover, archives being transferred and already available with NAI and other established and emerging provincial archives because of reorganisation or creation of States by merger or otherwise, had to be studied for accession, arrangement, description and servicing.[83]
- NAI had shortage of space and could not provide a separate Lecture Room or accommodation for trainees and students in Delhi.
- Shortage of technical books was another impediment. The Department was expected to publish books and pamphlets with technical information on various aspects of Archives Keeping. Stipends for deserving candidates had to be given out.

The Committee observed that a large number of trained archivists were needed for the reorganisation of Provinces by merger or reformulation and the Record Offices were hard-pressed to take care of old records and archives in the post-war period.

83. F.No.13/45-C, Committee Report on Post War Reorganisation of Archives Offices and Historical Researches in India

In anticipation of the demand, the IRD had already formulated a training scheme with the approval of the Government. The Committee felt that the newly offered training facilities should not be restricted, and instead become a permanent feature of the normal activities of the IRD. Meanwhile, the Government was advised to encourage students to enroll in large numbers for the full training courses and apply for suitable stipends and scholarships.[84] The committee recommended that:

1. Early steps be taken to air-condition the Muniment Rooms of IRD to secure uniformity of temperature and relative humidity,
2. Vacuum fumigation and laminating machines to be installed in IRD at an early date,
3. Imparting Instructions in theory and practice in Archives Keeping became recognised as one of the normal duties of the IRD.[85]

At the Nagpur IHRC Session in December 1950, Rajasthan State Government also introduced a Resolution for making provision for Mobile Centres for training in Archives Administration. However, the Resolution was dropped in view of Training being provided by NAI and other practical problems such as training being limited to people in the administration and preservation of records. Preference was usually given to candidates actually working in a Public Records Office or Manuscript Libraries.[86] The archival training was mostly practical and could only be imparted in a fully equipped Record Office. Mobile training centres were, therefore, dismissed as the wrong medium. There was also no possibility of NAI introducing any

84. Ibid, pp.180-181.
85. Ibid.
86. IHRC Proceedings, Nagpur, December 1950, Part I, pp.20-21

extensive training scheme, unless sufficient opportunities existed for employment of the trained people. That, in turn, depended on the existence of a proper Records Office in the country with the policy of employing only trained personnel.

The Director of Archives while delivering a course of lectures on Records Administration for the benefit of Indian Administrative Service probationers, then under training at the Indian Administrative Service Training School, Delhi, also included the topic as a permanent part of extra-curricular lectures for IAS probationer's training.[87]

The Union Government had requested NAI to arrange for training of officers of the Ministries, government departments and states in Archives Administration and Preservation of Records, so that they could be entrusted with the work of organising Central and Divisional Records Offices on an All-India level. Several states, including Rajasthan welcomed the Director of Archives, NAI, who was authorised by IHRC and endorsed by the Indian Government to inspect their records offices.[88]

But the many deficiencies in the courses conducted by NAI, and the overlapping content caused stress to the staff and other logistics problems. The course in Library Administration was not of much relevance. Even the rule for preference of science graduates was not justified as besides preservation, other aspects of archival science were getting neglected. The course for specialisation in Archives Keeping, for instance, needed candidates who had knowledge of history.

In May 1952, the Government decided to do away with two courses: the two-year Diploma course and the six months course

87. F.No. 14/50-C, pp, 20-21/corr.

88. Ibid. p.47/ATR.

in Preservation. A one-year Diploma course was made more comprehensive and the latest developments in Archives Keeping were added to it. Further, the syllabus was modified with more emphasis on practical training. Subjects covered now were Archives Administration, Preservation, Calendaring and Indexing. Only graduates were admitted with preference to those with an MA or Honours Degree in History with special reference to Modern Indian History. Two stipends of Rs 125 each per month were awarded on the basis of written examination. Examinations were held at the completion of the training course, and a Diploma awarded by the Government of India. The first Course began on 1 October 1952, with 7 students. Earlier that year, in January, a three-month course was started, to be held twice a year from January to March and July to September and restricted to officials of the Union and State Governments. Matriculation was the minimum qualification for this course and certificates were issued at the end of the course.[89] (For curriculum details, see Annexure IV of the Report.)

The modified syllabus with different time durations that had been accepted by the Government now provided training to a larger number of candidates for archival positions. Revised syllabus now provided training for the one-year full course, six months course in Preservation of Records and three months special short course mainly for staff in the Records Rooms of the Ministries and offices of the Indian Government and State Governments.[90]

The Curriculum of the revised one-year course was as follows:

- **Archives Administration:** Accession, Servicing, Filing technique, Control of over-production of documents, Weeding of documents,

89. National Archives of India, 1948-1952, A Quinquennial Review, p.25.
90. Ibid. pp. 45-47. Annexure-IV Schedule of Courses and Curriculum as revised in 1952.

Classification of records, Central and local archives business, Institutional archives, Active and dead archives, Current and non-current archives, etc.

- **Preservation:** Methods of Repairs, Rehabilitation, Mechanising process of repair, Cleaning, Fumigation, Photo-duplication, Maintenance of Records, Enemies of Records, Storage, etc.
- **Indexing and Calendaring:** Principles of Indexing, Descriptive cataloguing, Précis writing, Calendaring, different methods of Calendaring, collation and establishment of the texts, elimination of non-essential elements, identification of names, compilation of topographical, biographical and historical notes, use of typographical conventions, preparation of introduction, special explanatory notes, chronological details, conversion of dates, practical work in Calendaring, general principles of indexing, Indexing of Records, arrangements, main entries, sub-entries, chronological, alphabetical, and subject grouping of sub-entries, punctuation and spacing, treatment of personal and place names, subject Indexing, pitfalls in Indexing and editing, etc.

An admission criterion too was revised to enhance standards of eligibility of applicants. Candidates seeking admission needed a second-class MA Degree, or BA Hons Degree in History, with Modern Indian History as a special subject. Preference was to be given to students sponsored by State Governments, and learned Institutions, although private candidates were also admitted, with applications endorsed by the Heads of Institutions they last attended. Stipends were awarded to the two students who secured the best in a written examination, held a month after the one-year diploma course commenced.[91]

91. Roy. S. 'Professional Archives Training in India', Archivum, Vol III, 1953, p.79.

Instructions to the trainees were divided into theory and practice. The morning sessions were devoted to practical work, and afternoons, to theoretical classes. Saturdays and Sundays were weekly offs. The training also included:

- Seminars, where students exchanged views with the Officers of the Department on related topics
- Symposiums, which included reading of papers by the candidates on special subjects, with a senior staff member in the chair followed by a discussion in class. Personal attention by a staff member earmarked for training in theory, and whose duties included welfare and discipline of the students, in addition to lecturing.[92]

In August 1953, a Grade 1 Assistant Archivist was designated to supervise the work of the trainees of both courses. A Board of Examiners was constituted, comprising the Director of Archives, also Chairman and moderator, besides the State Directors.[93] There were six papers in all:

- **Part I** with three papers, each carrying 100 marks, on Archives Administration, Calendaring and Indexing, and Preservation.
- **Part II** consisted of three practicals of the same three papers as of Theory.
- Students securing 35 percent marks in theory, 50 per cent in practical exams and 40 per cent in aggregate to pass in all the examinations at the end of twelve months were awarded a Diploma by the Government of India.
- Those scoring 70 percent marks secured distinction.

The results were notified in the Gazette. The Diploma was

92. IHRC proceedings, Hyderabad, 30th Session, 1-3 February, 1954, p. 57.
93. Ibid, and Annual Report of NAI, 1953, p.9.

signed by Director of Archives and Educational Adviser, Ministry of Education. This new system came into effect in1953.[94] Two students were awarded the Diploma after completing the one-year course in 1949, one in 1950, four in 1952, and five in 1953. In the last batch, there was one woman student. The Diploma Examination also had a provision for passing in compartments. A candidate, who had failed in Part 2 in 1952, secured the Diploma in 1953, thus six diplomas were awarded in 1953. Seven students joined in 1953-54.

The three months course was strictly confined to employees of the Central and State Governments. Certificates were issued to the trainees after completion of their course. Nine successfully completed the short course in January 1952, and 18 completed the second course held from July to September 1952.[95]

Two categories of officers and officials were now ready to be appointed as Archivists or in administration of these archives in Government Repositories and in archives maintained by the Government of India.

But much more was still required to be done than simply getting the officers or officials trained. The emerging challenges posed by the post-War and post-Independence period of India, also saw the organisation and re-organisation of Provinces and Indian Princely States due to a Federal system of Indian Government, abolition of the Zamindari system and development of archival practices in the international arena.

The Government set up the National Committee of Archivists in 1953, to bring together all Directors/Heads/Keepers of Archives of the States and Director, National Archives of India

94. Ibid, and F.No.14-1/50-C.

95. Ibid.

on a common platform so that they could discuss technical problems relating to conservation and preservation of Archives/ Records and share best practices on training on scientific lines.[96] The Director of Archives was appointed as Convener and Secretary and all Directors of State Archives were nominated as members of the Committee. It was to meet twice a year, once at the Session of the IHRC and second on invitation by any State Archives by rotation in the country. It was not an appendage body of IHRC, but an independent body comprising only of Archivists unlike IHRC, which had official representatives of all State Archives and Records Offices in India. It emerged as an important body besides IHRC and concerned itself with training of Archivists both at professional and sub-professional level apart from addressing technical issues on conservation and preservation of Archives, and on archival training, further growth and development of archives on scientific lines in the country.

96. F. No.14-4/53-CA-3, pp.1-5/corr.

Growth and Development of Archival Science Education

Post-Independence (1947-1993)

Independence of India was a landmark for growth and development of Central and Provincial Records Repositories in India. The name, National Archives of India (NAI), in itself indicated that the Repository was not merely a storehouse of Records of a colonial administration but was a proud custodian of the documentary heritage of the country. There was a continuous flow of records to NAI, but not always in a systematic manner. In practice, only a few ministries and some of their attached and subordinate offices transferred their records to NAI, and that too, haphazardly. Minutes of the meeting conducted by Lord Harding on 23 February 1912 states that every Department is expected to transfer its records to the Imperial Records Department after 10 years. But this practice was not really followed. The usual transfer procedure happened only whenever an agency felt that it was saddled with a body of records it no longer wanted to keep by itself, so they would request that the IRD/NAI take them over.[1]

1. IHRC proceedings, 1950, Session XXVII, Appendix B (II),pp. 77-78

In the absence of rules and regulations, determining the destruction and transfer of records to NAI or States records repositories, IHRC had passed a number of resolutions demanding that the Government pass legislation to control and regulate archives and records management practices, archival education and training.

After Independence, the two-year course was shortened into a more comprehensive, one-year Diploma course in Archives Keeping with stress on practical training. All the positive changes have been outlined in Chapter 1. The Government now introduced 8 stipends for each state-sponsored candidate of Rs 75/month, to promote in-service training with the expansion of Record management activities in the Ministries and Departments. It also introduced a Special Short Course of Training in Archives Keeping in NAI.[2] Director of Archives, Dr BA Saletore wrote to the Secretary, Education in a letter dated 23 May 1953, about the steps being taken for archives maintenance in India.[3]

The National Committee of Archivists (NCA) was established with the approval of the Government including Director of Archives and State Directors with the objective to work closely working together for the common good.[4]It was a small unpretentious body of technical experts to exchange views on how to tackle problems in their day-to-day work efficiently and economically. The Government was requested to recognise the existence of NCA and to bring it to the notice of State Governments. The Ministry of Education wrote to all State Governments on 1 September 1953 about NCA, seeking their support while elaborating on its advantages.

2. IHRC proceedings, 1951, pp.183-185, 1951
3. F. No. 14-4/53-CA-3, pp.1-5/corr.
4. F. 92-16/53-A-2, pp. 92-93/c. vide letter dated 1 Sept. 1953, p., 29/c.

In the first six NCA meetings, preservation and other related issues dominated the deliberations.[5] At NCA's seventh meeting, a suggestion from West Bengal's Keeper of Records, GN Chandra, came for the training of menders and binders and a suggestion to make provision for systematic training of such personnel of Records Repositories. It was suggested that non-matriculates, menders and binders could should also be allowed to take the three-month course, so far, open only for matriculates. It was suggested that an even shorter course in mending and binding for staff of Record Offices be introduced for such staff. Dr Baliga of the Madras Records Office supported the proposal, and said that his office was already providing such training. The Chairman and Director of Archives of the NAI felt that rather than a short course, few people could instead visit the NAI or the Madras Record Office for short periods to learn this. A previous resolution (Res. IV of the NCA fourth meeting, 1956) had raised this point when the Committee had recommended a four-week Course for Keepers of Records, but so far, no one had opted for it. NCA now recommended a short course for staff in Archival Repositories and Record Rooms. With the course, with practical training, was to become effective by July 1958.[6]

Reorganisation of States and Record Offices

With the reorganisation of Provinces and the merger of the Princely States after Independence, the problem of Records Offices also became acute with the division of records taking place between the Provinces and the erstwhile Princely States. Deployment of trained staff became an immediate need in these Record Rooms. At the

5. F. No. 19-2/57-C. pp. 79-80/corr.
6. F. No. 19/58-C, NCA 8th Meeting, pp. 6-8/notes.

IHRC 34th session in Trivandrum in Jan 1959, a resolution was adopted recommending financial assistance for State Governments for Archives Development Plans under the Third Five Year Plan. NAI examined the proposal and said that this development should form part of State Development Plans, and not as part of the NAI development plan.[7] It was referred to Ministry of Education to forward to the States for necessary action. The Ministry wrote to all the State Governments on 28 April 1959 urging development of State Archives in their State Plans, and stressing on the need for their own Records Offices. For funding, the Ministry suggested approaching the Planning Commission under the Third Five Year Plan. Uttar Pradesh, Maharashtra, Assam, Bihar, Punjab, Andhra Pradesh, Rajasthan and Tamil Nadu worked accordingly and deputed staff to NAI for training.[8]

NCA developed Guidelines for Department Record Rooms' (DRRs) entitled *Minimum Requirements of Small Records Offices*, for all State Archives after reorganisation of States.[9] NAI had, so far, been helping State Governments in establishments of Records Offices in the States by deputing its own trained officers till 1960, many States like Tripuraand Kerala had no archives and Records were kept within departments. Now they too followed recommendations of the Legislation Committee and from IHRC.[10]As an outcome, State Archives were established by Uttar Pradesh, Rajasthan, Bombay, Jammu and Kashmir, and Assam.[11]All of them requested for funds under the Third Five-year

7. F. No. 3-3/59-C, pp.1-2/notes.
8. Ibid. p.7/corr.
9. F. No. 3-4/59-C, p. 1/corr.
10. F. No. 16-8/60-C
11. F. 3-3/59-C, pp. 27-29/corr., p. 35/corr., pp. 38-51/corr., F. 16-8/59-C, pp. 16-21/corr., F. 16-8/59-C, pp. 32-37/corr.

Plan. They also sought recommendations from NAI for financial support, but NAI wrote to the Planning Commission for inclusion of development of State Archives as part of State Plan Schemes.[12]

Development of Archives and Education as part of State Development Plans

During Third Five Year Plan (1961-64), some States did get some financial assistance from the Government of India for development of their archives and archival education and training. Rajasthan was given a Rs 3 lakh grant to collect records from all Princely States, consolidate and preserve them in a scientific manner; Rs 19 lakh was given to Andhra Pradesh, Rs 15 lakh for the building and Rs 4 lakh for office development, reorganisation of staff, training of staff by deputation to major archival repositories in India and abroad, besides refresher course for archivists in India.[13] In due course, they deputed their officials for the Diploma course in Archives Keeping, and for short-term courses. This is recorded in the minutes of NCA's sixteenth meeting.[14] Tripura Administration deputed two candidates for training, one in 1948 for the full Diploma course; another candidate, a, Lower Division Clerk for the three-month, short-term training in 1957.

As a policy decision, the State Government of United Provinces in 1958 decided that Record Keepers of Divisions, Districts and sub-Districts will undergo a thorough course of training and pass the examination, prescribed by the Keeper of the Archives so that they can look after the records, scientifically.[15] Even officials of

12. Ibid. p. 3/notes
13. F. No. 19/63-C, pp. 27-28/corr.
14. F. No. 19/63-C
15. Ibid. U.P. pp. 116-120, and121-142/corr.

the UP State Archives went abroad for training. The Assistant Keeper of Archives went for higher studies at University College, London in 1959-60, and also visited archival institutions in UK, Denmark, Sweden, France, West Germany, Canada, and USA. In 1960-61, its Keeper of Archives visited the USA for observation and studying advanced archival techniques in a few State Archives Offices, National Archives and Records Office, Washington and US Library of Congress, Washington. Two technical assistants underwent a year's training in NAI during 1959-60 and 1962-63, while one Preservation Officer underwent training at NAI for three months in Micro-photography and Preservation in 1961.[16]

Recommendations of National Committee of Archivists (NCA) for Education and Training of Candidates from State Record Offices

The NCA in its twelfth meeting at Srinagar in 1959 adopted the Report of the Sub-Committee appointed at its eleventh meeting at Allahabad in April 1959. The Committee of Dr PM Joshi as Convener, and T Balakrishnan Nayar, Dr GN Saletore and V Bawa as members to collect information about training schemes in Archives Administration for deputing candidates from the States for training abroad. The sub-committee proposed an **immediate programme** and also a **Long-Term programme** for training of candidates from State Records Offices. For the immediate programme, members said foreign scholarships might be made available for State candidates, if the proposal received the support of the Government. NCA recommended that the candidate to be sent abroad for observation and training, should

16. Ibid. p. 17 of the Report. Item-88. P. 138/c.

hold a first-or second-class MA Degree or research degree in History or Political Science, with experience in Archives for at least three years with independent charge of a State Records Office. The trainees on their return would have to work in their local Archives for a minimum period of three years.[17]

For the Long-term programme, the Sub-Committee recommended that since several posts in the State Records Offices were vacant, in the absence of qualified candidates, the State Governments should recruit eligible candidates, under the age of 30 who held an MA degree in History or Political Science with research experience and knowledge of language of records of the concerned State. It was proposed to send such recruits for training to NAI for six months, before taking up assignments in the State Record Office. In the long-term programme of training of archivists abroad, these recruits were to be considered along with Category I. It was hoped that these recommendations would create an unfailing supply of manpower for the existing and soon-to-be established Records Offices.[18]

The Committee further recommended that the Diploma Course be introduced at the university level as per the revised Scheme. It was to include the following Papers:

1. History of Administration in India, Central, Provincial and Local from 1500 AD
2. History of India including study of Genealogy, Heraldry, and Chronology from 1500 AD, Paleography and Diplomatic, Mediaeval and Modern from 1500 AD
3. Theory and Practice of Archives Administration and Description of Material

---

17. F.No. 19-3/59-C, pp.105-107/corr. Extracts Proceedings of the 12th NCA meetings.
18. Ibid.

4. Management of current records in Government and non-Government Institutions
5. Calendaring and Indexing, Editing material for Press
6. Preservation: Methods of preservation of Manuscripts and Documents, Photographic techniques
7. Practical and Viva Voce[19]

The Committee while recommending universities to start the Diploma Course, recommended classroom instruction at the university and practical training at NAI along with discussions and seminars. The course of post-graduate training in Archival Science should be open to graduates who had obtained a Master's Degree in History. The Committee observed that once the course was instituted by the universities in cooperation with NAI and State Records Offices, NAI would not need to conduct its one-year Diploma course over time. But it supported the continuation of short-term certificate courses from NAI.[20] However, NCA did not support the revival of the short-term course that had been suspended under the revised scheme of training by NAI in 1959as it did not serve the purpose for which it had been started—that of training archivists competent enough to take up independent charge of Records Rooms of Departments and other Records Working Agencies either at the Centre or in the States.

NCA supported the new revised scheme of training and recommended that it be tried for a couple of years, and then to come up with an alternative along with improvement suggestions, if needed. NAI accepted the inclusion of five subjects recommended by the sub-committee of NCA for the University

19. Ibid.
20. F.No.19-3/59-C, Proceedings of the 12th NCA meeting, Appendix 'A', pp. 101-110.

course for the NAI Diploma Scheme; it was to seek help from Delhi University and other agencies, if needed.

The syllabus of the new, one-year course was therefore revised, and opinions for improvement were to be factored in, before it was introduced by the NAI.[21]The NCA chairman had given an assurance of providing training to nominees of the State Governments but he also supported the proposal of opening of training centres in various State headquarters in collaboration with Museums, Laboratories, and Archaeological Chemists by State Records Offices in the Repair and Preservation of Records and other perishable materials, by specialists, who could impart practical training. These could be independent organisations working in collaboration.[22] Both courses received a good response from State Archives.

The Scheme was reviewed in 1959, on the basis of the Parliamentary Estimates Committee's suggestion in their sixteenth report of the second Lok Sabha and the stipend amount increased to Rs 150/month in each case, and the number of stipends raised to five. Provision was made for eight candidates sponsored by Central Ministries/State Governments at a special monthly allowance of Rs 75/month if they were from outside Delhi. The course was to commence from 1 March, every year.[23]

Seven candidates joined the one-year Diploma Course in October 1952, while ten officials of various departments of the Union and State Governments enrolled for the three-month course in January1953. In August, an Assistant Archivist (Grade I) was posted full-time to supervise the work of these trainees with a

21. Ibid
22. Ibid
23. Annual Report of NAI for the year 1959, p.12.

time table to cover both the practical and theoretical syllabus. For the one-year course, a Board of Examiners was constituted with the Director of Archives as the Chairman and Moderator and two State Directors as paper setters and Examiners monitored the examination process.[24] Besides regular classes, a series of seminars were held under the guidance of the Director of Archives and Assistant Director of Archives. Two officers deputed by the Government of Afghanistan also attended the course for a few months. Two sessions of the three-month course were held during the year and a total 25 trainees enrolled from Ministries and offices of the Government of India and State Governments.[25]

All due care was taken to maintain the quality of the courses. The Government of India decided to continue both the one-year and three-month course for three years.

Selections of candidates was done through interviews by a duly constituted Selection Committee and stipends were also awarded on their recommendations. The number of candidates admitted to the course and stipends awarded since 1954 were:

Year	Number of Students Admitted	Number of Stipend Awarded
1954	4	1
1955	5	2
1956	4	2
1957	4	1
1958	7	2
1959	9	5
1960	9	5

24. Annual Report of NAI for the year 1953, p. 9.
25. Annual Report of NAI for the year 1955, Archival Training, p. 8.

The Board of Examiners included the Director of Archives, NAI, as Chairman and Chief Examiner and moderator; and a State Director of Archives and a non-official expert (if none is available another State Director) as Paper setter and Examiner.[26]

The revised training Scheme commenced on 1 September 1959 with nine trainees on the roll, including four sponsored by State Governments. The syllabus was enhanced and study of Administrative History of India was included in the course. The Department also arranged special short-term training course for nominees of a few outside agencies like National Botanical Garden, Lucknow, Central Secretariat Library, UP Government Secretariat, Directorate of Archives and Monuments, Government of Maharashtra and National Library, Calcutta.[27]

Apart from the one-year training course, practical training was held whenever asked for by the sponsoring organisation and had no fixed time schedule.

Planning Commission Endorses Development of Archives and Training in State Plans

During the third Five-Year Plan (1961-1966), NAI received Rs 16, 00,000 for Development of Archives;[28] a list of proposed Central Government's Schemes to be undertaken during the Third Five Year Plan period by NAI also included expansion of a Scheme on Training in Archives based on recommendations of the Archival Legislation Committee (ALC). The Ministry of Education also informed all State Governments on 7 September, 1968,[29] that the Government had accepted 'Archives' as a Plan

26. F.N. 2-7/61-PR, p.1/notes.
27. NAI Annual Reports for the year 1959-60, pp.12and 9
28. F.N. 3-3/59-C, pp.25-26.
29. F.N. 4-4/70-C, pp. 59-60/corr. Ref. letter no. 6-29/66-CAI-2.

Item for inclusion in State Plans, as development of Archives was important both for meeting current needs of administration and for historical research. Development of Archives was included in State Plans from 1968-69 to 1973-74 as instructed by the Planning Commission.[30]

Recommendations of ALC to Strengthen the Scheme of Archival Science Education and Creation of Archival Cadre for India

The IHRC had adopted two resolutions in 1930 and 1948 after Independence, recommending need of archival legislation on the lines of the Public Records Act of England, enacted in 1938. But till 1993, India had been denied of a statutory basis for archival law, as it required amendment of the Constitution of India for enacting a law for the nation. The Government appointed an Archival Legislation Committee by a Resolution of the Ministry of Education, dated 19 August 1959, under the Chairmanship of Dr Tarachand, MP, to examine inter alia, the condition of public records in India, problems of ownership and custody, and the need for legislation for governance and disposal and measures for protection of records of historical value in private custody.[31]

The Committee submitted its report on 29 December 1960, and was circulated to all the State Governments by the Director, National Archives of India, in his letter dated 17 June 1961, followed by a letter from the Deputy Secretary, Ministry of Education dated 13 July1961, to all State Governments, seeking comments on 5 main issues including Archival education.[32]

30. NAI, F. No.13/68-Cpp. 141-142/corr.
31. M/Edn. F. No. 6-13/59-A.10
32. Ibid, copy of letter ref. F. No. 6-1/61-A-10. M/Edn., endorsed to DA, NAI.

These five main recommendations were:

1. Reorganisation of Archives-Creation, Administration, Management and Retirement procedures
2. Public Access to Archives
3. Legislation enshrining principles in regard to these matters and making of statutory rules for its proper enforcement
4. Establishment of an Indian Archival Council to coordinate all archival activities, whether of the Union or of the States or of the public bodies in the country, and advise on problems of archival administration
5. Pre-appointment archival training in the National Archives of India of candidates selected by Union/States Public Service Commission or other selecting Authority for appointments in the Central/State Archival Offices.

The recommendations of the Committee regarding the courses in Archives Keeping were to be considered in conjunction with paras 77(2) and 172 of the report, which pertained to recruitment of Archivists in the States and the Union Government, respectively.

Para 77(2) stated '.....we strongly recommend that the members of the archival service in the States should be recruited by open competitions at a young age and should be promoted to higher officers as they acquire experience, and that no responsible post in archives should be filled except by men of experience in archival work. The end we have in view will be met if a special archival cadre is created consisting of not more than three ranks of Officers: Keeper (the Head of the Archives), Assistant Keepers (Senior), and Assistant Keepers (Junior), all recruitment being made only at the level of Assistant Keeper (Junior). It may be profitable to examine as a long-term plan, the possibility of transforming the archival service into an All-India Service....'

Para 172 '….. Recruiting Archivists at a very young age and promoting them to higher posts as they gain experience of archive work is, we believe, the only way by which the shortcomings in the present system of recruitment or selection can be removed. We would suggest that should start at the level of the Archivist (or the lowest supervisory post in the Department) and once a person has been selected, his promotion to the highest post should be assured, provided he is able to acquire the necessary experience in archive work and the requisite knowledge of records. The appointees in our view should be selected by the UPSC on the basis of a written test, after which they should be given training in different aspects of archives keeping in the National Archives. Only on the successful completion of such training should an appointee be regarded fit for being posted in the appropriate Division…'[33]

The two paras summed up the Committee's viewpoint on the mode of selection of archivists and the formation of their cadre in the States and the National Archives of India. Their suggestions for reforms in the Training Course were based on the presumption that the recommendations regarding recruitment of Archivists would be acceptable to both State Governments and the Government. S Roy, the then officiating Director, NAI, in his UO Note dated 19 May 1961 to Ministry of Education, wrote that rules and regulations for the new Training Scheme should be framed only after getting the decisions of the State Government's and Union Government of India on the recommendations of the Committee, contained in paras 77(2) and 172, respectively.[34] It was essential because it involved substantive changes in the administrative structure also, of the respective archival

33. Ibid
34. F.No. 4/61-R.5. NAI, pp.3-6.

organisations including selection of the requisite staff.

The Ministry of Education took in comments of IHRC members, State Governments and ALC, and suggested that training in Archives Keeping be imparted to those recruited against archival vacancies in States and the National Archives. The Government accepted the recommendations in principle and wrote to Director, NAI, in a letter dated 27 July 1962 about the Diploma Course and archival training.[35] Accordingly, NAI was directed to re-examine the recruitment rules for the grades of Archivists in the Department.

Should Elements of Archival Science Education be Included in the Library Science Curricula in Universities?

The Government further suggested to the Inter-University Board of India to include elements of Archival Science Education in Library Science Courses in Indian Universities, to meet the demand for qualified and trained archivists for public and private archives in the country. A draft memorandum on the subject was prepared to be forwarded to the Ministry.[36]

However, NAI, did not support the government decision to include archival science in Inter-University Boards' Library Science curricula and instead, requested the government to reconsider their decision. The reasons given were the short duration of the of the 9-month course conducted by the universities already had seven to eight papers, and students were fully occupied with lectures and practical classes. Combining the two training courses in a limited time period of nine months was not sufficient as one could not even introduce one paper on Archives Keeping in that short period. Moreover, both subjects were different from each

35. Ibid.
36. Ibid.

other and students and even faculty had different qualifications.

For Library Science, a graduate in any subject was eligible, whereas for Archives Keeping, a student had to hold an Honours or Master's degree in History. Facilities for practical training like those conducted by the NAI, and which was considered the most important part of training in Archives Keeping was not possible elsewhere. Without it, the training would be incomplete or lopsided. Also, the demand for employment was very limited and accordingly, the Department had to cut down the number of private students for the course. And if this demand increased, the persons to be appointed should have been trained at NAI or at the Madras Records Office.[37] It was further observed that clubbing the two courses would be contrary to the government decision to limit training in Archives Keeping to persons selected for archival jobs in NAI or States Archives. The Tarachand Committee had categorically recommended a system of post-appointment training and it wasn't possible to include Universities in such a system.[38]

Had they accepted the Government's proposal, their training would have been of no use to persons likely to be appointed in Archives, as they had no qualified faculty to maintain the desired standards. He rightly suggested revising the NAI Scheme, if necessary, to meet the country's requirements for trained archivists. If the demand continued, a separate School of Archives Keeping could be started under the auspices of the NAI. The Government was requested to reconsider its decision, and the diploma course was provisionally continued on an year-to-year basis till a final decision was taken.

37. Ibid F. No. 2-7/61 PR, Letter dated 3 November, 1962, pp.6-9/corr.
38. Ibid

Should Archival Education be Continued on a Permanent Basis?

While the scheme was under review and being considered for further extension and modification in the light of the recommendations of the Archival Legislative Committee in consultation with the States and the Union Government, the Government's view was that the time was perfect to continue archival education on a permanent basis, as it had also been found useful by the Committee.[39] Final modifications were awaited as State Governments were being consulted apart from NAI and IHRC members. Approval of Ministry of Finance was also necessary. The Ministry of Finance did not agree to give extension to the scheme as an interim measure, as training more people and incurring an expenditure on them if they are not suitably employed was not considered wise. They were advised to first modify the scheme according to the recommendations of the Committee.[40]

It was hard to think of suspending or deferring the Training Scheme subject to the final decision of the Government on the recommendations of the Archival Legislative Committee. The task involved many vital issues and careful consideration and time to arrive at a decision. It was not advisable to keep the scheme in abeyance either as it would have been harmful to the task of archival recordkeeping in the country. Neither could one deprive nominees of State Archives from such training facilities being conducted by NAI. A number of nominations and enquiries had already been received for the next training session.

This category of trainees was not going to be affected by the commendations of the Archival Legislative Committee, as there

39. F. No. 2-7/61-PR, p.8/notes, vide U.O. dated 20.05.1961 of Deputy Secretary

40. Ibid. p.12/notes

was no obligation to give them employment. Neither was the training a wasteful expenditure as it was a well-known fact that there was a dearth of trained archivists in the country. Some of them did find employment, even though public demand for trained archivists was low as this group was still not well-organised officially as a group. Moreover, efforts should have been put in to make this an attractive career choice and revision should have been made in pay scales and perks. Trained archivists were definitely required for Records Rooms both at the Centre in the Ministries and Departments and in the Provinces after reorganisation of Princely States and the Provinces after Independence, and for emerging archives in the public and private sector. These facts had to be taken cognizance of and the scheme allowed to be continued as it had also attracted many foreign students from Asian countries. The Government had committed to some of them for the next Diploma training course to commence from 1 September 1961.[41] It would have been embarrassing if the commitment was withdrawn. For implementation, Director, NAI proposed to reduce expenditure by reducing the number of stipends of Rs 150 from 5 to 4 and of Rs 75 each to four from 8, thereby reducing expenditure to Rs 10,800 from 16,200. The Ministry of Education was to approach Ministry of Finance for necessary approvals.[42]

Implementation of ALC's Recommendation in Centre and States on Education and Training of Archivists

Finally, the Ministry of Education referred the matter to NAI for comments.[43] After carefully examining the issue, Dr Bhargav,

41. M/Edn. Memorandum No.F.3-15/61-A-10, nominating 2 Malaya students for the One-year Diploma Course
42. F.No. 4/61-R-5., U.O. dated 30 June 1961.
43. Ibid pp.16-17/notes.

Director of Archives opined that it would not be possible to introduce the system of training in archives as recommended by the Archival Legislation Committee for the next few years. He reasoned that the scheme did not get much support from State Governments, both for training and for the method of recruitment as suggested by the Committee. IHRC members generally did not express their opinion, except for the Director, Central Records Office, Hyderabad, and VK Bawa, who said it would not be practical to implement the recommendations of the Committee and felt that continuation of the existing training facilities in NAI was the best. Views of 11 out of 15 State Governments had been received, while Maharashtra, Bihar and Assam did not offer any comments. The Governments of Mysore, Punjab and West Bengal agreed with the proposal but did not state clearly if they agreed with the recommendations of the Committee about recruitment and promotion of Archivists as in paras 77(2) and 172 of the Report. The Government of Madras had given conditional acceptance and wanted archival posts to be declared technical, their pay scales made more attractive, and support from the Centre for their implementation. They doubted if the Government would give financial assistance to State Archival repositories.[44]

Andhra Pradesh (including today's Telangana), Kerala and Orissa approved the recommendations with Andhra Pradesh vetoing the idea of pre-appointment training of State Archivists as impractical, since it would mean planning the staff requirements three years in advance, as all schemes fell under Five Year Plans. Andhra and Orissa had also suggested promotion of archival training courses in universities with the idea of setting up Schools

44. Ibid, pp. 19-20/notes.

of Archivists in universities to cater to the needs of Central and State Governments. Kerala wanted the selected candidates to possess knowledge of vernacular scripts in use in the States and be trained in special methods of preservation of palm leaves, before going for training at NAI.[45]

There were divergent views on ALC's recommendations on the training. Though ALC had suggested an ideal scheme for the organised cadre of Archivists, implementation was a problem as it pre-supposed the existence of Central and State archival repositories maintained with certain minimum professional standards by staff employed by them. The Committee's presumptions were apt that although the candidates were trained, they lacked talent. Thus, a talented pool was generally not available for archival posts because of relatively low pay scales and low status assigned to archivists in the State Governments.

These observations even hold well and are valid even today! The suggestions by the State Governments for Archival Training in universities, was for a model followed by universities of London and Washington, but Indian universities also did not possessed neither the facilities or the competent staff for the lectures. Even the universities of London and Washington depended on staff working in their National Archives.

Delhi University was the only university, perhaps, which could have started the programme with part-time support from officers of NAI for lectures and practical training. In the given scenario, the only practical approach was to continue the existing Training Scheme for some years with modifications, till a final decision was taken.[46]

45. F. N.2-5/61-PR, p.17/corr.
46. F.No. 4/61-R-5, pp.21-22/notes.

Since salaries and placement was still a matter of concern, some of the trained Archivists even left their jobs for better opportunities in other fields. The Director of Archives sought extension of the NAI Scheme of Diploma Course by submitting a revised proposal to the Ministry of Education.[47] In all probability, NAI believed that the scheme had to be continued in the long-term basis with minor modifications and the practical difficulties involved in implementing the Committee's recommendations and keeping in view the different stages of development of Archives in the states. While sanctioning the continuance of the training scheme, for the year 1962-63, the Government reduced the number of the Rs 150 stipends from 4 to 2 for private candidates and increased the quota for the Rs 75 stipend for State nominees from 6 to 8.[48]

NAI had reservations about introducing Archival Science as part of the Library Science curriculum and so, Ministry of Education referred the matter to Director, Central Secretariat Library (CSL). For two years, till 1965, there was no response from CSL and the Diploma Course continued with a modified syllabus. Recommendations of the ALC could not be implemented in letter and spirit under the existing circumstances relating to archival science education and training.[49] The scheme continued with some modifications and students of the one-year Diploma Course in Archives Keeping were sent for field visits to understand the working of other State Archives on recommendations made by the National Committee of Archivists. This also developed bonding among the archival community. This practice has continued till date, and remains an important aspect of field

47. F.No. 5/62-PR, dated 28 May 1962, p.23/notes.

48. NAI Annual Report for the year 1961-62, p.8

49. IHRC Proceedings, 38 Session, Calcutta, November 1967, p. 65

training of students of the one-year diploma course.[50]

Indian Archival Council or Indian Historical Records Commission

One of the recommendations of the ALC was that 'An Indian Archival Council may be constituted by a Presidential order (under Article 263 of the Constitution) to advise both the Union and State Governments on the management, administration, preservation, disposal, and public use of records and to coordinate archival activities of the public offices in the country. This made setting up of a Statutory Advisory Council, possible.[51] The Council was to have fifteen members from fifteen States and ten additional members to be nominated by the Central Government including the Director of Archives. The Education Minister or any other minister in charge of Archives was to be the Chairman of the Council. The President could appoint members for 5 years. A Director of Archives was to be the Secretary and was to be supported by a full-time administrative Secretary. The Council was to have a Standing Committee of 7 members, selected from the Council. The Council was also to take charge of the work of the National Register of Private Archives. It was to have had its own staff and expenses were charged to Central Revenues. After the body was constituted, the IHRC and all its adjuncts were to be terminated.[52]

Some States did not favour the statutory status, which meant that while they supported the need of archival legislation, they did not support the single law and amendment of the Constitution to establish an Archival Council with a statutory status. The

50. Proceedings of the National Committee of Archivists, 15th meeting, Vol I (1954-64), pp.86-87. NAI publication
51. Ibid, pp. 68, 73, 79-80
52. Ibid. pp. 82-84 and 86.

Council could be constituted by an executive order of the Government to advise both the Union and State Governments on the management, administration, preservation, disposal and public use of records and to coordinate the archival activities of all public offices in the country. They supported separate laws for the central and state Records offices passed by Parliament and state legislatures. All States were to utilise whatever opportunities the NAI might offer to get their staff trained. They also realised that it would not be possible to send all employees for training.

It would suffice only if 40 per cent of the staff to be recruited in future against technical posts, were sent for training to NAI.[53]

Finally, the recommendation of the ALC to substitute IHRC by an Indian Archival Council was rejected by the Government due to lack of support from the States, historians and scholars. This support was necessary in a democratic set up. Most of the functions contemplated for the Council were already being performed by IHRC and NCA put together.[54] Like IHRC, NCA also continued without any change, but the two sub-committees of IHRC, Research and Publication Committee and Local Records sub-Committee were not revived.

Empowering IHRC

Paucity of funds affected the development of Archives in the States and NAI and it was still hoped that Archives be accepted by the State Governments as a Plan Item of development.[55] Many States like Mysore, Madhya Pradesh, Gujarat, Haryana and Union Territories, and centralised archives in Kerala had

53. Ibid, p. 1/corr., O.M.dated 20 February 1961, F.N. 6/7/61-A.10, endorsed to D.A, NAI.
54. IHRC proceedings, October 1966, pp.1-2, and10.
55. IHRC Proceedings, 37th Session, Delhi, 7-9 October 1966, pp. 9-19.

not yet organised their Record offices. It was argued that the revised IHRC had no financial or other powers to watch the implementation of its resolutions/recommendations, even at basic levels. It was, therefore, suggested that these powers be vested with the IHRC, so that it be empowered. It would involve constitutional and administrative issues, and the Secretary of the Commission was to write to the ministry, but the Government after examination decided that since all the powers recommended for the Council had already been given to Indian Council of Historical Research (ICHR)[56] and NCA, it could not be empowered with additional financial powers.[57]

The Commission resolved that henceforth 'the Secretary to the Commission should furnish at its next session a comprehensive report on the question of vesting the Commission with any or all the powers of the Archival Council as recommended by the Committee on Archival Legislation.' Besides following Resolution (XVII) was also recommended to the Government of India and the State Governments for liberalising access to records:

- All records in the custody of the Union and State Governments which are more than 30 years old should be open to bona fide researchers,
- The system of scrutiny of excerpts from open records should be abolished and no permission should be required for publication of such records and of results of researches based on them.

By now both Ministries of Home and External Affairs had allowed access to 30-year-old records.[58] NAI had recommended to the Government that 'Archives' be included as a Plan Item

56. A statutory body of Government of India, to give grants for historical research.
57. IHRC Proceedings, 40th Session, Madras, 18-22 February 1970, p. 80
58. Ibid, p.50.

in State Plans. To meet current needs of administration and of historical research, State Plans from 1968-69 to 1973-74 now included Development of Archives.[59] Ministry of Education and the Planning Commission also approved inclusion of Archives as a Plan Item in State Plans from Fourth Five Year Plan onwards, when all State Governments included 'Development of Archives', archival education and training as a State Plan Item as recommended by the Indian Government. This was done to ensure that sufficient attention was given to both administrative and cultural aspect of the course so that Archival development in the states was ensured. They also recommended that construction of archival buildings be included as a Plan Item. It was accepted both by the Central and State Governments.[60]

After a lapse of 5 years, the thirty-seventh session of the reconstituted IHRC was held in October 1966 at Delhi. Director of Archives, as Secretary of IHRC presented a comprehensive report to the Commission, covering major developments in Archives over five years both at the Centre and the States. Reportedly, most of the recommendations of the Archival Legislative Committee were accepted by the Government for liberalisation of access rules to public records with some restrictions to records of Ministries of External Affairs, Home and Defence, transfer of public records to NAI after twenty-five years, preparation of Retention Schedules for weeding of Records common to all, two-stage review of Records, once after 5 years by the Administrative Unit and at the end of twenty-five years, jointly by the Administrative Unit

59. NAI, F. No.13/68-C. pp. 141-42/corr.

60. IHRC Proceedings, 39th session, Patna, 25-27 December, 1968, p.17.

and NAI.[61] Other achievements of Archives in the centre and states included success in accessioning public records, private papers, microfilm copies of records and papers from India and abroad and other publications.

Training in Archives Keeping in the years 1961-66had been completed by twenty-nine persons, which included thirteen from State Archives Departments, 2 from the Indian Government, 1 from University of Jammu and Kashmir, and 1 each from Malaysia and Nepal (under the Colombo Plan) besides 9 private candidates. Thirty-four had trained under various short-term courses in preservation and photo-duplication. NCA had been promoting State Archives to explore whether training could be conducted locally, particularly in preservation and records management.[62] In1966, 8 persons were awarded Diplomas, from Andhra Pradesh, Utter Pradesh, West Bengal, University of Jammu and Kashmir, Ministries of External Affairs and Works, Housing and Development, besides 2 private candidates. Since April 1967, three batches of trainees for the Diploma Course in Archives Keeping completed the course and 14 persons took home their diplomas. Three from Central Public Library in Patiala, the Visva Bharti University and a person from HMT Ltd, Bangalore were trained in Preservation and Photo-duplication. The Director of Madras Records Office spent two months in the Department of NAI for study and observation.

With increasing awareness in the archival community in the states due to efforts of IHRC, NAI and NCA State archives, many of the archivists were now taking the course. State Archives

---

61. Ibid, pp. 9-10.
62. Ibid pp.11-16.

were also taking initiative to start in-house training of short duration. Andhra State Archives arranged training in Persian Paleography held by a PhD and post graduate members of the State Archives. Andhra Pradesh trained 12 persons in Persian paleography during 1967-68, including university teachers, PhD and post graduate students. They also started training of Record Clerks in the Collectors' offices. Kerala also started with an in-service training course in Archives Keeping for their staff and gave intensive training to 15 persons in Archives Preservation and Administration. The Madras Records Office imparted training in Mending and Binding to persons deputed by Governments of Kerala, Orissa, Mysore, University of Mysore and High Court of Madras.[63] Similarly, the Punjab Record Office made arrangements for training of mending and binding.[64] As per NAI report submitted to the Commission at its Fortieth Session at Madras in February 1970, two batches of trainees, in October 1967-September 1968 and October 1968-69, received training from State Archives of West Bengal, Orissa, Andhra Pradesh, Survey of India, Dehradun, University of Mysore, Government of Nepal besides 5 private candidates. Ten people were trained in Preservation and Photo-duplication, including one student from the Philippines.[65]

Need to Modernise Scheme of Archival Science Education and Training

For addressing all problems and issues in the development and modernisation of Archives in India, it was stressed to enhance the

63. IHRC proceedings, December 1968, 39th session, Patna, pp. 76-77, 96, 118-119 and126.
64. IHRC proceedings, November 1967, 38th Session, p.17.
65. IHRC proceedings, February 1970, 40th Session, Madras, pp. 201-202.

'professional competences of Archivists and their numbers had to be increased considerably to cope with these tasks. It was accepted that every Records Room of the Union and State Ministries and Departments should, as far as possible, be placed in the charge of a competent and trained Departmental Records Officer, who in all the advanced countries now forms the most important cadre for dealing with records in their semi-current stage.'[66]

All through, funds were low, and archival repositories were burdened with the additional problems posed by shortage of properly trained and experienced cadre of Archivists. India too had to take quicker and longer strides to catch up with advanced countries in the field of Archives Administration through education and training to understand the impact of computers on Archival problems. An Archival law was needed for India to regulate these activities. The Government was considering the feasibility of issuing a Policy Resolution on Central Archives since it would take time. The proposed policy resolution was expected to cover archives administration, including education and training.

This was what was needed to be done to modernise the scheme of Archival Training and Education in Archival Science.

A resolution was moved by Prof OP Bhatnagar in the IHRC Madras session in 1970, recommending that the Government, Universities and University Grants Commission (UGC), to facilitate Archival Training and create a Department of Archives along with History in Universities.[67] But the resolution was modified and the Secretary, informed members about the ongoing one-year diploma course in Archives Keeping conducted by NAI,

66. IHRC proceedings, October 1971, 41st Session, Trivandrum, p.7-9.
67. Ibid p. 29.

and that a short-term course in Records Management suggested by the Estimate Committee of the fourth Lok Sabha (1968-69), and recommendations by the Committee of Officers appointed by the Department of Administrative Reforms, Government of India in 1969 would be conducted.

The problem was two-fold: lack of availability of arrangements for training in universities, and second, lack of scope of absorbing trained archivists. While agreeing with the Secretary, some members recommended attracting more students, to increase the number of stipends for trainees at NAI. The Chairman suggested that a survey be done to ascertain the number of trained archivists required in the country over the next 10 years. As UGC was not in a position financially to support a new proposal during the current Plan, a revised resolution was adopted: '...Universities may provide facilities for archival training, during the fifth Five-Year Plan period, if UGC could provide financial assistance for the purpose.' The Secretary also highlighted two resolutions adopted by the Commission at its thirty-eighth session in 1967and at the fortieth session in 1970, recommending inter alia that universities be requested to entrust the care of their records to officers who were trained in Archives Keeping from NAI. Several universities welcomed the resolution. In 1970, a proposal urging the universities to set up a Model Archival Cell was invited by the UGC Secretary.[68]

Adoption of Archival Policy Resolution, 1972 and Training in Archives and Records Management

Adoption of Archival Policy Resolution of 1972 by the Indian Government was a landmark development in the history of

68. Ibid, pp.29-30, Annual Report of NAI for the year 1972, pp.7and13.

Archival Science and records management in India. IHRC in resolutions adopted in 1938 and 1948 had recommended the enactment of an archival legislation. There was also a persistent public demand for legislation for proper maintenance and management of records of the Union and State Governments, and for reasonable access to these records for the purpose of research. The Committee on Archival Legislation had made recommendations in its report that steps be taken to amend the Constitution of India by making a suitable entry in the Concurrent List to enable the framing of a single Central law that could take care of both the Union and State Archives. Pending the amendment proposed, separate Archival laws were to be enacted for the centre as well as the States. It was observed that amendment of the Constitution could take time, so till then, a common Archival Law for the Union and States under Article 252(1) of the Constitution would apply.[69]

For this, an amendment of the Constitution was needed. Entry 67 in List 1 of the seventh Schedule of the Constitution empowers the Union Government to legislate Ancient and Historical Monuments, Records and Archaeological Remains declared by Parliament to be of national importance. The amended Antiquities (Export Control) Act enacted in 1947 did not properly define the term 'Records' till it was amended in 1972 and the discrepancy removed. Till the passing of the Public Records Act of 1993, Records in India were managed by Executive Orders. In reply to a query from the Estimate Committee of Parliament (1968-69) of the fourth Lok Sabha,[70] on the delay in undertaking such Legislation, it was felt that statutory

69. A Handbook of Record Managers, Appendix-III, p.35.

70. Report of Records Management Committee, 1976, p.42.

obligations would have created more complications, because the central organisation would not be able to fulfil the obligation of enactment. Finding that it was not possible to fulfil the increasing demand for Legislation immediately, the Government issued an Archival Policy Resolution (APR) in December 1972 to serve as a guide for the proper maintenance and management of records of the Union Government.[71] State Governments were suggested to issue similar Resolutions for their records.

The Archival Policy Resolution (APR) with its eighteen clauses, was approved by the Union Cabinet and promulgated by the Department of Culture, on 11 December 1972. The clauses defined the responsibilities of the Ministries, Departments and Offices for the proper management of Records in their custody and selection and retirement of records of permanent value to National Archives of India. It listed NAI's responsibilities for Public Records in its custody and those of Ministries/Departments and other offices. It prescribed conditions governing public access to records.[72]

The APR laid down that Departmental Records Rooms with semi-current records be placed under a properly trained, suitable and responsible full-time staff. Andhra Pradesh, Assam, Delhi, Goa, Karnataka, Nagaland, Kerala, Maharashtra, Punjab, Rajasthan, Tamil Nadu, UP, and West Bengal accepted the APR. Maharashtra even considered establishing a centre for imparting training in Archives Keeping. Mizoram planned to take action after setting up its Records office. Because of the APR, NAI decided to start two short-term Certificate Courses on Records Management for Departmental Records Officers and Preservation of Records of Ministries/Departments of Union Government

71. Ibid p.53. For details of background work of passing of Public Records Act, please see Chapter III

72. NAI Annual Report, 1972, p.1.

of India. Fifteen candidates completed their training in 1972 in the one-year Diploma Course.

Many states such as Andhra Pradesh, Gujarat, Orissa and Tamil Nadu were considering appointment of Director of State Archives as inspecting Authority of their non-current Records. In West Bengal the question of implementation of the resolution did not arise as all non-current records of the Departments that were more than three years old were being transferred to the Central Records Office. Haryana, Himachal Pradesh and Madhya Pradesh were to consider the resolution while Arunachal Pradesh, Lakshadweep and Minicoy, Manipur, Nagaland and Pondicherry till then had no Records Offices.

NAI Collaboration with Department of Personnel and Administrative Reforms

Collaboration and cooperation with the Department of Personnel and Administrative Reforms, (D/P and AR) was crucial for implementation of recommendations of the Archival Legislation Committee of 1960. In 1959, Ministry of Education and Scientific Research had appointed Archival Legislative Committee, after submitting its report in December 1960. The report had made recommendations not only on Archival Legislation but also on reforms required for improving the archival economy of the Union and State Governments including archival education and training. The Department of Personnel and Administrative Reforms incorporated some of the recommendations of the Archival Legislation Committee in the revised Central Secretariat Manual of Office Procedure. But some very pertinent recommendations, such as those relating to files in the transfer of functions from one Department to another were not incorporated in the Manual. Consequently, the Manual of Office Procedure carried instructions contrary to accepted archival principles.

The Department of Culture and NAI stressed that after issuing of APR 1972, the Department of Personnel and Administrative Reforms' role should be limited to overseeing the work of Records Management through the former (NAI). However, the latter insisted on issuing direct instructions to the Ministries about the management and administration of current and semi-current Records. This caused confusion and efforts were made to resolve this issue; records management was done scientifically in accordance with correct archival principles both in theory and practice. The Department of Administrative Reforms has been primarily responsible for all policy directives for management of public records of the Government. While considering the Report of ALC, a landmark decision taken by the Government was the formation of a Committee on Management, constituted in 1969 by the Department of Administrative Reforms for discussion of various aspects of the problems of management of records. NAI was its member.[73]

The Committee of Officers on Records Management and on various recommendations of ALC, constituted four sub-groups to discuss various problems relating to creation, recording, indexing, and weeding of files in late December 1969. Sub-group IV deliberated on Archival training and the organisation of Departmental Record Rooms, essential for a well-planned Record Rooms to ensure survival of records and their working. Contrary to their expectations, many Record Rooms had no proper ventilation and had unhygienic working conditions

73. F.N.4-4/70-C, pp.22-23/Notes.

posing health hazards for the largely untrained staff. To make working conditions in DRRs attractive, trained Records Officers were appointed. The idea was to improve records management practices at the end while ensuring transfer of records to NAI.[74]

The Ministry of Education had also referred the Report of the Archival Legislation Committee to Organisation and Method (O and M) Division of the Cabinet Secretariat, vide letter dated 13 July 1961 for framing of statutory rules for enforcement of procedures for creation, custody, management and retirement of public records, in consultations with O and M Divisions of various Ministries and Departments.[75] The Cabinet Secretariat decided to amend the Manual of Office Procedure to incorporate recommendations accepted by them. A Working Group was constituted to consider the recommendations of the Tarachand Committee in the light of the comments received from O and M officers.[76]

The Working Group submitted its report on procedures for creation, custody, management and retirement of public records to the extent possible, after factoring in recommendations of the Archival Legislation Committee. The report was considered by the Government in consultation with Central Ministries and was accepted. The Department of Cabinet Affairs (O and M Division) was requested to implement the decisions including all Ministries/ Departments, President's, Prime Minister's, Lok Sabha and Rajya Sabha Secretariats, UPSC, Comptroller and Auditor General's office, Department of Atomic Energy, Bombay, Department

74. F.No.4-4/70-C, p.-45a-.

75. F.N.2-6/61-PR,p.1/cor. Memo.dt 21.12.61,F.N.2/34/61- 0 and M, D/Cabinet Affairs, Cabinet Secretariat., addressed to all O and M Officers in the Ministries/Depts.

76. Ibid.

of Parliamentary Affairs, besides all State Governments and Administrations of Union territories for information and action if any. NAI was also directed to take necessary action concerning them by Ministry of Education.[77] Subsequently, necessary amendments were made in the third edition of the Manual of Office Procedure, ed 1958, in consultation with NAI after trial and experimenting in some sections of few Ministries on various aspects including filing system, training of Departmental Records Officers and their supporting staff, etc.[78] By then, an O and M Division had also developed Retention Schedule of Records of Common Interest of all Ministries/Departments, with the help of the Working Group, covering files and other types of records, laying down retention period. The new system was to be implemented from 1 January 1963.[79]

The Department of Cabinet Affairs now wrote to all O and M Officers to appoint experienced staff in Departmental Records Rooms, who would be responsible for the maintenance of records directly under the guidance of the Section Officer in the O and M Unit, who would supervise to ensure that proper maintenance; weeding and transfer of records to NAI were done at the appropriate time. Persons in charge of DRRs or even Section Officers of the O and M Unit would be given training through Orientation Courses in the maintenance of records by NAI.[80] This course was soon implemented. On the request of the Cabinet Secretariat, a detailed Scheme of Departmental Records Officer's Training was worked out by NAI.[81]

77. Ibid, P.17-A/corr. andF.No.6/15/61-A.10
78. Ibid, pp. 52-59/corr.
79. Ibid, pp. 66-70 and 87/corr.
80. Ibid, pp. 83-84 and 86/corr.
81. Ibid, p.85/corr. vide their letter dated 1.2.1963, F.N.13-3/63-OandM,

The Department of Administrative Reforms had been responsible for all policy directives in the management of public records of the Government. After approval by the Government for amendments on recommendations of ALC, a landmark decision taken for the formation of a Committee of Officers on Records Management, constituted in 1969 by the Department of Administrative Reforms.[82] Sub-Group I-IV were formed to deal with the Central record room, procedures for records management, measures for toning up records management and training in records management, respectively.[83]

The primary responsibility for effective records management lay with the Ministries/Departments. The Department of Administrative Reforms would work its own, appropriate role in collaboration with NAI as and when necessary.

It was also agreed that there should be closer liaison between the Department of Administrative Reforms and NAI and that the latter should be associated in all policy matters, as recommended by ALC. Paras 108 and 114(iii) of the Manual, stated that NAI could advise Ministries/Departments on the correct period of retention during their survey of Departmental Records Rooms and revision of Retention Schedules done every fifth year. No confidential files could be transferred unless declassified as non-confidential. A functional File Index was to be introduced as soon as possible. Sub-headings of files were to be decided by the Section Officer and it was his responsibility to ensure that records were maintained with the prescribed procedures. O and M Divisions in every Ministry/Department were to monitor the recording and indexing of files monthly, by overseeing

82. F.N.4-4/70-C, pp.22-23/Notes

83. Ibid, pp.-45 (a-xxx)/corr.

reports in standardised formats.[84]

Sub-group IV observed that the root cause of the problem was lack of training in Records Management practices. Even a trained assistant performed better than a senior after training.[85] Quality of work was just as important as the process to be followed. Based on these observations, illustrative training material was introduced into the syllabus for training Departmental Records Officers and Assistants. The Committee accepted the recommendation that Departmental Records Rooms should be placed only under officers trained in Records Management and Finding aids. Assistants also had to have trained in Records Management especially in appraisal of Records. It agreed and recommended that NAI should develop brief training material for Departmental Record Officers (DROs).[86]

Cadre of Archivists and Records Managers; Training in Record Management Practices

The issue was discussed but did not get much support. Though attractive in principle, it was suggested that it be examined only after success in streamlining records management practices and issues in all the reorganised provinces/states and if need is felt for such a cadre. IHRC did not adopt even a Resolution, moved by a plea from FM Hassnain who said that the All-India Cadre of Archival Service must be constituted for the whole country as for other cadres to focus on efficiency in the administration of Archives Offices in various States.[87]At that stage, the question of constituting a full-fledged cadre of Records Keepers and

84. Ibid
85. Ibid p.45 (a-xiii)
86. Ibid p.45 (a-xiv)
87. IHRC Proceedings, 40th session, Madras, 18-20, February 1970, p.38.

Archivists was considered premature (though recommended by ALC), and it was decided to re-examine after 5 years.[88]

Issues of Archivists vs. Historians

After adoption of the ALC Report, IHRC and Director of Archives wrote to Ministry of Education to discuss problems faced by archivists and historians on liberalising access rules and supplying of extracts/photocopies and pushing for archival legislation. It was hoped that problems would be resolved and enactment of the Legislation be expedited once an appropriate Bill was introduced in Parliament.[89] But the Ministry of Home Affairs did not favour the enactment of a Law for Central Records and opined that a Policy Resolution of the Government to govern, maintain, retire and access Central Government Records would suffice. The Ministry of Home Affairs favoured instead a national law to cover Records of National Importance throughout the country. They believed Parliament could enact such a law within the framework of the existing Constitution of India. However, the Ministry of Law and the Tarachand Committee did not think Parliament could do that unless the Constitution is amended. The matter was thus, referred to Ministry of Law for their opinion and constitutional position.[90] It was decided to arrange a special session along with the next IHRC session to discuss the problems faced by archivists and historians and enable them to exchange views with the Education Minister on the progress made on recommendations of the AL Committee.[91]

Clause 5.1 of the APR stated that NAI was to organise

88. Ibid p.45 (a-xii)
89. F. No. 22-3/70-CA I-2 and of NAI f. No 4-6/70-C, p.3.
90. Ibid p. 3
91. A Handbook for Records Managers, Appendix III, pp.35-39, NAI publication, 1981

suitable training/reorientation programmes for officers in charge of the Departmental Record Rooms and their assistants, to enable efficient discharge of duties entrusted to them.[92] It did not tackle the issue of the Training Scheme of Archives Keeping.

The Archival Policy Resolution of 1972 had been issued as an interim measure in the hope that in due course with a comprehensive Public Records Act under Article 252(1) of the Constitution; a new training course would emerge. Neither did any State Government come forward to be covered under a Central law for the management and administration of its Public Records. NAI prepared a Draft Bill covering Records of Union Government and Administrations of UTs and referred to the Legal Department for advice and approval of the Union Cabinet.[93]

APR of 1972 helped in streamlining the work, as it laid down a well-defined policy on all aspects of Records Management, appraisal and retirement of records, for the APR noted the need for trained personnel to run the Departmental Record/ Muniment Rooms, besides other aspects of Records Management to improve the functional relationship between the DRRs and NAI as all records that were thirty years old or more were opened for consultation by bonafide Research scholars. The necessity of having trained Records Managers in the Departmental Muniment Rooms, had already been outlined by the 1972 APR, and NAI had even started two short-term in-service training courses from October 1973 in Records Management (8 weeks duration) meant for the officials to be employed in DRRs and the other in Repair of Records (6 weeks duration), meant for subordinate staff.

By March1975, NAI had imparted training to 18 officers in

92. Ibid p.36 andNAI F. No 4-6/70-C, p.5/notes,

93. Ibid, pp. 36-37.

Records Management and 18 officers in Repair of Records.[94] After adoption of Archival Policy Resolution in 1972, there was a greater demand for trained personnel at professional and sub-professional levels within the Government Ministries/Departments in India.

Establishment of Institute of Archival Training/School of Archival Studies

In the absence of trained personnel at professional and sub-professional levels within the Government Ministries/ Departments in India, there was indiscriminate destruction of Records in several States in 1975, and this alarmed Archivists and Historians. At the IHRC's forty-third session at Lucknow on 28-29 January 1975, a Records Management Sub-Committee was appointed and this committee submitted its report in June 1976. The report affirmed the ideas of the APR and recommended that Archival buildings be given high priority in the construction programme of State Governments and interim Repositories be set up till then. The report stressed that DRRs be managed by archival-trained full-time personnel, and that a combined Archival service be created for the Centre and Union Territories and States. IHRC was associated closely with the actual disposal of non-current Records. The recommendations were gradually implemented in the NAI archival programs of the country.[95]

NAI's status was raised to that of an Attached Office to deal with Ministries and Departments directly[96] and the Fifth Plan Scheme of NAI to set up a full-fledged Archival School was approved. The Institution would function at a national as well

94. Third report of Director of Archives, GoI, on the Implementation of APR 1974-75, pp. 9 and12
95. Report of the Records Management Committee, June 1976, NAI publication, pp. 36-38, and third report of Director of Archives, GoI, on the Implementation of APR, for the period 1974-75
96. Ibid pp. 13-14

as regional level to impart archival science education and was expected to be a major landmark in archival development in the country. As a result, the Institute of Archival Training was established as a separate branch of NAI, with full-time staff at New Delhi on 11 December 1976.[97] In due course with the expansion of the Records Management activities in the Ministries/ Departments of the Union Government of India and after the adoption of Archival Policy Resolution in 1972, based on the recommendations of the Archival Legislation Committee, there was a greater demand for trained personnel at professional and sub-professional level within India and in the Afro-Asia region in the absence of archival training facilities.

NAI records showed that every year, a number of students were being nominated for the Diploma course from the Afro-Asian region as the result of the establishment of SWARBICA (South West Asia Regional Branch of International Council of Archivists) in 1976 at New Delhi. In 1980, the Indian Institute of Archival Training at NAI was recognised as a UNESCO-approved Regional Centre for Archival Training for South Asia and South-East Asia Region, thereby enhancing the credibility of the Institute of Archival Training. The visiting team from UNESCO found the archival training at NAI in line with international standards.[98]

Already, NAI had a track record in running its Post Graduate one-year Diploma Course in Archival Studies, besides other short-term certificate courses. It had been attracting students from most of the neighbouring Asian and African countries.

97. Seventh Report of Director of Archives, GoI, on the Implementation of APR, for the period 1979-80, pp. 32-33.

98. For details please refer to an article by Frank B. Evans, published In Indian Archives, Vol XXX, No.2, (July-December 1981) pp.1-14

The Archival Training Institute was now renamed as School of Archival Studies in February 1980, and also approved establishment of a Board of Studies, with Director of Archives as the Chairman, to design the syllabi and mode of implementation of the various courses by the School.[99]

Board of Studies and Modernisation of the School

The Board of Studies was constituted as an advisory professional body with nominated experts, two each from Archives and History as members with duration of 2 years. The first Board consisted of six members with Prof SAI Tirmizi, Director of Archives as its Chairman. Other members included Dr P Basu, Dr BS Keswani, Prof PB Mangla, Prof Bipin Chandra, and Deputy Director, School of Archival Studies, was the Member Secretary. The Board was to examine the course contents of the new curriculum of the one-year diploma course in Archival Studies. While framing the curriculum, the Board was to take into account the latest modern archival trends and training needs of the archival Institutions in India and abroad.[100]

The first meeting of the Board was on 28 July1980 when the Board reviewed the syllabus of the one-year Diploma Course.[101*] Their recommendations included:

- Reading list to be restricted to 20-25 items for each paper.
- Schedule of work to be designed on the basis of 25 hours a week, out of which practical content should not be less than 10 hours.
- Standardising scheme of marking. The maximum marks were to be 600.

---

99. F. No. 4-2/81-AT, p.10/corr., letter from D/C, F.N. 32-8/80-Lib dt 26 May 1980.
100. Ibid, p.11/corr.
101. Ibid, pp. 12-13/corr. Minutes of the first meeting of the Board, held on 28 July 1980
 * There were 2 Core +3 optional papers out of seven that a student had to choose, besides dissertation.

- Each paper to carry 100 marks, out of which 60 was to be reserved for final theory examination, 15 for final practical test and 25 for internal assessments throughout the year.
- In addition to five papers*, Dissertation project work on an archival subject, was to carry 100 marks, of which 75 was to be reserved for the assessment of the project study and 25 for Viva-Voce. The project was to be assigned in the early part of the Session to enable each student to devote adequate time and attention to it.
- Specialists in various fields were to be invited in addition to regular lecturers. They were to be given an honorarium of Rs 100 per extension lecture + TA and DA. The Board authorised the Chairman to work out the details for each session.
- Appointments of examiners for the final test/exams were approved. One-third of the paper setters and examiners could be external and two-thirds, internal.
- The issue of affiliation of the School was unanimously approved for Delhi University and it recommended members of the Board be associated with the selection committee for Admission.
- The Board also examined the Scheme of Correspondence Course and opined that such a course could not impart practical training necessary for Archival Studies.

For the first time, the Board of Studies approved the appointments of examiners for the one-year Diploma Course. In their second meeting, the Board constituted a Moderation Committee with the Director of Archives as chairman with another two members. The committee decided that exams should be of three hours and the students answer four out of eight questions, apart from one question that was compulsory. Suitable guidelines were provided to the paper setters to set the papers in a way that would check the students' knowledge of different topics. The Board approved the syllabus of the short-term course of Servicing and Repair of Records at a sub-professional level.[102] Curriculum was revised on professional lines. It was hoped that affiliation would bring academic accreditation of the School by some university, so that the Diplomas and Certificates would carry greater acceptability. Delhi University was approached for affiliation and experts were invited for a series of extension lectures.[103] Delhi University after examining the matter, did not find it feasible to give affiliation, in their letter dated 24February 1981, No. CB-11/81/10 (0)/70572.[104] The Board suggested approaching the University again to reconsider their decision in the light of UNESCO's inclination to convert the School into the UNESCO Regional Centre for Archival Studies in South Asia.[105]

Another significant development was the start of a number of Short-Term Training Courses in all disciplines of Archival Science such as Archives Administration, Records Management, Conservation and Reprography at professional levels and Repair and Servicing of Records at sub-professional levels. The purpose of different Certificate courses was to accommodate sponsoring agencies who were unable to depute their staff for training for a full year. The Certificate courses met specific archival requirements of professionals and sub-professionals both of governmental and non-governmental agencies.[106] The Department conducted two short-term Certificate Courses of training—in Records Management and Preservation of Records for the first time.

Fourteen trainees were nominated for the course in Records

102. F.N. 44-2/81-AT, pp.33-34/corr.
103. F.No. 44-15/80-AT, p. 31/corr.
104. F. No. 44-2/83 AT, p. 42/corr.
105. Ibid.p.33
106. F.N. 44-2/81-AT, p.33

Management. Two nominees from the Department of Education and UGC underwent training in Preservation of Records. There was even a Special training session for a nominee of Namgyal Institute of Tibetology, Gangtok, concentrating on different methods of photo duplication of records.[107]

The School of Archival Studies also experimented with starting a One-Year Diploma Correspondence Course in Archives Keeping through Distance mode in 1978 as an in-service training. This was a major step in the field of Archival Training, introduced initially as a recommendation by IHRC in its 1975 session. The course would be of one year duration and candidates who had completed minimum one year's service and were holding regular posts were eligible for the course.[108] The Correspondence Course was finally introduced in August 1978, and was designed specifically for persons engaged in Records Management and consultation work in the Government. It also catered to professionals working in archival institutions all over India and for students living in distant parts of the country interested in Records Management and archival profession. The first session had 154 candidates on its roll in 1978.[109] Practical Training was provided to the first batch of the Correspondence Course at NAI, and at State Archives of Orissa, Rajasthan, and Andhra Pradesh. Sixty-five candidates completed their course from this batch.[110]

Practical training for these candidates was found to be tough as getting back assignments on time turned out to be a problem. The

107. NAI Annual Report, 1973, pp.7-8

108. IHRC Proceedings, 43rd Session, Lucknow, January 1975, pp.37-39.

109. NAI Annual Report, 1979, p 9.

110. Ibid

Board of Studies had earlier examined the Correspondence course feasibility in its first meeting and had concluded that imparting practical training in Archival Studies would not be feasible. Accordingly, the course was discontinued with the approval of the Government vide Ministry's letter of 13 October 1980.[111]

But numbers of students taking up the course had vastly improved. The one-year Diploma Course in Archives Keeping saw 106 students completing the theory and practical training classes during 1973-1980. Another 106 students were imparted theoretical and practical training. A record 227 students had completed their 6 and 8-week Certificate Courses from Central/ State Government Departments in Record Management and Repair of Records. The Repair and Preservation of Records course of 4 weeks duration had 8 candidates, including two from Bangladesh and one from Indonesia. Special Training in Microphotography and Preservation of Records was also provided to nominees of Geological Survey of India, Calcutta and Visva-Bharti, Shantiniketan, during 1973-74.[112]

The NAI Archival Training Institute provided a 4-month special training in Archives Administration to 10 trainees under the Indo-Afghan Cultural Exchange Program from 1976 to 1980. A 3-week training was organised for seven students of the National Museum in Conservation of cultural properties, sponsored by UNESCO. Special training was provided to two nominees of the Malaysian National Archives and Vrindavan Research Institute, besides two from Maharashtra State Archives in Repair

111. F. No. 44-5/81-AT, pp. 1-2/c. Minutes, 1 meeting of the Board of Studies, held on 28.7.1980, F. No. 32-32/80-Lib.

112. NAI Annual Reports for the years 1975, 1976, 1977, 1978, 1979 and 1980, pp 8, 9-10, 9, 1and9, and 8, respectively.

of Records and Reprography techniques and methods. One nominee from Burma under the special programme of Technical Cooperation of Ministry of External Affairs in September 1976 in Microfilming of Records also completed the course.[113]

During 1978-79, special facilities for observation-cum-training in Records Management, Repair of Records and Microfilming were provided to nominees each of Regional Records Centre, Jaipur, NAI, Malaysia and Radhsaomi Satsang Sabha, Agra. One nominee each of the Governments of Tanzania and Guyana, sponsored by UNESCO were given training in various techniques of Conservation of Records for 6 weeks and 6 months, respectively from 1 December 1978.[114] Nine candidates were trained in the field of Conservation, Reprography and Records Management, of whom four were deputed by the Governments of Afghanistan, Ghana, Guyana and Tanzania under the United Nations Development Program; three nominated by Ministry of Defence and one each of the State Governments of Jammu and Kashmir, and Kameshwar Singh Sanskrit University, Darbhanga.[115]

Changes in examination patterns had also been made. Passing percentage was 40 in individual papers and 50 in the aggregate. A first division was at 65 per cent. Fourteen candidates who joined in 1977 appeared for their annual exams in July 1978. There were foreign students from Nepal and Malaysia, besides nominees from Andhra Pradesh, West Bengal, Gujarat and other colleges. One paper was tough, and some failed. So, passing marks were relaxed to 40 per cent and students with 50 per cent in aggregate

113. NAI Annual Report, 1977, p.-9

114. NAI Annual Report, 1978, pp.-1and9.

115. NAI Annual Report, 1979, pp.-8-9

were declared successful according to the Director's orders, dated 23 November 1978.[116]

Still, 2 candidates failed. If the candidate had failed in one paper, the candidate was allowed to reappear with the next batch. Feedback from one student (from NAI, regional office, Bhopal) was that the two students should not have been failed as less time had been given for Dissertations, only after completing of classes. Question papers were too tough to assess the knowledge of students and he said that there was an urgent need to change the pattern of questioning. Suggestions were given for setting objective questions besides oral questions for viva voce. It was argued, that this was embarrassing for foreign students, and harmful for their self-prestige. It wasn't good for our reputation, either. Indian students could answer their papers in either English or Hindi, but if foreigners were weak in English, they were likely to fail. A candidate from Malaysia and one from Gujarat Archives were failed. It was argued that weightage should have been given to their experience and that other issues deserved consideration. Both candidates reappeared and passed. This information is highlighted here just to point out that feedback from students also matters.[117]

Dissertation work was given to students after they completed theory and practical exams in July. Trainees were, therefore, left with little time to submit their dissertation on the last day of the course. This period was called Internship project period. This situation continued for a long time.[118] The trainees had also been visiting two of the State Archives in the country as part of their

---

116. F. No. 4-12/78-AT,p.2/notes
117. Ibid. Sr. No. 13/corr.
118. F.N.4-1/78-TR

regular training programme introduced on the recommendations of NCA in its fifteenth meeting[119] at Srinagarin1962.The State Archives that were visited frequently included Uttar Pradesh, Tamil Nadu, Karnataka, Madhya Pradesh, Kerala, Andhra Pradesh (now Telangana, as the divided State of Andhra Pradesh is now establishing its new Archives at Amravati), Maharashtra, West Bengal, Orissa and Rajasthan. The 1980-81 session commenced on25 August 1980 with 13 students. Among them were five sponsored candidates: two from Nigeria, one from Kenya, and two sponsored by Government of Delhi and Visva Bharti University, and eight private candidates.[120]

Dr Frank Evans, Program Specialist in UNESCO, visited NAI in February 1980, before NAI was recognised as a Regional Training Centre. He delivered a talk on 'UNESCO and Archives' in NAI. Relations of NAI with UNESCO have been detailed in Chapter V. UNESCO also provided financial assistance to augment and strengthen NAI resources. Senior Officers of NAI had also been deputed abroad for conducting training in Afro-Asian countries. NRR Chari, Deputy Director of Archives and an expert in Reprographic Techniques and Methods and Dr TR Sareen, Assistant Director were deputed to Nairobi, Kenya, in April 1980 to conduct training in Reprography and Records Management, respectively.[121]

For selection and admission of private candidates for the one-year Diploma Course for 1981-82 sessions, thirty-eight applications were received and letters issued for interviews.

Written tests were introduced in 1987, with the approval of

119. Proceedings of the National Committee of Archivists, 15 meeting, Vol I, (1954-64), pp.86-87.NAI publication

120. NAI Annual Report, 1980, pp. 9-10

121. Ibid, p. 14

the Board of Studies and Department of Culture.[122] A University Professor conducted the interviews along with a Selection Committee constituted with the approval of Department of Culture with Director of Archives as its chairman, with a nominee of D/Culture, one History professor from a reputed university and the dealing officer, Deputy Director of Archives/Assistant Director of Archives of the Institute as members.

Later, one member of the Board of Studies was included in the expert committee to interview candidates. Eight candidates were selected. Thirteen sponsored candidates were admitted including 3 candidates from Nigeria and 2 each from Sudan and Malaysia. Candidates by Indian States Archives were 2 from Karnataka, and the rest from Madhya Pradesh, Haryana, Delhi Administration, and Devasahayam, Tirupati. Point to be noted here is that there were more sponsored candidates then private students as per the requirement of the archival institutions from within and outside India in the Afro-Asia region as recognition of the School of Archival Studies by UNESCO had given it credibility.[123]

The short-term Certificate courses were meeting specific archival requirements of professionals and sub-professionals in governmental and non-governmental agencies.[124]

Modernisation of curriculum was also being done, alongside. There were nine papers in the old curriculum.[125] The syllabus was divided into Core curriculum, compulsory for all students and Optional subjects, of which any three were to be offered and approved by the Director.

---

122. F.N. 44-1/87-SAS, p.20/notes

123. F.N. 44-2/81-AT, Minutes of Board of Studies, extracts. F.N. 32-33/80-Lib.pp.20-23/notes, F.N.44-1/87-SAS, p.20/notes

124. F. No. 4-2/81-A.T., p.54/corr.

125. Ibid

The Subjects included the following:

I **Core Curriculum:**

1. Archives Administration
2. Record Management

II **Seven Optional Subjects:**

1. Conservation,
2. Reprographics,
3. Administrative and Institutional History of India (Post 1500 period)
4. Reading and Interpretation of Documents Persian or Rajasthani or Marathi, or Malayalam or Portuguese
5. Ancillary Disciplines–Sigillography, Cartography, Diplomatic and Paleography
6. Archival Development in Developed countries and Developing countries
7. Archival Libraries and Information Systems.

Most of the students opted for subjects at serial numbers 1, 2, 6 or 7, besides two compulsory Core papers.

III **Dissertation based on archival sources (compulsory).**

The Board of Studies was reconstituted in 1982 and now had seven members to examine the curriculum, including short-term courses. The Government also increased scholarships to private candidates from two to five, and the amount was enhanced from Rs 200 to 300/month and stipend to sponsored candidates from States/Union Territories increased from Rs 125 to 200/month. Department of Culture, approved the continuation of one-year Diploma Course in Archival Studies, for five years from 1982-83 to 1986-87. Earlier, it had been approved for five years

1976-77 to 1981-82, with consent of Ministry of Finance vide their letter dt 2 July 1976, F. No. 8-13/76-CA (I) (2)], but it had not agreed to give approval on permanent basis, as the Finance Division did not agree. The approval was subject to conditions of executing of Bonds (already approved vide Ministry letter no. F. 50-46/54-CI dated 20 October 1955), by the trainees receiving Scholarships.[126] A Bond was to be executed by the candidate while availing Scholarship.[127]

The revised curriculum was approved in the sixth meeting of the Board on 25 August 1983.[128] The number of papers were now rationalised to six, based on choices of students during the previous sessions.

The approved six papers:

- Archives Administration,
- Records Management,
- Conservation and Reprography,
- Administrative History,
- Archival Library and Information System,
- Dissertation.

These courses were preceded by an Orientation Course in History and Evolution of Archives. The Board of Studies constituted a Committee to examine and finalise the detailed syllabus of Director of Archives as Chairman with Miss DG Keswani, YP Kathpalia and PK Ghosh as members.[129] Annual examiners were also appointed. Out of eleven examiners, four were to be external. The marking scheme was 60 per cent for

126. Ibid
127. F. No. 44-5/81-AT, pp. 1-26/corr.
128. F.No.44-10/81-AT, pp.24-25/corr. F. No. 32-2/82- Lib, letter dt 22nd June 1982
129. Ibid,NAI Annual Report, 1982, pp.13-15

Theory, 15 per cent for practicals and 25 per cent for internal assessments per paper and Dissertation 75 for content +25 for Viva Voce. Altogether, there were six papers. The marking scheme has been mentioned earlier.[130]

The Syllabus of Administrative History of India had been restructured to provide the trainees with an overall view of the growth and development of the Secretariat and dealt with the teaching mechanism of the Government, organisational structure of major Ministries and impact of the constitutional development on administrative machinery and the system of record keeping of the Government during the colonial period and that of the different archives/records connected with it. Constitutional History of India was not covered in the course as it had a sizeable number of trainees from foreign countries.[131] Other recommendations of the Board were to procure syllabi from Centres and Schools abroad conducting similar training courses. There was provision for extension lectures every year on non-governmental records for students of the one-year Diploma course. A synopsis of the lectures was to be provided to the trainees along with bibliography.[132] Appointment of paper setter and examiner for the paper Administrative History was done vide letter dated 12.5.1986 and an honorarium of Rs 100 was paid for Theory papers and Rs 50 for practical papers.[133]

The School of Archival Studies was now recognised as the foremost of its kind in the Afro-Asia region, and catered to candidates from many developing countries like Afghanistan, Bangladesh, Botswana, Kenya, Malawi, Malaysia, Nigeria, Sudan,

130. F.44-2/83/AT, pp.90-92/corr.

131. F. No. 44-3/82- AT and K W

132. F.No. 21-44/87-Lib., extracts of the Minutes of the Board of Studies, held on 4 Nov.1987 in NAI, p. 56/corr.

133. Ibid

and Thailand. Forty-four candidates were given training in One-year Diploma Course during 1981-84, while 164 had pursued short-term courses. Even some of the States like Rajasthan, Tamil Nadu, Uttar Pradesh and West Bengal began short-term training courses for their own employees and other States were encouraged to do the same by using their own trained professionals.[134]

While conducting the twelfth course in Records Management from 26 March-20 May 1980, applications were invited from private candidates associated with private businesses/temples/churches. Under the Archival Policy Resolution of 1972, adopted by the Government as an interim measure, NAI had an obligation to train persons in Records Management for Government departments. Admission was restricted to 20 candidates.[135] Short-term training courses for private candidates had been started in 1987-88 in Care and Conservation and Reprography to widen the scope of the training and provide trained personnel for induction in the archival profession in States and Union Government offices.[136]

Extension lectures were held often by eminent persons and faculty drawn from Universities, and from within NAI besides the School. Apart from routine subjects, Information Systems and Services of the United Nations Organisation, and its Agencies, International Organisations, their programs and activities, IFLA (International Federation of Library Associations), Modern Public Records and Measures for their efficient Management, and Conventional Archival Sources were taken up by eminent speakers such as Dr P Basu, TN Rajan, OP Gupta, and Prof KA

134. IHRC Proceedings, February 1985, Surajkund, Haryana, p.131

135. F. No. 44-5/86-AT, Annual Exam Diploma-1985-86, session

136. F. No. 45-1/80-AT.p.23/notes

Issac on subjects as varied as Indexing and Abstracting, Role of Library in Archival Science, New Trends in Information Services, Special Problems in Restoration of Wax Seals, Palm Leaves and Paintings, Functioning of an Archival Repository in the interest of an Administrator and General Public, Archival Development in Developing Countries with special reference to India, etc.[137]

Courses were increasingly getting popular in the Afro-Asia region but total seats available for admission to the one-year Diploma and short-term courses were restricted to twenty to match the facilities and infrastructure available for theory lectures and practical classes. From the 1987 session, an entrance test had been introduced for private candidates, while sponsored candidates continued to be admitted on nomination basis. The School introduced a registration fee of Rs 25 from Indian citizens and $ 25 from foreign nationals as registration fee from applicants.[138]

There were three semesters, the first from 1September to 30 November, covering Orientation and papers 1 and 2, Semester II was from December to January, in which Part I of paper 3, Reprography and paper 4, Administrative History, and beginning of Dissertation work began. Semester III was the longest, stretching from February to August, and covered Conservation, part 2 of paper 3, and teaching of paper 5 on Archival Libraries, Documentation and Information Systems, and completion of paper 6 with the writings of Dissertations and submission. Teaching was to be completed by May end. June was for revision and preparation of annual exams held in July. August was for Study Tours conducted to two State Archives. Results

137. F. No. 44-1/87-SAS

138. Ibid. Minutes of meeting of Board of Studies, dated 12.6.1986, and NAI Annual Report, 1981, pp.11-12.

were declared by 31 August. Christmas break was for 10 days. At the closing of teaching of each paper, periodical and internal tests were conducted internally. Besides theory papers, practical exams were held for Papers 1, 2, 3 and5. Practical note-books in each of the above 4 papers, were prepared by students and evaluated internally. The Viva Voce was held by a Board chaired by Director of Archives (Director General wef June 1990), an expert in History and Head of the School.[139]

Examiners were now being appointed by the Board and subsequently approved by Department of Culture which gave financial approval for Honorarium to examiners. Some suggestions were also received from Dr NH Kulkarni, the then Assistant Director of the School and some Guidelines were again framed for paper setters and examiners.[140]

School Fellowship Programme

To augment the faculty, a Fellowship programme was introduced in 1985, as approved by the Board of Studies in its sixth meeting in 1983.[141] The scheme-initiated research and development work in the field of archives, preparation of suitable teaching and learning material for trainees of the School and for professionals in archives repositories in Third World countries. The scheme offered two Senior and two Junior Fellowships (later amended as only Fellow), for renowned Archivists and Conservators for teaching, specified research work and to consultancy. The fellowship was for a period of two years, extendable yearly on the basis of performance. In 1989, the Board amended the

139. NAI Annual Report, 1982, pp.13-15

140. F. No. 44-5/85-AT, one-year Diploma Course, Annual Exams(1984-85)

141. F.N.44-2/83-AT.p.92/corr. Minutes of sixth meeting of BoS. and F.N. 44-1/89-SAS,pp.117-118/corr.

Fellowships scheme to be offered for one year only.[142] Fellowships were advertised and circulated on the basis of rules framed by the Board of Studies, governing the award of Senior and Junior Fellowships in SAS, NAI, to all State Archives. Some responded with remarks that no suitable candidates were available so no one could apply. Some recommended names of retired officers from National and State Archives. Selections were made by the Board of Studies and a Fellow's work was monitored periodically. The Fellows were attached to various members of the Board of Studies. The Honorarium paid to Sr Fellow and Fellows was Rs 2,000 and Rs 1,600/month, respectively. A contingent grant of Rs 4,000 per annum was also given, subject to certain conditions. Administratively, they reported to the Director of Archives.[143]

The scheme worked for only six years from 1985 to 1991. As an outcome, the School produced some standard text books on Conservation, Reprographics and Records Management for teaching and reference purposes. These included books titled 1. Guide to Restoration of Documents, 2. Micrographics for Archives and Libraries, 3. A Select Bibliography of Literature on Reprography. 4. Elements of Conservation and Records Management. The School was also able to develop and design a small Fumigation Vault, a vacuum-operated Chamber, for use by small archives, libraries and manuscripts repositories that were economically priced to be available to organisations with limited resources.

Before the passing of the Public Record Act of 1993, 139 students had passed out with diplomas during 1985-1993. The number included fifty-eight foreign students from Malaysia,

142. Ibid

143. F.N. 44-1/89-SAS, pp.112-113/corr.

Kenya, Malawi, Thailand, Tanzania, Sudan, Nigeria, Sri Lanka and Uganda. The Government had meanwhile, further raised the value of scholarship/stipend for trainees from Rs 300 to Rs 500 for private candidates and from Rs 200 to Rs 300 for sponsored candidates. More than 500 students had benefitted from training programmes, including private students. With the support of Board of Studies and its faculty, the School had gained academically and administratively. More than a hundred extension lecture programmes were delivered by experts in the field of conservation, information, dissemination and publication.[144] Some of the State Archives were also running short-term training courses in Archives Administration and NAI would support them willingly.[145]

Three senior faculties of NAI, Dr RK Perti, NRR Chari and PK Ghosh were deputed during 1985 for imparting training in Archives Administration, Records Management and Reprographics to Malaysia.[146] The School also organised a seminar on Records Management in collaboration with British Council in April 1990 with Dr Nicholas George Cox, Head, Records Administration Division, Public Records Office, London, as the principal Speaker. Twenty-two delegates of State Archives and other institutions besides NAI Regional offices, senior officers and students of the School attended. Various aspects of Records Management prevalent in UK vis-à-vis Indian practices were discussed in detail.[147]

For augmenting Training facilities in SAS, UNESCO was also supporting by funding many of the foreign students during the

144. Ibid. F.N. 44-1/89-SAS, pp.112-113/corr.

145. IHRC Proceedings, March 1988, Bikaner, pp.99-100.

146. NAI Annual Reports for the years 1984-85 to 1993

147. NAI Annual Report, 1986, p.22

period of their training under various programmes and by giving financial assistance to the School. UNESCO offered US$ 12,000 for upgrading of the School, as aid.[148] It also funded training of some of its faculty by supporting their deputation abroad. This is detailed in Chapter V regarding NAI and its collaboration with foreign bodies in the field of archival education and training.[149]

148. NAI Annual Report, 1990, p.18.

149. Ibid

Public Records Act and Public Records Rules

Role in Archival Science Education and Training

Recommendations of the Tarachand Committee on Archival Legislation, 1960 had already built a strong case for archival legislation and suggested the framework of such a law. But it took 33 years for enactment of the Public Records Act in 1993. One of the recommendations of ALC had been centralisation of all records of the Union Government at the centre at NAI and of the State Governments at the States archival repositories. To do this, trained officers and officials in archival education and Records Management practices at all records creating agencies and archival repositories was necessary.

The National Committee of Archivists (NCA) considered the recommendations of the ALC in its fifteenth meeting at Srinagar on 28-29 September1962[1]. NCA declared that centralisation of all records was not possible as State Archives could not provide space to accommodate huge bulk of records if transferred to

1. F.N.7/62-C, pp. 12-15/corr.

State Archives. NAI[#] too had been facing a space crunch, as it could not provide additional shelf space of 40 miles or 176 miles shelf space, as estimated by the Committee to accommodate the permanent records of Ministries and their Subordinate Offices all over the country. NCA thought that an All-India Cadre of Archivists should be taken up only after the formulation of Central and State archival laws. This would help in evolving a uniform pattern of archives administration in the country. It requested the Government to frame an archival law quickly, which could serve as a model for the States as recommended by the Committee on Archival Legislation. NCA agreed on setting up an Archival Council with the same composition and functions as suggested by the Committee. It, however, did not favour the discontinuation of IHRC after formation of the Council. It was also resolved that NCA may be continued in its present form.[2]

Consequently, NAI voluntarily took up a Pilot Project of Records Management to help various Government agencies get rid of their burden of ephemeral Records. The objective was to evolve appraisal standards and procedures for locating records of permanent value. The Government agencies cooperated and annually, around 1 lakh files were appraised. Subsequently, NAI also helped the Department of Administrative Reforms in drawing up Retention Schedules of Records for various agencies

Ministries itself had records of about 40 miles. In average as information received from subordinate and attached offices could have approximately 68 miles? If put together all such offices it will not be lesser than 176 linear miles of shelving or a repository 11 times the size NAI had at that time. (Having a room for 16 miles of shelves). In addition the new accruals were estimated to cover 8 miles of shelving space. So every year will require a new Repository of the size of NAI, to house fresh accrual of Records. The multiplying numbers of new offices, being established every year were adding more requirement of shelf space. So volume of records was a very big challenge to be addressed. Though being increased due to increase in government business but this was also due to existing documentation procedures and disposition of records. (Tarachand Committee Report, p.11)

2. Ibid

to facilitate appraisal. Records Management Procedures had to be toned up to accommodate the progressive increase in the number of offices and their records. Appraisal of records by trained archivists continued to be undertaken on priority by NAI.

Since 1954, the responsibilities of the Ministry of Home Affairs affecting archival matters was being looked after by Organisation and Methods Division (O and M) of the Cabinet Secretariat, which now formulated Rules for Records making and Record-disposal procedures. Since Archives continued to be with Ministry of Education, it was often consulted on disposal, retirement and accessibility of records. But the advice tendered did not help the Government in determining the archival policy of the Central Government due to NAI in the absence of an archival law. The role of NAI was of a mere custodian and powers were very limited, as it could not control the manner in which records were to be retired nor how they should be borrowed or returned to their parent departments. In reality, they were enjoying conceivable autonomy and overall control, albeit in an illogical manner.

Secretary, IHRC while presenting the Report of Development of Archives for the first time at the Delhi session in 1966, informed members that the Report of the Archival Legislative Committee is a great landmark in the history of the country and most of its recommendations had been accepted by the Government. Besides liberalising access rules, it was to transfer 25-year-old records to Archives, following a 'Retention Schedules Common to All', that had been framed by the Department of Administrative Reforms in consultation with the Working Group, and NAI, to guide in weeding of records, common to all ministries, a practice that would guide them in a two-stage review. The Manual of Office Procedure had also been amended for documentation and disposal practices and this helped in streamlining Records Management and disposal practices in Government offices. The Ministries of External Affairs and Home had to reorganise their Records Rooms in consultation with NAI. NAI accepted its advisory role outlined by the Government on the basis of recommendations of the Committee in Preservation of Records on scientific lines. Recommendations for Private Archives were also accepted in principle, by the Government.[3]

Practical problems now emerged. Many Record Rooms had no proper ventilation and these led to unhygienic working conditions that posed health hazards. Moreover, the staff was untrained. To make working conditions in DRRs attractive, it necessitated deploying of trained Records Officers-in-charge, as recommended by ALC, who would improve records management. As was agreed to, NAI developed brief training material indicating the nature and scope of each item of the syllabus proposed for the training course for Departmental Records Officers.[4]

Training of Record Officers at NAI

Only two types of training in Archives Keeping were being conducted by NAI before the adoption of the Archival Policy Resolution of 1972.

- **Regular training programme** or the one-year diploma course in Archives Keeping, open to candidates having second class MA degree in History, preferably in Modern India or an honours degree in History. Selections were based on their proficiency in History and an oral test (the written test for admissions started in 1987) conducted by a selection committee, constituted by the

3. IHRC proceedings, October 1966, p.5.
4. Ibid

Government. Many seats were reserved for candidates sponsored by Ministries/Departments, Government and State offices. The main focus of teaching had been theory of Archives Keeping/ Administration and archive preservation, and national and international practices of progressive countries like USA, UK, France, and Germany, role of NAI, IHRC, Administrative History and its bearing on archival records and development. Practical training included entrusting trainees with difficult assignments in various Branches/Divisions which they were expected to complete. On the conclusion of the course, trainees took written and practical tests before receiving their diplomas.[5]

- **An informal arrangement for training** was also available for candidates sponsored by Government Departments and the Records Offices for shorter durations in practical aspects of record-keeping or record preservation. There was no fixed time schedule for this kind of training. The date and duration was fixed in consultation with the sponsoring body and was useful to those who already had a background in archives keeping. The programme was suitable and appropriate for officers and officials who had worked with current and semi-current files in Departmental Records Rooms of the Ministries and Departments.[6]

The Archival Legislative Committee took note of recommendations made by the Weeding Sub-Committee, constituted by a local sub-committee of IHRC, on disposal of records and recommended that the task be assigned to especially qualified/NAI trained Departmental Records Officers. The

5. Ibid. pp.97-102/corr.
6. Ibid

proposal was endorsed by NAI. The Committee recommended DRO'S should also be responsible for the general care of all departmental papers from the time they were created or received till they are disposed of either by destruction or retired to the National Archives. They were also to be responsible for deciding, together with administrative staff, which record was necessary for the Department to be kept for use during first review and to collaborate with NAI for the second review when due for retirement to NAI. But NAI did not decide on the level a DRO should possess in the office structure, but recommended, that the DRO be higher than a Section Officer. It stressed on the importance of appointing a capable and trained official for the post. Realising that Departments would not be able to spare officials for extended trainings, a short-term training of minimum two months, with a comprehensive curriculum of the general principles of archive keeping and different processes connected with it, was recommended. The trainee was guaranteed to receive a basic and elementary knowledge during archival training at NAI.[7]

The scheme included practical training by NAI in some processes of archive keeping and preservation, and fifteen lectures on the general principles of the subject with stress on Dos and Don'ts. Preparation of a Ministerial Records Room was part of the practical training for current and semi-current files were also given importance. The benefits that the trainees derived depended on their educational background, experience of records and knowledge of modern Indian history; this criterion was to be considered by Ministries/Departments while deputing officials

7. Ibid, pp.101-102/corr.

for training. NAI had experimented with short-term training courses between1952 and1959, and yet, the right candidates were not forthcoming. NAI now proposed to start the course from 1 October1963, with 10 trainees, after seeking concurrence of O and M Division of the Department of Cabinet Affairs. But they still recommended the one-year Diploma Course in Archives Keeping in the first instance.[8]

NAI had also been providing training to students sponsored by foreign countries. In 1962, four trainees sponsored by Nepal Government had been given special training in microfilming, hand lamination and other processes of preservation of records from October 1962 for six months under the Colombo Plan. Similar training was also given to employees of the Central Road Office, Hyderabad, Delhi Administration, Asiatic Society, Calcutta, and KM Institute of Oriental Languages, Agra University.[9]

Archival Policy Resolution of 1972 and its Implementation[10]

The Government, finding it difficult to enact Archival Legislation, as the amendment of the Constitution was not immediately feasible, had issued an Archival Policy Resolution in December 1972, as an interim measure to serve as a guide for the purpose of proper maintenance and management of records of the Union Government.[11] State Governments were to issue similar Resolutions for their records.

It was possible to have a common archival law, applicable to the Union and States who had given their consent under Art.252 {1}

8. Ibid.
9. Ibid.
10. For APR Resolution of Government of India, N.F. 7-6/71-CAI (2), dated 11 December 1972. Please see Appendix XVI, pp. 241-243.IHRC Proceedings, 42nd Session, Goa, January 1973.
11. Ibid.

of the Constitution. The reasons for the delay in legislation have already been discussed in an earlier chapter. Accordingly, the NAI had approved certain measures for all Departments/Ministries of the Union Government, their Attached and Subordinate offices, all Committees and Commissions, and the Union Public Service Commission (UPSC). However, these guidelines did not apply to the Supreme Court, the Comptroller and Auditor General, the Election Commission, and the Parliament or of autonomous bodies set up by the Union Government, including nationalised undertakings and enterprises. These bodies could seek assistance of NAI in any matter coming within the scope of the Resolution and retire their non-current records of permanent value to it, if they so desired. The term records for the purpose as given in the resolution, included documents, rolls, codices, sheets, files, dossiers, microfilms, photographs, charts, plans, diagrams, maps, and sound recordings, among others.

The Archival Policy Resolution of 1972 had 18 sections that defined and regulated the responsibilities of Ministries, Departments and offices of the Union Government for custody, care and management of their records, and their subsequent selection and retirement after 25 years to NAI. It had also laid down the responsibilities of the NAI in respect of public records in its custody and those of ministries and other offices, prescribing the limits and conditions governing public access to records retired to NAI. They also had to organise training/ reorientation programmes as described earlier. Vide sections 6, 7, 8 and 9 of the APR and sections 11,12,13,14, and 15, it defined the duties and responsibilities of the Director, National Archives of India for coordination and to guide in all operations connected with public records. They were given the task of ensuring and preserving records of permanent value by their transfer after 25 years to NAI, then making them available to research scholars after the records were more than 30 years old. Ministries/Departments and other offices could grant special access to records not transferred to NAI, in consultation with them.[12] But APR 1972 had nothing to say about the one-year Diploma Course in Archives Keeping that was running.

After APR 1972, NAI's Status was raised to that of an Attached Office in September 1975, with Director of Archives providing executive direction in the implementation of policies or matters laid down in the APR and serving as a repository of technical information of records of the Government of India and of agencies and organisations which the Government assigned to it.[13] NAI and Ministries and Departments could directly correspond with each other on matters related to Archival Policy Resolution, or for technical advice for the execution of the policies of the Government as laid down by the Department of Culture on archival matters including training of personnel for upkeep and preservation of records.

Section 16.1 of the APR stated that Director of Archives was to submit a report to the Government every year on the management of public records, with reference to the actual working of the records management systems in the Ministries and Departments of the Union Government. Till the enactment of the Public Record Act of 1993, Reports of Director of Archives on the Implementation of the APR for the period 1972-1993, for nearly 30 years makes it clear that APR was not an adequate substitute for archival law.

The information was received in response to a circular issued

12. Ibid. pp.38-39
13. Ibid. pp.33-34, Ann. III.

by NAI every year to all Ministries/Departments and their offices including Secretariats of the offices of President of India, the Prime Minister, Cabinet Secretariat, and UPSC. The information required was on:[14]

- Appointment of Departmental Records Officers and their training besides training of the subordinate staff,
- Setting up of organised Departmental Records Rooms,
- Possibility of sharing space and services of NAI and its Records Centres,
- Progress made in recording, classification, and reviewing of semi-current files and compilation of indexes for records of A and B category,
- Compilation/revision of Retention Schedules for Records,
- Downgrading of classified files/records for their appraisal and transfer to NAI,
- Compilations of organisational history and defunct Commissions and Committees,
- Total record holdings of Ministries/Departments,
- Annual accruals and bulk of records more than 25 years old, awaiting final appraisal before retirement to NAI.[15]

An analysis and review of the Archival Policy Resolution annual implementation Reports before enactment of Public Records Act in 1993 reveals that efforts and repeated attempts made by NAI in drawing attention of the Ministries and Departments for streamlining records management had been ignored by Ministries and Departments and not too many positive steps had been taken. They further reaffirmed and

14. 2nd Report of Director of Archives on the Implementation of the APR-, 1974-75. pp. 1-2.
15. APR Report 1977-1978 ending March 1978, pp.1-2.

justified the need for replacing APR by a comprehensive law on public records, affixing the responsibility of records creating agencies for proper maintenance and upkeep of records.

The Table below indicates the kind of response the Archival Policy Resolution of 1972 evinced from Government Ministries and Departments from 1978 to 1994 as tabulated from the APR Reports for this period.

Year (1)	No. Ministries/ Depts./ Offices addressed (2)	No. Ministries/Depts./ Offices Responded to the Circulars (3)	No. Ministries Depts./ Offices Furnished Complete Information (4)	No. Ministries/ Depts./Offices Furnished Partial Information (5)
1978-79	721	72	26	2
1979-80	721	105	52	7
1980-81	721	133	57	9
1981-82	721	120	68	9
1982-83	721	119	75	1
1983-84	721	136	89	7
1984-85	721	146	88	7
1985-86	721	145	99	13
1986-87	721	156	105	3
1987-88	721	150	104	6
1988-89	721	140	93	10

1989-90	721	140	102	7
1990-91	721	104	68	7
1991-92	721	130	73	9
1992-93	721	120	74	5
1993-94	721	136	86	8

Year (6)	**Ministries/ Depts./ Offices seeking clarification (7)**	**No. Ministries/Depts./ offices giving vague replies (8)**	**No. Ministries/ Depts./ Offices sending Nil reports (9)**	**No. Min./ Depts./Offices acknowledging the Circular and those who didn't respond (10)**
1978-79	10	3	6	25- 649 No Response
1979-80	10	13	15	8- 616 No Response
1980-81	3	5	35	1- 588 No Response
1981-82	3	1	22	Nil -601 No Response
1982-83	Nil	1	25	Nil -602 No Response
1983-84	Nil	1	22	Nil -585 No Response
1984-85	Nil	Nil	35	Nil - 575 No Response
1985-86	1	Nil	22	Nil - 576 No Response

1986-87	Nil	1	32	Nil -565 No Response
1987-88	Nil	6	18	2-571 No Response
1988-89	1	2	19	6-581 No Response
1989-90	Nil	4	15	3-581 No Response
1990-91	Nil	3	16	Nil -617 No Response
1991-92	Nil	3	15	5 -591 No Response
1992-93	Nil	5	23	Nil -601No Response
1993-94	Nil	3	16	6 -585No Response

Remarks- It is clear from these tables that as per the implementation Reports of Archival Policy Resolution of 1972, barely a handful of Ministries and Departments had agreed to abide by the provisions of this Resolution. An Archival Law was therefore, the need of the hour. In addition, there was lack of coordination in Records Management. The situation could have improved if the Government acted urgently and appointed DROs in each ministry (see para 3 of APR).

Equally important was the appointment of trained DROs of the minimum rank of Section Officers, and supporting staff, duly trained in methods and procedures for maintenance and upkeep of records. The School of Archival Studies, NAI were easily accessible. But NAI needed empowering with a Statutory Act for management and control of records throughout their life cycle. The ministry of Finance had agreed to follow a selective approach, but later backtracked, citing economy measures. But the Government's measures proved shortsighted in avoiding expenditure on appointment of DROs that, in the long run, would have ensured that they weeded out records of ephemeral value that occupied costly shelf space.

DRRs continued to be under part-time charge of Under Secretaries, Senior Analysts or Section Officers and defeated the very purpose of APR. Despite starting of two short-term in-service training courses from October 1973 in Records Management for preparing officials to be employed as DRRs, few Ministries/ Departments had shown some interest in getting their officers trained in the Short-Term Records Management or Preservation courses being provided by NAI.[16]

The Director of Archives had always stressed on the need of whole-time and trained Departmental Records Officers to achieve the best results in the appraisal and transfer of records in Ministries/Departments and other offices with sizeable Records holdings to NAI in the interest of historians and research scholars. For the assistance of these officers, a full complement of trained junior Records Officers should also be appointed without delay. These trained officers would then ensure quality appraisals of semi-current Records as well as indexes of permanent records. The Director also recommended that posts of Departmental Records Officers be declared as ex-cadre posts to enable DROs to perform their duties more effectively. This would have ensured a proper status of DROs in official hierarchy.[17] Ministries/ Departments did not even bother to respond, as it lacked the statutory obligations to do so as inherent in the APR. Archival law was, therefore, absolutely necessary not only in this, but in another context as well.

Para 50 of the fourteenth Report of the Committee on

---

16. Ibid. p.12
17. Ibid. p.13.

Subordinate Legislation (fifth Lok Sabha) enquired about the reasons for issuing executive instructions for the destruction of Records in the Central Ministries and for not framing statutory rules for these under the Destruction of Records Act, 1917. An Inter-Ministerial Committee meeting held on 30 September 1975, concluded that under the present constitutional set-up, the Destruction of Records Act had become obsolete and should be replaced by a comprehensive Archival Law, which would also include a clause enabling Departments to frame rules for the destruction of ephemeral records.

A few organisations felt hindered due to a ban on creation of posts. By 1975, only 21 offices like Ministries of Home, External Affairs etc. had confirmed having organised DRRs, although they still lacked trained officials. In all, 330 out of 500 Central Government Organisations had some 18,301,601 files, 415,970 registers and 9,950 ft of other recorded material. These were staggering figures that awaited appraisal and weeding as per Procedure.[18]

To further improve our record management practices at the initiative of NAI, the Government constituted an inter-Ministerial Working Group in January 1978 to look into the appointments of properly trained and responsible whole-time staff for DRRs and the additional space required by them. This Working Group consisted of the Officers of Ministries of Home Affairs (Department of Personnel and Administrative Reforms), Finance, Works and Housing, Department of Culture and NAI.[19] The first meeting of the Working Group was held in NAI on 15 April 1978 under the chairmanship of Director, NAI. It was unanimously agreed that

18. Ibid.

19. F.N.8-6/78-RM-I,pp.5-6/notes.

these DRRs would be in charge of Record Rooms all the Ministries/ Departments/Offices of Central Government and that this staff should not be saddled with any other responsibility. Further, the staff strength for each Records Room should be determined on the basis of quantum of records it held:

- Records Room with one lakh or more files tobe treated as Major Records Rooms,
- Those housing 50,000 to one lakh files should be treated as Medium Records Rooms,
- Those with less than 50,000 files could be considered as Small Records Rooms.

It was, however, felt that the staff requirements of these Records Room could be determined only after the individual items of work in the Departmental Records Rooms had been enumerated in detail. Information on these points was collected by NAI. Equally important was setting up of organised DRRs. This problem continued as Records Management was awarded only a very low priority among administrators. By 1978, only forty-six Central Government Organisations had their own Records Rooms, thirty-five of them were well-organised, while others were not well-equipped at all. Thirty-four had no records Rooms.[20]

In spite of submission of these reports by Director of Archives, no serious efforts were made for enactment of an Archival Law. There was, by now, a huge backlog of files in Ministries and its offices, due for appraisal and retirement. It was estimated that more than 30 lakh un-appraised files were

20. Ibid. pp. 45-47/corr.

lying pending with Ministries/Departments. NAI had estimated that the Government would continue spending large amounts of money on the storage of unwanted files @ Rs 1 per file per year, in metropolitan cities. Scientific appraisal of these records by trained personnel would be more economical than spending on their storage.[21] The Tarachand Committee Report had been valuable, and perhaps the first and the only comprehensive survey ever done in assessing the archival problem of India, both at the National and local levels and Public Records and papers of historical value with private institutions and individuals. Accordingly, the Director of Archives in all APR Reports till 1993, had always emphasised that the important issue of archival law had got stuck in legal tangles and procedural delays since 1960, in spite of strong recommendation for its enactment. He appealed to the authorities to expedite the enactment of the Public Records Act. In1974-75, 139 out of 508; 1975-76, 105 out of 500; 1976-77, 94 out of 500; 1977-78, 68 out of 740 responded. Percentage-wise responses had reduced roughly from 20 per cent in 1974-75 to 11 per cent in 1975-76, 7 per cent in 1976-77, 6 per cent in 1977-78, and only 4 per cent in 1978-79.[22]

Some Ministries and Departments issued circulars to their Attached and Subordinate Offices to implement APR, but surprisingly they, themselves were defaulters. The Director had accordingly pleaded that improvements in management, administration, and preservation of records could be made only if this subject was placed under statutory obligations.[23]

It was observed that, by and large, the Ministries and their

21. APR Report 1977-1978 ending March 1978, pp.30-31
22. APR Report 1978-1979, ending March 1979, pp.1-2.
23. Ibid. pp. 2-5.

offices which had reported their willingness to appoint full-time, trained and experienced staff for their Records Rooms had not done so, either because their proposals were still under consideration or because they were not acceptable to the Government for one reason or the other. An Inter-Ministerial Working Group, during its second meeting at NAI on 9 February 1979, NAI submitted all data/information received from Ministries/Departments.[24] The Working Group observed that by and large, level of personnel looking after the Records Rooms was low and at senior levels, the responsibility of supervising the work of Records Rooms, in particular, and Records Management, in general, was divided. The Working Group recommended the deficiency be removed immediately as otherwise it would not be possible to start a speedy implementation of the APR.[25]

This is precisely what Director of Archives had been stressing in NAI annual APR reports, when he had pointed out that 80 per cent of shelf space was occupied by files that should have been weeded out much earlier if only fully trained and experienced officers had been available to handle complex, subject-like appraisal of files at both semi-current and non-current stages. And this was just one aspect of the responsibilities of Departmental Records Officers as envisaged in the APR. There are plenty of other aspects of Records Management, which had been highlighted to the Ministries through annual reports on the implementation of the APR. The Working Group made the following observations:

- The Records Management of each Ministry/Department should be placed under the whole-time charge of an Officer of the level of Section Officer, who should be designated as Departmental Records Officer.

24. F.N.8-6/78-RM-I, pp.145-149/corr.
25. Ibid. p.147/corr.

- In the case of Attached/Subordinate Offices, the Departmental Records Officers should similarly be of the level of a Sectional heads of the organisation concerned.
- The persons to be appointed against these posts should be selected and given training in Records Management by National Archives of India.
- The posts of Departmental Records Officers in the Ministries/ Departments and their attached offices should be made ex-cadre posts so that the persons appointed can continue long after their training for at least,3 years.
- Pending evaluation of their workload, Departmental Record Officers may be assisted in their work by one Lower Division Clerk and one Daftry.
- The Departmental Records Officers should be given target dates to compile comprehensive data in the form required by the Director, NAI to enable the Working Group to assess staff requirement in each case. If need be, the Internal Works Study (IWS) Units of the various Ministries/Departments should work out staff requirements based on guidelines provided by the Working Group.[26]

The Working Group's recommendations were forwarded to all other Secretaries to the Government in various Ministries to ensure prompt and adequate action, in compliance of para 3 of the Archival Policy Resolution of 1972. All the Ministries/ Departments were to be persuaded strongly to post 'properly trained, suitable and responsible full-time staff' at least in the major Records Rooms. Secretaries were requested to post an officer, reporting to them, of the level of Deputy Secretary, who

26. Ibid. pp.147-148.

would be made responsible in each Ministry for taking quick action for implementation of the APR.[27]

This was an important step initiated by the Department of Culture and NAI. It was stressed that proper Records Management is fundamental to an efficient administration, and called for urgent action.[28] Many replies were received assuring follow-up action in consultation with their Finance Division. Ministries of Defence, Department of Expenditure, Tourism, and Atomic Energy reported that their proposals had been turned down by Ministry of Finance, as they had been told to cut expenditure and this made it very difficult for various Ministries to implement the Archival Policy Resolution. It would have been very difficult to work with the redeployment of the existing staff.[29] It was decided to take up the matter with the Ministry of Finance. NAI asked them to sanction minimum staff for DRRs in various Ministries/Departments as was recommended by the Inter-Ministerial Working Group on the appointment of minimum staff in DRRs. The matter was referred through Department of Culture and they approached Ministry of Finance for sanction of posts and staff for DRRs by Department of Culture.[30]

Many now either dropped the idea or explored the creation of posts for their DRRs within their budgetary allocations. Some Ministries/Departments did appoint Departmental Records Officers of the level of Section Officers with part time or with additional charge. Departments like Social Welfare stated that workload in the Records Rooms did not justify the appointment of full-time staff.

27. Ibid, pp.145-146/corr.
28. Ibid, pp.156-171/corr.
29. Ibid. p. 178
30. F. No. 13-3/80-RM (PandL)

Since Ministry of Finance did not sanction even limited staff requirements for the DRR, the Additional Secretary, Ministry of Education and Social Welfare, took up the matter with the Secretary, Department of Expenditure, who finally agreed to have a selective approach in this matter.[31] But Ministry of Finance, Department of Expenditure eventually turned down a concrete proposal citing economic reasons. It was argued that 'setting up of a separate cell in each Ministry for Records Management might only help to dilute the responsibility of the normal Sections concerned for this work and this might ultimately lead to more expenditure to Government and less work.' It was opined that this would add to non-Plan expenditure at a time of extreme budgetary constraints. The whole matter needed to be reconsidered.'[32] It simply pointed out that the time was not opportune to implement the provisions of APR for maintenance of DRRs and that such appointments should be deferred for the time being. But it had no objection to the Ministries finding such staff from within their existing staff strength.[33]

Thus, the matter got shelved and was not pursued further by Department of Culture, and NAI was also advised accordingly. There was hardly any progress. DRRs continued to be looked after by Under Secretaries, Section Officers, and Senior Analysts, who looked after the Records Management programme in addition to their regular duties. In many cases, DRRs were manned by Assistants/Clerks/Records Keepers/Daftaries. NAI continued to train DROs and supporting staff sponsored by various Ministries/Departments.

---

31. F. no. 8-6/78-R.M.(PandL), p.240/Corr. APR Report 1979-80, p.11
32. F.No. 13-3/80-RM (PandL), p.54/corr. Letter No. F. 1(81)-E (Coord)/79, dt 30 June 1980 to Add. Secretary, D/Cul, from V.S. Jafa, J.S. (Per.), M/Finance, D/Expenditure.
33. Ibid. p.80/notes and APR Report for the year 1980-81, p.5.

Another important issue that demanded attention was dual control of two different Departments of the Government over one field of specialisation. The NAI and Department of Personal and Administrative Reforms (DoPT) were confused over Para 6 of the APR, which had laid down that 'the authority given to Departmental Records Officers to draw up Retention Schedules in consultation with National Archives of India should not, however, override the instructions contained in the Manual of Office Procedure, (MOP) according to which officers dealing with the Records at appropriate levels had to take decisions regarding the period of retention of different records. The function of the Departmental Records Officer was only advisory.'

This provision meant that the Department of Administrative Reforms only had a limited say in the Management, Administration and Preservation of Records. In spite of this limitation, 'Administration and Management of Records' continued to be handled simultaneously in the Department of Personnel and Administrative Reforms and by the NAI. Both Departments issued instructions on the subject, which also led to confusion and called for early delineation of the functions of each Department, something possible only by the enactment of an archival law. The Department of Personnel and Administrative Reforms continued to maintain that the subject of Records Management forms a part of the wider and more comprehensive Organisation and Methods Work, (O and M Units).[34]

The best course would have been that after the issuing of APR, the Department of Personnel and Administrative Reforms should have been entrusted with the task of overseeing Records

34. Ibid, pp.37-38

Management of Government offices through the expert agency of the NAI. But that did not happen. They did not even agree to incorporate even all recommendations made by the Committee on Archival Legislation for improving the management and administration of Public Records in MOP. For example, the Legislation Committee's most important recommendation- 'in the event of transfer of functions from one Department to another, only the current files should be transferred to the successor body', continued to be flouted and the Manual carried instructions which were not in conformity with this universally accepted archival principle.[35] This meant that we were often unable to locate records in the interest of research scholars and historians. With mass creation of records, the problem to house them and keep them in a proper manner was growing by the day.[36] The only way out was that Ministries/Offices should have cooperated with NAI to appraise their non-current Records, and yet also made concerted efforts for expediting appraisals of semi-current Records, so that the already limited shelf space could be spared to accommodate fresh files, by destruction of ephemeral records. But the situation continued, year after year. One of the essential requirements of sound Records Management is that there should be a reasonable ratio between the creation and destruction of records. This could be achieved only if older records were subjected to periodical reviews and timely destruction of ephemeral Records was undertaken. But this had never been the priority of Ministries and Departments. Only an archival law could empower NAI to take up such duties and responsibilities with a sense of responsibility and power.

35. APR Implementation Report for the year 1979-80, p. 38, (Para.72, 1978 Ed of MOP).

36. APR Implementation Report for the year 1980-81, p.19

The Institute of Archival Training, continued running their long as well as short-term courses and started a new course in Reprography in January 1980, with two students from the Institute of Islamic Studies. Another training course in Care and Conservation of Books, Mss. and Archives was also introduced in 1980. Three sessions of this course were conducted by the School. Eighteen candidates were sponsored by educational and research institutions, State Archives Department, and Public Sector Undertakings. Ten candidates attended the second session of Reprography Course held in November-December 1980. Special training facilities were also provided in the field of Conservation, Preservation, Reprography and Records Management to this batch, which included 3 students from Afghanistan, Guyana, and Ghana under UNDP. Foreign Governments like Afghanistan had sought advice from NAI on Records Management, in filing system, storage and preservation of records. Similarly, the Royal Thai Embassy in New Delhi was advised on procedures for disposal and preservation of classified documents.[37]

Efforts of National Archives of India for Enactment of the Public Records Act,1993

NAI continued to push for archival legislation in the hope that in due course, it would come up with a comprehensive Public Records Act under Article 252(1) of the Constitution. Since no State Governments came forward to be covered under a Central law for the management and administration of its Public Records, the Act had to be limited to the Central Government and Administrations of Union Territories. Accordingly, National Archives of India had

37. APR Implementation Reports for the year 1979-80 and 1980-81, pp.31-32 and pp. 24-25.

prepared a Draft Bill covering Records of Union Government and Administrations of UTs first in 1975 and again in 1980 and was referred to the Legal Department for advice.[38]

A Law on Records of National Importance was also being discussed at the same time to prevent clandestine trade in manuscripts, documents and records, which were less than 75 years old. This was in line with the decision taken by the Government in the Department of Culture in 1971 to frame a separate law to prevent illegal export of Antiquities and Art Treasures. On the advice of the Department of Legal Affairs, NAI prepared a Note on the subject to secure the approval of the Cabinet before further steps were taken.[39]

The Department of Culture convened an inter-ministerial meeting on 10 November 1980 to discuss the Draft Note on Archival Law submitted by NAI, before approaching the Cabinet for approval for enactment of a Public Records Act. The meeting, attended by representatives of the Departments of Legal Affairs, Expenditure, Culture and Personnel and Administrative Reforms and Ministry of Home Affairs, was chaired by Dr Kapila Vatsyayan, Jt Educational Advisor. It was decided that NAI would draw up a Note for circulation amongst the concerned Ministries showing:

(a) How Destruction of Records Act of 1917 had not been effective in solving problems of Records Management,
(b) Appropriate machinery for effective implementation of Records Management Procedures, and
(c) What would be the financial implications in the proposed Public Records Act?

---

38. APR Report 1979-80, pp.36-37.
39. Ibid, p. 37.

Comments from Ministries and Departments were received and examined in NAI.[40]

NAI had also been trying for a Legislation on Records of National Importance to prevent illegal trade and unwarranted destruction of manuscripts, documents and records that were less than 75 years old. NAI, on advice of Department of Legal Affairs had prepared a Note seeking approval of the Cabinet.[41]

Talk on the enactment of a law on Public Records was considered in an inter-Departmental meeting on 7April 1982 comprising Department of Culture, Department of Personnel and Administrative Reforms and NAI.[42] The Department of Personnel had furnished a list of illustrative points for incorporation in the proposed law on public records. NAI and DoPT agreed on the contents and suggested a few modifications, and it was again considered by the Department of Culture.[43]

Suggestions also came from the Ministry of Home Affairs on inclusion of para 7(ii-vi) of the Archival Policy Resolution of 1972 in the illustrative points for the proposed Public Records Act. They were:

- The President's Secretariat, the Cabinet Secretariat, the Prime Minister's Office and UPSC may prescribe a period longer than 25 years for transfer of their non-confidential records.
- An individual file or record series can be retained by the Ministry/ Department beyond the stipulated period, with National Archives being apprised of the position.
- Files once transferred may be withdrawn from NAI by the Ministry/Department or Office concerned after apprising the NAI of the reasons for this action.

40. APR Implementation Report for the year 1980-81, p. 27.
41. Ibid.
42. Report of Director of Archives for Implementation of APR, 1982-83, pp. 31-32
43. Ibid, p.31

- The administrative Ministries would have sole authority to decide on the consigning of particular records of the attached and subordinate offices to NAI.
- Classified files remaining un-transferred to the National Archives at the end of the stipulated period should be appraised once in five years, and if downgraded, be transferred to NAI for permanent preservation.

Another suggestion of Ministry of Home Affairs was to prescribe a penalty for unauthorised removal/destruction of records.[44] NAI examined these suggestions to enact a Public Records Act. The plan of action and revised illustrative points were incorporated on the basis of discussions held with Department of Personnel and Administrative Reforms and Department of Legal Affairs and were referred to the Cabinet Secretariat for their consideration.[45]

NAI had also been trying for Legislation on Records of National Importance to prevent clandestine trade and unwarranted destruction of manuscripts, documents, and records more than 75 years old. In a meeting on 8 April 1982, it was decided to frame a law on the lines of Ancient Monuments and Archaeological Sites and Remains Act of 1958. The Historical Monuments and Archaeological Remains and Sites (Declaration of National Importance) Act of 1951 and Antiquities and Art Treasure Act of 1972 were also taken into account and illustrative points submitted to the Government for approval. The Government had been debating on giving a 'Statutory base' to these valuable papers under the proposed 'Bill on Records of National Importance'.

44. Ibid, pp.31-32.

45. NAI Annual Report for the year 1984, p.9.

Accordingly, illustrative points for the law had been framed to prevent the unwarranted destruction of records, fraudulent dealings, their export, and above all to ensure their maintenance. Another meeting was convened on 24 November 1984 under the chairmanship of the Education Secretary, where it was decided that comments of Education Secretaries of the States on these points be obtained before proceeding further with the Bill.[46]

The Note on the Public Record Act was considered by the Cabinet in its meeting of 28 October 1983, and later by the Committee of Secretaries on 17 November 1983. The Additional Secretary and Director, NAI also attended. (Minutes recd. vide ref. 6/1/7/83-Cab.dt 29 Nov 1983). It was suggested that:

- The Department of Culture prepare a comprehensive plan for records management after a study of one or two typical Ministries,
- A study of the State of Archives in some of the States be conducted,
- The proposed line of legislation for records be re-examined so that it covers regulations of private records.[47]

Accordingly, NAI was to conduct:

- A comparative study of two typical organisations of the Government of India, i.e. Director General, Posts and Telegraphs and Ministry of Social Welfare in New Delhi to study various aspects of records management.
- A study of the State Archives of Gujarat and Bihar were conducted to study their records management practices.[48]

The studies revealed that none had undertaken a systematic review of files for disposing of records of ephemeral value.

46. Ibid.
47. F.No. 16-1/85-RM, p.3/corr.
48. F.No. 16-1/85-RM, p.16-17/corr.

Indexing was either not done or was incomplete. Besides, their Records Rooms were manned by untrained staff. A comprehensive plan of action was prepared on records management in the Ministries/Departments, indicating procedures for timely weeding of records, and for training needs for personnel working in the Departmental Records Rooms. The study was also to enable Director of Archives to discharge his obligations towards preservation and maintenance of records of permanent value, which were to be transferred to NAI. Notes were prepared for Director of Archives for a rationalised system of records management and for microfilming of records in NAI.

In a meeting on 29 July, 1984, the Education Secretary considered these Notes and found the issues administrative in nature to be resolved by the Department of Personnel and Administrative Reforms. Two meetings were held on 7 and 21 August 1984 under Chairmanship of SP Tuli, Deputy Financial Advisor and Director of Archives and a representative from the Department of Personnel and Administrative Reforms to resolve this. It was decided:

- Though general instructions/guidelines for management and maintenance of records would continue to be issued by the Department of Personnel and Administrative Reforms, NAI, would be consulted on all matters concerning records management,
- Training courses would continue to be conducted by the Institute of Secretariat Training and Management and NAI, being the nodal organisation on records management would review their Records Management Course content policy issues on the subject.
- Despite rules, the system had not yet functioned properly, either because the officers in charge were either on the verge of retirement or were unwanted elsewhere. These officers were not fully complying with instructions for better records management and hence, records continued to occupy 11 to 24 per cent of space

against the designated10 per cent. Indexes were not appropriately done. It was, therefore, recommended that DRRs be manned by persons who were trained and interested in the task. But this could be possible only if the post of the Departmental Records Officer was made attractive and declared as a Junior Class I post of pay scale, Rs 700-1,300, supported by a Grade II stenographer and a few class IV employees in his functions. The Department of Personnel and Administrative Reforms, however, expressed reservations.

- The NAI should be authorised to inspect departmental records and record rooms.
- The study in State Archives of Gujarat and Bihar revealed a very gloomy picture. Both States lacked basic infrastructure. Accumulation of records, lack of manpower and equipment, and untrained staff needed urgent attention. The compilation of a Retention Schedule for records, an administrative tool for selecting records on scientific lines, had never been drawn up in both States.
- With reference to enactment of a suitable legislation on public records and other documentary collections of historical and national importance, the National Archives opined that an exclusive Act on Public Records was necessary for enabling Director of Archives to wield legal authority over documents, as they have evidential value. An enactment on public records was necessary for declaring Director of Archives as legal custodian of all records of the Central Government and for allowing access to records more than 30 years old for consultation by research scholars. It was recommended that this law be made applicable to records of the Union Government including the Union Territory Administrations.
- Similarly, a separate Act for documents of National Importance was considered necessary for empowering the Director of Archives to declare any document(s) in the custody of any institution(s) or individual(s) irrespective of their age, as that of national importance.

> It would prohibit sale/export of documents in private custody without specific permission from Director of Archives. In case, the records were in danger of getting destroyed, these could be taken over by Director of Archives and compensation be paid to their owners.

The legislation for records issue was deeply discussed in a Department of Legal Affairs meeting on 6 September, 1984. The meeting recommended two separate laws, one on Public Records and another for Records of National Importance presently with individuals and institutions, so that these are properly preserved. Public Records Act would indicate that the Director of Archives is the legal custodian of all records of the Union Government. All records which are more than 30 years old should be made accessible to research scholars for consultation. There should be a separate law on private records. The law should empower the Director of Archives, to declare any document/group of documents in the custody of any institution or individual, irrespective of their age, as that of national importance. It should prohibit the sale/export of documents in private custody without specific permission from the Director of Archives. A severe penalty was to be imposed on all those who might break this law. If records were in danger of getting destroyed, they could be taken over by Director of Archives and compensation be paid to the owner.[49]

Accordingly, revised illustrative points along with status papers were again forwarded to Department of Culture. Education Secretary wrote to all Chief Secretaries of all States and Union Territories and Secretaries of the Government of India on 4 June 1985, seeking their comments about legislation on public

49. Ibid, p.109/corr. Record of Discussion of the meeting held on 6th September, 1984.

records and records of National Importance. The enactment of Public
Records Act was further processed by Department of Culture.[50]

The response was discouraging. Only ten Ministries Departments responded, besides 5 States/UTs. In February 1986, the Department of Culture transferred the enactment of Archival Law proposal to NAI stating that since it was technical in nature, they were not in a position to contribute much towards its examination. NAI, thus, resubmitted draft Bills for Records of National Importance and amended the Draft Bill on Archival Legislation, incorporating points suggested by Department of Administrative Reforms and Public Grievances to Department of Culture for approval.[51] The Draft Bill for Records of National Importance was circulated to all States/UT administered States and comments were received from 16 State Governments/University/ Union Territory Administrations, after many reminders.[52]

IHRC, however, recommended that this law receive active consideration. The draft Bill was, therefore, finalised in consultation with the Department of Administrative Reforms and Public Grievances and submitted to the Ministry for Human Resource Development for permission to get the Bill drafted and finalised by the Legislative Department. On the advice of Department of Legal Affairs, a draft Bill for Public Records was finalised and sent to Ministry of Law by Department of Culture.[53] It again went through a round of drafts and consultations.[54] After the approval of the Committee, the Bill on Archival Legislation

50. Ibid, pp. 1-3/notes.
51. Annual Report, NAI, 1989, pp. 20-22.
52. Annual Report, NAI 1987, p.18
53. IHRC Proceedings, April 1992, Rohtak, 54 Session, p.156.
54. Annual Report, NAI 1990, pp. 14 and 17.

was finally introduced in the Lok Sabha and was passed on 21 December 1993, as the Public Records Act of 1993.[55] The Act became operative from 1 March 1995 after gazette notification. To implement the various provisions of the Act, action was initiated for constituting an Archival Advisory Board. Draft Rules were sent to the Ministry of Law for vetting.[56]

The enactment of this Act mandated National Archives of India to organise training programs in Archives Administration and Records Management. Director of Archives (Director General wef June1990) was empowered to lay down norms and standards for course curricula, assessment and examinations for training of Archivists and Departmental Records Officers in the Union Ministries/Departments, and for Attached and Subordinate Offices manning Departmental Records Repositories. Public Sector Undertakings were also brought under the purview of NAI and mandatory training of officials was initiated by the School of Archival Studies in record management practices of current and semi-current records. More than 2,000 organisations benefitted from these training courses. This is discussed in Chapter IV.

Proper maintenance of public records is an obligation on the part of the government in a democratic set-up and it is imperative that this instrument of administration is not left to be managed by an executive order. The Government had issued an APR in 1972 to streamline the administration and management of records. Area of responsibilities of various agencies should have been clearly defined and the mandate should have been followed through. Reports submitted by Director of Archives for implementation of APR, between 1973 till enactment of the Public Records Act in 1993,

55. Annual Report, NAI 1993, p. 43.

56. IHRC Proceedings, December 1995, Jadavpur, p.175

and the practical experience with the Ministries, Departments and other Offices, clearly indicates that the Resolution failed to create the desired impact on the administration. The only remedy lay in a Public Records Act, as part of Statute Book defining responsibilities of record-creating agencies and of their maintenance. This Act was enacted only in 1993.

Only the State Archives of Maharashtra, Orissa, Haryana, Delhi, Gujarat, Kerala, Himachal Pradesh, Manipur, Orissa, Rajasthan, Delhi, Goa, Daman and Diu and Pondicherry were reported to have issued their Archival Policy Resolutions in the seventies. Andhra Pradesh had dropped the idea because of additional expenses. All these APRs invariably included paras on archival training/re-orientation programme for the officers' in-charge of DRR and their supporting staff. Efforts had been made to bring in uniformity in archival theory and practices. Fifteen years' time limit was recommended for Gujarat, keeping in view the date of creation of the State as not old enough, as formed in 1960, while Mizoram was keen to adopt the APR. Karnataka had adopted APR on national lines with some difference to meet requirements of the State as it was performing dual functions of State Archives and of a DRR.[57]

In Chapter IV, we will further explore how the Public Records Act impacted the record management practices in the working of the Government's Ministries and Departments and in particular, how archival education and training in India in an electronic environment with the enactment of the Information Technology Act of 2000 and Right to Information Act in 2005.

57. F. No. 16-5/83 RM and IHRC Proceedings, June 1985, SurajKund, Haryana, p. 127.

Public Records and Curriculum Reform Act in the Digital Age

The National Archives of India is the nodal agency, responsible for the administration, management, and preservation of public records of the Union Government according to the Public Record Act of 1993. Public Record Rules were now framed, so as to make the Act operative and notified in the Gazette in January 1997. The Act** became operative from 1March 1997. For the first time, the Act covered Record Management activities of Central Ministries/Departments, Public Sector Undertakings, Commissions and Committees and other statutory bodies which were so far functioning under their own rules without proper experience in management of records.

The Government constituted an Archival Advisory Board under Section 13(1), under the Chairmanship of Secretary (Culture), comprising an officer each from seven key ministries, not below the rank of Jt. Secretary. These officers came from the Cabinet Secretariat, Ministries of Home Affairs, Defence, External Affairs, Finance, & Personal, Public Grievances and

**For Public Record Act, please see Annexure 6.

Pension, besides two representatives of the rank of Jt. Secretaries also from Union Territory Administrations, nominated by the Central Government. The advisory board also had three persons, two Historians and one Archivist nominated by the Central Government for a period of three years, with Director General, NAI as Member Secretary (ex-officio) of the Board. The members were expected to facilitate the Board in deciding on sensitive key issues.[1] The constitution of the Board was notified on 1 November 1995 and Public Record Rules declared on 18 January 1997. The Board's first meeting was convened on 30 May 1997 under the Chairmanship of Secretary, Culture. As per recommendation of the Board, an order was issued on 6 October 1997, authorising Director General of Archives to discharge all functions under the Public Record Act.[2]

NAI's first task was to educate the various offices about the provisions of the Public Record Act and its proper implementation through archival education and training in the School of Archival Studies, NAI. Thereafter, a phased programme for appraisal of records, inspection of Departmental Record Rooms, and an Orientation Course for Departmental Records Officers was launched to streamline records management activities. DRRs had been in existence in many of the main Ministries/Departments of Government of India since 1972, but now, they became mandatory in all offices of the Government.

After the Board's second meeting on 6 October, 1997, a circular was issued to all Government Organisations and Public Sector Undertakings, for implementation of the Public Record Act, 1993, setting up of an organised Departmental Record

1. IHRC, 1997, p.142
2. IHRC Proceedings, 2001, Mysore, p.200-202

Room, designating a Departmental Record Officer and declassification of classified files. Record Rooms of Government Departments at the Centre and States were to be organised on scientific lines and managed by trained personnel, and special training programmes in Records Management to be organised on regular basis by the State archives were to be held for the benefit of the staff posted in the record Rooms.[3]

To ensure that DRRs are manned by trained personnel, NAI designed a short, five-day Orientation Course in Records Management for Departmental Record Officers at the instance of Department of Administrative Reforms. Accordingly, NAI launched the special course from 1998 for DROs of Ministries, Departments and PSUs. The results have been positive, and till 2001, NAI had conducted 21 special courses, training 294 DROs.[4] By 2003, NAI had conducted 39 Orientation courses training 482 officers, according to the Secretary in an IHRC presentation at Raipur. Special 17 Orientation Courses were conducted for the North Eastern Region, and 159 DROs were trained between 2001 and 2003. Special training Workshops in Records Management were also conducted at Aizwal, Paradeep Port Trust, and Vishakhapatnam Port Trust.

Training on Care and Conservation of Records was conducted in Shimla, Kolkata, and Vrindavan Research Institute. Some 676 Ministries/Departments/Organisations nominated an officer to function as the Departmental Records Officer and set up their own Departmental Record Rooms.[5] The courses acquainted the Records Officers with relevant acts, rules, and provisions

3. IHRC Resolution II of the Jabalpur session, 1997,
4. IHRC Proceedings, 2001, Mysore, p.200-202
5. IHRC, 2003 Raipur, pp.198 &173-174,

of the Central Secretariat Manual of Office Procedure, Central Secretariat Manual of e-Office Procedure, besides instructions and guidelines of the Government on Records Management.

State Archives also started training programmes besides NAI. State Archives of Andhra Pradesh, Gujarat, Karnataka, Madhya Pradesh, Orissa, Rajasthan, Kerala, Uttar Pradesh, Tamil Nadu, and West Bengal had already started short-term training courses for their staff. Other State Archives were advised to follow suit.[6]

NAI has consistently attempted to raise the level of awareness in management and administration of records in their semi-current stage in DRRs before their transfer to NAI. This was to be done regularly, as many of the trained DROs often got transferred or moved on. These officers also regularly needed orientation to understand the importance of the Public Record Act, so that it could be better implemented in letter and spirit ensuring survival of records for administrative and cultural use. A letter was sent by the Chairman, Standing Committee, IHRC, to Heads of important Ministries and Departments requesting them to seriously address the provisions of the Public Records Act, 1993.[7]

Dr SN Prasad, former Director of Archives and member, IHRC, moved a resolution in the fifty-eighth IHRC session at Raipur in 2003, drawing the attention of the Government to the persistence violation and non-implementation of the provisions of the Public Record Act 1993, in many ministries. He urged effective and corrective steps by fixing individual responsibility of Secretaries to the Government. By then, the Act was 10 years old and one can only visualise the sorry state of affairs, till then. He

6. Ibid.

7. Ibid. pp. 8-9.

observed that violation of the Act by the Government itself was a serious matter and embarrassing too, if a question were raised in Parliament or taken to court as public interest litigation.

It was seen that the Director General of Archives, NAI, could not push the Secretaries of the different ministries to comply with the Act after it was passed in 1993, even after ten years. 'Records of historical value are in danger of damage and destruction in ill-kept, poorly-manned Record Rooms of various offices. Learned IHRC members need hardly be reminded that archival records are unique, single-copy documents, irreplaceable, and held in trust by the present generation for future generations. Something must be done, and quickly,' Dr SN Prasad, had explained. Prof SR Mehrotra and RC Agarwal called for mandatory accountability for implementation of the Public Record Act, 1993. After some discussion, the following amended resolution was adopted:

> 'The IHRC expresses deep concern at the serious and persistent violation and non-implementation of the provisions of the Public Record Act, 1993 by many Ministries/Departments and urges upon the Government of India to take necessary corrective measures at the highest level, in order to ensure proper compliance of the Act.'[8] (Resolution III)

NAI gained further experience of enforcing the provisions of the Public Record Act till 2005. It was now found that the Act and its rules be made more relevant and effective in the changed scenario of Information Technology (IT) Act of 2000, electronic records, and Right to Information (RTI) Act of 2005. This called for amending the Act and also the curriculum of courses of the

8. IHRC 2003, Raipur, April 2003, pp. 8-9

School of Archival Studies. Some provisions of the Act needed to be amended and strengthened, like transfer of non-current records to NAI after appraisal within a time frame, liberalisation of access to public records, management and preservation of e-records. New enabling clauses needed to be introduced to make the Act effective for electronic records, which had since been given legal recognition under the IT Act 2000. The RTI Act, 2005, had necessitated the need for redefining the role of the Records Officers (ROs) and their relationship with the Central Public Information Officers (CPIOs) to ensure transparency, efficiency, accountability and citizen-centric good governance through effective records management.

All of it had to be done keeping responsibilities of Archivists and NAI, in mind. Section (4)(a) of the RTI Act 2005 states that every public authority shall maintain all its records duly catalogued and indexed in a manner and form which facilitates the right to information under this Act and ensure that all records that are appropriate to be computerised within a reasonable timeframe and subject to availability of resources, be so done and connected through a network all over the country on different systems. This meant that capacity building programmes too had to be taught at the School of Archival Studies NAI. The matter was discussed by the Archival Advisory Board in its ninth meeting on 7 February, 2008. The Board recommended setting up a Review Panel under Chairmanship of Joint Secretary, Ministry of Culture with members from Legislative, Department of Personnel &Training, National Informatics Centre, Information Technology Department besides scholars and other stakeholders, who were using Archives. The Review Panel was constituted under the Chairmanship of Lov Verma, Jt. Secretary, Ministry of Culture.[9]

9. F.N. 16-11/2008-RM, dated 16 February, 2009, pp.39-41/corr.

The Review panel was to study the Public Record Act, 1993 and Public Records Rules, 1997 in relation to the IT Act, 2000 and the RTI Act, 2005, and to suggest changes as draft amendments to them. The Review Panel had also to strengthen the weak provisions of the Act and introduce new enabling clauses in view of the RTI and IT Act of 2000. In the case of electronic records, this had since been given legal recognition under the IT Act. Moreover, the Right to Information Act, 2005 had also necessitated the need to redefine the Role of Departmental Record Officers and their relationship with the Central Public Information Officer so as to bring about transparency, efficiency, accountability and citizen-centric good governance through effective record management.

The Review Panel had to study the Act and make recommendations for harmonisation of the provisions of both the Public Record Act and Public Record Rules of 1993 and 1997 and study the implications of the IT Act of 2000, RTI Act 2005, Destruction of Records Act, 1917, Manual of Departmental Security Instructions on classified categories of records, and study it according to the Central Secretariat Manual of Office Procedure, and Companies Act of 1956. The Review Panel finally submitted its Report on 10 February, 2010, to the Ministry of Culture.

The Report was placed before the Archival Advisory Board in its twelfth meeting on 5 August 2010. After reviewing the Report, the Board recommended that a Consultative Committee be set up to act like a Regulatory Committee for the management of electronic records and any other key area which had not been covered by the Review Panel.

The Consultative Committee constituted on 25th October, 2010, had DG, NAI as its Chairman besides two legal experts, representatives from the Legislative Department, Department of Information Technology, Department of Administrative Reforms and Public Grievances and a professional Archivist. Its initial term was 3 months and could be extended further by 3 months up to 15 May 2011. During this time frame, the committee held three meetings and submitted its final report on 30 August 2011 to Secretary (Culture) and Chairman Archival Advisory Board. The report was overseen by the committee's chairman, Director General, NAI Prof. Mushirul Hasan. The recommendations included:[10]

- Setting up of a Regulatory Committee to review the working of the Act and empowering it to seek clarifications and justifications for violations and imposing penalties, if required.
- Inclusion of Electronic Records under the Act and curriculum of the training courses.
- Redefining the period of transfer of records from 25 to 20 years and of access from the twenty-first year.
- Users over 18 years could access public records on furnishing proof of identity. Users over the age of 14 years could be allowed to consult records with the prior approval of the Director General or Head of Archives.

Subsequently, the report of the Consultative Committee was submitted to the Archival Advisory Board in its thirteenth meeting on 18 December 2013. The Board recommended that amendments be incorporated in the Public Records Bill 2014 for amending the Act. But on some observation made by a nominee of the Ministry

10. Report of the Consultative Committee on Public Record Act, 1993 & Public Record Rules, 1997, dated 30th August, 1911, NAI, p.3.

of Home Affairs, Board members were given a week's time to study the provisions of the Public Record Bill 2014. Since then, further follow up action is still pending, as no meeting of the Board has taken place since 2013.[11*]

With the amendment of the Public Record Act and Rules still pending, what steps could NAI take to meet the challenges of the IT Act of 2000 and the RTI Act of 2005, especially on Computerisation, Education and training? Both sectors are closely linked. Since 1998, NAI had made considerable progress in the field of Computerisation of Records, and all facilities are available for online consultation of Catalogue of Records and Library materials for Research Scholars. NAI is also trying to introduce an e Office Management System in consultations with the Department of Personnel & Training and NIC. Similarly, the School of Archival Studies has built up a reputation for excellence in providing training on various aspects of archival science. The enactment of Public Record Act of 1993 gave a mandate to NAI to organise courses and training programmes under section 3(2)(k) of the Act and authorises Director General or Head of Archives, for 'organising training programmes in various disciplines of Archives Administration and Records Management.' Section 6(b), lists laying down guidelines for training of Archivists as one of the functions of the Board. The Act empowers DG, NAI to lay down standards for courses curricula, assessments and examinations in archival science and other ancillary subjects for training of Archivists.

11. F.No.46-2/2018-SAS,pp.48-52/corr.

*I was nominated member of the Archival Advisory Board in December 2017, for a period of 3 years, till December 2020, as notified in the Gazette; but still looking forward for the Board to meet before its term expires.

Till 2013, 95 Orientation courses of 5 days' duration had been conducted in which 1,340 Record Officers successfully underwent training.[12] During 2011-13, nominations of DROs were invited from 85 Ministries/Departments and approximately 2,000 Public Sector Undertakings. Seminars and workshops are also regularly organised by the NAI, RTI Cell in collaboration with State Archives and Government Offices and Departments throughout India on RTI Act, 2005, Record Management practices and access to records and information. A series of extension lectures were also organised for the trainees besides other workshops on techniques of management and conservation of records for Government officials all over India. Special training programmes were also conducted for nominees of the Governments of Afghanistan and Bhutan. The DGA's Report for 2013, published in 2015, in response to a letter from Secretary (Culture), (vide F.N. 16-16/2014-RM), dated 11 June 2014, to all Secretaries, 29 Ministries had nominated their Nodal Officers of the rank of Joint Secretary to interact with DG, NAI, on Implementation of the Public Record Act/Rules, and persuade them to nominate DROs for the training courses.[13]

Cooperation from the Ministries and Departments was essential and the programme could succeed only if the Public Record Act is further amended and strengthened on recommendations of the Consultative Committee, a matter, still under consideration.

Some of the State Governments also continued with short-term training courses. West Bengal state Archives conducted a

12. Sixteenth Report of the Director General of Archives on the Implementation of the Public Record Act, for the year 2013, pub. 2015, p. 40.

13. Ibid. p. 10-12.

3 Month training Course on Paper Conservation during 2012-13 and trained candidates from Rabindrabharti University and Bidhan Chandra Krishi Visvbidyalaya.[14]

Modernisation of SAS and One-Year Diploma Course Curriculum

An archivist is essential to store valuable records and documents professionally through digital archiving. But one cannot master skills of all fields. At best, one can acquire knowledge in all related disciplines, but focus on one area to gain expertise. But shortage of manpower compels one to have knowledge of all disciplines including digital archiving to remain relevant to the job and for survival in this competitive world. The curriculum therefore had to be comprehensive. And of course, efforts were being made to introduce computerisation.

At the Trivandrum, session, Education and Culture Minister stressed on the age of Computers and the need to undertake studies to understand the impact of computers on archival problems.'[15] Shri SAI Tirmizi, Director, NAI in the 1982 session at Gandhinagar, Gujarat, had said:

> Archives are no longer considered Luxuries. We have succeeded in creating congenial climate for according Record Management its rightful place in the administration of the country. Archives are increasingly looked upon as an essential component of information—a vital national resource for development. Thus, much had been done but much more remains to be done to meet the technological challenges of the age we live in. Modern

---

14. IHRC Proceedings, October. 2013, p.290
15. IHRC Proceedings, 1971, Trivandrum, pp.7-8.

> technology has revolutionised information systems all over the world. Computers, video-cassettes, audio-visual discs and space-satellites have no doubt provided faster and better techniques of information, but they had also created problems for the archivists. Complex technology with its storage and retrieval systems is likely to bring about in the coming decades, a revolutionary change in the information sector of which archives constitute a vital ingredient.[16]

He had sounded confident that his successors would tackle these problems under the mature guidance of the Commission's members.

He had set the ball rolling. The syllabus was drastically rationalised during the 1980s by the Board of Studies and the Curriculum Committee. The Board of Studies in its 1996 meeting also reviewed the syllabus, but Computer Studies and ICT were yet to be introduced in the curriculum. After the IT Act of 2000, and RTI Act of 2005, it was necessary to modernise the curriculum and train archivists to meet Information and Communication Technology challenges. From 1991 to 1998,[17] the one-year diploma course in Archival Studies was attended by 153 students, including 30 foreign trainees from Sri Lanka, Botswana, Burma, Kenya, Lesotho, Mauritius, Sri Lanka, Malaysia, Malawi, Uganda, Bangladesh, Tanzania, Nigeria, Swaziland, Gambia, Ethiopia, and Zimbabwe. But during 1999-2000 and 2000-2001, only 13 students attended, 7 and 6 in respective sessions. This decline in number is not hard to explain.

16. IHRC, 1982, pp.17-18.
17. IHRC, Oct. 2013, p.290

The course curriculum needed modernisation.

Michael Cook of the Centre for Archive Studies of Liverpool University wrote in1990 that 'Archives services are rooted in the administration methods of the country. There can be no generally applicable model of training for it. Curriculum must be developed locally, and take account of: 1) the interests and capabilities of teaching staff, 2) the advice of practising archivists, 3) the nature of the practical training possible.' These had been the guiding principles for the School of Archival Studies (SAS) at NAI to prepare the course curriculum for training programmes.

Even today, existing skills in National Archives of India are drawn for teaching work in the School of Archival Studies-though on a part-time basis and without disturbing one's substantive work, besides Archivists posted in the School to serve as main faculty and by inviting experts and guest faculty from outside. The training now required to be modernised not only for the students, but the faculty also was to be trained to take up challenges of the Information and Communication Technology. Rigorous training was needed in modern technological methods through seminars, workshops and extension lectures by inviting technical experts and eminent persons, Archivists, experts in digital conservation and preservationists from leading institutions and universities.

The Board of Studies in a meeting on 14 December 2000 decided to increase the intake of the students to the Diploma course of non-scholarship category on merit basis, in view of the decreasing number of students opting for the course. It also decided to reformulate the course so that the archivist was trained both as a technician and a managerial person. As an outcome, 2 candidates were admitted on merit in the non-scholarship category in 2001, then again, 2, and 5 candidates each in 2002 and 2003 sessions as the number of students in the Diploma course had been going down in the absence of sponsorship from State archives and from countries of the Afro-Asia region.[18]

Some significant decisions were taken by the Board of Studies while reviewing the Action Taken Report of the SAS in May 2005. The Board recommended revision of the syllabus to include Application of Computers, Fundamentals of information Technology in Paper I, II and V from the 2004 session. For attracting foreign students to the Diploma course, NAI had issued letters to National Archives of different countries in African and South East Asian Region. A Computer Lab was being established in the School. For attracting local students, the stipend for private candidates of the Diploma course had earlier been increased from Rs 500 to Rs 800 and of sponsored candidates from Rs 300 to 500/month.[19] Scholarships had been increased from 5 to 10 for private students and their amount raised from Rs 800 to Rs 1,500/month. For the sponsored candidates, 6 stipends of the amount were raised from Rs 500 to Rs 1,000/month.[20]

The Board invited suggestions from experts in different fields like Archives, History, Information Science, Conservation, Microfilming and digitisation for revising the syllabus. It was proposed to constitute an Academic Council from among the members of the expert Committee. This committee would also draw a Vision Plan for training courses conducted by SAS. All this was done to finalise course content by end of August 2005 so that the revised syllabus could be implemented from the next academic session, commencing in November 2005.[21]

The Board also decided to invite thirty percent of experts

18. Agenda Notes of the Seventh Meeting of the Board of Studies, 15.9.2004, p.1.
19. IHRC, 1997, p.187 and IHRC, 2001, Mysore, p. 161
20. Op.cit. p.3 of Agenda notes of the seventh meeting of the Board of Studies.
21. Agenda of the 13th meeting of BoS, held on 7.7.2010, Ann. Minutes of the BoS, 8th Meeting, pp.90-93,

from outside to deliver lectures as guest faculty. They were also entitled to TA/DA as per existing norms. Therefore, a panel of experts was to be drawn up along with their bio-data. The Board also introduced a feedback system from the students on the lectures delivered by the experts to ensure quality. Monthly talks on historical, archival and allied subjects by well-known experts for the benefit of students and faculty, and to be published by the Publication Division by the end of the year were also organised. The Board recommended Trainers' Training courses of a week's duration, encompassing Records Management, Conservation, Microfilming and Digitisation in different regions in collaboration with State Archives. A course calendar was designed every year for this. The short-term programmes would also train the trainers at Guwahati, Chennai, Pune, Bhubaneswar, Ahmedabad and Thiruvantapuram. It also decided to employ few successful candidates each year for project work in NAI on a contract basis for a year. SAS was now coordinating all the training activities at NAI and an honorarium was to be paid to faculty members of NAI as an incentive, as given in other institutes like Archaeological Survey of India.[22]

Three specialised papers were introduced in the one-year diploma course in 2005. These were Paper IV: Business and Private Archives, Paper V: Information and Communication Technology (ICT) – Practices in Archives, and Paper VI: Archival Library and Documentation. The study of these specialised papers was to begin only from July 2006.[23] The ICT paper was developed by SAS with support from National Informatics Centre (NIC) and for the first two years, they deputed their faculty to NAI for

22. Ibid. pp.2-4.

23. F.N. 46-3/2006-SAS, p.3/notes.

teaching, before officers in the Reprography Division mastered the skills. One condition imposed by the Board was that there should be minimum of 5 students for the teaching of a specialised paper.

The Board of Studies was reconstituted by the Director General on 5 January 2006 as the 2-year term of the existing Board had expired.[24] The newly appointed members were experts in Business Archives and ICT and included Prof Dwijendra Tripathi (Retd.), IIM Ahmedabad, Dr Gautam Bose, Deputy Director General, NIC, Dr Gyas Makhdumi, Head, Department of Library and Information Science, JMI.[25*]

The syllabus of the one-year Diploma Course in Archives and Records Management, approved by the Board in its ninth meeting was further reformatted and redesigned on professional lines by the SAS team. The courses were restructured in terms of teaching hours, and were divided into theory, practicals and assignments. Paper IV on Business & Private Archives was further developed and upgraded. Similarly, the specialised Paper V of ICT was updated and made more practical. The suggested reading list of the papers was also changed and the revised document placed before the Board. The members found the syllabus comprehensive and exhaustive, but recommended some measures to make it more attractive and value-oriented, such as associating with other universities/Institutes where Archival studies were conducted and asking for copies of their syllabus. They also recommended that SAS interact closely with these universities and Institutions.[26] The Board was advised to

---

24. F.N. 46-12/2005-SAS, pp.25-26/corr.
25. F.No. 46-3/2006-SAS, p.5/notes.
    * I was Headof the School from 2005-2012 as Deputy Director of Archives.
26. Ibid. pp. 20-21/corr. Minutes of the 10th meeting.

summarise the syllabus of specialisation papers in Unit form and to emphasise legal matters like Acts and laws. Company Secretaries were suggested for teaching Business Archives as they are well-versed in company business affairs. The School was advised to contact the Company Law Board and Institute of Company Secretaries, in Delhi. The Board also recommended that students be attached with institutes having Business and Private archives (NMM&L) depending on specialised paper they were opting for. The Board recommended an exclusive Library for the School with the required infrastructure and staff. Books were to be purchased immediately with multiple copies and a committee of 2 or 3 members was to oversee this.[27]

The Board also suggested the marking scheme to be adopted for evaluation. It was decided to raise marks for dissertation (earlier called Project Assignment) from 75 to 100. The Viva-Voce was to be restricted to dissertations rather than general Viva at the end of the course. 25 marks were to be earmarked for 'Study Tour and Report' which was to be objectively evaluated. To attract talented experts as guest faculty, an honorarium @ Rs 400 for each lecture was to be paid, plus conveyance. The Board also recommended that the School organise a national seminar on Electronic/Digital Management Practices in Government Offices/Departments and also in non-government Corporate, Private and Public Sector Bodies. The Member Secretary had to decide on this Workshop/Seminar in consultation with Dr Bose and Dr Gyas Makhdumi.[28]

These decisions of the Board were significant and introduction of specialisation papers of ICT and Business and

27. Ibid.pp.21-22/corr.

28. Ibid, pp.22-23/corr.

Private Archives became very popular with the students. This compelled the Board to make ICT a Core Paper. Studies in business and private Archives were predicted to open the doors of employment in archives of corporate bodies, Banks and Public Sector Undertakings. Students started to increase and once again, there was demand for the courses. But still many things had to be done and these were reviewed by the Board in its next meeting on 20 March 2007.

The Board felt that the revised syllabus should be circulated to all Universities, Departments of History for incorporation of the subject of archival science as part of their curriculum. A one-day interactive session was planned for Professors of History from various universities after circulating the syllabus for their comments and observations. A copy of the syllabus was also given to all the members of the Board for sending their comments and observations.[29]

Dr Basudev Chatterji, Director, West Bengal State Archives was concerned about the reduced number of sponsored candidates in the One-Year Diploma Course. The Board decided that letters should be sent to Chief Secretaries of State Governments for nominating staff working in State Archives/Museums/ Departments and Documentation centres for training in archival science. Members suggested that SAS develop interactive course material facilitating learning and reading of various Indian scripts during summer vacations for history teachers of central/state universities separately, without disturbing the current Diploma course in Archives and Records Management. The Board also decided to prepare a paper on Information and Communication Technology (ICT)–Practices in Archives as a compulsory paper

29. No.46-1/2007-SAS, 1-3 pages. Minutes of the 11th Meeting of the Board of Studies., dated 3.4.2007.

from the 2006-2007 session of the One-Year Diploma. There were two optional specialisation papers in Business and Private Archives (Paper IV) and Archival Library and Documentation (Paper VI) and students could opt for either one.[30]

The Board also took up the question of registration and course fees charged from trainees of SAARC countries, and from private and sponsored candidates of the one-year Diploma and other short-term courses. The Board decided to keep in mind the SAARC countries' economic development and bilateral relationship with India. It was decided that the school charge registration and course fees from trainees of these countries at par with Indian trainees. It was decided to enhance registration fee to Rs 100 for both Diploma and short-term courses and US$ 40 for both Diploma and short-term courses in case of other foreign students. There was no enhancement in the course fee.[31]

The Board now turned its attention on teaching and learning material being made available in Hindi and noted that it was within the power of the DGA to consider honorarium for such special assignments while outsourcing the work for developing such material. Some other special programmes like preparing material for the Trainers Training programme were already on. They further recommended the School to organise a 'Regional Workshop in Human Resource Development in Archives'.[32]

The Board also approved the School to organise two workshops during 2007-2008 on a) Hazards faced by records in tropical climate, and b) Business Archives in India. Prof Dwijendra Tripathi of IIM, Ahmadabad, volunteered to organise the workshop on

---

30. Ibid
31. Ibid. Minutes –pp.2-3.
32. Ibid

Business Archives in India with SAS. The Board also adopted a resolution stating that 'This meeting of the Board of Studies of the School of Archival Studies, NAI, places on record its appreciation of the leadership and guidance that Shri K Jayakumar, Joint Secretary and DG, NAI, had provided to its deliberations and to the programmes of School of Archival Studies during his tenure as Chairman of this Committee in his capacity as DG, NAI.'[33]

SAS implemented all its decisions with enthusiasm and shared the syllabus with almost a hundred universities who had a Department of History, besides State Achieves and archival institutions, invited them for a one-day interaction. But the response was not very encouraging.[34] According to some of the responses, it was observed that the syllabus shared was already very comprehensive. In contrast, even Universities with an optional paper on Archival Science had a very sketchy syllabus and covered topics covered in the short-term course on Archives Administration by the School. Some universities like Berhampur, Raipur, and Ajmer Universities, requested for a more detailed look at the syllabus. Some universities and Institutions were already teaching archival science as an optional paper in their MA History programme. Gujarat Vidyapith had been conducting an MPhil programme in Archival Science, which was also found very sketchy.[35]

The outcome of the exercise was placed before the Board of Studies in its twelfth meeting on 29 January, 2008, in which the members of the Board* felt the syllabus of the school was quite comprehensive.

33. Ibid
34. F.No. 46-5/2007 SAS
35. Ibid.

*(Board of Studies having been reconstituted with two new members, Dr. Arvind Sinha, Associate Professor, CHS, JNU & Sh. N. Narayanan, Principal Commissioner, TN State Archives, while retaining Dr. Bose, from NIC and Dr. G. Makhdumi from JMI).

The School was advised to take up the matter of introducing a paper on Archival Science in interested universities with the University Grants Commission. But for the interactive meeting, it was advised to restrict attendance from 15-20 universities only.[36]

The members also reviewed the eligibility criteria for the One-year Diploma course in Archives and Records Management and as suggested by Secretary (Culture) Abhijit Sengupta proposed that it should not be restricted to history students alone and instead be opened to students from other streams of social, linguistic and other sciences in view of the changing nature of archival records. It was also decided to increase the number of seats from 20 to 30 with10 seats earmarked for science and other streams. The entrance/aptitude test was to be moderated correspondingly and be based on other areas of science, social sciences, humanities, and linguistics. But this required amendment of recruitment rules for students joining from other streams to be eligible for employment after their diploma course. Once again, it was stressed that efforts should be made to make the course more popular so that quality students would apply both from India and SAARC countries. NAI was to write directly to these countries informing them about the training courses and scholarships available. It could also approach Ministry of Culture for help in this aspect. Amending recruitment rules meant that there were more employment opportunities for the new incumbents.[37]

The course fee pattern introduced in 1999 was revised and the registration process also streamlined.[38] The instant registration charges from Private Indian and sponsored students was Rs 40

36. Minutes, 12th meeting of Board of Studies, pp.10-13, (Annex) Agenda Notes of the 13th Meeting of the BoS.
37. Ibid. pp.10-11.
38. F.No.1-23/99-SAS

for the Diploma Course and US$ 40 from foreign candidates. No registration fee was charged for short-term courses, but an admission fee of Rs 25 was levied on both private and sponsored candidates and US$ 25 from foreign candidates vide approval orders dated 30 April 1994.[39] It was also noted that some Afro-Asian countries had opened their own schools with the help of UNESCO and other countries. Rates were slashed by 50 per cent from the academic session 2005 for attracting students in the Board's eleventh and twelfth meetings.[40] One trainee joined the course from Bangladesh, but left due to medical reasons. Another foreign student joined the 2006-07 sessions from Sri Lanka. The new approved rates by the Board of Studies were as under.[41]

New Approved Rates

Name of the Course	Application fee	Course fee
One-year Diploma course in Archives & Records Management	Rs 100 for Indian students US$ 40 for foreign student	Rs 1,500 for Indian student US$ 300 for foreign student
Short-term Certificate courses: 1. Archives Management (6 weeks) 2. Records Management (4 weeks) 3. Reprography (6 weeks) 4. Care & Conservation of Books, Manuscripts, & Archives (8 weeks) 5. Servicing & Repair of Records (6 Weeks)	Rs 100 for Indian students US$40 for foreign student	Rs 300 for Indian student US$ 300 for foreign student

To make teaching learning material available for students of Hindi medium, SAS was advised to explore IGNOU to find resource persons. The Director General could commission

39. F.N. 1-18/94-SAS

40. F.N.43-2/2005-SAS

41. Minutes, 12th meeting of Board of Studies, pp.11-12,

professional Hindi translators keeping copyrights in mind after seeking due permission from the publisher.[42]

As mentioned earlier, SAS was also gearing up for the interactive meet with other University professors. Professors attended from all the three universities of Delhi—Jamia Millia Islamia, Jawaharlal Nehru University, and Indira Gandhi National Open University besides faculty of SAS and members of the Board of Studies and senior officers of National Archives of India on 18 November 2009. The focus was on extending the duration of the Course. The majority supported the proposal of the Internship scheme for students who had already obtained their diploma. A move was made to promote study of Persian and other oriental languages to facilitate study of documents in these languages. However, they supported the syllabus with a suggestion from IGNOU to avoid duplication in Papers I and II on Archives and Records Management. It was decided to place the syllabus before the Board for final approval before it could be sent for printing.[43]

Modernisation of the course curriculum had started in May 2005 as recommended by the Board of Studies. Two new papers had been introduced—on Information and Communication Technology (ICT) as a compulsory paper and Business and Private Archives as a specialisation paper. Courses had been made more scientific and methodical by adding teaching hours with stress on practical working. SAS had to keep referring to material available on the internet as well. Efforts were also made to make material available to students based on project studies of the International Council on Archives (ICA). Moreover, the

42. Ibid.p.13.

43. Agenda of the 13th Meeting of the Board, Annex.II, Minutes of Interactive Meet, pp.14-21.

ICT syllabus was developed in association with NIC and for two years, faculty came from NIC for teaching the students. Later, NAI's new Computer Unit took over the teaching of the paper.

The infrastructure of the Archival School was gradually strengthened by installation of LCD Projectors in the Lecture rooms; one portable projector was also purchased besides a laptop for the workshops and seminars organised by the School. A workshop on Hazards faced by Records in Tropical Climate and Remedial measures was held on 3 Nov, 2007, at Lucknow in collaboration with Uttar Pradesh State Archives, besides 5 Trainers training workshops at Goa, Bangalore, Guwahati, Manipur and Chennai with their respective State Archives. A series of 7 workshops were held at the Central Social Welfare Board, at New Delhi and its 4 zonal offices at Chandigarh, Lucknow, Bangalore and Calcutta. Another Workshop on Business Archives in India was organised on 28 February 2008 at New Delhi. Besides a Computer Lab, a Modular Conservation Lab had also been developed in the School to facilitate practical work.

The Board of Studies in its meeting on 7 July 2010 noted that the quality of students in the one-year diploma course was improving as many students came from DU, Jamia and JNU. This was a result of the efforts by the team of officers in the School. In the Interactive Meet on 18 November 2009, the Board had decided to print the syllabus of the one-year Diploma course at the earliest. A new fee structure had been implemented, but the School was facing problems in developing teaching and learning material in Hindi, particularly for the very technical subjects, Conservation and Reprography. IGNOU did not respond to the correspondence by the School. Some material had been developed in both English and Hindi by the Fellows of the School appointed between 1985-1991, such as standard books in

Conservation and Reprography. Five books were recommended by SAS for the Board to decide if they could be recommended for translations. Besides 3 NAI publications, two books on Archives Administration by Michael Cook and Modern Archives by TR Schellenberg were subject to copyright and could not be taken up for translations without permissions.[44]

The Board suggested that the books for Hindi translation should be a post-1990 publication. Another small committee was to make recommendations and selection of books to start translation work. The members, however, wanted the school to pay more attention to the teaching of e-governance to enable ICT applications in official functioning and for storage of information. The School of Archival Studies had introduced one specialisation paper on ICT. Dr Bose from National Informatic Centre (NIC) had assisted in developing the syllabus and had provided faculty for the initial years for teaching of the paper.

The Archival Advisory Board of NAI, a statutory body constituted under the Public Record Act of 1993, in its eleventh meeting on 10 November 2009, under the chairmanship of Jawhar Sircar, Secretary (Culture), took an ad-hoc decision on the recommendation of the Board 'that the trainees of One-Year Diploma course be made to go through an internship for a period of six months and be used for archival work. They would be entitled for a stipend equivalent to JRF being given by UGC.'[45] It was placed before the Board of Studies for implementation and to decide on the stipend amount. After examining the scholarships being paid by ICHR and UGC, it was noted that NAI was

44. Agenda & Minutes of the 13th Meeting of the Board of studies, pp.

45. Agenda of the 13th meeting of the Board of Studies, Annex. IV, Minutes of the 11th Meeting of Archival Advisory Board, held on 10th November, 2009, pp.75-87. (p.80)

already paying Rs 15,000/month to Archival Assistants under NAI Critical Area Projects. The Board recommended that they be paid a consolidated amount of Rs 20,000/month. The Board also revised the earlier remuneration of Rs 15,000/month to Archival Assistants on contract. The Chairman of the Board and other members recommended that it be enhanced to Rs 22,000 and accordingly, the payments of trainees during internship for six months was fixed at Rs 20,000 pm. It was implemented with the approval of Ministry of Culture. The first batch to have benefitted with the SAS Internship scheme was the 2011-12 batch of the one-year Diploma Course. The honorarium being paid to the Guest faculty was also raised from Rs 400 to 1,000 per lecture of one hour duration. The department did not pay any conveyance charges to the guest faculty, hence the hike was justified.[46]

In December 2013, the Board approved an extension of the Internship from six months to one year and recommended internship of six months for the short-term training course in Reprography and Care and Conservation of Books, Manuscripts and Archives with the approval of the Archival Advisory Board. It was suggested that the interns could prepare the Reference Media in the Records Division of National Archives of India.[47]

The Board was satisfied with the archival interns and the strategy followed by the School for deployment of the interns on a rotational basis in Branches/Sections of the Department.[48]

Sadly, the affiliation of the School with the National Museum Institute (Deemed University), Ministry of Culture or other university was dropped to retain its identity. The School of

46. Minutes of the 13th meeting of Board of Studies held on 7th July, 2010. pp. 2-3.
47. F. No. 46-2/2018-SAS, Agenda of the 13th meeting of AAB, and Minutes of the meeting dt 18.12.2013, pp. 39-52/corr.
48. Ibid., Minutes of the 14th meeting of Board of Studies, held on 27.03.2018. pp. 1-3.

Archival Studies would continue to function as per the present status.[49] It was an important issue being pursued by NAI since long and deserved more attention from the Board to enhance the credibility of the School, which had a certain reputation, internationally, in the past. This issue, has been further discussed in the last chapter.

Other important issues taken up by the Board were on the infrastructure development of the School, increase in the honorarium paid to both internal and guest faculty for lectures, and to examiners, enhancement in the Scholarship/stipend amount for private and sponsored candidates of the Diploma course in Archives and Records Management. These had been agreed to by the Board and were being implemented with the approval of Ministry of Culture. Another important development had been the re-introduction of the Scheme of appointment of Senior and Junior Fellows in 2018, due to shortage of manpower, mainly for the preparation of teaching learning material in Hindi for Archival Science papers, apart from teaching.[50]

Infrastructure includes maintenance and sustaining the already existing facilities with a certain budget in mind. This was among the biggest challenge for the SAS team. Because of lack of manpower, the maintenance of Classrooms, Computer Lab, Conservation Lab, Library and other facilities had been through outsourced. A full-time employee was required to maintain the School library and reading room, who was well-versed in cataloguing, and could cater to the needs of the students and also perform routine librarian duties. Internet was needed in the

49. Minutes of the 13th meeting of Board of Studies held on 7th July, 2010, p.3 of the Minutes.

50. NAI website, www.nationalarchives.nic.in, posted list of selected candidates for SRF &JRF dated 29.5.2018, site visited on 21.08.2020.

library for students to access online sources for study purposes.

Currently, the course is open to post graduates in other disciplines besides history by increasing the total number of seats to 35 and the addition of new papers has already been described. It is noticed that the current lot of students prefer to specialise in Business and Private Archives for better employment opportunities and find employment in archives established by Business houses and corporates, Banks, and PSUs. Many trained archivists from SAS are now holding top positions in these organisations. The compulsory assignment, the dissertation that students write on a topic of their own interest is research based on archival sources that prepares them to serve, help and guide research scholars and gives them a feel of future archivists working in a repository. They learn how to conduct research, write a synopsis by using material in the library. The dissertation contains chapters, including proper bibliography and other related details. Many students have produced a thesis of excellent standard, at par with MPhil programmes.

The infrastructure in the School is now fully upgraded with a Modular Conservation Lab and a Computer Lab. The School's Lecture-cum-Conference Rooms are equipped with modern teaching aids. The system of examination at the conclusion of the School year includes both theory and practical exams; Marks are awarded based on one's performance besides internal marking for the practical assignments during the year. Finally, there are mandatory internships for all courses that include a handsome stipend. During internship, they are attached for one month in important Divisions like Records Repository, Records Management, Conservation, Reprographics and Computers, Reference and Research, Private Archives, Publication & Exhibition. It provides them an opportunity to work and earn at the same time and gain valuable experience. It keeps their interest alive in the subject and prepares them for the profession of an archivist. But the scheme needs to be more intensive and requires constant monitoring to get even better.

According to the Plan Document of NAI submitted to the then Planning Commission in 2011 for the XII Five Year Plan, in the previous Plan period, a total of 52 students had been trained including 4 foreign students from Sri Lanka and Bangladesh, in 2007-08, 2008-09, and 2009-10. The fourth session 2010-11, was underway with student strength of 24 trainees. The SAS team had revived the School and their hard work was paying dividends!

The professional qualification has also been recognised by UGC and the Public Service Commissions of the States besides UPSC, as a qualification for appointment to the Post of Assistant Archivists/Archivists at the Centre and the States Archival Repositories, University Archives and other such Institutes and Documentation Centres. Currently, the student strength is in between 25-30 for the one-year course. But SAS had to work harder and to keep up the momentum, needed support of the Government for money and competent manpower.

After the Public Record Act of 1993, and during the period 1993-2011, short-term courses had proved popular. Almost 2,000 students, both sponsored and private, had benefitted through the various short-term certificate courses in Records Management, Archives Administration, Care and Conservation, Reprography at Professional and Repair and Servicing of records at Sub-professional level. The methodology for all the courses included Lectures, Practical, written assignments, and for the Diploma, included field study to any of the two State Archives/ Business Archives, Guest Lectures, Workshops on latest trends of Indian History, Archives Management, Information Technology, Conservation, Technology for Archival Storage and Reproduction and Seminars based on Historical/Archival themes.

Many State Archives had also started giving greater importance to archival training.[51] Andhra Pradesh State Archives* started a one-year Post Graduate Diploma Course in Archival Science and Manuscriptology in collaboration with Osmania University in 1992-93 with 12 students and the University had recognised State Archives as a Research Institute. The State Archives had introduced a Research Fellowship scheme since 1966 with full-time and part-time stipends. It proved a very successful scheme, leading to PhD degrees. They also run a short-term course in Records Management.[52]

Kerala established a State Institute of Archaeology, Art, History, Conservation, and Museology at Hill Place, Tripunithura, and at Ernakulum to provide qualified and trained professionals in the field. The Institute conducts a one-year Diploma Course in Archival Studies and Manuscriptology, besides other courses. A Regional Archives is located in Ernakulum. Gujarat State Archives provide training facilities to Government officials in the state.

The State Archives of Rajasthan conducts one month training course in Records Management, three times in a year while the Tamil Nadu State Archives also conducts a short-term course in Records Management. West Bengal State Archives provides short training courses in conservation of different durations, ranging from 4weeks to 3 months. Other states are encouraged to give serious thought to Archives Keeping, which could provide a background for professional and sub-professional courses. Such

---

*Now divided into Telangana and Andhra Pradesh. Now Institute is part of Telangana State Archives.

51. IHRC 1995, p. 191 and IHRC, 2001, Mysore, p. 161, (apstatearchives.ap.nic.in)

52. IHRC Proceedings, Raipur, April 2003, pp. 196-97, & apstatearchives.ap.nic.in

a programme could be applied to all the states in the country with support of NAI.[53]

Thus, School of Archival Studies at NAI has become a Hub-Centre for Archival Science Education in India. Efforts are being made by the Ministry of Culture to start a National Heritage University by upgrading National Museum Institute (Deemed University), with a view to bring all cultural training Institutions of Archaeological Survey of India, National Museum Institute and National Archives of India under the umbrella of this new upcoming University. It remains to be seen how it will work out.

53. IHRC Proceedings, Raipur, April 2003, pp. 196-97

India's National Archives and its Relations with its International Counterparts

UNESCO, International Council on Archives (ICA) and Archival Education in India: A Beginning

The Imperial Record Department (NAI after Independence) in its memorandum for its Post-War Reorganisation programme, had emphasised on establishing educational contacts with archival training institutes outside India, duly supported and approved by the standing committee of the Indian Legislature on Education in March 1945. It marked the beginning of the growth and development of archival institutions in India. The progress report of the Imperial Records Department also reported about its training scheme, having trained twenty-three students since 1942 with a definite syllabus. The report highlighted the shortcomings of the course and suggested improving the technical services further by establishing educational contact with progressive archival institutions of Europe and America.

The Government, in general had accepted the principles and subjects of the schemes prepared by the Central Advisory Board of Education for Post-War Educational Development of India, subject to finance. This included development of Imperial Records

Department/National Archives of India and Indian Historical Records Commission, under the General Branch of the newly constituted Department of Education wef 1 September 1945.[1] It was an important aspect of the Department's activities, which was showing promise of further development in strengthening of educational contacts. The Department believed that in archival matters, no records office can be self-sufficient. To avoid stagnation, it must avail of the superior technical knowledge within India and abroad.[2]

The Department had, thus been corresponding with several progressive archival institutions and experts in including National Archives, Washington, the Huntington Library, the Colorado Archives, the Library of Congress, the Archives of Illinois State, the Society of American Archivists, the British Records Association, the Institute of Historical Research, and many others. There was regular exchange of pamphlets, publications and technical information. Foreign Archivists and historians had contributed articles in the Indian Archives journal, being published by NAI since 1947. Contributors had included Sir Hillary Jenkinson, Sir Harold Bell, Sir Cyril Flower, Rev Claude Jenkins, Prof CH Phillips, M Charles Samaran, M Jean Filliozat, Signor Eugenio Casanova, Dr Solon J Buck, Prof Holden Furber, Dr Lester K Born, Dr Ernst Posner and Dr Arthur E Kimberly.[3]

The Department had derived immense benefits from such cooperation and to strengthen relationships further, the Government had been nominating some of these archival experts as Corresponding Members of Indian Historical Records

1. NAI F.No. 13/46-C, pp. 21-22/corr.
2. Ibid, pp. 99-100/corr.
3. The Quinquennial Review, NAI, 1948-1952, p. 22.

Commission (IHRC) since 1942. After 1972, this practice had been confined to persons residing outside India only, who were actively interested in records and also had published works of sufficient merit.

IHRC had been constituted purely as a consultative body in 1919 to make enquiries and recommendations for promoting historical research in the country, encouraging publication of historical documents and preserving records for use by scholars. Initially all its eight members were government officials only. Such a body was, therefore, unlikely to inspire public confidence or carry any weight with the Government. Finally, in 1942, as a matter of policy archival experts acclaimed internationally in records and archives management, having published work of sufficient merit were to be appointed as Corresponding Members. Though, some experts were invited as co-opted members since 1921for some select sessions, some Corresponding Members from each province and few universities had been invited in 1928.

The reconstitution of the Commission on 3 January 1942 converted the IHRC as a representative forum of historians, administrators and archivists. The Education Member to the Government now became its ex-officio President, and the Keeper of Records continued as its ex-officio Secretary. The Government's nominees were reduced from eight to five. Nominees of the Provinces with Record Offices were Ordinary Members and those with relatively inactive Records Offices were classed as Associate Members including nominees of universities. The number of Corresponding Members was fixed at forty. Indian history research scholars were alone to be considered for inclusion in this category and could only attend meetings by special invitation. All categories of members were to be nominated for a fixed period of five years. After Independence, the Commission underwent some changes but retained its general outline.[4]

In 1951, members were divided into two categories: the first was formed by the Union Minister for Education and Scientific Research and included five nominees of Government, one member from each State with organised Record Rooms, all members of its Research &Publication Committee and Director of Archives, who officiated as ex-officio Secretary. In the second category, members comprised of scholars both from within India and abroad and this continued till 1965, when its membership was made more broad-based. In 1972, the corresponding membership was restricted to only scholars residing abroad. Broad categories were now ex-officio members, nominees of the Government, representatives of Central and Semi-Government Institutions, State Governments/Union Territories/Regional Records Survey Committees, and representatives of universities. Only those history scholars teaching post-1600 period were included, apart from representatives of certain Institutions and Corresponding Members. The composition remained the same till recent times. Till 1990, Corresponding Members were there[*] but when this category was abolished is not clear.

In 1982, there were 7 corresponding members from African countries, 4 from USA and Latin America; 9 from Asia, 9 from Europe, 2 from Australia and 1 nominated from ICA. Most were Directors/Chief Archivists of the National Archives in their own country. Presidents of Regional Branches of ICA, subject experts or nominees of ICA on various Committees had been nominated, and this enriched the IHRC academically, besides fortifying

4. Indian Historical Records Commission, A Retrospect, Vol II, pp. 1-5. NAI, Publication, 1995.

*Indian Historical Records Commission, A Retrospect, Vol II, (1948-1994, pub. 1995, pp.54-59

contacts with foreign archival repositories and institutes for acquiring microfilm copies of records and private papers related to Indian history.[5]

At the Silver Jubilee session of IHRC at Delhi in December 1948, invitations had been extended to UK, France, USA, USSR, Belgium, and Austria. The Government offered to bear their entire hotel and travel expenses. Only UK accepted, but the delegate could not attend. The session was, however, attended by members from Burma, Nepal, and Ceylon, including two delegates from the Superior Council of Scientific Investigation from Madrid (Spain), and of course, by archivists, historians and scholars from all over India.[6]

The most encouraging was the response to Resolution VI of the twenty-third Indore session in 1946 of the IHRC, recommending establishment of cultural relations with foreign countries. Eighteen Corresponding Members from UK, USA France, China, Iran, Burma, Nepal, Australia, and Ceylon had been appointed by 1949-50.[7]

It was a matter of pride that NAI had attracted the attention of foreign archival authorities and received appreciation. Notes on Preservation of Records compiled by NAI were acclaimed in the USA as 'one of the best comparisons between silking and lamination that has ever been made'. The research by the Department in its Conservation Research Laboratory, for the physical protection of records against insects and fungus growth had aroused interest among well-known archivists like Dr SJ Buck, Margarate Norton, Dr Hiller and JJ Barrow. Hand lamination

---

5. IHRC Proceedings, Gandhinagar, Gujarat, June, 1982.pp.223-225, IHRC corresponding members as in 1982.
6. F. No. 13/49-C, pp.123-124/corr.
7. Ibid. p.386/corr.

was perfected by the NAI in 1953, and was known as the Indian process of lamination, and adopted as a repair technique in advanced archival institutions in the world. In France, a firm marketed a machine based on the Indian practice as India-7.[8]

Even the Post-War Reconstruction Plan of the NAI was acclaimed by American archivists as a significant document. It had been printed as a pamphlet and distributed widely in India and abroad and was published in the American Archivist issue. Many foreign archival repositories had furnished interesting and useful information on documents of Indian interest in foreign repositories.[9] This had also increased expectations and responsibilities of the Department, who realised that they needed trained staff in the latest methods and techniques of preservation, archival storage and administration.

The syllabus of Training in Archives Keeping was revised and circulated among leading institutions in India and abroad. It was well-received by distinguished authorities like Prof VK Galbraith, Director of the Institute of Historical Research, London; Sir Hilary Jenkinson, Deputy Keeper, Public Records Office, London; and by the Secretary of the British Records Association. Appreciation for the new syllabus had also been published in the American Archivist. The new syllabus was subsequently approved by the Standing Committee of the Central Legislature on Education in its Shimla meeting of May 1946. Financial assistance to encourage students was also sanctioned.[10]

It was decided to depute one of its senior officers, Dr. P. Basu, Assistant Director of Archives for training at the National

8. IHRC proceedings, Delhi, October 1960, p.17.

9. Ibid. & IHRC proceedings, Jaipur, Feb. 1948, pp.154 & Appendix 'A', pp. 174-176.

10. F.N.2/48-C, p.5/corr.

Archives, Washington for nine months followed by RC Gupta, Preservation Officer, and sometime later. Both were awarded Overseas Scholarship by the Government for advanced study in archival economy and conservation, respectively. S Chakravarti, a senior chemist was sent in 1946 to National Archives, Washington for a year's training in Archives Preservation and Microfilming. A proposal was submitted to depute three more members of NAI to USA and elsewhere, for further training and the Government was requested for funds. It was requested that to maintain an efficient archival service, candidates should be regularly sent abroad.[11]

NAI took an active interest in acquiring microfilm copies of Indian interest from foreign repositories and to also establish educational contacts. The NAI had established good contacts with the Public Records Office, London; British Museum; National Library, Scotland; Historical Manuscript Commissions of England and Scotland; Public Records Office, Scotland and Northern Ireland; State Archives in Norway and Sweden; Society of Intellectual Cooperation, Geneva; Society of Comparative Legislation, Bibliotheeque Nationale, Paris; Council of Learned Societies, USA; American Society of State and Local History and many others.

Many of these bodies had placed IRD in their free distribution list of publications and cooperated in maintaining an archival news service for its journal Indian Archives. During 1946, the NAI officer deputed for training to National Archives, Washington, in up-to-date methods of archives keeping had, according to reports from USA made a very good impression

11. NAI F.No. 13/46-C, pp.100-101/corr.

on the archivists there and this prompted Dr Ernst Posner of the American University and Dr Solen J Buck of the National Archives to invite IRD to send more staff for training in future years. This, they believed would help build friendly relations between Indian and American Archivists. The Department fully endorsed the views.[12]

UNESCO, ICA, and NAI

The Government is a member of the United Nations Educational, Scientific and Cultural Organisation (UNESCO), a specialised Agency of the United Nations since 1946. Article VII of the Constitution of UNESCO requires that 'each Member State shall make such arrangements as suit its particular conditions for purpose of associating its principal bodies interested in educational, scientific and cultural matters with the work of the Organisation, preferably by the formation of a National Commission broadly representative of the Government and such bodies' and further defines that 'National Commissions or National Cooperating Bodies, where they exists, shall act in an advisory capacity to their respective delegations to the General Conference and to their Governments in matters relating to the Organisation and shall function as agencies of liaison in all matters of interest to it.'

In fulfillment ofUNESCO's requirements and to ensure active participation of the people of India in the implementation of its various programmes, an interim Indian National Commission for Cooperation with UNESCO was set up in 1949 by the Ministry of Education. By 1951, the interim Commission was firmly established, when the constitution was approved, it was for better

12. NAI F. N. 15-3/47-C, p.17/corr. & 13/47-C, pp.22-23, Report of the Development of IRD 1946-47, submitted to Standing Committee of Indian Legislature on Education for its Shimla Meeting.

implementation of UNESCO's programmes within India.[13]

In January 1949, the Government had approached the Secretary, IHRC, to nominate a representative of the Commission to the proposed Indian National Commission for Cooperation with the UNESCO. According to its original report, IHRC was entitled to nominate a representative on the Education Sub-Commission of the National Commission.

Minister of Education nominated Director of Archives & Secretary, IHRC, to represent the Commission in the meeting of the Indian National Commission for UNESCO, held in April 1949. Its Executive Board revised its composition and grouped IHRC with five others, to be represented by rotation. IHRC felt that under the revised system, representation of historical associations and institutions was inadequate. But IHRC felt it should be individually and permanently represented on the Indian National Commission for Cooperation with UNESCO, instead of 'taking its turn in rotation'.[14]

IHRC again nominated the Secretary, IHRC to represent it on the Education Sub-Commission of the Indian National Commission for Co-operation with the UNESCO. Dr BA Saletore, Secretary IHRC, forwarded two proposals—one on the compilation of a 30-volume History of Asia and Africa on scientific lines and the other on the close co-operation of Asiatic and African Nations on archival matters—for the consideration of the Indian National Commission at its first Conference in New Delhi.[15] UNESCO had been providing financial support for many programmes of the Government.

13. F. No. 12/69-C, pp. 129-130/corr., Resolution No.F.134-27/50-A-5 dated the 16 October, 1951
14. Ibid. pp. 60-61 (IHRC proceedings, Bhopal, 29th Session, 10th February, 1953
15. IHRC proceedings, Hyderabad, 30 Session, 1-3 February 1954, p. 73.

Establishment of International Council on Archives and Contribution of NAI

Some leading archivists were proposing an International Archives Organisation with the support of UNESCO. A circular letter dated 2 May 1947 was issued by Dr Solon J Buck from the National Archives of USA reached Dr S Sen, Director of Archives, with enthusiasm for the establishment of a permanent, international archives organisation. The letter invited views, suggestions and advice globally to determine what kind of organisation should be set up.[16] The matter was placed before UNESCO at its first General Conference at Paris in December 1946, and included in its approved programme.* UNESCO had recognised the importance of the subject and offered its encouragement.[17]

Three recommendations were made at the Paris meet:

a) To call the Session of the International Congress of Archivists.

---

16. F.N. 15-3/47-C, pp. 1-12/corr.,
    Along with the letter some documents were also forwarded including statements of Proposed Archives Program for UNESCO, and a suggested draft statement of 'General Purposes', of an International Archives Organisation. Enclosures included:

1. Suggested Statement of 'General Purposes', 2. Basis of members and representation, 3.General questions relating to forming of International Archives Organisation, steps to be followed in its establishment, basis of membership and representation, association with National Governments, nature of its governing body, permanent headquarters & secretariat, appropriate name, suggestions for programme and activities, etc. 4. A Note on National Archives of USA, September 1946 and proposed archives programme for UNESCO, stating the problem, background considerations elaborating from the first and only International Congress of Archivists and Librarians, held in Brussels in 1910. Dr. Waldo G. Leland, who attended the meet, stated that 'this congress permanently influenced archival conceptions and practices in the United States.' It reported to have a comparable influence in many other countries and its papers and discussions, printed in a volume of 800 pages, still recommended as reading material for students of Archives Administration. Among the major problems of the professionals for which a call had been made for Archivists of all countries to unite, highlighted the instant problems of rehabilitation of war damaged archives, preservation of archives of international organisations, archives in the international field settlements, and handling of modern types of archives and records besides the training of Archivists. Regarding training of Archivists, it made recommendation for cooperation for making provision of better facilities in training of Archivists and archival technicians should be studied and encouraged. This should include the institution of channels for the international exchange of leaders and teachers and also for the international exchange of students.

   *Mimeographed 'Report of Program Commission adopted by the General Conference,'p.26

17. F.N. 15-3/47-C, pp. 1-12/corr.,

b) For constitution of a provisional International Committee of Archivists to plan the Agenda for the International Congress and to guide UNESCO for related activities for archives in the interim, and to be reconstituted at the International Congress and made a permanent liaison agency between Archivists and UNESCO.

c) To constitute a small but permanent unit in its regular organisation to have responsibility for archives. This would have a permanent Executive Secretary of the ICA as its Head and have responsibility for all aspects of documentation.[18]

Secretary Education, Sir John Sargent, who had represented India at the UNESCO meet, had assured India's support, if the new Archivists' international organisation is affiliated to UNESCO. Director NAI further suggested that membership be extended also to individual archivists, archivist's offices and regional associations. He also supported its proposed activities and programmes for ICA, holding of the first ICA meet at Washington, and subsequently in different countries. He also supported formation of a provisional International Committee of Archivists to expedite the preliminary work and to draft a Constitution of the Congress.[19] IHRC endorsed the Draft Constitution prepared by UNESCO and approved of the suggestions made by Director of Archives with a proviso that out of the five co-opted members, at least one should represent the 'user' of archives.[20] Dr Buck appreciated the suggestion of the Commission and promised that it would be laid before the Provisional Committee along with his other comments and

18. Ibid

19. Ibid.,pp.13-15/corr.

20. IHRC Proceedings, Jaipur Session, Feb. 1948, pp. 160 & Appendix 'B', pp. 184-85. Ibid. pp. 20-21/corr.

suggestions, in its summer meeting in Paris.[21]

With the Government's concurrence, IHRC, thus, became an 'Associational' Member of ICA, according to para 3(a) of the constitution with a subscription fee of £50 for membership of the International Council. This entitled the Commission to receive all publications for the benefits of the students of the archival school, services and privileges of the Council and to send two delegates to each Congress.[22] While NAI's request of becoming an 'Institutional' member of the Council was being considered, the President of the Council, Dr Charles Samaran, appointed Dr SN Sen as a member of the Admissions Committee of the Council.

ICA's first meeting was held at Paris during 23-26 August 1950, with a registration fee of 1,000 French Francs for students of recognised archival schools. University students were admitted on a fee of 300 francs. The subjects to be discussed were control of archives in the process of creation, archives and microphotography, economical archives (archives of private enterprises), and publication of an international bibliography of Guides to archives. The IHRC nominated Dr Sen to represent IHRC at the ensuing ICA meeting at Paris. However, Dr Sen could not attend the meeting due to financial stringency.[23]

To obtain information on the status and working of archives in India, two questionnaires sent by ICA, had been circulated by NAI to all State Governments and Records Offices in India. NAI also forwarded its information as disclosed in its meeting at Nagpur.[24] Dr Sen had retired and Dr P Basu, the new

21. Ibid. / op.cit. pp. 20-21/corr. & pp. 29-30/corr.
22. F.No. 15-3/48-C, p. 9/notes & 71-72/corr. IHRC Proceedings, Jaipur Session, Feb. 1948, p. 160 & Appendix 'B', pp.184-85.
23. F. No. 15-3/48-C, pp.84 & 97-110/corr. & IHRC Proceedings 1950, pp. 20-21.
24. F. No. 15-3/48-C, pp.84 & 97-110/corr. & IHRC Proceedings 1950, pp. 20-21.

Director of Archives, was appointed by ICA as a member of the Admission Committee.[25] It was also proposed that the State Archives also become members of ICA. Representatives of West Bengal, Bombay, Madras and Bhopal Governments had already become members of ICA.[26]

Secretary General and Chairman of 'Committee on the Protection of Archives in time of War' of ICA had written to Director of Archives on 21 August 1952, if anything was being done by India on protection of cultural heritage during the time of armed conflicts. If not constituted, the letter urged to initiate efforts to form one for protection of cultural objects such as Archives, Libraries and Museums. On the basis of recommendation of ICA, IHRC unanimously adopted a resolution recommending to the Government that a Committee of Experts representing Archives, Library and Museum interests to study the problem of protection of cultural properties during the periods of war be set up and suggest measures for affording these, maximum security.[27]

The Secretary, IHRC attended the second International Congress on Archives, held at The Hague during 15-20 June 1953 as representative of the Commission. The Report submitted by him was recorded in the thirtieth IHRC session. The third ICA meet was to be held in Florence in 1956.[28] Dr Saletore recorded that the first Congress, held within two years of ICA's establishment was highly successful compared to the second Congress attended by him. The issues at the first Congress were more relevant, he

25. N.15-3/50-C, p.18/corr. IHRC Prods. Dec.1950, Nagpur session, App. (I) & C, pp.73-89, 91, Questionnaires.
26. IHRC proceedings, Jaipur Session, 26-27 December 1951, para 9, p.31. Report on the ICA
27. Ibid. Bhopal, 29th session 1953, pp. 60-61.
28. IHRC proceedings, Hyderabad, 30 Session, 1954, p.67.

had said. His talk gave rise to the following questions:

a) What should be done to enable archivists to know in advance what was to be discussed at such meets? This knowledge would prevent knowledge gaps for future reference.
b) What archival means should be adopted?
   (i) To reduce the volume of Archives to be preserved, and
   (ii) To keep in different places, their copies so as to increase the chances of their survival and make them available for research.
c) How to save the very important class of economic archives which were increasing at a pace beyond control? and
d) How to establish a system which would enable archivists all over the world to exchange their views, their methods and their experiences?

The work of the ICA was being, carried forward by the Committee on Microphotography and Archives, Committee on Archives in times of War, and Committee on Accessibility of Archives. The ICA also started a new periodical, Archivum, to serve as a medium for disseminating the constructive results of activities among archivists.[29]

The Government had permitted the Secretary, IHRC to attend the second ICA Congress as Dr Sen could not attend the first due to financial constraints. The archival issues being discussed at the Congress meet at The Hague included discussion on development of uniform terminology for use in archival work. India was to gain much by this form of intellectual cooperation as the development of archives and archival education and training in India was still at a rudimentary stage and much could be learnt by personal discussion on technical problems with other Heads

29. F.No. 14-2/53-C, pp.4-5/notes.

of Archives and could facilitate the availability of historical material not available in India, as it was only after Independence that India had taken up the project of acquiring microfilms of such material from foreign repositories.

The Secretary reported that as most of the discussions were in French, it was difficult to participate in the proceedings. But the talk on 'Training of Archivists' by Sir Hillary Jenkinson, Deputy Keeper, Public Records Office, London, was brilliant and would guide NAI on training of Archivists in India. The agenda included discussions on useful subjects-Uniformity of Archival Terms, Archives and Documentation, Archives and History of Art, Professional Training of Archivists, Historical Museums of Records, and Communication and Lending of Documents. The crux of his talk was that it was not necessary for Archivists to know every subject in existence. The English translators were not efficient enough and out of 300 delegates, only about twenty delegates could not follow French. He, however succeeded, in generating members' interest in the manuscripts in the possession of NAI, the training courses in Archives Keeping being conducted by NAI and the journal, Indian Archives maintaining, arranging and preserving records. After visiting the National Archives of Netherlands, he found NAI was definitely ahead. Netherlands had no proper fire-fighting arrangements, no sand bags or water hoses and he even witnessed mildew and fungi between the leaves of many volumes. But their Library Room was indeed excellent, for it was spacious, well-lighted and well-ventilated.[30]

The report of Dr Saletore was taken by the Ministry with a pinch of salt. The report of the proceedings from 16-19 June

30. Ibid, pp. 10-17/corr.

1953 was not found very encouraging either, especially for the Government to consider again deputing its representatives to attend the forthcoming Congress Meetings in the future.[31] At the next ICA Session at Florence in September 1956, there was no Indian delegate. Questionnaires received from ICA on Private Archives for Archivum, besides a questionnaire on International Directory of Archives were circulated to all State Archives and other archival institutions for collection of information and information was sent in both cases. The questionnaire sought general information on archives, locations, history, access to records with restrictions, loan facilities of records to other institutions, microfilms and readership, principal qualified Archivists and their Departments, with names, bulk of records, date of oldest record, if purely historical repository or increases with periodical accessions, were also sought. Replies to ICA questionnaire are available in IHRC proceedings Vol XXVI, pp. 75-91, Pt. I. The answers contain valuable information on archival activities in the country.[32]

ICA continued sending invitations for their International Congress of Historical Science and meets. NAI would circulate information among the Records Offices in India. IHRC was also a member of ICA. State Governments could also enroll as institutional members of ICA, as some like the Bombay Records Office had done. However, no information is available if anyone was deputed for these ICA conferences. IHRC who could only make recommendations. But it was for the Government only to make nominations for international conferences.[33] Further there were foreign exchange difficulties and the Government had

31. Ibid, pp. 24-25/notes.
32. F. No. 18-2/1955-CA-3.
33. F. No. 18-2/59-C

been restricting sending delegations abroad. The Commission had only accepted the proposal in principle and recommended that the Government secure UNESCO and other foreign fellowships for the purpose.

The agenda of ICA so far had included subjects for discussion (a) the Archives of the States and their organisation, (b) new methods, materials, and practices introduced since 1950 in the field of restoration (documents and seals) & preservation (maps & plans) and photography, archival training and c) the Archives of the modern economic and social research. The ICA Secretariat had also circulated questionnaires on these subjects to all the member countries to elicit information on them.

Director NAI could not attend the Fifth International Archives Congress held in Brussels from 1-5 September 1964 as IHRC was in a state of suspended animation due to the recommendation of the Report of Archival Legislation Committee of 1960 to abolish IHRC and establish an All India Archival Council to regulate Central and State Archives in India. VC Joshi, Project Director in the Indian Institute of Public Administration, (IIPA, on loan from NAI) of the Project 'Guide to the Sources of Modern Indian History,' of Ministry of Education attended the ICA Brussels Congress. As advised by the Ministry of Education, he forwarded a copy of his tour report to Director, NAI, for follow up action and record.[34]

The visit sponsored by IIPA enabled him to meet several eminent archivists and scholars. He was also able to visit several leading archival repositories of Europe and study their organisation and working, especially of Manuscript repositories

34. Ibid, pp. 74-91/corr.

during his six weeks' tour of Belgium, The Netherlands, UK, France, Ireland and Germany. He also examined important records and manuscripts series relating to modern Indian history which proved useful for not only his project but for NAI projects also for acquisition of microfilm copies of material of Indian interest in foreign repositories. His report was very positive than the one submitted by Dr Saletore of his participation in the second ICA meeting.[35] His report mentioned that the meet was attended by 600 delegates from 48 countries registered from Europe, and America with negligible participation from Asia and Africa. The arrangements for the conference were good including interpretations available in English, French and German. The Business meeting was presented with the multilingual Lexicon of Archives Terminology in French, English, German, Spanish, Italian and Dutch, prepared by the Archival Terminology Committee, constituted in 1953. This valuable document serves even today as a manual for archivists, historians, librarians and for others interested in archives keeping and documentation. Besides, discussing about types of documents, he also discussed about the physical and structural aspects of archives and methods of preparation, processing, utilisation and preservation. Some members in the General Assembly sought better representation from Asia and Africa and the need for promotion of archives work in developing countries. The Council's secretariat assured that greater interest would be taken in the development of archives in this region. The themes of the Conference were:

1. Publication of Archives and Methods of Publication
2. Ecclesiastical Archives: Legislation, Organisation and Classification

35. Ibid

3. Sigillography: Preservation and Description of Seals
4. Introduction and adoption of Mecanographic Devices at the Archives,
5. Recruitment and early stages of the careers of professional staff in State Archives.

Shri Joshi could attend sections 1, 3 and 5 as these were being held simultaneously. In the discussions pertaining to Recruitment (Theme 5), some delegates spoke about the lower positions and emoluments given to Archivists. It was encouraging to note that Archivists in many countries were recognised as officials concerned with scientific research and enjoyed privileged positions unlike India. They played an important role as intellectuals in their countries and had links with universities and learned institutions by giving courses in specialised fields and by undertaking editing of texts.

He was able to discuss NAI publications during the first section, where the emphasis was on publishing Guide to Archives of each country on a priority basis. In the Sigillography section, the International Committee on Sigillography presented its report and adopted the new form of Cataloguing seals which the Committee had prepared. The next Congress was to be held in Madrid in 1968.[36]

The Technical Committee of ICA had also invited Director of Archives, NAI, being a great repository of such material for the compilation of the Guide to the Sources of History of Africa. India was to collaborate in the programme. Director of Archives could not attend the Brussels ICA Congress, but NAI decided to work in collaboration with Delhi University, Department of

36. Ibid.pp.76-79/corr.

African Studies on the project. NAI worked out the strategy to work in consultation with the Department as a Unit, under the supervision and technical guidance of NAI and the Department.[37] Since NAI had no funds for the project, it requested for sanction of $ 6,000 as funds for the project, in favour of Department of African Studies, Delhi University, as NAI could not accept any such grant. For all this, they were requested to write to Director of Archives.[38] He further gave details of record series available in NAI and other State Archives of Bombay, West Bengal, Goa and Madras.

NAI cooperated with ICA and responded to a questionnaire on archival training, received from ICA.[39] Archival science education and training was only given by National Archives of India and universities have yet to start teaching the subject.

ICA has been promoting Archives as a profession globally and had brought the archival community on a common platform. ICA convened an extraordinary meeting from 9-13 May 1966 at Washington, which the Director of Archives attended. The meeting of the Extraordinary International Archives Congress was hosted by Library of Congress and other United States Government Agencies including Society of American Archivists. Accesses to archives turned out to be an issue with most archival repositories including India as outlined by historians and research scholars.

The Congress discussed liberalisation of rules on access to these records. It reaffirmed that ICA's principal objectives is 'to facilitate more frequent use of Archives and the effective and impartial

37. Ibid, pp.43-44/corr.
38. Ibid
39. F. No 12/66-C, pp. 33-39.

study of the documents they contain by making their content more widely known and encouraging greater freedom of access' as listed in article 2 of the ICA Constitution. The Congress wanted researchers, of any nationality be accorded equal and easy facilities for access to archives and that every means should be employed to make the principle effective. It recommended that international reader's card be created to serve as recommendation to foreign archival institutions. Other lists of the Congress were very crucial for its growth and development in India. It included:[40]

- Accelerating the arrangement and preparation of finding aids.
- Publishing comprehensive guides to documentary sources.
- Archival depositories are provided with qualified personnel insufficient numbers to carry out work rapidly.
- Permitting access to increasingly voluminous archives of contemporary times.
- Promoting publication of documentary sources in each country and the Committee to study the use of microfilms as a means of publication.
- Strengthening microfilming programmes, including drafting agreements concerning the exchange or the provision of microfilms regulating their reproduction or their further transfer.
- ICA Executive Committee initiating a study of the conditions under which films may be preserved in tropical climates like India.
- Mobilising finances for increasing operating funds for ICA projects and programmes and to establish a permanent secretariat. This needed UNESCO giving a substantial increase in the subvention granted to the Council. It requested delegations present in Washington to recommend to the National UNESCO Commissions

40. Ibid, pp. 166-170/corr.

of their respective countries that they take forceful action on behalf of ICA during the next general UNESCO Conference.

- Suggesting to UNESCO that special items be added to their technical assistance budget for helping developing countries to organise their Archives.
- The Congress approved UNESCO's idea to start an archival pilot project in Africa's two sub-regions; English speaking East Africa and French speaking West Africa and assured ICA collaboration. It also aimed to strengthen operations of the UNESCO Mobile Microfilms Units and to incorporate them in sub-regional projects. While awaiting the start of these sub-regional projects, it was recommended to train qualified personnel for African archival institutions by using local opportunities.**
- Under the sponsorship of the International Council on Archives, another series of Guides devoted to sources preserved in Latin America, Africa and Asia was to be taken up.
- The Congress established a permanent working group of representatives of the UNESCO secretariat and of the ICA, whose principal function would be to investigate ways of assisting archival institutions in developing countries, to oversee their Implementation and to coordinate activities in the field.
- The Congress Working Group was too created by the President of the ICA to continue the work started at Washington. The Round Table Conference was to take special interest in the measures recommended by the Congress and report submitted to the General Assembly in 1968 at Madrid.[41]

41. Ibid.

** These projects once implemented, provided lot of opportunities to Indian experts as they were called upon to work in Africa in these ICA-UNESCO projects to train African archivists and officials or they were deputed in large numbers for training at Institute of Archival Training at National Archives of India during 1970s & 1980s as discussed in Chapter II and further elaborated in Section II in the chapter dealing with UNESCO and NAI.

Based on these recommendations, ICA prepared a five-year programme for 1967-1972 for submission to the General Assembly at the Madrid Congress, for circulation to member countries.[42] Highlighting the objectives of ICA, the then President of the ICA and Archivist General of Belgium, E Sabbe pointed out that rendering technical archival aid to developing countries had become one of the pre-occupations of the Council. India also benefitted from these programmes. They had projects carried out with financial assistance from UNESCO, and with ICA's own funds or third-party organisations (regional institutions, national governments and private foundations). The Council also had direct ties with independent international organisations such as libraries, museums, documentation, and social sciences projects. Major programmes included in the brief were:

- Problem of Organisation & Administration
- Recruitment of new members with a target of 90, from Africa, Asia and Latin American countries between 1968 to 1972, from Madrid to Moscow.
- To organise Round-table Conference in 1967 (Copenhagen), 1969, 1970 and 1971. Regional conferences were to be held in America, Africa and Asia.
- Creation of Permanent Secretariat of ICA before 1970.
- Reviewing of Documentation Centre of ICA in Paris to make it more active.
- Creation of Regional Branches of ICA to promote regional cooperation among archival institutions of South East Asian countries, (SWARBICA ICA branch was launched in New Delhi during 1976, as discussed in detail in SWARBICA section of

42. Ibid, pp.247-262/corr. Translated English version of Five year program, as was received in French only.

this chapter) English-speaking countries of East Africa, French-speaking countries of West Africa.

- Formation of Work Groups/Commissions as per projects of the programmes such as Congress, The Round Table, *Archivum,* the Executive Committee, office of the International Technical Committee of the Guide, etc.
- The combined Work Groups for ICA/UNESCO for technical archival assistance, for study with liberalisation of access to documents, Commission for study of modern methods of publication of documents, audio-visual and mecanographic archives.
- Expansion and empowerment of the General Assembly to determine the general policies of the Council and ratify its long-term programmes.
- Assistance to developing countries and to implement a standard programme of Archival instruction during 1967-68.

II

Archival Legislation

- A brief history for publication by UNESCO and to make available ICA's services for Archives Departments or Government Organisations. To publish a Manual of Archival Legislation in 1967/68.
- To develop a Manual on Construction of Archival Buildings by 1966 and assist the member countries in their plans.
- To conduct preliminary studies for implementing Pilot archival projects in Africa by 1967/68 in collaboration with UNESCO and to assist it in implementing other archival projects in the future.
- Enquiry on technical assistance of *Archivum* Volume XVII dedicating to the problems of archives of developing countries.

III

International Cooperation of Archives for Historical Science

- Publications and methods of publication-of the Guide to the Sources of History of Latin America (already being printed), and of History of Africa which was nearing completion. ICA together with UNESCO would take up editing of the **Guide to the Sources of History of Asia**. Preparatory studies were on to complete it by 1968 and its compilation was to start by January 1969.[43]
- Publication of Collective Guide to Archives of Latin America, Africa and Asia before 1970. The Pan-American Institute of Geography and History was to take up the work with Inter American Technical Council of Archives.
- To set up a Commission for finding amore economical and rapid method of publishing archival documents and utilisation of microfilms as a means of publication.
- To study methods of cooperation on bilateral, regional and international plans on reference media and documentary sources attempted before 1972.
- To facilitate exchange of archival publications between member countries of ICA, and liberalisation of access to archives in Rules for consultation of documents, policy of microfilming for foreign countries, creation of an international plan for serving the needs of archives organisations of foreign countries. A Working Group was constituted to study and submit a report in 1968.

43. Note: Guide to the Sources of History of Asia was part of the ICA-UNESCO's project Guide to the Sources of History of Nations, initiated in 1959. The Asian chapter of the project was inaugurated at a Planning meeting held at Kuala Lumpur during 2-6 July 1979 where compiling National Guides were discussed. India launched the project in June 1984 with an advisory Committee, which set guidelines for preparing the Indian chapter of the Guide to the Sources of Asian History. Of the twelve Asian countries participating in the project, India was allocated number 3 for its Guides. National Archives of India brought out 6 Volumes of Guides under the project (3.1 to 3.6) which has hopefully served as a useful reference media for holdings of archival repositories in India).

IV

Study of Scientific, Technical and Professional Problems

- The methodology of the history of Archives was to be discussed in the Congress in 1968.
- Manual of Methods of treatment of contemporary archival documentation was to be prepared by 1967-68.
- The Council was to study current and non-current archives in 1968.
- The new rules regarding rights of the author on the utilisation of archival documents was to be studied by the ICA.
- A Round Table Conference was to complete study of international law by 1969. The study had commenced in 1961.
- The application of mecanographic methods in archival work and their preservation was to be taken up before 1970

V

Publications

- To continue all publications as given under various chapters besides Archivum, International Bibliography on Archives.

VI

Cultural Programmes

- Holding international Exhibitions on Seals in 1967-68 by the Committee on the study of Seals under ICA, of national and international exhibitions of historical documents, formation of an Educational Service at different archival depots for the children of primary and secondary schools.[44**]

After deliberations on the *Guide to Sources of African History*, NAI with Department of African Studies, Delhi University and

---

44. Ibid

** National Archives of India also developed its Sigillography Unit for developing Seals replicas.

UGC joined hands with a UNESCO-ICA project in 1965. They also wrote to CH Phillips, Secretary Director, SOAS, for advice, as the matter was getting delayed. The Project was to collect information on Records available in NAI and State Archives. US$ 4,000 was given for the African History Project, through Department of African Studies, University of Delhi.[45]

ICA had provided guidelines and details for compilation of the Guide.[46] Department of African Studies estimated the cost of the project as Rs 85,000. Since funds were short, UGC was approached for additional funding. But UGC declined, saying that UNESCO had given sufficient funds.[47]

India's Concerns at ICA Meet on Access, Preservation of Microfilms and Availability of Conservation Material

Director of Archives now wrote to Secretary ICA on 25 July 1969 on problems of microfilms preservation in India. He recommended a survey and help from ICA for a special fund for developing countries to procure raw material like acetate foil, tissue paper, raw films, etc. because of lack of foreign exchange.[48] He sent the ICA letter and circular to all State Archives for necessary action and to correspond with the Executive Secretary, ICA if interested to attend Madrid VI Congress.[49] Shri KD Bhargava, Director, NAI was elected as a member of the Executive Committee of ICA for four years from September 1968, at the ICA VI Congress held at Madrid, 3-6 September 1960. This was a first for India.[50]

45. F. No 12/68-C, p. 168/corr.
46. F. No 12/66-C, p. 279/corr.
47. Ibid, pp.22-31.
48. F. No. 12/69-C, pp. 97-98/corr.
49. F. No. 12/1968-C, p.46/corr.
50. F. No. 12/1968-C,p.100/corr.

Many of the Committee's recommendations were on issues raised in the letter of Director of Archives which were considered and approved by the General Assembly such as access to records, including access to 30 years old records with defined reservations where necessary. Longer periods in specific cases should be imposed only to meet realistic needs and in no case, was to exceed 80 years. For private papers deposited at archival institutions, access was governed by the same regulations as for public papers, with longer delays applied to documents of a strictly confidential nature, and where the donor reserved certain rights to himself and his successors for access.[51]

The Congress recommended that treatment of national and foreign researchers be equal and condemned any discrimination against foreign scholars. It recommended a **national reader's card** to replace formalities of identification and serve as an introduction to public archival institutions in the country. These national card systems could later be adapted for international use. The Congress recommended Directorate of Archives to ease its microfilming policy for foreign scholars in exchange of materials. The Congress recommended liberalisation of Access on exchange agreements, technical assistance agreements, prices of microcopies, and utilisation of microfilms. Accordingly, it adopted a resolution on the report of the Microfilming Committee, which stated: 'Since the microfilm publication of entire series of records and the making of copies of them freely available to scholarly and scientific researchers is the most effective, rapid, and economic way to promote greater access to archives, microfilm publication work should be regarded as a normal activity of archival

51. Ibid, pp. 79-89/corr.

institutions.' A reference list was to be prepared for microfilms and they were to be shared if free from copyrights in the interest of scientific research and production. A small group of experts in microfilming were to give advice and render assistance and study how microfilms can be preserved in tropical climates.[52]

A Working Group of both historians and Archivists to study current records, problems of classification and filing and of appraisal for retirement

ICA recommended that an International Working Group of historians and Archivists study current records, problems of classification and filing and of appraisal for retirement, if possible of regional authorities, and international organisations. The Congress accepted recommendations of the Restoration Section for an international seminar to study restoration methods and procedures and identify future areas of research and study. It was concerned at the slow pace of the Committee on Sigillography and accepted recommendations of Business Archives Sections to promote Business Archives and to train business archivists.[53]

ICA released a booklet on Training of Archivists, and through this, NAI received courses of Instructions from Germany, Argentina, Austria, Belgium, Spain, USA, France, Great Britain, Hungary, Iran, Israel, Italy, Holland, Poland, Portugal, Czechoslovakia, USSR, Vatican, Venezuela, etc. Dr Desikachar, Assistant Director of NAI had been thanked in the preface for

52. The NAI and State archives complied with many of these standard international guidelines in giving access to Indian and foreign research scholars especially for exchange and acquisition of historical material of Indian interest in microfilms. Subsequently NAI developed and established an excellent Microfilming Unit and repository with multiple Microfilm Cameras and other accessories. Students of the one-year Diploma course learn reprographic methods and work in a Microfilm repository for paper III on Conservation & Reprography.
53. Ibid

providing Information on India. The Booklet is, not available, but notes and information are available on pages 10, 43, and 68 and acknowledging the contribution of Dr Desikachar, who acknowledged the booklet and thanked the Secretary, ICA, and Mons C Kecskemeti, in his letter dated 26 April 1967.[54]

ICA had also invited information for a Handbook on Archival Legislation under contract with UNESCO. In the absence of an archival law, Director of Archives forwarded related documents including Destruction of Records Act 1917, relevant extracts from Manual of Office Procedure, the Report of the Archival Legislative Committee and a copy of the Report and a brief note relating to Rules of Access to Records in NAI.[55] NAI sent twelve documents on Indo-Afghan relations to the cultural exhibitions held at Kabul by ICA, along with photo-prints of twelve seals for display at the mobile exhibition, organised by UNESCO.[56]

At the ICA meet at Bucharest, Romania, in September 1969, subjects like Basis of Investigations, Archaistic Responsibility and Degree of Autonomy, Legislation and Regulations, Organisation and Contents (holdings) of Archival Depositaries, Personnel of Archives, Recent and Prospective Evolution were discussed.[57] Ms DG Keswani was nominated for a further term as a permanent correspondent from India, for *Archivum*, the ICA Journal on Bibliographies, Archival Legislation, and the Chronicles of Archives.[58] India always participated in activities of international organisations and ICA, but in a limited way.

54. F. No. 12/67-C, pp. 3/notes, 12/corr.
55. Ibid (Archival Policy Resolution based on the Report of Archival Legislation Committee was adopted only in 1972.)
56. IHRC Proceedings, 38th session, 16-18 November 1967,
57. F. No. 12/69-C, p.19.
58. Ibid, pp.127-28/corr.

The Treasurer of ICA wrote to Director General, UNESCO seeking increase in UNESCO subvention to ICA in the next budget period. This information was sent to all member countries of ICA, including India. Director of Archives, Dr SN Prasad recommended to Jt Educational Adviser, Ministry of Education & Youth Affairs that India should try to obtain full support of Indian National Commission of UNESCO at New Delhi to meet the Council's request. He agreed that ICA be supported financially as it would help India also.[59]

Dr SN Prasad, Director of Archives, had contributed significantly in consolidating and making India's presence in the global archival community felt. His journey had first started when he attended the thirteenth International Congress of Historical Sciences in Moscow during 16-22 August 1970 and also been a part of the meeting of the Executive Committee of the ICA in London in September 1970. While attending any international meet, Dr Prasad always visited the country's national archival repositories. He also visited Public Records Office, London and India Office Library, to arrange for procuring microfilms of records of Indian interest facilitating historical research in India.[60]

Director of Archives also led the Indian delegation of all Officers-in-Charge of State Archives who were sent to the seventh International Congress on Archives at Moscow from 21 to 25 August 1972.[61] The Director, NAI, was accompanied by Directors of State Archives of Andhra Pradesh (Dr (Ms) Sarojini Regani), Maharashtra (VG Khobrekar), and of Uttar Pradesh (Dr KP

59. Ibid, pp. 144-146/corr.

60. IHRC Proceedings, 1971, p.118

61. IHRC Proceedings, 1973, 42nd Session, pp. 58-59. & Ibid. ATR, pp.47-48/corr. 26th NCA Meeting proceedings.

Srivastava), besides two others that included BK Basu, Director, Historical Division, MEA and SK Mishra, IAS, Secretary and Commissioner, Goa& Haryana. The Indian delegation projected an appropriate picture of our achievements, and the results were very positive for several years afterwards. Proposals had already been received for Indian technical assistance from Nepal and Indonesia for archival development. Dr Prasad was nominated as a member of the Committee on Archival Development and was invited by UNESCO to a planning Seminar of Archival Consultants held at Paris from4-6 December 1972.

NCA also recommended deputing archivists for training abroad from State Archives. Selections were made by the Ministry of Education. Directors Dr KP Srivastava from UP and JK Jain from Rajasthan were deputed for training abroad. TS Sinha from Bihar State Archives had visited France for training. He also went to London for training in Archives Administration Orientation on a British Council Bursary in January 1969 for four months. The question arose of who will pay for their travel; only ICA members could attend the meeting. If permitted as Director of Archives had discussed at the Executive Meeting in London, State Governments would have to pay their own bills; it was not easy to attend these meetings and conferences without financial assistance from the Government.

Director of Archives attended the ICA Executive Committee meeting at Brussels from 20-23 May 1973, at Paris and an International Seminar on Public Records Management at Washington from 17-30 March 1974 besides attending a meeting of the Committee on Archival Development of ICA at Darmstadt in West Germany from 20-22 May 1974. SN Sharma from NAI visited UK in August 1974 to attend a Seminar on Automated Data Processing in Archives organised by the Public

Records Office, London in collaboration with ICA.[62]

Close collaborations with ICA and UNESCO continued, and some State Directors also participated in International events. RK Kelavadi, Director, of Karnataka State Archives and Director of Madhya Pradesh Archives, MD Khare, also attended the ICA meetings in Nairobi and London, respectively. Dr PP Shirodhkar, Director, Goa State Archives, attended an international seminar at Lisbon.[63] Dr NH Kulkarnee, Assistant Director of Archives attended the annual meetings of the Committee on Archival Development of the ICA at Nairobi (Kenya) from 7-13 October 1978. Ranbir Kishore, Assistant Director was deputed to Nairobi to attend a seminar and conduct a 'Conservation Workshop' organised by the Kenya National Archives from13-25 December 1978.[64]

There was both growth and development in NAI's activities during Dr SN Prasad's tenure as Director of Archives from 1969-1979,[**] as Regional Rapporteur and member of the Executive Committee of ICA for many years. He also attended the meeting of the ICA Bureau at London in April 1979. Dr Kulkarnee was also invited to attend the UNESCO-sponsored Consultation on Development of Records and Archives Management Programme at Paris in May 1979. Dr Prasad and Dr Kulkarnee also attended a seminar on Strategies for Archival Development in the Third World, organised jointly by German Commission for UNESCO and ICAin Berlin during June 1979,sponsored by UNESCO.[65]

Four years later at the Washington Congress, Dr Prasad

62. IHRC, Proceedings, January 1975, pp. 155,159 &160.
63. IHRC Proceedings, Delhi, 1981, pp.17-19.
64. Ibid, p. 167.** Indian Historical Records Commission, A Retrospect, Vol II (1948–1994), pp.31-32. NAI publication
65. Ibid, 1981, pp.173-74.

presented his article on Liberalisation of Access Rules in India that was acclaimed widely. India had already by then, adopted the Archival Policy Resolution in 1972. He was also elected as Vice President of ICA, a rare distinction and the first Archivist from the Third World to achieve this. He also set up the South and West Asian Regional Branch of International Council on Archives (SWARBICA) in 1976. He must be lauded for his initiative in deputing so many from National Archives as experts on the invitation of UNESCO to visit other developing countries like Saudi Arabia, Kenya, Ghana, Singapore, and Afghanistan to organise workshops, and on consultancy missions. Many of these countries signed Cultural Exchange Programmes with India, which helped in promoting bilateral relations in Archives and Archival Education. (INDIA, 1995, pp. 31-32)

The Director of Archives participated in the XX International Round Table Conference on Archives in Oslo (Norway) from 3-7 September 1981, and at the Executive Committee meeting of ICA at The Hague during 8-12 September 1981, as a representative of SWARBICA and succeeded in getting three Indian Archivists nominated on different Committees of the ICA.[66]

NRR Chari, Deputy Director of Archives attended the annual meeting of the Committee on Archival Reprography of ICA, at The Hague from 26 to 29 May 1982. Ranbir Kishore, Chief of Reprography & Conservation attended the Conservation and Restoration Committee meeting of ICA at Brussels from 11-13 October 1982.[67] Officers of the Department were getting recognition worldwide and were participating in various seminars and conferences as experts in various subjects of archival Science.

66. IHRC, June, 1982, Gujarat, p.128.
67. Ibid, p. 132.

NRR Chari, Deputy Director, attended the meeting of the Committee on Archival Reprography of ICA at Toledo, Spain, in September 1983. Ranbir Kishore attended the meeting of the Conservation and Preservation Committee at Rome from 30May to 2 June 1983. YP Kathpalia, Scientific Officer, as a member of the ICA's Professional Training and Education Committee attended a meeting of the Committee at Stockholm, Sweden in May 1983. PL Madan was also appointed as member of ICA Committees on Professional Training and Sigillography for 1982-84.[68]

Dr RK Perti, new Director of Archives attended the inaugural meeting of the Commonwealth Archivist Association in September 1984 at Bonn and also the Executive Committee meeting and the International Congress on Archives held in the same month. At the tenth International Congress on Archives, he presented a paper on Management of a Conservation Programme. Ranbir Kishore, Chief of Repair and Conservation attended the meeting on Conservation and Restoration and a joint meeting in collaboration with the Committee on Sigillography of the ICA also in Germany during September 1984.[69] Dr Perti, attended ICA meetings of the Commission on Archival Development at Ottawa, Canada in October 1985, and also the Executive Committee and Round table Conference on Archives at Austin, Texas, USA in October 1985. Dr Perti also attended the first International Congress on Records Management at Manila, Philippines, in November 1985.[70]

The Director also participated at the ICA Conference on Microfilming Programmes for Developing Countries, held

68. IHRC 1985 session, Surajkund, Haryana, p.196.
69. Ibid, p.178.
70. Ibid, p.201.

at Trier, FRG in March 1987. TR Muniswamy, Director of Karnataka State Archives, along with Director of Archives, NAI, attended the twenty-fourth International Round Table Conference on Archives in Helsinki in September 1986. He also attended the twenty-fifth International Round Table Conference on Archives held at Gardone, the Riviera, Italy during 21-24 September, 1987 and presented a paper on Problems and Studies in Conservation of Archival Heritage in Tropical Countries.[71]

All this increased India's participation internationally and helped in acquiring archival material and literature of Indian interest for historical research and in developing close relations and exchange of ideas with the archival community internationally and also in India.

Dr (Ms) Meena Gautam, Assistant Director of Archives, was deputed to Ottawa, Canada during 15-26 May 1989 to attend a symposium on Current Records: Converging Discipline in the Management of Recorded Information, and a Round Table Discussion. She also attended a course in Current Records, Future Use: The Public Role of National Archives Institutions in the same month in Ottawa. She also presented a country paper on National Archives of India: Current Status and Achievements, at the Round Table Discussion, held under the auspices of the National Archives, Canada and International Council on Archives.[72]

In the international field, NAI continued its cooperation in different ways even seeking funds from UNESCO. Since 1963-64, under UNESCO's assistance for archival programmes, the proposal for Fellowships in Archives Keeping was in the form of

71. IHRC March, 1988, Bikaner, pp.151-52.
72. IHRC, 1990, Guwahati, p.119.

services of experts, and fellowship for training and observation abroad and of equipment.[73] NAI decided to submit a proposal for training for the Disposal of the archival accumulations of the Government of India, and of the Compilation of a National Register of Private Archives, as there was no trained person with sufficient experience in Archives for both the projects.* UK had staff trained both in Archives and National Register work. Director of Archives thus recommended to Ministry of Education for short-term fellowships during 1963-64 and 1965-66.[74] NAI proposed two short-duration fellowships for each project on Compilation of National Register for Records and Records Management & Administration for inclusion in the UNESCO participation programme. These were forwarded to UNESCO for assistance for the year 1965-66, but were again not approved.[75]

Yet, UNESCO, in consultation with ICA invited YP Kathpalia, Scientific Officer to be a consultant and advice Florence and Venice Archives in Italy on restoration of records, and setting up of model restorative workshops for six weeks.[76] Ms DG Keswani, OSD, of the Department was deputed to Accra to teach Archival Science in the School for Archival Training, Regional Centre for Archivists in Ghana, established under UNESCO and UNDP due to the initiatives of ECARBICA (East Central Africa Regional Branch of ICA).[77]

During the year ending 31 December 1978, UNESCO administered nearly 140 projects relating to training, record

73. F.N.1-7/62-PR, p.2/notes.
*Mimeographed 'Report of Program Commission adopted by the General Conference,'p.26
74. Ibid, p.3/notes, U.O. dated 26.10.1962. & p. 15/corr. Letter from M/Education dated 4.6.1963. F. 3-26/62- A.10.
75. F. No. 18-5/64-C.
76. IHRC proceedings, 40th session, Madras, 18-20 February 1970, p.205.
77. NAI Annual Report, 1975, p.13.

management, archival buildings, restoration and reprographic laboratories and regional and sub-regional fellowships. A book, Basic International Bibliography of Archives Administration with publications of the last 10 years was published, with a special chapter on problems in developing and tropical countries.[78] National Archives of India received UNESCO's support to augment its resources and its development as a UNESCO recognised Regional Centre for Archival Training in South Asia.[*79]

SAI Tirmizi, Director of Archives (1979-82), in his UO note dated 15 January 1980, wrote to Department of Culture,[80] requesting them to issue an invitation to Indian National Commission, for deputing members for an exploratory mission for upgrading of the Institute of Archival Training, as a UNESCO Regional Centre for archival training in South Asia. He writes that '...The training courses have been unique inasmuch as no such instruction facilities are available in the whole of South Asia. Consequently, our neighbouring countries have been availing of these facilities more or less regularly during the past 25 years or so. A large number of foreign trainees from Nepal, Afghanistan, Malaysia, Philippines, Singapore, and Burma, etc. have been trained. Similarly, even African countries such as Kenya and Nigeria have availed of these facilities. Many of these India-trained persons are holding eminent positions in the archival organisations of their respective countries. Thus, the Institute of Archival Training is not only a National Training Centre but has become in course of time a pedagogic archival training institute for the entire Asian Region, particularly in South Asia.'

---

78. Indian Archives, July-December, 1978, News Notes, p.67.

* This has also been discussed in Chapter II, may please see.

79. Indian Archives, July-December, 1978, News Notes, p.67.

80. F. 3-4/79-A.6,

Appreciating the services rendered by the Institute, the meeting of UNESCO experts on the harmonisation of Archival Training Programmes (Paris, 30 November 1979) made the following recommendation:

'While noting with satisfaction the efforts already made by Inter-Governmental Organisations including UNESCO and OAS to ensure the training to qualified personnel for archives services within the framework of the regional schools, the meeting recommends, in the interest of improved coverage, the creation, reinforcement and upgrading of additional institutes of regional character where basic infrastructure exists and where national efforts have been made to the regional needs, such as at New Delhi.' He pointed out some deficiencies: '....while the Institute of Archival Training has been serving the needs of the region to a certain extent the facilities available for the same cannot be regarded as sufficient. The trainees have no hostel facilities whatever and have to make their own lodging and boarding arrangements. While some of the foreign trainees received scholarships under various international agreements, others have to be funded by their own Governments for a whole year. The Institute itself is struggling on with the resources which cannot be regarded as adequate by any means.'

The UNESCO and ICA had designed and developed various audio-visual teaching aids which made the training interactive, interesting and easy for the trainees, but these are not available with the Institute. Similarly, latest reading material is also lacking. More equipment for specialised training in reprographics and conservation is required. Guest-lectures, workshops, seminars, etc. by specialists from other countries would enhance the value and dimensions of instructions. He also added that 'the association of UNESCO with the Institute of Archival Training will open up possibilities of improving the existing facilities in the Institute to suit the requirements of a Regional Centre in South Asia.' The manner of upgrading the Institute as recommended by the UNESCO Expert Committee was to invite UNESCO to depute its member for an exploratory mission for about a week. He suggested that the Indian National Commission for UNESCO be requested to issue such an invitation to the General Information Programme, UNESCO, and Paris at an early date.'[81]

The note gives an honest assessment of archival science education in the 1980s. It was further modernised after the UNESCO team visited and recognised the School. To streamline the training curriculum, it was renamed as School of Archival Studies (SAS) in 1980, and a Board of Studies constituted to design and modernise its syllabus. This has been discussed in detail in Chapter II. In the same year, the Indian Institute was recognised as a UNESCO-approved Regional Centre for Archival Training for South Asia and South East Asia. The team found the archival training at NAI attuned to international standards.[82] Tirmizi also attended the meeting of experts on Harmonisation of Archival Training Techniques sponsored by UNESCO at Paris, during 26-30 November 1979. He was elected to chair the meeting.[83]

UNESCO sanctioned US$ 12,000 for the development of the School in 1981.[84] The assistance was to finance study tours or similar activities for developing skills and knowledge of the staff. The SAS upgraded and restructured its syllabus and introduced short-term courses on the advice of Board of Studies. Out of

81. F.No.46-2/80-AT, pp. 2-5/notes.
82. Ibid, 1981, p.11.
83. NAI Annual Report, 1979, p.11.
84. F.No.1-14/81-AT, p.1/corr.,

this grant, an offset printer was also purchased for the School besides teaching aids, books, and periodicals.[85] NAI continued to maintain close cooperation with ICA and UNESCO.[86]

But NAI considered the grant too meagre. The Director of Archives wrote to UNESCO Division of Central Information Program, in Paris, justifying the requirement of US$ 1,10,000 for the School to be utilised for using archives experts, purchase of books and journals, audio-visual equipment, instructional and administrative equipment, and fellowships for training and internships abroad.[87] But UNESCO said it could not provide such a big grant under its regular programs and advised NAI to approach the UN Development Programme (UNDP).[**] UNESCO had earmarked US$ 12,000 for 1982-83 to the School for which they were awaiting approval from the Director General. They suggested that this grant be used for staff development, or for the purchase of books, and equipment. It advised the Indian National Commission to try for funding under the Regional Participation Programme. But for this, they needed to be supported by two other countries in the region, which was perhaps not easy.[88] Subsequently, senior Archivist PK Ghosh was deputed to Public Archives of Canada at Ottawa, in October 1981 for training in Records Management. Another Archivist was sent to France and UK, to survey and list 'Removed Archives'

85. F.No. 31-4(6)/81-IR, p.80/corr.
86. F.No.1-14/81-AT,p.1/corr.
87. F.No. 31-4(6)/81-IR, pp.63-68/corr.

**The UNDP was founded on 22 November 1965 with the merging of the Expanded Programme of Technical Assistance (EPTA) and the Special Fund. The rationale was to 'avoid duplication of [their] activities'. The EPTA was set up in 1949 to help the economic and political aspects of underdeveloped countries while the Special Fund was to enlarge the scope of UN technical assistance. The Special Fund arose from the idea of a Special United Nations Fund for Economic Development (SUNFED) (which was initially called the United Nations Fund for Economic Development (UNFED).

88. Ibid, p.99/corr.

under the UNESCO Program in late 1982.

Another positive development was that NAI wrote to NIC on 15 March 1982, to develop a computerised system for NAI's Automated Information Storage and Retrieval System.[89] But this programme finally began only in 1998, as described in Chapter IV. Computerisation in NAI and teaching of ICT by SAS started only in 2006.

UNESCO had asked for information on the courses being conducted by the School and eventually sponsored a number of foreign students under its Fellowship Scheme for training at NAI. Students came from Afghanistan, Tanzania and Guyana, each sponsored by UNESCO wef 1 December 1978.[90] In an article, Indian Archival Training and the Archival Training Needs of Asia: Some Observations, Dr Frank B Evans records that between 1961 to 1979-80, thirty-two foreign students had joined SAS for training. During 1979-80, 9 of the 21 students in the Diploma course were foreigners from African and Asian countries.[91] He described the syllabus, 'in terms of coverage ... more comprehensive than the courses offered in many European countries.'[92] He pointed out that the reputation of the School and the quality of its programmes, as well as the absence of tuition fee, had attracted trainees from neighbouring countries, especially Africa. However, it lacked academic affiliation with a University* and accreditation for its programmes.[93] Tirmizi with the experts he interacted with on Harmonisation of Archival Training Techniques sponsored by UNESCO, as Chairman

89. Ibid, pp.95-96 & 100/corr.
90. NAI Annual Report, 1978, p. 9.
91. Indian Archives, July-December 1981, pp.4-5.
92. Ibid, pp.6 & 8-9.
*In spite of its best efforts, NAI failed to secure affiliation from any of the universities in Delhi.
93. Ibid, p.9.

of the Committee, agreed to recommend the reinforcing and upgrading of the Institute of Archival Training at New Delhi as a Regional Training Centre for South Asia. As a result, Dr Frank Evans, Program Specialist in the General Information Program Division of UNESCO, had visited the Department in February 1980 and delivered a lecture on 23 February 1980 on UNESCO and Archives for creating archival consciousness in the people.

UNESCO approved Fellowship for five months for Thuthu Ntjona of the National Archives of Lesotho for a Special Training Course in Conservation at NAI from March to July 1982 under UNESCO Fellowship Scheme. He also went on a study tour with Diploma Course students to Rajasthan and UP State Archives.[94] Likewise, the1982-83 session had 3 students sponsored by Malaysian Government, one each by Governments of Thailand, Kenya and Afghanistan, two from Malawi and Sudan supported by the German Foundation.[95] NAI received thirty-one books from UNESCO as Aid and a total of sixty-one books (foreign publication) were received and UNESCO paid for it during 1982.[96] One UNESCO Fellow from Burma, Mr Mya Than Tun, Archivist, from National Archives Department, Rangoon, Burma, attended the twentieth Certificate course in Records Management from Dec1994 to Jan 1995.[97] Under the UNESCO's participation program, NAI also deputed an officer to UK, USA, and Canada for a month's training in Automated Data Processing.[98]

RC Gupta, Deputy Director and Ranbir Kishore, Chief of

94. F. No. 46-5/80-AT,p. 6/ notes & p. 35/corr.
95. NAI Annual Report, 1982, p. 14.
96. F. No. 1-14/81-AT. p. 3/ notes.
97. F. No. 45-10/84-AT, p. 10/ corr.
98. IHRC Proceedings, 1988, Srinagar, p. 187.

Repair and Conservation Division were deputed to Accra (Ghana) on a UNESCO consultancy mission for six weeks in 1980. Dr TR Sareen, was sent to Nairobi, Kenya at the same time to conduct a course in Records Management under the Commonwealth Fund for Technical Cooperation. NRR Chari and YP Kathpalia had also conducted training programmes earlier.[99]

Dr RK Perti, Director of Archives, visited as a UNESCO Fellow, Mexico, Cuba, and Brazil under the South-South Cooperation Program and gave suggestions for improving the Conservation and Repair facilities in 3 countries. The objective was to assess the state of preservation of Archives under UNESCO Mission and it had been quite a success.[100]

Thus, we see that NAI continued its efforts to promote archival development in the Third World countries in a big way and maintained close ties with ICA and UNESCO. In collaboration with ICA, NAI organised an international seminar on Disposition of Government Records, in Delhi in October 1981 and was attended by delegates from Iraq, Malaysia, Nepal, Pakistan, and Sri Lanka, besides Dr TA Wadlow from USA as the main Resource person. The seminar was based on his handbook, Disposition of Government Records. Dr Charles Kacskemeti represented ICA at the seminar.[101] With UNESCO's assistance, another Archivist was deputed to Canada for a course in Records Management and agreed to provide US$ 5,000 to locate and list the 'Removed Archives' available in other countries from Asia.[102] At the UNESCO's Colombo meeting in October 1981, Director of Archives was unanimously elected as the Chairman of the

99. IHRC Proceedings, 1981 session, pp. 183-84.
100. F. No. 1(Int.)/89DA.
101. IHRC, June 1982, Gandhinagar, Gujarat, pp. 13 & 128-29.
102. Ibid, p.14

Regional Co-ordination Committee of the UNESCO Project for the Guide to the Sources of Asian History for 1981-84, for which UNESCO sanctioned US$ 1500.[103] Six volumes have been published under the project.

NAI had also been associated with UNESCO Memory of the World programme and Director General; NAI attended its Experts Meeting at Kuala Lumpur in 1994. He also attended UNESCO's Memory of the World Conference at Oslo in June 1996 where recommendations were made to preserve endangered collections in various archival repositories.[104] Dr S Sengupta, OSD, was deputed to attend the first Regional Committee Meeting and Workshop on Strategy Formulation and Resource Mobilisation for the same programme in Asia Pacific held in Beijing, China in November 1998.[105]

Serious efforts were also being made to use the offices of the Indo-US Sub-Commission for promoting fruitful collaboration with American Institutions. The Department also received officials and delegations from various countries including Greece, Iran, Russia, and Poland for promoting bilateral cooperation with India in Archives.[106]

From 1995-96 to 2005-06, this author could only find scanty information in NAI files except for activities relating to ICA or UNESCOO undertaken under cultural exchange programmes or through bilateral agreements.

Cultural Exchange Programmes (CEPs)

The key objective of a country's international cultural policy focuses on helping leading Indian art and culture institutions

103. Ibid.p.128

104. IHRC Proceedings, 1997, Jabalpur, p.143

105. IHRC 2001, Mysore, p.230.

106. IHRC Proceedings, 1997, Jabalpur, pp.140 &143.

to achieve international standards, strengthen the international market position of Indian artists and institutions, handicrafts, ethnic arts and indigenous cultural industries of India, strengthen Indian economic interests by emphasising on cultural, trade and economic ties; and strive for ease of access in export and outsourcing as per UNESCO guidelines. Cultural diplomacy means strengthening international relations by using Indian art and culture and participating in the formulation and implementation of policies and programmes relating to India's external cultural relations, thereby strengthening cultural relations and mutual understanding between India and other countries in the field of art and culture. Such programmes require funding which is usually provided both by the Government and other private and national and international organisations like UNESCO, German Foundation, Indo-American Foundation and some NGOs, including non-government heritage organisations.

NAI and State Archives were being supported financially by both the Government and international bodies like UNESCO and benefitting from various scholarship and fellowship schemes from UNESCO. The organisation was also sponsoring foreign students to undergo training at the School of Archival Studies at NAI.

Through Cultural Exchange Programs, NAI had established that Indian Archivists were comparable to the best in the world and their services were being requisitioned by Archives of the Third World countries. But that was till the 1990s. Our Archivists are now, no longer active in the international field or getting any recognition by the archival community, globally.

What are the reasons behind this and where have we failed? These issues are addressed in the following chapters of the Project Study. But before that, let us examine how much we could achieve bilaterally through our Cultural Exchange Programmes. Under

CEPs with foreign countries, India had been able to develop and promote respect for each other and provided opportunities in exchange of expertise and sharing of experience in different fields including archives.

Inclusion of Archives Alongside Subjects like Archaeology and History

National Committee of Archivists (NCA) resolved to approach Ministry of Education and Social Welfare to include Archives alongside subjects like Archaeology, History, etc. for sending delegations under Cultural Educational Programmes to foreign countries for exchange of information.[107] The Ministry accepted the resolution in principle and NAI was advised to make specific proposals on archives as exchange programmes are normally on a reciprocal basis. States of Mysore, UP, West Bengal, and Assam supported the resolution. Andhra Pradesh didn't respond and Tamil Nadu deferred the scheme for CEP with USSR on financial grounds. Maharashtra left the matter in the hands of the Government.

Under Indo-French CEP (1971-73), Director, NAI proposed to Ministry of Education & Youth Affairs for inclusion of two items: (1) Specialisation Study in the field of Archives preservation including reprography services and planning of Archives Building; and (2) Research and acquisition of microfilms of French Records pertaining to the erstwhile French Territories in India for favour of inclusion in the Indo-French CEP, 1971-73.[108]

NAI had been dealing now with more than 25 countries under CEPs in archival matters. The countries exchanged publications

107. Proceedings of the 25th meeting of NCA.
108. F.N. 16-2/1972-A-1.Ref.to the Ministry's letter dated 29 July 1970 (F.N.21/32/1967-CAI (2),

and microfilms of records of each other's interest, exchange of Archivists for Study-cum-observation tours, and training of foreign officials in School of Archival Studies of the Department. The CEPs strengthened India's relations with other countries by promoting goodwill and harmony through fruitful interaction at international seminars and conferences. The Department has successfully carried out exchange of publications as well as officials for study-cum observation tours, besides providing training facilities to officials from different countries.[109]

In all the CEPs signed during 1970-2000 and beyond with France, German Democratic Republic, Italy, USSR, Belgium, Federal Republic of Germany, and also with Czechoslovakia, Afghanistan, Mongolia, Turkey, Mauritius, Iran, Syria and others for items related to archives were for exchange of Archivists and archival material.[110] State Archives were also taken into account while implementing these programmes. In 1988, the Director of Uttar Pradesh State Archives was deputed to Finland under CEP. In 1989, Gujarat was requested to depute its nominee to South Korea; likewise, Goan officials visited Portugal to prepare lists of records of Indian interest in their repositories. Similarly, when foreign archivists visit India under CEPs, they also visit State Archives to study matters of common interests. UP State Archives has played host to a number of foreign archivists from Korea and China in 1989 and 1994 and from Russia back in the 1960s. Often, financial constraints prevent candidates from visiting another country.[111]

Under bilateral arrangements, Indian consultants had been

109. IHRC, Feb.1997, Jabalpur, p.140.
110. IHRC, Gandhinagar, Gujarat 1982, pp. 110-111.
111. IHRC Proceedings 55th session, December 1995, Jadavpur, pp.5 &112.

called to countries like Indonesia, Singapore, Nepal, Afghanistan, Saudi Arabia, Malaysia and Nigeria. The international archival community and UNESCO had long since recognised the status of archives and the competency of Indian Archivists, who were comparable to the best in the world, a fact that the Secretary, IHRC observed, at the 1979 session at Aurangabad, Maharashtra.[112] Indian Archivists were also invited to Ghana, Kenya and Iraq on consultancy missions. A request had also been received from Oman. The Secretary had been selected as a member of the Executive Committee as also of the Sigillography Committee of the ICA and was assisting the UNESCO Consultation Group on harmonisation of Archival Training Techniques and was elected Chairman of the Committee. It was on his insistence that the Institute of Archival Training had been upgraded as a Regional Training Centre for South Asia and been renamed as School of Archival Studies in 1980. Its syllabus had been restructured and many Short-Term courses were offered apart from the one-year Diploma Course.[113] The School of Archival Studies had been attracting candidates from countries as far away as Nigeria, Botswana, Lesotho, Somalia and Kenya and as near as Thailand and Malaysia.[114]

Study of the files at NAI reveals that CEPs had provided a useful avenue for promoting bilateral cooperation between different countries. Items relating to archives are invariably included in the CEPs finalised with FRG, GDR, France, Egypt, Italy, Hungary, Tunisia, Algeria, Sudan, Republic of Korea, Yugoslavia, USSR, Syrian Arab Republic, Australia, Czechoslovakia,

112. IHRC Proceedings, January 1979, Aurangabad, pp. 106 & 155-56.
113. Ibid, p.18 & IHRC Proceedings, Delhi, 1981, pp.17-19.
114. IHRC 1985, Surajkund, Haryana, p.196.

Pakistan, Bangladesh, Belgium, China, Cuba, Greece, Mauritius, Mongolia, Democratic Republic of Yemen, Portugal, Finland, Tanzania, South Korea, Netherlands, Maldives, Singapore, and Zambia between 1988 to 2003. India continued collaboration with ICA and other bodies besides CEPs during this period.[115]

The CEPs were finalised with various countries, in phases and in different years. We note that CEPs for the years 2012-14 were also finalised with Brazil, Myanmar, Vietnam, Tajikistan, and Russia. Director General of Archives visited Surinam and signed an MoU for Archives in December 2012.[116]

Two officers visited GDR under CEP in 1972 and 1973 and exchanged catalogues of material of mutual interest in their archival repositories.[117] Dr SN Prasad visited Kabul in October 1975 for attending a seminar on Indo-Afghan Relations through the Indo-Afghan CEP for 1973-75 and read a paper on Afghanistan as a Centre for Indian Nationalists and Revolutionaries.[118] Another officer visited Kabul to advise the Government in setting up their National Archives. A conservation expert also visited National Archives of Indonesia. Under Cultural Exchange Agreements, RC Gupta, Deputy Director of Archives was deputed to Kabul for 10 days in 1975 to assist the Afghan Government in setting up their Reprographic Unit.[119] Under Indo-Afghanistan CEP, Shri. KL Arora, Deputy Director of Oriental Records visited Afghanistan in June-July 1988. Dr RK Perti visited FRG for two weeks in September 1979.[120]

---

115. IHRC Proceedings June, 1985 (Surajkund) & October 1988 (Srinagar), p.178 and pp. 134-135, respectively.
116. IHRC Proceedings, December 1995, Jadavpur, pp. 109-110, IHRC, 2001, Mysore, p.221, &IHRC Proceedings, October2013, pp.271-72.
117. IHRC Proceedings, 1976, Bikaner, NAI Development Report for the year 1975.
118. IHRC Proceedings, January, 1975, Lucknow, p. 78.
119. IHRC Proceedings, 1990, Guwahati, p. 170.
120. IHRC Proceedings, 1981, p. 174.

A number of officers were deputed to undergo training under the 'International Technical Training in Archives' programme launched by the French Government, on the French Government Scholarship at Archives Nationales, Paris, France.[121] The Indian government also deputed two officers of NAI for microfilming records of erstwhile French possessions in India, lying in French repositories. The Indian team visited France in 1995 to prepare microfilms of removed archives and acquired 77 rolls. Continuing the work under Indo-French CEP, HD Singh, Deputy Director, visited Paris along with other Microphotographists for selecting and microfilming records. Together, they prepared and brought 115 rolls of Microfilms (containing 71652 exposures) to India.[122] Thus, besides imparting archival education and training, these CEPs acquired material of Indian interest from abroad by microfilming for historical research.

Tirmizi, Deputy Director of Archives, was deputed to advise the government of Saudi Arabia on planning their archival infrastructure. After a detailed discussion with their Minister of Higher Education, he visited records repositories of Riyadh, Mecca, Medina and Jeddah in 1976, and gave necessary advice. On his return, he submitted a detailed comprehensive report which was then forwarded to Saudi Arabia for further action.[123] In October, he was deputed to London for identifying gaps in the record series of NAI as available in India Office Library and Records. He also visited Paris Archives Nationale, holding discussions with the Archivists and Sigillographists and submitting a report.[124]

121. IHRC Proceedings, 1981, p. 174.
122. IHRC Proceedings, 1979, January Aurangabad, p.143, IHRC Proceedings, Delhi, 1981, p.17-19, and IHRC, Gandhinagar, Gujarat 1982, pp. 110-111.
123. IHRC Proceedings April 1992, Rohtak, p.110-111, IHRC Proceedings, December 1995, Jadavpur, pp. 109-110 and IHRC Proceedings, April 2003, Raipur, pp.175-76.
124. IHRC Report 1975, NAI,

Gulf countries have been requesting for services of Indian experts from Archives as part of education and training and advice on archival matters in conservation of records. Another Archivist from NAI was deputed to Yemen. The services of Indian Archivists/Librarians/Conservation experts were requisitioned by Iraq, Oman, and Saudi Arabia. Ahtashamuddin, Assistant Librarian, was deputed as Senior Abstracter/Indexer to Saudi Arabian National Centre for Science and Technology; BL Razdan as Technician for the Repair of Manuscripts and Documents in the Ministry of National Heritage and Culture, Sultanate of Oman, Muscat; and YK Bukhari, Keeper of Records, NAI, Bhopal, deputed to Peoples Republic of Yemen for selection of material under CEP.[125] Tirmizi visited Saudi Arabia to advice in planning their archival infrastructure in 1976 and later as Director of Archives, delivered a series of lectures on Modern Archival Practices at Baghdad in 1980.[126] YP Kathpalia, Scientific Officer, was invited by ICCROM to deliver lectures on 'Deterioration of Paper and Preventive Conservation' at the Regional Centre for Conservation of Cultural Property in Arab States, at Baghdad, Iraq, in 1981.[127] Dr RK Perti, Director General, NAI, was invited by the Government of Iran in 1990 to organise a short-term course in Records Management for the benefit of young archivists of Iran National Archives.[128]

The Indian archivists and other technical officers of the preservation and reprography divisions always looked forward to CEPs with the European countries because of their developments in different fields of Archival Science. Under the Indo-Hungarian

125. IHRC, June 1982, Gandhinagar, Gujarat. p.14.
126. IHRC, Delhi, May 1981, pp.191-92.
127. IHRC, 1982, p. 132.
128. IHRC Proceedings, April 1992, Rohtak, pp.110-111.

CEP, RC Gupta, Deputy Director of Archives, visited Hungary in 1972 while Dr Ivan Borsa, Deputy Director General, Hungary, visited India in 1973 and listed materials of Indian interest available in the National Archives of Hungary. Similarly, he was also provided with a list of material of Hungarian interest available in NAI.[129] ML Ahluwalia was deputed to USSR and Hungary in 1978 under CEP with these countries. Likewise, Dr Joseph Kanyar, Director, Somogy County Archives, Hungary, visited NAI in 1980 under Indo-Hungarian CEP.[130]

Having good relations with the USSR, Dr SN Prasad, Director, NAI, visited Kiev (USSR, dismembered in 1991) in 1975.[131] Under CEP, two senior officers of Russian Archives visited India in 1977,familiarising with the workings of the NAI and State Archives of Andhra Pradesh and Tamil Nadu.[132] This exchange of officers continued as Dr RK Perti visited USSR in 1984 under Indo-USSR CEP, followed by a visit of SN Sharma, Deputy Director of Archives, in 1988.[133] NAI also participated in the Festival of India organised in Moscow, Russia, and in an exhibition called 'Druzhba-Dosti', depicting close links between the two countries, in 1988 inaugurated by the then Union HRD Minister, PV Narasimha Rao.[134]

After independence, NAI had been trying to procure copies of records from India Office Library and Records, London, to fill up the gaps in our different records series. After a lot of deliberations, they eventually agreed to provide them on payment basis. In 1987, officers were deputed to the IOLR, London, under Charles

129. IHRC Proceedings, June 1982, pp. 140-141.
130. IHRC session, 1981, Delhi, pp.166 and 174.
131. IHRC Report, 1975, NAI, p.127.
132. IHRC Proceedings, January 1979, Aurangabad, pp. 106 and 155-56
133. IHRC, 1985, Surajkund, Haryana, p.178, and IHRC, March 1988, Bikaner, pp.151-52.
134. IHRC, October 1988, Srinagar, p.138.

Wallace (India) Trust Scheme.[135] The Director of Archives also visited London under the Charles Wallace (India) Trust Grant in 1989 to discuss the progress made. They surveyed and prepared priority lists of records which could be acquired on microfilms.[136]

In 1987, under the Technical Cooperation and Training Program, an Assistant Librarian was deputed for training in Library and Information Service at Loughborough University, London.[137] NS Mani, a Microphotographist, was deputed to Kent, UK, and to Frankfurt, Germany, in 1999 to attend a training programme on Hybrid Scanner cum Camera.[138] In 2010, Prof Mushirul Hasan, Director General of Archives, NAI, also visited London accompanied by Dr Meena Gautam, Deputy Director of Archives, to examine and select records of Indian interest in British Library and allied Institutions, for mutual exchange of information and archival material of Indian interest. A detailed report was submitted to Ministry of Culture, suggesting short-term and long-term projects for exchange of archival material.[139] Prof Mushirul Hasan also attended the 42 CITRA Conferences and Annual General Body meeting of ICA held at Oslo in 2010 to mark NAI's participation.[140]

In 2008, Dr Meena Gautam was deputed to National Archives of Netherlands under CEP to exchange Archival views, experiences and practices. She was also invited by the Netherlands government to participate in a two-day conference in Hague organised by the National Archives of Netherlands on Mutual Cultural Heritage (MCH) Archives, along with other archivists

135. IHRC, March 1988, Bikaner, p.151-52.
136. IHRC Proceedings, February 1990, Guwahati, p.119.
137. IHRC, October 1988, Srinagar, p.138.
138. IHRC 2001, Mysore, p.230.
139. IHRC Proceedings, November 2011, p.183.
140. IHRC Proceedings, November, 2011, p.183.

from Sri Lanka, Burma, Ghana, Indonesia, etc. As an outcome of the MCH meetings, India can share information with other partner countries like Surinam, South Africa, Sri Lanka, Indonesia, Netherlands, etc. JK Luthra, a Microphotographist, was deputed to Hague to attend the Encoded Archival Descriptions (EAD) workshop held in 2011.[141]

India has close archival association with the South Asian countries too as most of the countries in Asia-Africa region have been deputing their officials for archival training in the School of Archival Studies since 1961. NAI faculty has also been visiting these countries for sharing of expertise and archival material of mutual interest. RC Gupta visited Singapore in 1976 under Colombo Plan for advising the Singapore government on constructing their archival building on scientific lines.[142] An MoU was signed with Singapore National Archives to facilitate exchange of archival materials of each other's interest on reciprocal basis.[143] Dr S Sarkar, Director General, NAI, attended the 30 Anniversary Celebrations of Singapore Archives and delivered a keynote lecture at the seminar on 'Role of the Archives of the 21st Century' at National Archives of Singapore in 1998. The Singapore government gifted NAI with a Leaf Casting machine to augment the repair and rehabilitation facilities in the department, besides continuing to share microfilms containing information of mutual interest.[144]

Although other countries from Africa and the South region have stopped sending their archival personnel for training, Sri Lanka National Archives had been regularly sending its officials

141. IHRC Proceedings, February 2013, Lucknow, p. 304.
142. NAI Annual Report, 1975, p.13.
143. IHRC Proceedings, December 1995, Jadavpur, pp. 109-110.
144. IHRC 2001, Mysore, p.230, and IHRC Proceedings, April 2003, Raipur, pp.175-76.

to India. In 2010, Dr Meena Gautam was deputed for the SWARBICA meeting in Colombo, and was authorised by Birender S Yadav, Counselor (Press, Information and Culture), Indian High Commission in Colombo, to discuss the terms of collaboration between Indian and Sri Lankan National Archives. Accordingly, it was discussed with the Director, National Archives of Sri Lanka, to mutually exchange professionals for understanding the practices followed in conservation and digitisation of records, and also for exchange of professionals for training. It was also agreed to send preservation and digitisation experts between the two countries under CEP (Extracts from the Report submitted by the team).[145] Subsequently, two officers from NAI were deputed to the National Archives of Sri Lanka, Colombo, in 2013. They conducted a survey to locate the records of Indian interest under the Ministry of Foreign Affairs. A mutual exchange programme of archival experts was also recommended, either bilaterally or through SWARBICA, to co-opt mutual best practices in records management.[146]

NAI continued to support development activities of archives in various countries in the Third World. Candidates from countries like Kenya, Madagascar, Lesotho, Thailand, Tanzania, and Malaysia participated in various training programmes run by the School of Archival Studies. An NAI Officer was deputed to National Archives of Zimbabwe for conducting a 4-weeks Training Course on Conservation, and for participating in the ESCARBICA Conservation seminar in 1988. Dr Yashodhara Joshi, Scientific Officer, was deputed to Nairobi, Kenya, to present a paper in a conference on 'Preservation and Conservation of Library and Archival Material' at

145. F.No.24-4(2)/2010-CC.

146. NAI website: www.nationalarchives.nic.in, e Abhilekh, NAI Quarterly News Letter, Vol I, July- Sept. 2013. No. 2. Site visited on 13.8.2020.

the Pan-African Conference in 1993. Her paper was titled 'Protection of Collections from damages caused by Pollution.'[147] India was also invited to an international seminar on 'Evidence based governance in the Electronic Age', organised in 2002 by World Bank and International Records Management Trust (IRMT) in South Africa. It was followed by a series of interactions with various institutions through electronic video discussions and conferences. In 1996, the NAI hosted the visit of Mr LI Mawangi, Deputy Director, National Archives of Kenya, under Indo-Kenya CEP.[148]

In 1992, NAI received two senior officers from Smithsonian Institution, USA, Dr John Fleckner and Dr William Moss, to discuss acquiring microfilms of records of Indian interest available in USA and to utilise their expertise for Conservation programmes in India. They also delivered two lectures on American Presidential Libraries as an extension of National Archives System and Archival Profession in the USA. NAI also conducted a workshop on Conservation of Archival and Library Material organised under Indo-US Sub-Commission by National Research Laboratory for Conservation of Cultural Properties, Lucknow. Five experts from the USA also participated in the workshop.[149]

Besides participating in several international events and activities, NAI had hosted a number of foreign delegates. Some of them are Deputy Secretary and Scientific Officer, Embassy of Federation of Russia, Ms Penny Brook, Head, India Office Library and Records, London, Principal Secretary and Second Secretary, Embassy of Singapore, India, dignitaries from Turkish Embassy, Ambassador of Poland, Charge 'd' Affairs, Embassy of Switzerland,

147. IHRC, October 1988, Srinagar, pp134-35, and IHRC, Feb.1997, Jabalpur, p.140.
148. IHRC Proceedings, April 2003, Raipur, pp.175-76, and IHRC, 2001, Mysore, p.221.
149. IHRC Proceedings, December 1995, Jadavpur, pp. 109-110

Director, National Library Bhutan, Director, Asian Civilisation Museum, Singapore, Dr Louis Fillip Pereira Thomaz, Prof of Sanskrit and History, University of Lisbon, Mr Vicky Lenieux, Consultant, IRMT, UK, Mr Graham Shaw, Deputy Director, British Library (Oriental and India Office Collection), London, UK, Director, State Heritage Museum and Member of the Russian Academy of Sciences, St Petersburg and Second Secretary, Embassy of Russian Federation, and Dr Suzanne Summer, Associate Professor of Mathematics, Mary Ashington College, Virginia, USA.[150]

Many other delegates visited NAI from Singapore, Oman, Harvard Business School, Poland, Afghanistan, National University of Malaysia, Ethiopia, Japan, USA, and Iran Cultural House to share information, collaborate in latest technology of preservation and digital archiving, and exchange ideas and material. Under the MoU, a delegation from Surinam visited NAI in 2013 and discussed issues of mutual interest with Director General of Archives and other senior officers of NAI. A host of other foreign dignitaries from Malaysian National Archives visited NAI and the trend continues.[151]

Under the auspices of the Indian Ocean Rim-Association for Regional Cooperation (IOR-ARC), NAI, in collaboration with Ministry of External Affairs hosted a two-day meeting of the Heads of the Archives of the IOR-ARC providing them with a common platform. Out of 22 member countries, 15 countries participated, including Ambassador KV Bhagirath, Secretary General, IOR-ARC Secretariat, Mauritius. An exhibition on 'Documentary Heritage of IOR-ARC Countries' was mounted at the NAI, based on archival heritages received from the Heads

150. IHRC Proceedings, April 2003, Raipur, p.228
151. IHRC Proceedings, February 2013, Lucknow, pp. 304-, (IHRC Proceedings, October, 2013, pp.271-72.

of the Archives of the IOR-ARC. The meeting focused on various aspects of the Indian Ocean as an area which is a testimony to the cultural diversity of the various existing countries. Each member country presented a paper based on the holdings of records in their respective countries under the following themes: Significance of the Indian Ocean-Historical and Contemporary; Social and Cultural Profile of the Indian Ocean; Sharing and Dissemination of Knowledge and Information: Creation of a Database-documentation centres of information of Records of other countries and Augmentation of Training facilities; Access to information and RTI and the Future.

The member countries discussed the recommended suggestions received from each country. Those were summarised and the same were adopted for further collaboration by the member countries of IOR-ARC as listed below:[152]

- Developing a virtual archives/documentation centre comprising a comprehensive database of archives of common interest lying in the Repositories of IOR-ARC member countries to facilitate sharing of knowledge. Efforts should be made to add link of other RIM countries' website on their website.
- Appropriate steps to be taken by all countries to digitise their records holding so that information can be 'Shared' by all stakeholder countries/archives.
- Developing training programme in the field of records management and preservation with the help of new technology, including e-records management.
- Listing rare records/archives regarding IOR-ARC countries in the Memory of the World Programme of UNESCO.

152. IHRC Proceedings, February 2013, Lucknow, pp.259-60 and IHRC, October 2013, pp.270-271.

- Framing guidelines to address legal and copyright issues for digital document.
- Establishing regular forum of National Archives of RIM Countries with an approved constitution and mandate.
- Framing suitable guidelines to ensure free flow of information and culture, trade and commerce. Moreover, step should be taken to ensure that no visa is required for scholars travelling among member countries.
- Exchanging archivists and technical experts among archival institutions of the member countries for studying and sharing their experiences in the field of archives.
- All member countries should have MoU/CEP with other countries.

Regarding meeting of South West Asian Regional Branch of International Council on Archives (SWARBICA) and the active role that NAI played in its establishment and working has been discussed in next segment of this chapter.

The Growth and Development of South West Asian Regional Branch of International Council on Archives (SWARBICA)* and Role of NAI in relevance to Education of Archival Science and Training in the Region

Establishment of SWARBICA to Promote Regional Cooperation Amongst Archival Community

Presenting the development report of NAI at the IHRC 43rd session in 1975, Dr SN Prasad, Director, NAI, informed the Commission about the proposal to form a Regional Branch of the ICA for South and West Asia (SWARBICA) covering Bangladesh and Bhutan in the East to Iran in the West. He

*SWARBICA objectives as per the Constitution, please see ANNEXURE-5.IHRC Proceedings 1975, January, Lucknow, p.70.

emphasised upon the benefits of regional cooperation among the archival community for India and other countries. He reported that several officers of NAI have gone to our neighboring countries, like Indonesia, Afghanistan, and Singapore, as Archival Consultants. Similarly, nominees of government of Indonesia, Malaysia, Sri Lanka, Burma, and Nepal have already been deputing their officers for archival education and training in the one-year Diploma Course in Archives Keeping organised by NAI since 1943. He was certain that such professional contacts are mutually advantageous, promoting regional cooperation and preserving old records which are part of cultural heritage of mankind.[153] He reported that the SWARBICA had been approved by both ICA and the Indian government. It will include archives of eight countries: Iran, Pakistan, Afghanistan, Nepal, Bhutan, Bangladesh, Sri Lanka, and India. Some of these countries have already extended their support for setting up the Regional Branch, and steps have been taken to frame the Constitution for the proposed organisation. SWARBICA is expected to promote regional cooperation in the field of Archives.[154]

The Presidential address of the Union State Minister of Education and President, IHRC, states that the experience and expertise of Indian Archivists had been frequently utilised by friendly countries in Asia and Africa to train their personnel. But international cooperation and exchange need not be confined to training alone, nor need it be one-sided. Though we can acquire archival material of Indian interests from the advanced countries, India has much more in common with the Third World

153. SWARBICA objectives as per the Constitution, please see ANNEXURE-5.IHRC Proceedings 1975, January, Lucknow, p.70.
154. Ibid. p. 79.

developing countries in Asia and Africa. This commonality is evident in problems of climatic conditions, limited resources, comparative lack of public awareness of the value of records, and many other factors. Hence, exchanging ideas, technology and professional contacts in the archival field among the Asians and African countries would be mutually beneficial.[155]

It was proposed that India should host a symposium on archives of mutual interest inviting Indian Ocean countries to participate. ICA had also been thinking of providing a common regional archival platform for developing countries and proposed forming a regional branch of the Council for South and West Asia (SWARBICA).[156] The NAI report mentioned that setting up SWARBICA was already approved by the Indian government. The preliminary meeting was to be held in Tehran to draw up a constitution for SWARBICA and to work out other organisational details. The Indian government offered to hold the inaugural meeting of SWARBICA at New Delhi, hoping that it would promote regional cooperation in this part of the world.

The SWARBICA was inaugurated in 1976 to promote the archival development in the region through cooperative efforts. Besides India, delegates from Afghanistan, Bangladesh, Iran, Nepal and Sri Lanka participated. Mr Cyrus Parham, Archivist of Iran, and Dr NH Kulkarnee and Ranbir Kishore, Assistant Director, NAI, were elected President, Secretary and Treasurer, respectively. Besides, an exhibition was organised and two papers were presented by the delegates on the cultural cooperation among the regional countries.[157] The countries joining SWARBICA were

155. IHRC Proceedings, Bikaner, Feb. 1976. P. 73
156. IHRC Proceedings, 1976, Bikaner session, p.81
157. Ibid, pp.113-114.

India, Bangladesh, Iran, Nepal, and Sri Lanka. Afghanistan and Pakistan were also likely to join. This helped in fostering closer regional cooperation and improving preservation and utilisation of the national heritage of this part of the world.[158]

Dr NH Kulkarnee attended the 8th Annual meeting of ICA Committee on Archival Development in 1977.RC Gupta, Deputy Director, and ML Ahluwalia, Assistant Director, were also appointed as members of the Training Committee and the Business Committee of the ICA. The SWARBICA project study of the source material on Asian history and culture, as available in the archival organisations in South West Asia, was completed by KD Gupta, formerly Assistant Director of Archives in NAI. He submitted his report to the ICA in 1977.[159]

Pakistan and Afghanistan had also become members of the Branch, represented by Mr Atique Zafar Sheikh, Director of Pakistan Archives, and Mr Hedayatullah Akram, Deputy Director, UN and International Affairs, Ministry of Foreign Affairs, Kabul. Dr Kulkarnee also attended the Bhubaneswar History Congress as Secretary General of SWARBICA in 1977, targeting institutional and individual enrolment to the Branch. As a Regional Rapporteur, he offered his comments on the applications of Sri Lanka and Bangladesh for International Archival Development Fund support, and suggested projects to member countries for similar assistance. The SWARBICA News Bulletin was brought out towards the end of the year. RC Gupta, Deputy Director of Archives, NAI, also completed his preliminary Working Paper, a study for the proposed training requirement of the region to be presented at the proposed symposium, scheduled

158. IHRC proceedings, 1 Feb.1977, Mysore, p.68.
159. Indian Archives, Jan.-June 1977, News Notes, pp. 67-68.

to be held in January 1979 at Colombo.[160]

As a part of the UNESCO programme on Asian Cultural Studies for 1977-78, KD Gupta had completed his study for listing and describing source material on Asian history and culture available in the archives of the SWARBICA region. The study was entrusted to NAI through the Branch. The scope of the study had been restricted to public archives of the eight member countries in SWARBICA, including information about such material in the custody of more than 40 national and provincial archives organisations functioning in those countries.

But, the report also provided significant information about records and documents held by important semi-public and private institutions. Considering the volume of public records available in the countries in the region, and prohibitive cost of preparing the descriptive lists, compiling separate guide for each country was recommended.[161]

The Executive Board held its meetings in 1978 under the Chairmanship of Mr Cyrus Parham (Iran). The Board gave approval for setting up of a Regional Reprography Demonstration Centre at New Delhi as a part of the Institute of Archival Training; deputing its Secretary General to Dacca and Islamabad for better liaison; and exploring the possibility of surveying records in private custody in the region through country-wise committees. The Committee on Archival Development (CAD) summary forms for assessing archival needs was to be sent to institutional members. Iran expressed the possibility of imparting archival instructions to some Afghan trainees with possible assistance by CAD.[162]

---

160. Ibid, pp.96-97.
161. Ibid, p.97.
162. The Indian Archives, Jan.-Dec. 1977, News Notes, p.82.

The most important work of the Board was to make preliminary arrangements for the forthcoming SWARBICA meetings to be held at Colombo in 1979 and to finalise the list of special invitees, including expert archivists from outside the region. The Sri Lanka Archives had agreed to host the meetings. Besides the Executive Board meetings, a two-day symposium on 'Archival Training Requirements of Personnel in the Region' was to be held, followed by the first General Conference, and a full-day Business session on the theme 'Problems of Promoting research and raising Archival Consciousness at all levels in the SWARBICA region'. The meeting was followed by a panel discussion over All India Radio, Srinagar, on 'Preserving the Past' in which was attended by all the Board members and moderated by Dr SN Prasad, Director, NAI, Dr NH Kulkarnee also addressed a press conference to explain the objectives and achievements of SWARBICA. The first issue of SWARBICA Journal (1978) was also released, briefing on the inaugural proceedings of the Branch. So far, the State Archives of Delhi, Haryana, Sikkim, Goa, Uttar Pradesh, Orissa, and West Bengal, the Universities of Bundelkhand, Calcutta, Gorakhpur, Mysore, Osmania, Patna and Visva Bharti, and ICHR had enrolled themselves as institutional members. The other departments of State Archives of Assam, Jammu and Kashmir, Tamil Nadu, the Research Department of Arunachal Pradesh, various universities, archival institutions and individuals in India and other neighboring countries actively considered enrolment.[163]

SWARBICA had promoted the spirit of cooperation and mutual assistance in the entire region. The first General

163. Ibid, pp.82-83.

Conference of SWARBICA was inaugurated on 22 January by the Minister, Cultural Affairs of Sri Lanka, Mr BL Hurulle. Besides delegates from Afghanistan, Bangladesh, India, Nepal, and Sri Lanka, a number of institutional and individual members from India attended it. Other foreign and important dignitaries who attended the conference were Dr Evans, representing UNESCO, Dr Franz, ICA, Dr Riegar, CAD, Dr Bousso, Senegal, Mrs Talib, Malaysia, Mrs Arcangel, the Philippines, Dr Haellquiest, Scandinavian Institute of Asian Studies and Dr McLaws representing Genealogical Society of Utah.[164]

In the absence of the Chairman of the Branch, C Parham, the meeting was chaired by A Dewaraja, Vice Chairman. The conference adopted the report of the Secretary General and Treasurer, and approved the budget for the year 1979. The general conference elected the next Executive Board of SWARBICA with A Dewaraja as Chairman, Dr KM Karim as Vice Chairman, Dr NH Kulkarnee and Ranbir Kishore, both re-elected unanimously as the Secretary General and Treasurer respectively for the term1979-80. The meeting of the outgoing Executive Board was held on 22 February 1979 with A Dewaraja. It proposed amendment of the Constitution for creating new category of Associate Members by enrolling archivists and scholars from outside the region who were interested in the archival activities of countries in SWARBICA. The newly constituted Board had two sittings, one at Anuradhapura and the other at Colombo, under the chairmanship of A Dewaraja. One of the major projects approved by the Board was to prepare descriptive list of microfilms of Dutch records in the NAI with assistance of

164. Indian Archives, July-December 1978, pp. 76-78, and IHRC Proceedings. January , 1979, Aurangabad, p. 167

scholars from Sri Lanka and CAD funds.[165]

In the academic session of 1979, a number of papers were presented by members on various subjects relating to promoting research and archival consciousness in the region, and information about the records available in their repositories of other member countries. The important two-day session was related to the symposium on Training Needs in Archival Technology and Management in South West Asian region. Based on RC Gupta's working paper, a resolution was passed urging UNESCO to provide Consultancy services for a complete study of the needs of the training institution.[166]

The next Executive Committee meeting of SWARBICA was held at Madras in July 1980, and was attended by SAI Tirmizi, Director of Archives. He was unanimously elected as executive member of the SWARBICA.[167*] Dr RK Perti, Director of Archives, attended the next meeting of Executive Committee of SWARBICA at Kathmandu in 1983. He was also elected Chairman of the SWARBICA.[168*] He attended the Executive Board meeting and 2 General Conferences of SWARBICA held at Islamabad in July 1984, and was also elected as its Chairman.[169*] As the Chairman of SWARBICA, he attended a seminar on 'Archives Awareness' held at Kathmandu, Nepal, in 1985.[170] Unfortunately, proceedings of none of the meetings referred above and in subsequent paras, are available.

---

165. Ibid
166. Ibid, p.78
167. IHRC, 1982, Gandhinagar, Gujarat, p.110.
168. IHRC proceedings, 29-30 June 1985, Surajkund, Haryana, pp.134-35.
169. Ibid. p. 178

 * (details of the proceedings of all these meetings are however not available either in DRR files or NAI Annual Reports)

170. NAI Annual Report 1986, p.22.

An international seminar on 'Conservation of Traditional Records' was held in 1985 at Vigyan Bhawan, New Delhi, under the joint auspices of SWARBICA and the NAI. The seminar was inaugurated by YS Das, Secretary, Department of Culture, Ministry of Human Resource Development, Government of India. Besides delegates from Iran, Nepal, Pakistan, and Sri Lanka, representatives from different State Archives in India also participated in it. Mr John Davies, an internationally renowned conservationist from the New South Wales Archives Authority, Sydney, Australia, attended the seminar as a 'Resource person'. The seminar focused on using microfilms for a better dissemination of information and specifying standards for production, storage and use of archival microfilms. The seminar highlighted India's progress in conserving records.[171]

Dr Perti attended the ICA Conference on Microfilming Programs for Developing Countries (1987) held at Trier, Federal Republic of Germany.[172] He also attended the Executive Board meeting of SWARBICA in 1989 at Colombo, Sri Lanka, besides 3 plenary meetings of the Regional Coordinating Committee for the Guide to the Sources of Asian History at Colombo, a UNESCO project.[173] In 1990, Dr Perti was invited by the government of Iran to organise a short course in Records Management for the benefit of young archivists of Iran National Archives. He also attended Executive Board meeting of SWARBICA and its IV General Conference held at Colombo and Tehran, respectively, where matters of regional interest were discussed. India was again elected as Chairman of the SWARBICA at its 15th Executive

171. NAI Annual Report, 1985, pp. 1-2, and IHRC Feb. 1987, Lucknow, pp.199.
172. NAI Annual Report, 1987, p.25.
173. IHRC Proceedings 1990, p.170.

Board meeting held in 1991 at Goa.[174*]

The Constitution of SWARBICA lays down its aims and objectives as sponsoring professional training of archivists in the region in keeping with ICA, organising training workshops as a prerequisite for developing archives, and facilitating international and regional collaboration. The proceedings of the SWARBICA meetings held from 1976 onwards reveal that thematic conferences are being held regularly along with the meetings of its General Body and Executive Board. This has promoted regional cooperation and development in the field of archives as a profession by sharing their expertise and experiences, and by deputing their officers for various short-term and long-term training programmes.

Based on bilateral cooperation, the School of Archival Studies had provided customised training to people of Afghanistan, Bhutan, Myanmar, Iran, Gambia, Korea, Malaysia, Mauritius, Nigeria, Sudan, Tunisia, Uganda, Genealogical Society, Utah, USA, Oman, etc., under CEPs or otherwise.

The School of Archival Studies has been attracting students from the neighboring and African Countries. The training of the foreign students had been funded either by CEPs or by some international funding agencies, such as Asia Foundation, German Foundation for International Development, or Ford Foundation, or by the International Archival Development Fund. All the sponsored candidates joining the one-year diploma course from Africa and Sri Lanka were financed by the German Foundation for International Development, Bonn, Germany,

---

174. IHRC, April, 1992, Proceedings, pp.110, 113.
*(details of the proceedings are neither available in files of Departmental Record Room of NAI or the NAI Annual Reports)

and Colombo Plan, UNESCO.

Besides private and sponsored students from State and archival institutions in India, significant number of students sponsored by one National Archives of Afro-Asian Countries has also joined the one-year diploma course. Some of the countries who have sponsored students are Nepal, Sri Lanka, Bangladesh, Myanmar, Malaysia, Indonesia, Singapore, Afghanistan, Bhutan, Tanzania, Zambia, South Africa, Kenya, Nigeria, and South Africa among others. NAI has trained over 20 officers from the Kenya National Archives and Documentation Service, and a similar number from the National Archives of Sri Lanka. Until recently Bangladesh, Sri Lanka, and Myanmar had been deputing their students.

India has offered more training opportunities than all the developed countries put together. This is certainly one of the best examples of Soth-South Cooperation. The alumni from the School of Archival Studies have been occupying the top-most positions in their respective countries like National Archives of Malaysia, Singapore, South Africa, Nepal, Kenya, Sri Lanka, Myanmar, Bangladesh, etc. The member countries of SWARBICA and SAARC region too have benefitted significantly.

The SWARBICA Secretariat had always worked with complete transparency. The accounts were duly audited and the Treasurer report presented in the Executive Board and General Body meetings. In the 1990s, the annual subscription for the member countries was Rs 3,000 or US $250. The State Archives of India were also SWARBICA members, paying an annual fee of Rs 500/- only. A SWARBICA meeting was held in Pakistan in December 1989, and a regional seminar was held in December 1989 in Islamabad. Mr MR Abbasi from Iran was the Chairman of SWARBICA. The 13th Executive Board meeting of SWARBICA was to be held in New Delhi in 1990, with Bhutan's membership on the agenda, among other issues.[175] The 14th Executive Board meeting was held in Pokhra, Nepal.[176] Another Executive Board meeting was held in Goa, in 1991. Dr Perti had written to the Director, National Archives Nepal, to consider hosting the Executive Board meeting in Nepal. As Nepal expressed its inability to host the meeting, Mr M R Abbassi, Director General, National Archives of Iran and Chairman SWARBICA, requested NAI to find an alternative Venue.[177*]

SWARBICA had been unable to work effectively from 1990 to 2008-9, even though efforts were made to revive it at ICA Kuala Lumpur Congress meeting in 2007. As per NAI records, this was largely due to a shortage of funds, as is evident from the correspondence between the member countries. The Director General, NAI, had raised this issue in the report, dated 24 May 1995, on the Inter-Regional Conference on Archival Development, held in Tunisia in 1995. He reported that the conference discussed the development of archival activities over the last three decades, with an emphasis on mutual cooperation in training, the conservation of archival heritage, and its dissemination. The subject of regional ICA branches was also discussed at length and noted that SWARBICA has not been working effectively. It was proposed to have a permanent secretariat in any of the member country to ensure proper functioning and co-operation amongst the member countries.[178]

In 1994, Mr Marcel Caya, Editor ICA Bulletin, Canada,

175. F. No. 1/90, T. R. SWARBICA, p. 53/corr. Subject of the file is Report of SWARBICA, 1991 Audit Report; deals with the subject of transfer of treasury to Iran from India. Contains SWARBICA News Letter, Sri Lanka.

176. Ibid, p. 78/corr.

177. F. No. 2(SWAB)/DG/91, pp.1-2/corr.*Proceedings of Goa meeting not available in DRR files of NAI.

178. F. N. 31-1(6)/95-CC and Report by Dr. Sarkar, F.N. 1/95.DGA, pp.10-11/corr.

requested for details of the activities of SWARBICA since 1992, as they had information only about the Executive Board meeting held in Montreal in 1992 under the Chairmanship of Dr Perti. By now the SWARBICA treasury had also been transferred from India to Tehran, Iran, adjusting the bank charges. There has been financial crunch due to non-payment of dues by the member countries. As per the records, even India had paid dues only till 1992.[179]

In spite of these limitations, the Chairman and the other member countries, Sri Lanka and India, wanted to hold the SWARBICA meeting before the ICA Congress meeting in Beijing. This was due to the impressions of the ICA and CAD (ICA Committee on Archival Development) regarding the workings of SWARBICA, as revealed in the discussions. The Director General, NAI, reported this after his return from the Inter-Regional Conference on Archival Development, 1995.[180] Meanwhile, the ICA Secretariat wrote to SWARBICA Secretary General (ICA ref.CK.CT.96/148) requesting Quadrennial Reports for the XIII meeting of the General Assembly, and some information on the functioning and achievement of the ICA bodies and SWARBICA.[181] The SWARBICA General Secretary invited information and suggestions from all the member countries to draft the SWARBICA progress report for the last four years, which was to be placed before the Executive Committee of the ICA on the fourth Medium Term Plans. The report required information regarding administration—the General Conference meetings, membership, term of office of the current Executive Committee, Executive Board, co-option of members, and

179. Ibid. p. 13/notes, and reminder at Sr. No. Receipts.7.

180. F.No. 24-2(2)/96 CC, p.17/corr.

181. Ibid. pp. 20-40/corr.

details of the meetings of these bodies. Under programmes, it sought information regarding symposia, seminars, publications, and other activities like inter-branch events, cooperation with NGOs, missions, surveys, types of projects, implementation, funding, etc. Under suggestions, it required to include difficulties encountered, suggested solutions, and suggestions to improve ICA's function, programme or image.[182]

The minutes of the ICA Committee on Archival Development held in Washington, in1995, was attended by Mr Atiquue Zafar Sheikh, Secretary General, SWARBICA, who reported to have never shared the meeting details with other member countries.

As per the minutes, the action points applicable for the regional branches, including SWARBICA, were—identify new members in their regions and urge them to join ICA (1.4), suggest new programme activities (2.3), and submit archival development projects to national governments and UNESCO commissions (3.1 and 3.2).[183]

Likewise, the minutes of the Tunisia ICA-CAD Inter-Regional Conference on Archival Developmenthad some action points recommended for the Regional Branches by adopting some resolutions besides holding Extra Committee Meeting for the Regional Branches. The minutes of the Extra Committee Meeting recommended constituting a small committee to discuss actions based on the recommendations and resolutions from both the Abuja and Tunis conferences and to propose guidelines for future CAD action.[184]

When the Regional Branch representatives stated their

182. Ibid.p.22/corr.
183. Ibid. pp.27-30.
184. Ibid, p.37/corr.

opinions on the immediate archival needs, training at all levels, got the highest priority. There was a need for expert assistance in creating university courses in records and archives management, and for scholarships to send young archivists to recognised archival schools. The records note that special attention should be paid to two branches that, for various reasons, are not functioning well at the moment, CANARBICA and SWARBICA. It was crucial to find ways and means to revitalise them. The committee proposed that (ICA Commission on Archival Development) CAD should:

- urge the Regional Branches and their member countries to contribute as much as possible to development projects;
- request the Regional Branches to establish closer links within the region and to encourage inter-regional cooperation;
- request that CSP extends its efforts to identify possible financial sources for development projects;
- request that the Secretary of CAD, in cooperation with ICA Secretariat, establishes a programme for identifying and registering the archival needs in the various regional branches. The programmer should record the archival assistance that can be offered by National Archives in UNESCO-Europe, national aid organisations, and other offers of assistance; and
- request that the Secretary of CAD, in cooperation with the ICA Secretariat, develops appropriate documentation and evaluation tools.

The Director General, NAI, wrote to the Secretary General, SWARBICA, expressing his concern for SWARBICA's dismal performance over the last few years due to paucity of funds. Since this hindered implementation of ICA programmes, he suggested revitalising its activities and bringing out the Journal of the Branch regularly. It was suggested that the membership should be increased by enrolling Maldives and Bhutan to the Council.[185]

The meeting of Executive Board and of General Assembly of SWARBICA Branch had not taken place since 1991. The Committee issued a meeting notice to all the member countries of the Branch for holding SWARBICA meeting on 1 September 1996 in Beijing. There was a two-point agenda, (i) activating the Regional Branch, and (ii) addressing matters related to SWARBICA treasury. However, further details of the proceedings of the SWARBICA meetings in Beijing are not available in NAI records. As an outcome of the SWARBICA meetings in Beijing, and the participation of other member countries in the ICA Congress, SWARBICA received a grant of US$ 5,000 from CAD for a single project—organising SWARBICA General Conference.[186]

The Executive Board Meeting and General Conference, held in Tehran, was attended by Mr H D Singh, Deputy Director of Archives, as Director General of Archives was unable to attend. The agenda points of the meeting included electing the office bearers, sorting treasury problems and payment of dues and arrears, re-activating and coordinating the archival relationship between the countries of the region, publishing the SWARBICA Journal, enrolling Maldives as a member, and nominating SWARBICA representative for the 14 Biennial Conference of the ESARBICA of the ICA to be held in 1997. The following decisions were taken at the meeting:

- For the Executive Board, SH Sehrastani, Director General, Iran National Archives, was elected as the Chairman; Director General, NAI, as the Vice Chairman; Mr Atique Zafar Sheikh, Director General, National Archives of Pakistan, as the Secretary General;

185. Ibid, p. 53/corr.
186. Ibid, pp.56-57/corr.

and Dr KDG Wimalratne, Director, National Archives, Sri Lanka, as Treasurer.

- It was agreed that the treasury had problems due to procedural gaps in settling the payments. All the member countries were requested to remit their annual dues for 1996, including arrears to the External Account, National Archives Organisation, at the earliest, to enable the new treasurer to submit detailed accounts of the treasury.
- To reactivate the branch, the National Archives of Bangladesh will organise a 3-day Awareness Seminar in April-May 1998. The host country will bear the hospitality expenses, while air fares of the SWARBICA member countries were to be announced after ICA's approval.
- The next meeting was decided to be held in Colombo, Sri Lanka, in October 1998.
- It was resolved to publish SWARBICA Journal yearly, with Pakistan bringing out the next issue. Iran will publish a SWARBICA Newsletter and all member countries were requested to send the material by 30 June 1997.
- Bhutan and Maldives were advised to become members of ICA before enrolling as SWARBICA members.

On 6 May 1997, a General Conference was held. Papers were presented and discussed by the members of the Iran National Archives and representatives of other records repositories of Iran on various issues related to the development of archives in their respective countries and organisations. It was also decided to cooperate with each other in archival field.[187]

187. Ibid, pp.79-81/corr.

The Iran National Archives issued the SWARBICA Newsletter in August 1997, which contained information of SWARBICA Executive Board meeting and General Conference held in Tehran in May 1997, with the support of ICA and the SWARBICA treasury. Other information was from the National Archives of Sri Lanka, and Bangladesh. There was no news either from India or Pakistan.[188]

The Chairman submitted SWARBICA Professional Development Report for the period 1992-2000 to ICA and shared it with other branch member countries. As per the report following the Beijing meetings (2-3 September 1996) held during the13th International Congress on Archives, the primary agenda was to reactivate the SWARBICA branch of ICA after a six-year recess. The next SWARBICA Executive Board Meeting and General Conference were hosted in 1997 by Iran National Archives with the financial support of ICA and SWARBICA treasury. The meeting included information like archival awareness seminar by Bangladesh, Journal by Pakistan, and the next Board meeting by Sri Lanka, etc.

By 1998, only two activities were accomplished. Iran issued the Newsletter in August 1997 and Sri Lanka organised the next SWARBICA conference and the Executive Board meeting. But Pakistan deferred the release of journal due to lack of articles and funding, and Bangladesh could not organise the seminar due to financial stringency and other limitations. ICA and UNESCO did not offer financial support to Bangladesh. After the first issue, Iran could not release the SWARBICA Newsletter either. Pakistan could bring out the SWARBICA Journal only in 2000.

188. Ibid, pp. 106-117.

Under Guide to the sources of Asian History, India had brought out the volumes starting in 1992—India (1992, 1994), Pakistan (1994) and Sri Lanka (1996). This ICA UNESCO Project has since been completed. Individual member countries did bring out a number of publications as mentioned in the report.[189]

Though there had been little professional development in SWARBICA region over the period 1992-2000, the Conference in Tehran in 1997 showed promise, followed by Colombo Conference in 1998. However, things slowed down after the Colombo conference due to factors like lack of efficient trained staff, limitations of digital technology, and shortage of funds. But, lack of cooperation among the member countries of the Branch Region was the biggest factor. The ICA too had neglected the Branch by not giving the desired support and financial assistance for its proposed activities. The Branch cannot survive on meager annual subscription of 6 member countries, which are also the developing countries of the Third World. Its survival requires immense technical and financial support from ICA and its various Committees.[190]

In response to the SWARBICA Report for 1992-2000 and development of the Branch during 2001-2008, Dr S Sarkar, Director General, NAI, shared his concern for under-performance of SWARBICA and gave some suggestions. He pointed out that more attention must be paid to improve interaction amongst the member countries through exchange of publications, information, training etc., if not through meetings, which invariably gets hampered due to financial constraints. Although the 1997 meet looked promising for the proposed activities, financial and other

189. F.No. 24-2(1)/99-CC, pp. 13-20/corr.
190. Ibid

limitations slowed down SWARBICA. Hence, ICA can play a crucial role as a parent body by financially supporting the branch. It can help SWARBICA survive and sustain itself by facilitating its annual meetings and encouraging technical cooperation among the member countries of the region through seminars and workshops. Without regular financial or technical support, SWARBICA will not be able to make the desired progress. This was the reason behind SWARBICA's inability to progress over the 10-year period (1999-2008).[191]

Revival of SWARBICA and Contribution of NAI

An Indian delegation comprising of two senior officers, SMR Baqar and Dr Meena Gautam, both Deputy Directors of Archives, was deputed to Tehran, Iran, to attend the Executive Board meeting and General Conference of SWARBICA in May 2009. The team actively participated not only in reviving the SWARBICA, but also in preparing the agenda notes and minutes of the deliberations on behalf of the Regional Branch to make it a vibrant body, at least for the next five years as meetings were being held regularly. Financial support was necessary to continue its activities and to keep the branch alive. The Executive Body decided to increase the subscription fees of the member countries from US$ 250 to 500, and to request ICA for funding and supporting its activities and programmes in its annual meetings. The Board also recommended taking up joint research projects, to make SWARBICA a success. It will also assure ICA to extend financial support.

A resolution was adopted for the purpose. Five sub-committees were constituted to discuss and finalise the areas of

191. Ibid, p.13/corr.

mutual interest and to propose a plan of action. The five sub-committees were: Preservation and Conservation Committee (chaired by Sri Lanka), Processing Committee (chaired by Iran), Archival Training/Education Committee (chaired by India), Acquisition and Appraisal Committee (chaired by Bangladesh), and Digitisation and Dissemination Committee (chaired by Pakistan). The member countries also agreed to exchange their publications. All the member countries presented their country reports and decided to hold the next annual meeting in Sri Lanka and to approach ICA for financial assistance.[192]

The Tehran meeting of SWARBICA was followed by a meeting of the Executive Board in Colombo in 2010, besides a workshop on Electronic Records Management of the Member Countries, organised by the National Archives of Sri Lanka, with the financial support of ICA. Dr Meena Gautam, Deputy Director of Archives, was deputed to represent the DG, NAI, and NS Mani, Senior Microphotographist, was deputed to represent India at the Executive Board meeting and the workshop. Both the meeting and the workshop were inaugurated by the Minister of National Heritage of Sri Lanka, and the keynote address was delivered by the Secretary to the President of Democratic Socialist Republic of Sri Lanka. The delegates from SWARBICA member countries—India, Iran, Pakistan, Sri Lanka, Bangladesh, Nepal, and Bhutan attended the meeting. Mrs Mahfuzah Yusuf, an expert from National Archives of Malaysia, was the Resource Person for the workshop. All the delegates from Iran, India, Pakistan, Nepal, Bangladesh, Sri Lanka and Bhutan made presentations about their progress in electronic records management of their

192. F.N. 24-4(2)/2010-CC, Minutes of the SWARBICA Tehran meeting.

respective archives. At the end of the workshop, the following recommendations were made:

1. Every member country should have a legal framework to meet individual requirements aligning with the UNESCO convention relating to preservation of Digital Heritage adopted by UNESCO in 2003.
2. All the member countries of SWARBICA agreed to share their knowledge, best practices and challenges in the field of e-records management, digitisation and management of archives in project mode regionally and globally.
3. Conducting training or orientation programmes for skill development in the field of archives and digital records management.
4. Developing a new training module to address electronic records issues and challenges through strategic partners for specialised solutions.

The formal meeting of the Executive Board of SWARBICA was held on 2 December 2010. Mr Martin Berndse, the President of ICA and Director General, National Archives of Netherlands, also graced the meeting by his presence. The ICA President appreciated the efforts of the member countries in the region over the last two years in reviving SWARBICA. But he regretted ICA's inability to fund digitisation and preservation projects on account of being a self-supporting international organisation. Iran assured to support Pakistan by sending a team of experts to assess the damage caused to their records due to floods, and to prepare a report on their restoration and preservation. The Executive Board also adopted the recommendations from the workshop on e-records management.

The Executive Board agreed to increase the subscription fee to US$ 400, not US$ 500 as was decided at the Tehran meet since the amount seemed too high in view of the economies of the member countries and the resultant paucity of funds. The Board agreed to hold the next meeting in India as was offered by the Director General, NAI. It was also decided to have a workshop on Archives and RTI, a burning issue, in all the member countries. Moreover, Maldives and Afghanistan were to be accepted as observers of the SWARBICA. Mr Ali Akbar Ashari, the President of SWARBICA, agreed to inform this to the concerned countries.[193]

Birender S Yadav, Counselor, Press, Information and Culture, Indian High Commission in Colombo authorised Dr Meena Gautam to discuss the terms of collaboration with National Arhcives of Sri Lanka. Accordingly, it was discussed to mutually exchange professionals both for training purposes and for understanding the practices followed in respective countries for conserving and digitising records. It was also agreed to send preservation and digitisation experts under CEP between the two countries. The next SWARBICA Executive Board meeting was held in September 2012, at NAI, New Delhi. The meeting was assisted by ICA and SWARBICA treasury. It was attended by all the member countries i.e. Bangladesh, Iran, Nepal, Sri Lanka, Pakistan, Bhutan and Afghanistan (as an observer) besides the host country India. Since Dr David A Leitch, the ICA Secretary General, was unable to attend the Executive Board meeting, he shared an inspiring message with the branch.[194**]

In his email to all the member countries of the branch, Dr David A Leitch advised SWARBICA to post all its news and information on the ICA website, instead of maintaining its own separately. To quote him, 'This would undoubtedly serve to increase the visibility of the branch in ICA. ICA had also developed some

193. Ibid, pp. 93-98/corr. And IHRC Proceedings, October 2013, p.271.

194. Email dated 27th September, 2012, from Dr. David Leitch, Secretary General ICA, in the name of the Branch.

**Please see the verbatim text of the email at the end of the chapter V.

central guidelines for the use of ICA bodies, including branch, on the use of the organisation's logo. ICA stands for cultural diversity but I hope you agree that everything we produce should be seen to come from one and the same organisation.'[195]

While discussing the minutes of the Colombo meeting, the member countries sought a clarification on the issue of recognition of School of Archival Studies and its university affiliation. It was informed that the SAS is already recognised by the UNESCO since 1976, and the short-term courses and one-year diploma course in Archival Studies conducted in the NAI are duly recognised by the University Grants Commission. SWARBICA adopted the resolutions proposed by the Director of Sri Lanka National Archives for exchanging expertise in the area of digitisation of records from India. He had suggested the member countries to invite experts from NAI through SWARBICA to deliver lecture on digitisation. The entire expenditure, including air-fare, board and lodging, and local transport, of the expert will be borne by the host country. The duration of the training will be mutually agreed upon by the two governments. NAI offered to provide training facilities to all the member countries for no additional costs.

It was decided that every member country should have CEP or MoU with other member countries for exchanging experts for 5-10 working days. The duration will depend on the mutual agreement and understanding between the countries.

Summary of Recommendations Adopted for Executive Board Meeting

- The SWARBICA constitution should be revised and amended on the lines of the revised constitution of ICA.

195. Ibid

- SWARBICA strongly recommends that the governments of the respective countries extend full support for modernising and upgrading of archives and records management practices.
- Special effort should be made to develop private archives among the member countries.
- Efforts should be made to establish close cooperation bilaterally or multilaterally among the member countries to facilitate exchange of experts.
- SWARBICA meetings should be held regularly by rotation among the member countries to facilitate better participation and close cooperation.
- The National Archives of the member countries should take steps to undertake digitisation projects of rare and vital records and manuscripts in respective countries.

Office bearers for a new term were elected. Following the suggestions from members, it was decided that the Board members would continue for a term of 4 years. The following office bearers were elected by the House:

1. Sri-Lanka: President, SWARBICA
2. Pakistan: General Secretary, SWARBICA
3. India: Treasurer, SWARBICA.

After Delhi, the next SWARBICA meeting was held in Colombo in June 2017. Initially, the Director of Sri Lanka National Archives had planned the meet with the SAARC Centre in Sri Lanka, which was organising an international conference on archives earlier scheduled to be held in October 2014. However, SWARBICA meeting could not be held as proposed by the President, Director of Sri Lanka National Archive, in the absence of all the member countries.[196]

The Colombo meeting was held in 2017 and was attended by two Deputy Directors from NAI, namely T Hussain and Ansarul Haq. They attended the Executive Board meeting of SWARBICA and the international workshop on the digital management and establishment of digital archives. Nepal, Pakistan, and Sri Lanka presented their papers on the first day of the workshop, highlighting their digital initiatives and progress. The second day's programme included lectures and hands-on exercises on tools and methods, access and use, consideration from process to programmes, institutional models and priorities for digital curation.

The Executive Board meeting was held on 24 June 2017.[197] The minutes of the seminar and the previous Executive Board meeting of SWARBICA were presented by the Secretary General and adopted. The Treasurer Report was presented by India and approved with an appeal to all the member countries to remit their annual dues in time. The new office bearers of SWARBICA were elected.

The meeting strengthened the bond between the member countries and gave them an opportunity to further promote the activities of the archival science and the preservation of documentary heritage among the member countries. It was emphasised that SWARBICA should make its presence felt in the ICA meetings by actively participating in its deliberations. The session emphasised upon the need for exchanging archival experts and documents of mutual interest. The member countries expressed their interest in getting their officials and staff trained

196. Email dt 7 March 2014, from Director, National Archives, Sri Lanka.

197. F. No. 24-2/2017-CC. pp. 137-140

in the School of Archival Studies. Besides, dedicated software for digitisation of archival material along with customisation according to the requirements of the country should also be developed. The meeting facilitated carrying forward the policy, programmes, aims and objectives of SWARBICA according to its constitution.

Message from David A Leitch, ICA Secretary General to the Members of SWARBICA Meeting in Delhi, 28-29 September 2012

I am very sorry indeed not to be with you in person for this important meeting of SWARBICA. However, I am deeply grateful to the Treasurer of SWARBICA, based in Sri Lanka, and the hosts, the National Archives of India, for taking the initiative in organising this meeting. I would like to mention specifically Saroja and Meena Gautam for all their help and understanding.

SWARBICA is perhaps not one of the better-known regional branches of ICA, but there have been encouraging signs in recent years that it is gradually becoming more active. I attended the meeting of the branch in Kuala Lumpur (July 2008) and the President was present at last one in Colombo, Sri Lanka (December 2010).At recent meetings of the ICA Executive Board, the branch has been effectively represented by the National Archives and Library of Iran as President of the branch. During the Brisbane Congress I was very pleased to receive from Iranian colleagues a handsomely produced volume relating to the origins and development of SWARBICA.

However, I should like to suggest ways in which the branch could become even more involved in ICA activities. ICA has set aside a fund for regional branches to finance their basic operations (including governance meetings). Some of this money has been used to support the meetings of SWARBICA in Colombo and here in Delhi. It is always good to have a meeting, but those meetings should also lead to outcomes and results. A branch has to do more than merely deliberate if it is to be considered fully operational–it must be much more than a talking shop.

For example, the branch could put together a proposal for funding by the Program Commission Mission (PCOM), which normally issues it annual call for project proposals very early in the year. The project could come under one of the approved themes, including good governance, disaster preparedness and digital record-keeping. This leaves potential proposers plenty of scope. However, applicants have to realise that the total amount of funding that is available is comparatively modest–only 100,000€ per calendar year. Only very rarely are grants of over 5,000€ awarded. Informal advice is available from the ICA secretariat in Paris as proposals are developed. Watch out for the call for proposals in 2013 on the ICA website!

In addition, there is a separate fund to help institutions and colleagues in developing countries who are working in particularly challenging situations, called the Fund for International Archival Development (FIDA). FIDA grants are not intended to fund great projects, but to provide pragmatic solutions to specific problems. There is a representative from each of the world's regions on the Board of Trustees, a role currently carried out for

Asia by Mike Kichuchi, the former President of the National Archives of Japan. The Trustees would welcome the opportunity to assess many more applications from SWARBICA countries.

It is important each regional branch keeps abreast of what is going on in ICA by constantly monitoring the content of the ICA website. ICA intends to continue with the publication of its bulletin Flash. However, it will increasingly comprise feature articles rather the latest news, which will be posted on the website. Details will be posted on the website about the right time to make funding applications to PCOM and FIDA. The development of major ICA projects, including ICA-A to M, the freely available multi-lingual archival description software, can also be followed through the website. And branches should also regularly publish news from their region on the ICA website. Much of what they do will be of interest to colleagues in other parts of the world who are trying to meet similar challenges. In other words, if a regional branch does not make very full use of the ICA website as the main communications tool, then it puts itself at a severe disadvantage.

I was pleased to see that in its Delhi meeting SWARBICA wishes to consider the subject of the Right to Information and its links to records management. As the White Paper on Freedom of Information in the UK (1997) pointed out, 'An FOI Act can only be as good as the quality of the records which are subject to its provisions. Statutory rights of access are of little use if reliable records are not created in the first place, if they cannot be found when needed, or if the arrangements for their eventual archiving or destruction are inadequate.'

In other words, effective records management is an indispensable precondition for any successful Freedom of Information legislation; it is a key underpinning function.

Now, with the advent of the Open Government Partnership, originally developed by the United States and Brazil, the emphasis is switching from making information available to the citizen, who requests it, to the pro-active disclosure of data on a large scale, without anyone having to ask for it. It is disappointing that, up to now, so few national archives are involved in their country's open government or open data programs or policies. What is the situation in your country?

In this context the approval of the Principles of Access to Archives at the ICA's AGM in Brisbane on 24 August is highly significant. How far are SWARBICA countries aware of these principles? Are they comfortable with them?

Finally, I should mention that the Universal Declaration of Archives, a succinct and powerful statement of the relevance of archives in modern society, was endorsed by the UNESCO General Conference on 10 November 2011. Although it has been translated into over twenty languages, it is not yet available in many of the languages used in SWARBICA countries. Volunteers to remedy this gap would be most welcome. It is now possible for individuals to indicate their support for the Declaration by signing the online register accessed through the ICA website.

I wish SWARBICA a very successful meeting in Delhi and it would be great if a report could be published about it on the ICA website in the near future.

David A. Leitch

DAVID A LEITCH
ICA Secretary General
27 September 2012

Archival Science Education in Academic Institutions
An Analytical Survey

Archival Science Education in the University Set Up

In the Presidential Address at the IHRC Bikaner session in 1976, the Union Minister of Education stated it is high time to set in motion a comprehensive programme for training of Archivists. As a beginning, it would be necessary to select for the archival organisation at the Centre and in the States, bright and motivated history graduates and post-graduates from universities. Selected persons should then be provided with intensive training in archives keeping for at least one year. Such in-service training should be obligatory and the money spent on it, an excellent investment. To acquire the necessary familiarity and experience of emerging trends of historical research, such students should then be associated closely for one year or two with the History Department of selected universities specialising in research in Modern Indian History. Staff members of the selected University History Departments should, in turn, spend a year or two with the National Archives or selected State Archives. Such an interaction would vastly improve archival work as well as historical research.'[1]

1. IHRC, Proceedings 1976, Bikaner, p.73

He made these suggestions to promote archival science education in the universities and to reinforce IHRC's recommendations.

The Commission had recommended that the universities may provide facilities for archival science education and training during the fifth Five Year Plan period (1974-1979) if the UGC could provide financial assistance for the purpose. Some universities had also submitted their proposal to UGC for starting a course on archival education. Delhi University replied that since NAI is already conducting the Diploma Course in Archives Keeping, they will not conduct a course in archival training. Bangalore University reported, 'One-year post graduate Diploma Course in Archival Science has been instituted.' Bombay University was also in favour of providing facilities for archival training during the fifth Plan period. The colleges Principals were also requested to grant paid leave to the teachers who desired to take advantage of the scheme.[2] By the middle of the twentieth century, the historians showed concerns about the neglect of university records too.

With the establishment of many universities# and other technical institutions the administrative work had also increased which required proper record management. However, this area remained neglected. The issue had been frequently taken up by the IHRC, following which resolutions were adopted in 1949 and 1967 sessions, stressing on the need for establishing archives in the universities established before 1900.

---

2. IHRC Proceedings, Bikaner, Feb. 1976, pp.94-95, and IHRC Resolution IX at the 41st session at Trivandrum, Oct. 1971.

As an outcome of the Charles Wood's Dispatch of 1854, three universities were established at Calcutta, Madras and Bombay in 1858, based on the model of London University, thereby laying down the foundation of the modern higher education system in India. (Report of the Indian Education Commission, 1882, pp.-25-26)

In response to the action taken by the NAI, it was reported that 'Aligarh and Delhi Universities have appointed an archivist each to look after their records. Osmania University has a Records Section and Universities of Berhampur and Magadh have decided to open Archives Cells. Bombay and Burdwan Universities have accepted the resolutions while Universities of Allahabad, Madras, Maharaja Sayaji Rao, Rajasthan and Venkateshwar are unable to implement the resolution due to financial reasons. The resolutions are under consideration of the Universities at Gauhati, Gujarat Vidyapeeth, Kurukshetra and Sagar.' It was further recommended that necessary assistance may be obtained from the UGC. Professors attending the IHRC sessions were also requested to take personal interest in the matter and ask for necessary funds from UGC and advice from NAI. As per 1977 proceedings of IHRC, only the Universities of Delhi, Aligarh and Berhampur had established their Archival Cells. The IHRC President emphasised that UGC had already agreed to consider such requests for funds and initiative had to be taken by the History professors who were members of the Commission. IHRC resolution (II) 'Resolved to reiterate the earlier resolutions that Universities should organise Archival Cells for preserving their records on scientific lines. It is further recommended that necessary assistance may be obtained from UGC in this behalf.'[3]

In his report on development of archives, the Secretary, IHRC, informed that the Institute of Archival Training, inaugurated on 11 December 1976, has started functioning. Besides diploma, short-term courses have also been initiated along with a one-year correspondence course. He believed that the universities

3. IHRC proceedings, 1977, Mysore, p. 9.

willing to start training courses in archival science still had scope. Besides, there is good scope in exchanging specialists between the Universities and the Institute of Archival Training for delivering lectures on archive related disciplines.[4] The Universities of Guru Nanak Dev, Amritsar, Saurashtra, Utkal, Bhagalpur and Kurukshetra had initiated steps to set up Archival Cells.

By 1980, only 7 universities had implemented the resolution discussed in the 47th IHRC Delhi session.[5] Universities were trying to obtain photocopies of the material from State Archives instead of their own records, and most of them had failed to establish Archival Cells for want of funds and official records. The Secretary of Education assured the Commission to take up the matter with UGC. A Resolution was moved by SAI Tirmizi for introducing Archival Studies as optional paper at post-graduate level. He stated that Archival Studies were an empirical method of filing, referencing and describing documents for a long time, but when historians began to use the documentary sources, Diplomatics emerged as a critical study of the documents. This science developed particularly from the seventeenth century onwards in countries which had been the first to revive written law. This revival has progressively setup written records as being the foremost source of evidence. Archival Studies initially emerged as an off-shoot of Diplomatics. With the remarkable development of historical research and the firm establishment of the science of Diplomatics in the nineteenth century Europe, Archival Studies evolved as a discipline related to history and began to be taught in France (1821), and other countries including Australia (1854). Though lagging far behind the European countries, India had made considerable progress in

4. IHRC Proceedings, January 1979, Aurangabad, p.106.
5. Ibid, Delhi Session, 1980, pp.25 and 37-38.

the field of Archival Studies. Hence, it was high time the Indian Universities should start teaching Archival Studies as a separate paper at post-graduate level.

As recommended by the IHRC Standing Committee, the Commission recommended that edited texts or calendars of unpublished manuscripts, records or documents, when accompanied by an adequate introduction and critical apparatus, should be regarded equally worthy of consideration for the award of a Doctorate degree. But, the resolution was not supported by all the universities, except a few like the Universities of Awadesh Pratap Singh, Gujarat Vidyapith, Jadavpur, Karnataka, Marathwada, Poona, Maharaja Sayajirao, Rajasthan, Sardar Patel, Shivaji, Utkal, and Visva Bharti. It was felt that introducing Archival Studies as a new discipline at the post-graduate level would immensely help the students wish to opt for historical or archival research after their post-graduation. The Committee felt that it could also be introduced in the syllabus of trainee probationers of Indian Administrative Services. The resolution deserved to be supported. During discussions, S Roy from NAI suggested substituting the term 'Archival Studies' with 'Archival Science' to give it a wider scope, and introducing practicals as a part of the paper. The following amended resolution was adopted, 'The Indian Historical Records Commission recommends to the Indian Universities to introduce Archival Science as one of the optional papers at the post-graduate level. This paper should include practicals in Archival Administrations to be conducted by archival repositories in respective areas.'[6]

6. IHRC Proceedings, 1982, Gujarat, Action Taken Report, pp.86-88. and IHRC Resolutions (1948-73) Vol II, NAI Pub. p.74

The resolution was forwarded to universities and few of them expressed their interest in introducing the Archival Science as an optional paper at post-graduate level. Gujarat Vidyapith was already conducting one-year post-graduate certificate course in Preservation and Management of Archives.*Other universities gave varied reasons like lack of resources for Delhi University, dearth of qualified teachers in Visva-Bharti, still considering the matter in Kurukshetra, Jabalpur, Baroda, Poona, Utkal, Shivaji, and Vikram University, while Ujjain and Universities of Madras, Mysore, Osmania, Sardar Patel University, Saurashtra expressed willingness to implement, and requested syllabus and booklist to consider the possibility of introducing the paper. The School of Archival Studies supplied the necessary material to everyone concerned.[7]

Since the fourth Five Year Plan (1969–1974), UGC has been providing financial assistance to central universities to establish their archives or Archival Cells. UGC circular, F.-22-2/81(H.E.-II) dated 24 September 1981, sent to all Heads of Departments of History in central universities, encouraged them to establish and develop archives or Archival Cells in the universities. The letter refers to the proposed grant for selected universities during the Sixth Plan. The purpose of the scheme was to provide assistance for 'augmenting facilities in the existing Archival Cells or for enabling them to establish such cells. These facilities shall be located in the Central Library of the University and the posts sanctioned for the purpose will be borne on the library cadre.

The work of the Cell may be over-seen by a committee consisting of the librarian and the users departments. The Cell

* Has since been discontinued for want of students by Gujarat Vidyapith
7. Ibid

should be available for processing historical records, manuscripts and University records. The Commission's support will be available for the following purposes:

a) Staff (Archivist, Chemist and other supporting staff.)
b) Library equipment, and
c) Chemicals'[8]

Though UGC gave it a wider scope to develop the cells into fully-fledged archives, it never happened. Many universities, though capable of establishing their own archives, were able to establish only Archival Cells as in the case of Universities of Punjab, Chandigarh and Guru Nanak Dev University, Amritsar.[#] This was due to lack of support and resources. Nonetheless, some universities have been able to do so in the recent past, such as Delhi University, Jamia Millia Islamia and Jawaharlal Nehru University. Many Indian universities have archives but they greatly differ from the conventional ones.

The UGC constituted a committee to examine proposals and make recommendations for establishing Archival Cells in the universities. The committee[9*] comprised of:

- Prof AR Kulkarnee, Department of History, Poona University,
- Prof VA Narain, Department of History, Patna University,

---

8. UGC circular F.-22-2/81(H.E.-II), dated 24 September1981; [covering letter]. (Copy courtesy Archival Cell, Punjab University, Chandigarh)
   # University Archival Cell of Guru Nanak Dev University, Amritsar has been now named as Khalsa Heritage Centre, occupying three floors. In the name of Archives they have no university records; but are only keeping prospectus of all the courses being run by various Departments of the University. For details please see Appendix A of the chapter VI, Survey and Field Work: A Status Report.
9. IHRC, 1982, Gandhinagar, p.135.
   *The deliberations of the committee are not available in IHRC proceedings or NAI records. Could not contact or visit UGC due to Covid pandemic, when the project work was being done in 2020, as deadline was August 2020 for submission of Report. Even tried to contact UGC vide email id—contact,ugc@nic.in with cc to latha.ugc@gov.in dated 8th January 2024.

- Prof JS Grewal, Department of History, Guru Nanak Dev University, Amritsar,
- Prof MN Das, Department of History, Utkal University, Bhubaneshwar,
- Prof Ravinder Kumar, Director, Nehru Memorial Museum and Library,
- Prof SAI Tirmizi, Director, NAI, New Delhi.

The meeting of the committee was held in June 1982. But NAI public records have no information regarding the workings of the committee.

The post-graduate department of History, Venketeshwara University, Tirupati, introduced Archives Keeping as one of the optional papers with effect from the academic year 1985-86, and seventeen students of MA History opted for it. The Archivist of the University Cell, Department of History, was assigned the responsibility to teach the paper.[10]

Talking about the difficulties faced by the Archival Cells, Prof AC Bose mentioned lack of trained and qualified personnel to manage the cells and take up the training programme. Prof Khurana cited the example of Kurukshetra University which was about to close the cell. JK Jain pointed out that the Archival Cells, as envisaged in IHRC resolutions, were for the older universities established prior to 1900, and were not meant to work as training institution. Archival Cells should take care of the older records of the university; training could be deputed to NAI. Training was not feasible in the university as they lack infrastructure required for imparting practical training.[11]

10. IHRC Proceedings, 10-11 February, 1987, Lucknow, p.156

11. IHRC Proceedings, March, 1988, Bikaner, pp.5-6.

Dr TS Banerjee, member of IHRC, appreciated the efforts of the School of Archival Studies in promoting training in Archives Keeping, which had evoked a considerable interest among Indian Universities. He referred to the proposal of Jadavpur University to set up an Archival Cell in collaboration with the State Archives of West Bengal. Suggesting that NAI should examine ways and means for modernising the training programme, he wondered why the correspondence course in Archival Science was discontinued by NAI.[12] Dr Amba Prasad suggested that a common syllabus be formulated by the NAI in collaboration with the State Archives. However, he doubted the success of such training programmes contemplated by some universities.

Therefore, he favoured a training programme which might include a course in Library Science, adding to the employment potential of the trainees. Prof Sriramamurty informed that Andhra and Annamalai Universities had recently started a course in Archival Science in cooperation with the State Archives. He also supported Muniswamy's suggestion for a re-orientation course. Dr JK Samal suggested formulating a scheme to develop Archival Cells in universities. Dr KK Sharma referred to the proposal of Meerut University for starting a course in Archival Science and sought central assistance for the same.[13]

The Secretary informed that the correspondence course was discontinued as it had not yielded the desired results. For in-service training, the School ran a number of short-term courses besides organising workshops on various aspects of Archival Science, wherein participation of different States/Union Territories are always sought. He agreed that a uniform syllabus was extremely

12. IHRC Session, 1990 Proceedings, p.2.
13. Ibid, pp.3-4.

desirable and subject could be discussed further at the meetings of National Committee of Archivists. However, he felt that universities do not have the required infrastructure and facilities for setting up archival cells and imparting practical training.[14]

Dr PP Shirodhkar, Director Goa State Archives, informed that the University of Bombay was planning to introduce a course in Archival Science and hoped that NAI would provide the material as well as its expert advice in the matter. The Secretary, IHRC, stated that universities may introduce archival courses after procuring the requisite infrastructure and expertise which was an essential component of any archival training course.[15]

Equally important is the conservation of archival heritage in the universities and the need for encouragement of active participation of the universities in the preservation of archival heritage of the country. The establishment of Archival Cells required priority in the universities, with proper infrastructure for the exchange of material of interest on microfilms, compilation of reference media and records on subjects of regional or local interest. Regular interaction between archivists and historians could also help achieve the objectives of establishing Archival Cells in the universities.[16] Gujarat Vidyapith has an Archival Cell that works under the university Department of History and Culture, and has its own building. Gujarat Vidyapith has two dedicated archival training courses—one-year certificate course in Archival Studies (for 12th pass candidates), and MPhil in Archival Studies for one year.[17]

All the three University Archives in Delhi—the University of

14. Ibid
15. IHRC 1992, Rohtak, April 1992, pp.3and6.
16. IHRC, 1997, Jabalpur, pp.129-30.
17. IHRC, Nov. 2011, Aligarh, p.203

Delhi, Jamia Millia Islamia, and Jawaharlal Nehru University—have been formally established recently. The study has discussed how these archives reflect the history and evolution of these universities, the circumstances leading to the establishment of their archives and records management practices and the reasons behind the delayed establishment of archives. To study the system of university education in India, one has to refer to public records available in the NAI and not university archives or records as they are not available in the archives of the universities. Even when they are available, they are not easily accessible for various reasons. The author's study of these archives identifies two primary reasons. Firstly, they are not part of university archives; rather they are under the control of an agency other than the archives department by virtue of their records management policies. Secondly, the available archives are not easily accessible; it took the author 3 months to get access to DU archives. Moreover, there is lack of awareness and financial support from the university authorities, historians and research scholars. This will become clearer on studying the working of these three archives. For details, please refer to the author's research paper presented at the ICA-SUV international conference at University of Salamanca, Spain, in October 2018, and published in ICA Journal, Comma.[18]

Though records of the establishment of these universities and monetary support from the government are available in NAI, their university archives hardly have any administrative records in their repository. A study of NAI records reveals the establishment of these universities, the election and nominations of members to executives, academic councils and university courts, the

18. ICA Journal 'Comma', Comma_2018_16_Gautam (2) pdf. Adobe Reader, pp.167-178.

appointment of faculties, reports from registrars of various universities, budgets and audits, sanction of land and grants and loans for the construction of buildings and other infrastructure development. Moreover, it also provides information on amendments to act and rules, ordinances, parliamentary questions, the establishment of health centres, the affiliation and setting up of colleges, the recognition of degrees, the constitution of various commissions and committees, the implementation of their recommendations and many more subjects related to problems of teachers, employees, salaries and so on.[19]

The archival science education in the universities required detailed curriculum and syllabus as developed by the School of Archival Studies and recommended by the Board of Studies. The members of the Board appreciated the syllabus revised by the SAS team and found it comprehensive and exhaustive. But they also recommended that the School should associate other universities/institutes conducting courses on Archival Studies to make the syllabus more value oriented. SAS was directed to write to them and to send copies of their syllabus to make it more uniform, dynamic and professional.[20]

Accordingly, the syllabus of the one-year diploma course was circulated to most of the universities to promote the study of Archival Science and to request their feedback and copies of their course curriculum. But the response was not very encouraging. As per the then survey done by the School, findings were quite startling. Very few institutions and universities in India offered courses such as PG Certificate Course in Archives, PG Diploma in Archives Keeping, PG Diploma in Archival Studies, PG Diploma in Archives, Documentation and Management, PG

19. Interested readers may visit the NAI website 'AbhilekhPatal' to consult online Records of Home Dept. Education Branch. At www.abhilekh-patal.in/jspui/ (viewed 25 July 2019).

20. F.No. 46-3/2006-SAS, pp. 20-21/corr. Minutes of the 10th meeting.

Diploma in Archival Science and Manuscriptology, etc. Many Departments of History in Indian universities offer only one or two papers in Archival Science, after its introduction by UGC as an optional paper in Post Graduate courses, offering MA (History in Modern India) in consultation with NAI. UGC wrote to NAI vide their letter dated 1 February 2000, F.N. 3-8/2000, (Desk, Panel/Academic), requesting NAI to develop a course outline (of a full paper of 100 marks) for consideration by the National Committee of UGC for Curriculum development in History and Archaeology. The committee had decided to introduce a number of optional courses at the MA level, including Archival Studies. Teaching one optional paper is not enough to train a professional archivist even though the curriculum was developed in consultation with NAI.[21] Many of the courses offered by these institutions and universities imparted only theoretical knowledge, whereas the role of an archivist also demands practical experience. This issue has also been examined during the field visits to various universities.

Besides the SAS, some of the colleges offering UG/PG/other related courses in archival science were Gujarat Vidyapeeth, Ahmedabad, Annamalai University, Tamil Nadu, Gandhigram Rural Institute, Gandhigram, Osmania University, Hyderabad, Pondicherry University, Pondicherry, Maharishi Dayanand Saraswati University, Ajmer, and Heritage Society of Kerala.*

However, these universities provide theoretical knowledge only. For practical training, they have contact programmes of one

21. NAI. F.N. 1-8/2001-SAS, pp 17-20/corr.

*On checking websites of these 7 universities, to my utter surprise, found that except 3 university of Osmania and Kerala Heritage Society none of the other universities are running these courses. Tumkur University has introduced one specialisation paper since 2018-19as per UGC Scheme. The project study gives an idea of the current status of Archival Science Education in India in chapter 6 and 7 based on field survey and online survey conducted under the project study.

or two months' duration with some local archival institutions, which, again, is insufficient for gaining expertise in the subject. The training offered at the SAS was found comparatively more comprehensive and intensive.

The German Foundation had also conducted a study in 1987-88 regarding the utility of the one-year diploma course offered at SAS, having sponsored a number of foreign students for archival training at NAI. During the survey, they received some suggestions from the participating countries:

- The period of training is too short as there is a lot of training material to be studied.
- Foreign students need time to acclimatise themselves to New Delhi before starting to study.
- The NAI course is more relevant to tropical countries in Asia and Africa and more emphasis should be given to conservation and reprography.
- NAI should offer an MA programme by affiliating SAS to an Indian university.
- Computer related archival programs should be introduced at NAI.
- The conservation component of the training was exceptionally good, especially the part of Preservation and Conservation of Documents.
- It was acknowledged that in some African Countries, the services of archival institutions would not have been good had the SAS not trained their archival personnel.

Since the findings of the above survey had been relevant NAI noted them all and even implement some. The academic environment involving the concerned officials in theoretical dissertations is limited as the SAS is not situated within a university system and only meets the archival needs of government and non-government offices. The demand for trained archival personnel is less due to the limited number of archival institutions in India. The profession of an archivist is usually not preferred and many people even look down upon it.

To make the archival education more relevant and up to date, it was necessary to introduce the study of Information and Communication Technology and business archives. Based on the suggestions of all the stakeholders, the SAS reviewed and scientifically restructured the curriculum in 2006 to emphasise the use of Information Technology for teaching, practical work and hands-on training. The course has also been opened for post-graduates in disciplines other than history. The course now includes four compulsory core papers on Archives Administration, Public Records Management, Conservation and Reprography, and Information and Communication Technology (ICT). There are two Optional/Specialisation papers on Business and Private Archives, and Archival Libraries and Documentation. Most of the students prefer specialising in Business and Private Archives for better employment opportunities as there are many archives being established by business and corporate houses, like banks, public sector undertakings, etc. Every student has to complete a dissertation on archival sources on any topic of their interest. It is aimed at preparing them to serve, help and guide research scholars in future, and help them understand how to conduct research, write synopsis, use published material in the library, find aids to access archival material for research work, collect material, classify them and write their dissertation including different chapters, bibliography and other relevant details. The course also includes a few lectures on Research Methodology. Many of the students have produced theses at par with MPhil programme as these dissertations are evaluated by university professors who also hold viva and award marks accordingly.

The current Curriculum Transaction Methodology includes theory lectures, practical work, written assignments, field-study of any two state/business archives, guest lectures (30 per cent), and workshops on latest trends in Indian history/ archives management information technology, conservation, technology for archival storage and reproduction and seminars on historical/archival themes.

Archival Science is a technical-scientific field of study, comparable to any other academic discipline. It is closely related to History, Religious and Family Institutions, Political Science, Business and Management Studies, Contemporary history, International Affairs, Information and Library Science and more to the scientific institutions because of their emerging archives. The subject touches almost all the areas of education and development including industry, labour, agriculture, applied sciences, multimedia, trade and commerce and many more. It can be studied both as an independent subject of study as well as an inter-disciplinary subject of study, as has been taken up in the West and China in particular.

However, the Indian system of Archival education in India and universities is facing a crisis. The study of Archival Science needs to be promoted in the country being one of the most neglected areas of study. Hence, raw data was collected in an online survey and personal interactions using two methods, questionnaire method and field work.

The data has been collected to ascertain the present status of archival science education and training requirements based on the existing public archival repositories of Central/State governments and universities, and other institutions in public and private/corporate sector, in addition to newly emerging archives in all areas.

Accordingly, two sets of questionnaires[22] were developed, the first was meant for the established archives in the public and private/corporate sector and the second for the archives and universities imparting archival education and training from under-graduation to post-graduation level, offering Diploma, MPhil or PhD programmes. The survey questionnaire was circulated to archival experts and students, university department of History and their professors and students, Vice Chancellors and Registrars of various universities, Archives of Centre/States/UTs, Central/State University Departments of History teaching Archival Science in consultation with Director General, NAI, and Registrar, National Museum Institute (Deemed University). Approximately, 30 institutions responded out of more than 300 institutions addressed.[23] Though it yielded only 10 per cent response efforts were made to supplement the information during the field work through personal interactions with the students, professors and officials in the State Archives, by visiting various Universities, State Archives and other institutions.

Though the responses to the questionnaire were limited, they came from significant and varied institutions with different nature of records, and express their concern for their basic requirement of expertise and skills to be developed through the training programmes. Many of them have also commented upon the training programme of NAI—its utility, weaknesses and strengths, suitability for Business/Corporate Archives, and if it needed any changes under the UGC scheme. The responses and observations received have been briefly analysed with comments

22. Sample Questionnaires; please see Annexure - 8, along with letter of recommendation from DG, NAI and Registrar, National Museum Institute (Deemed University).

23. Please see Appendix A and B at the end of the chapter with comments and observations.

and observations, and later summarised under Findings of the Project in Chapter VII.

The responses have been classified under 5 main categories as per the grouping of the institutions. These categories are (1) Government Archives, (2) Banking and Corporate Archives, (3) Institutional Archives of the Universities and Colleges, (4) Archives of Defence Departments and Autonomous Bodies, (5) Archives of Scientific Institutions besides upcoming Gender Archives (Gender archives as briefed under Field work). The QAMRA Archives, or the upcoming Queer Archive for Memory Reflection and Activism, is a gender and sexual minorities archive in India. It is a physical archive, located in Bangalore. While preserving memories through collecting and collating multimedia material, the archive aims to be a living one, creating and furthering activism around gender and queer issues. The idea of this archive emerged from the audio/video material that Miss Jayshree, In-charge Archives, had been collecting since 2001. The material in QAMRA is about the public history of the movement, while focusing on the private lives of individuals. Hopefully, this archive will serve both as a repository of collective memory and platform for collective action.

The information based on these questionnaires was sought on the following broad parameters: location, status of the institution, their clientele, the kind of records/collections they hold and preserve, quantum, qualifications and recruitments, basic skills and training, skill enhancement programmes, facilities for in-house training or through outsourcing, pre or post appointment training, etc.

The parameters for second questionnaire were: the kind of courses offered by the University/Institution, its length and duration, the target group, nature of certification/Diploma awarded, eligibility criteria and the course contents. It also sought information on evaluation methods, the extent of emphasis on reprography, digitisation and conservation using both conventional and modern methods of preservation and storage. Additionally, the questionnaire addressed the intake of students and the nature of faculty, whether outsourced by inviting experts/specialists of the subjects, historians, scholars, etc., their teaching methodology, lecture/practical methods, field and project studies, available infrastructure, use of modern methods of teaching, funding, etc. as has been grouped and briefed under respective groups. The comments and observations have been summarised along with the activities of the institutions. Before listing out the findings and recommendations, including the Training Scheme of NAI, observations have been reviewed, analysed and discussed in the chapters of the project study. The important observations of other institutions are noted in Chapters VI and VII under Findings.

Current Status of Archival Education in Government Archives and Universities

The nature and functioning of all government archives are same. They maintain public, corporate and historical records, serving not only their own governments but also historians, research scholars and the general public. Most of the archival institutions hire their archival staff with the basic qualification of a Master's degree in History, preferably in modern India, and a one-year diploma in Archives and Records Management recognised by Union and State Public Service Commissions, Staff Selection Commission, UGC and other public and private/business archives. Most of the archivists are trained at NAI or other Archival Institutions/Universities, or have 5 years of research experience in Modern

Indian history. The course targets students who have completed Master's in Social Science or MSc in Applied or Physical Sciences from a recognised university. However, the study found that this is hardly implemented despite the qualifications been duly recognised by UGC, UPSC, and all State governments and their Public Service Commissions.

Most of the State Archives sponsor their new Assistant Archivists for training at the SAS with pay. In some of the states, like Assam, West Bengal, and Bihar, no Assistant Archivist is promoted without NAI professional training which significantly helps an archivist in preserving archives and climbing the promotional structure in their institution. Though promotion is given on the basis of seniority, higher salary is not given for higher qualification. As per their analysis, on-going training is required for the staff, in the form of short-term orientation courses, workshops and seminars.

Some of the state archives, like Kerala after recruitment through Kerala Public Service Commission, offer a six-month customised training in Epigraphy before probation since they have many manuscripts and inscriptions in their vernacular language. Many state archives also provide regular in-house training in different subjects of archival science, and particularly in records management and conservation, to equip their officers with new developments under the guidance of experts. Kerala has the Centre for Heritage Studies under the Cultural Affairs Department, State government of Kerala. Even they depute their officers for training abroad in digitisation and conservation by signing MoUs.

All the archives are found to be running short of staff as recruitments are not regular as per the requirements, be it the National Archives, State archives, or any public or private archival institution. Most of the recruitments are either contractual or project-based, offering no incentives to the contractual Archival Assistants. These Archival Assistants are performing the duties of professional archivists trained from the SAS, and are well versed in the field of Archives Administration, Records Management, Conservation and Reprography, Business Archives and Information and Communication Technology (ICT).

Information and Communication Technology (ICT) requires every Archivist to cope with the latest trends in e-office, electronic records and digitisation work done on a large scale in all the archival repositories. Though there is a core paper on ICT under the NAI training scheme, they need to upgrade the curriculum and start a specialisation course in ICT.

Besides NAI and Kerala Heritage Society, Osmania University is also conducting PG diploma course in Archival Science and Manuscriptology in collaboration with Telangana State Archives, customised for the State Archives and other State government offices. The course was started in 1975 with 12 seats, 6 for private candidates and 6 for sponsored candidates from within the University, State Archives and other State government and other offices. The syllabus includes 4 Papers:

1. Archival Science, Theory and Practice
2. Manuscriptology, Theory and Practice
3. Indian Art
4. Indian History

The theory classes are held in the Department of Archaeology, in the University College of Arts and Social Science, Osmania University. For practical classes, the department has collaborated with Telangana State Archives. The Director of Telangana State Archives also delivers lectures on Archival Theory and Practice, and coordinates practical classes in Telangana State Archives. With only one regular faculty, they rely heavily on retired professors to work as guest teachers on honorary basis. The expenses are equally split between the University and the State Archives. There is no scholarship or hostel facility for the students. However, there is a Placement Cell to help in the deployment of trained diploma holders and archivists within the state.

The curriculum is old and does not include any of the modern theory and practices of archives management, like ICT, digitisation or e-Records and their management. The course is customised for their local requirements as majority of archival records of Nizam Darbaar and Osmania University are in Persian as per their holdings kept in Telangana State Archives and University Library. The holdings in the library are old collections of printed books and reports of the Nizam Administration on various aspects.

Barring NAI, currently there is no particular course related to archival science in any of the Indian or State universities or archival institutions, except one paper titled Archives and Museums, under UGC Scheme. The paper was introduced in 2016 in many universities and colleges as BA (Hons) and BA (Programme) under CBCS (Choice Base Credit System) of University Education. It comes under skill enhancement course in CBCS where a student has to choose the paper in 2nd year (3rd Semester). The syllabus in the University of Delhi includes:

I. Definition of Archives and Museums, history of development of Archives and Museums (including special case studies with reference to India).
II. Types of Archives and Museums:
    - Understanding the traditions of preservation in India, collection policies, ethics and procedures.

- Collection: field exploration, excavation, purchase, gift and bequests, loans and deposits, exchanges, treasure trove confiscations and others.
- Documentation: accessioning, indexing, cataloguing, digital documentation and de- accessioning.
- Preservation: curatorial care, preventive conservation, chemical preservation and restoration.

III. Museum presentation and exhibition.
IV. Museums, Archives and Society: Education and communication outreach Activities.

For outreach activities, the college students are engaged in various visits to archival repositories and in-house seminars with experts on Archives and Museums.

The prescribed syllabus is sketchy and needs a revision and upgrade. Teaching should be introduced in Modular Form in consultation with SAS, NAI. The syllabus focuses more on Museums than the Archival Studies. Besides stressing equally on both the subjects, it needs to include the study of subjects like Digital Archiving. For practical purposes, they must develop their university and college archives. They need to mobilise resources for college archives and approach UGC and NAI for grant-in-aid. Since the institutions are not funded adequately, they need to be selective in their preservation and development of archives.

Various universities offer courses at PG level in Museum and Archaeology, but there are none on Archival Science. There is a need to develop proper course curriculum at PG and post PG level, giving equal weightage to Archival Studies as well. There is a hidden academic linkage with NAI for teaching history courses. However, a formal linkage is required by formally signing

MoUs with individual colleges for providing certificate courses. Additionally, in case the UGC provides financial support for professional courses taught under the CBCS as part of regular History course, these colleges can tie up with the NAI.

There is only one paper, Archives and Museums, and the objective is to make the students familiar with the basic structure and functioning of archives and museums in India. The trained students will be able to examine these archival repositories of history from close quarters, contextualise the way in which museums are organised and managed, and examine the considerations governing the organisation of exhibitions in museums. The students are assessed on the basis of assignments and projects involving visits to the archives and museums.

Tumkur University, Tumkur, Karnataka

The Tumkur University has been conducting the course in MA History, and has introduced a one-year Specialisation paper on Introduction to Archival Studies for 2nd Semester from the academic year 2018-19, under the UGC scheme. The paper offers a basic introduction to Archival Studies for only one semester, including introduction to archives, types of archives, principles of archives management, conservation and reprography, etc. The paper targets students doing MA, and is treated as a part of MA course in History and Archaeology. These courses are of PG level, recognised by the State and UGC. Though there is no eligibility criteria for the course, history and/or archaeology are a compulsory component of the MA course.

Archival Studies is a single paper. Its syllabus is created to offer preliminary information to the students. At the base of the syllabus is the course offered by the NAI and UGC model. The paper emphasises on both conventional documents and electronic records.

Internal assessment tests, seminar presentations and assignments based on syllabus and field visits are the main modes of evaluation. Reprography and Conservation are part of one unit of the syllabus and are duly taken care of. The department is still in the nascent stage of the course, but the students have shown a keen interest.

Since it is a specialisation paper, the MA students opt for it based on individual choices. Currently, there are 13 students studying this paper under only one faculty, having knowledge in Ancient Indian History and Culture (AIHC) and Archaeology and Research and work experience at the Karnataka State Archives (KSA). The KSA conducts special lectures in the department; regular visits to the KSA are mandated for all the students. The university offers regular scholarships as per the State government rules. The Conservation and Reprography labs are yet to be developed. The KSA has provided specific grants for organising workshop on Research Methodology for SC/ST PhD scholars in 2017. In collaboration with the KSA, the department also organises exhibitions in the university.

As per the survey study, only Tumkur University has introduced this paper at PG level. While other universities also need to introduce this paper, the UGC has to ensure that Archival Studies is a single paper in itself. Practicals involve only visits to archives, which is insufficient. The students should have more activities with hands-on training in all fields of archival science.

School of Cultural Texts and Records (SCTR), Jadavpur University

The university is not teaching the subject currently but is keen on introducing and teaching Archival Science in the department of History. The university's department of History is also developing its own collection of private papers.

The School of Cultural Texts and Records (SCTR) is an interdisciplinary school in Jadavpur University, Kolkata. It has two units: Text Archive and Music Archive. The archive focuses on Bengali cultural material; thus, it is mainly based on private records. The archive stores some primary material, which is digitised and returned to the custodians of the material. The digital copies of such material are kept in the archive. Fellows at SCTR are recruited on temporary basis, as per the availability of project funds. With no permanent archivist/staff at SCTR, the total strength stands at 20. Fellowships usually begin from Rs 18,200 and go up till (depending on project budget and funds) Rs 25,000. The project fellows, with the minimum qualification of Master's degree, are recruited only for the duration of the project period. Some of the students, trained in the Digital Humanities and Cultural Informatics (DHCI) course offered by the archive, also work as fellows at the archive. Since the archive is a part of the university, offering a regular training course (DHCI) to students, there is a fairly consistent availability of trained archivists. Generally, the recruited fellows are former students of the university or former students of the DHCI course. Some projects have provisions for training workshops at the beginning of the project.

The DHCI course provides training not only to prospective fellows but also to students in general. If untrained persons are engaged in archiving projects related to Humanities and Social Sciences, they require foundational knowledge. Hence, basic introduction is given at the beginning of a project. Both the options are implemented, depending on the workflow of the project. However, external training through sponsored programmes outside the university are rare. Funds are limited at SCTR and do not covers travel expenses or related costs.

SCTR offers UGC approved one-year PG diploma course in Digital Humanities and Cultural Informatics with digital archiving in the curriculum. Though there are no hostel facilities for outstation candidates, the DHCI course provides thorough training. The one-year course started in 2013, but several workshops were held even before the course started. It's a stand-alone PG diploma course targeting MPhil and PhD scholars, as well as independent researchers. The course aims at:

- Conceptualising humanities research in the context of new digital technology
- Acquisition and processing of material (digitisation, metadata, tagging, mark-up)
- Organisation (system and platform architecture, information structure, systems of classification etc.)
- Data mining and processing (creating and optimising search engines, performing programming operations, querying data, generating results)
- Communication and presentation (user/community interaction, interface, front-end applications, standards).

No particular subject/discipline is compulsory for the course. The papers offered are:

1. Conceptualising the Digital Humanities,
2. The Photograph and its Digital Surrogates,
3. Digital Music Archiving,
4. Student Project

The course focuses on the practical aspects of archiving and data creation. Hence, students learn through hands-on assignments from the beginning of the course. They are encouraged to attend all the classes and participate in the hands-on sessions. Students learn operating camera/scanners and other necessary equipments, and handling fragile documents. Outreach activities include seminars, workshops, and student-led projects. The student intake is 25, and the faculty is sourced from disciplines, such as Humanities, Computer Science (Programming), Social Science, Library Science, and Archival Studies. Their current tie-ups are with Victoria Memorial, Maulana Abul Kalam Azad Institute of Asian Studies, and academic collaboration with international universities, such as the University of Exeter. Equipped with a reprographic unit and a library, SCTR is self-sponsored although it did receive grant from the UGC initially. Being a job-oriented course, SCTR offers job opportunities when projects are available.

SCTR needs to popularise its course to widen the scope of deploying trained personnel in the country's audio-visual/sound archives, like All India Radio and Doordarshan, along with television archives, multimedia archives of various government and private channels, National Film Archives of India, Pune, Archives of Indian Music, Bangalore, and many more.

Banaras Hindu University (BHU), Central Library

Banaras Hindu University does not offer any course in Archival Science nor does it have a centralised university archive.[24] Rather, it has a decentralised system for the official records where each department in the university maintains its archives. Central Library, BHU, has a dedicated section for manuscripts and rare collections which are duly preserved and conserved. The Central Library of BHU is one of the depository libraries in the country to receive the government and United Nations publications

24. BHU has introduced only recently MA in Archival Studies and Management a 2-years degree course at the PG level. Website https://www.bhu.ac.in, cite visited on 13th June 2024.

for free. Moreover, it maintains an Institutional Repository to maintain and provide easy access to the knowledge produced by the university. The archival records are maintained by individual departments, and hence are spread across university under the maintenance of the regular university staff. The university has a MoU with the National Mission for Manuscripts (NMM), under Ministry of Culture, and it provides trained professionals to the Central Library for conserving the manuscripts and rare documents of BHU. The Central Library has developed Mahamana Madan Mohan Malviya (founder of BHU) Digital Library and Mahamana Archives. However, the university does not teach the subject of Archival Science.

Punjab University, Chandigarh

Like BHU, the Punjab University also does not teach the subject of archival science, but is keen on developing a training unit in Punjab for the Northern states. They developed an archival cell for the Punjab University in 1981 under the UGC Scheme, in the premises of Punjab University Library as referred earlier.

The cell is not responsible for collecting any official records of the university. The university cell has a significant collection of rare books, and is managed by a trained Assistant Archivist with a pay scale of Rs 15,600-39,100+5,400, as per the UGC norms. The archival cell staff is a part of the Library Staff as per the UGC Scheme. However, the university now wants to have the cell as a separate unit from the Library.

There are currently no promotional avenues available. However, a proposal is being processed with the UGC to grant a separate identity to the Archival Cell and to offer avenues for its growth, similar to the provisions available for Teachers/ Librarians. The matter has been referred to the UGC, as recommended by the Punjab government. The staff is limited as there is no professional growth without the development of the cell. With the expansion of the cell, training will be taken up within the university programmes. In February 2019, the University Archival Cell received a grant of Rs 8 Lakhs under the NAI grant-in-aid scheme, with the amount disbursed in a 6:2 ratio between NAI and PU for developing the archival cell.

Currently, the university is not running any academic programme in archival science. The cell has recently received a sanction of Rs 50 Lakhs from the Board of Finance, Punjab University, to set up the archival cell on the 5th Floor of the University Library. They will also try to seek financial support from the Indian Council of Historical Research (ICHR) and UGC.

Delhi University (DU) Archives

Delhi University Archives was formally established in 2006, in a heritage building known as Viceregal Lodge. With the renovation of the Lodge, being a heritage building, DU decided to reorganise and relocate the university's archival material while commemorating 150 years of Indian Revolt of 1857. It collects old official records and private papers, including written and visual records. There was one Assistant Archivist, who has now retired without any replacement. With the post of Archivist lying vacant, it is presently looked after by the Dean/Registrar office while the students help with the record keeping. However, the teaching faculty was temporarily entrusted with the task. Dr Basara trained the students while they worked as interns, working on modules to develop the University Archives and Museum. They will prefer to approach the NAI for training purposes, as it can also provide funds to the university.

The paper in Archival Studies is being taught under BA

(Hons) history and BA (Programme) level, under CBCS, as a part of the course since 2016. It targets the undergraduate students of BA (Hons) and BA (Programme) with history as their subject at graduation level. The course is under revision since it offers only generic information citing some examples. However, hands-on experience cannot be provided through examples. There are written tests and student projects for evaluation.

The University Archives, with no Reprography or Conservation unit, does not teach the subject in depth. But, they do emphasise on preservation. Outreach activities will commence when certificate courses are offered to regular students like other courses of BA (Hons) and BA (Programme) with history/social science. The student intake falls in the range of 10-40. Most of the faculty is drawn from History department. There is no tie up with NAI or National Museum, although the students do visit them as a part of their study visit/tour. There is no regular or visiting faculty. Courses are job-oriented. Delhi University has also initiated digitisation of its records that are made available online by its own reprographic/computer unit. The funds were provided by the university. Currently, there is no other programme. They need to develop a proper curriculum at the PG level. They need to give weightage to Archival Studies as a discipline and introduce courses at undergraduate and post graduate level.

University Archives, Gujarat Vidyapith, Ahmedabad

Gujarat Vidyapith was established in 1920 by Mahatma Gandhi, and it later became a deemed university in 1963. The archive of Gujarat Vidyapith is under the control of Department of History and Culture. Prof (Dr) Mehebubbhai Desai is the Head of the Department and Dr Binduvasini Joshi, Associate Professor, is the Head of Archives, being a trained Archivist from the SAS. The rich archive holds private papers of Morarji Desai, it's first Vice Chancellor(VC), along with collections of other VCs, Congress Kranti Samiti, papers relating to Vidyapith, its publications, conference collections and their proceedings, periodical journals and other papers. They have a Conservation Lab and Reprography services in its Library.

The department of History and Culture of the Gujarat Vidyapith runs an MPhil programme, but only when there are students enrolling for the course. Vidyapith needs to revive the course and introduce the specialisation paper on Archival Science as per UGC Syllabus since they have the faculty to teach the paper at the MA level.

University of Hyderabad

Though the university does not offer any course in Archival Science, the university library has full-fledged Conservation Laboratory, Reprographic Unit, functional library, etc. to complement the library requirements as reported by Mr K Chaudhury. The department of History of the Hyderabad University should initially introduce the course approved by UGC on Archival Sciences. Similarly, Ms Sreeti Das, PhD Scholar, Hyderabad Central University, has reported that the university does not offer any such course.

Archives of Autonomous Bodies under Ministry of Culture and other Bodies

Indira Gandhi National Centre for the Arts (IGNCA)

IGNCA is an autonomous government body, fully funded by the government resources. They also get project-based funding from the NAI under grant-in-aid schemes. They have over 2.5 lakhs microfilmed and digitised copies of manuscripts in different languages and scripts, over 25 collections of private papers of eminent persons, out of print rare books, and over 1 lakh visuals on Indian Art collected from various sources, including mask and puppet collections. All these collections are looked after by trained archivists/personnel. IGNCA have their own building* divided into Kalanidhi, Janapada, Sampada, Kalakosa and Kaladarsana repositories. Besides regular staff, they have professionals, scholars and technicians and clerical staff. They deploy scholars and trained professionals from national/state level institutions for the projects as per requirement. Working in IGNCA is an enriching work experience as one learns on the job. The skills are further sharpened through workshops and seminars. IGNCA also sponsors professional staff for training in India and abroad. They have also helped new aspirants to get jobs in leading institutions in India.

Since 2018, IGNCA has been conducting 7 PG Diploma and Certificate Courses in Art, Culture and related subjects, recognised by UGC. They have PG diploma in:

1. Cultural Informatics
2. Preventive Conservation
3. Buddhist Studies
4. Digital Library and Data Management
5. Manuscriptology and Palaeography
6. Cultural Management
7. South-East Asian studies

But none of the above course caters to archival science, except the course in preventive conservation. These courses are professional, job-oriented courses where due weightage is given

* IGNCA is currently located at Janpath Building, near Western Court), Janpath, New Delhi-1. (shift to footnote on pg 294)

to study of Reprographics, and practical assignments are given for evaluation. They have in-house faculty from the department of Library science, Information and Communication Technology, Conservation, in addition to museum experts, photography experts, and dedicated scholars in the field of Indology. IGNCA has signed a number of MOUs with 25 leading academic and cultural Institutions and universities to collaborate, and share resources and expertise in various disciplines. They have both regular and visiting faculty as well as the desired infrastructure, including a full-fledged Conservation Laboratory, Reprographic Unit, functional library, etc. to take care of archival holdings.

Vrindavan Research Institute (VRI)

VRI is a Non-Government Organisation, registered under the Societies Registration Act of 1860. The VRI preserves manuscripts, Farmans and archival material in addition to its own official records. Their conservation staff is trained from NAI and other government institutes. VRI receives financial grants from Ministry of Culture, government of India, and Department of Culture, State government of Utter Pradesh. Though no qualified Archivist has been employed in VRI so far, they do have a Manuscript Conservator with the supporting staff. They have 29 staff, recruited as per VRI recruitment and Service Rules, with minimum qualification of Intermediate with Science at substantive level. The pay scales are in accordance with the government of Utter Pradesh and the VRI pay scales.

VRI provides in-service training and organises manuscripts conservation workshops and short-term training programmes.

The technical staff of conservation section is duly trained and has proven its efficiency time and again. The new employees get a general in-house training in manuscript conservation besides being sent to NAI and National Research Laboratory for Conservation of Cultural Properties (NRLC) in Lucknow for a specialised training. VRI needs archival training for its technical staff because now they have several artifacts in the Braj Culture Museum.

The VRI conducts manuscript conservation workshops under experts from NAI, NRLC, and NMM, besides its own experts. They are also planning to start a diploma course in the future.

Archives of Scientific Institutions

Archives of National Centre for Biological Sciences (NCBS), Bangalore

An archive of NCBS has been established as both an institutional archive and a collecting archive for the history of contemporary Biology in India. The Archives keep copies of official records as a secondary source. The original official records of its parent organisation, Tata Institute of Fundamental Research (TIFR), are most likely at TIFR or the Department of Atomic Energy. But the Archives at NCBS are primarily a public collecting archive for the private manuscripts and related materials of individual scientists and engineers. These are not institutional or corporate records. By March 2019, Archives had collected approximately 65 linear feet of papers kept in the NCBS. They have one contract staff and a host of project assistant/interns. Since they are contract staff, there is no salary range. Currently, they have no plans for hiring trained regular persons.

There is not enough data to assess the changes or future plans regarding the requirement and availability of trained archivists. NCBS has trained about 35 student interns from 10+ levels from various disciplines over the course of one year. They are trained not to be future archivists, but to be sensitive to historical contexts in their subject areas, from science to law, and design to journalism. They are taught archiving methods, including provenance, original order, handling disordered manuscript collections, developing finding aids, accessioning, arrangement, description, preservation and access, in keeping with archival description standards, compliance with ISAD (G), metadata structures, and others. It was noted that student's discipline does not matter as much as the intent and clarity of thought regarding the historical context of the material. The trained interns are from disciplines of basic sciences, law, education, journalism, literature, design, and biotech. One of the best things here is that the students learn archiving while working, something that can be experimented by other Archives too.

NCBS collaborate with a variety of individuals and archives in India and abroad to get up to date details on archival methods as well as preservation/conservation practices. For instance, the British Library will be setting up a digitisation standards workshop at NCBS archives. NCBS had a conservation practices roundtable hosted by a conservator from **Chhatrapati Shivaji Maharaj Vastu Sangrahalaya** (CSMVS) in 2018. They had also participated in online conferences with various archives around the world for conversations on description standards, and tools. Due to shortage of funds, conference visits had been partially supported in a limited and discretionary manner.

Though NCBS is not deploying formally qualified persons, the Archives would like to hire 2-3 permanent staff members in the near future. They are keen to acquire Degree/certification personnel and would definitely be interested in availing programmes offered by the Society of American Archivists, ICA, etc.

NCBS archives have developed over two years. Now they have an internship programme, a reading material list, on-site orientation, and specific project deliverables. It is not meant to train people formally as professional archivists, but works well as a mentoring/apprentice programme.

There is need to have an organised archival community for sharing resources and ideas through common mailing groups and likewise. Though there are many online resources today for individual queries, especially around archival arrangement, description, and conservation practices, but the Indian community appears to be spread out with insufficient routine interaction.

Indian Institute of Science (IISc), Bangalore

The Archives of IISc Bangalore have developed only half way through for want of trained manpower. Prof Kaushal Verma, Chairman of Archives and Publications Division, (APC) laid emphasis on the need of education and training for the upcoming archives. The IISc archive is very active in collecting and cataloguing all documents related to the history of the institute. All the work is collectively done by a small team at the archive. Though they could not significantly contribute to the study, they have provided suggestions which could be implemented. Some of these are:

- Students graduating from the NAI, or elsewhere, should be allowed to apply to various archives across the country for short-term positions. They can help the host institution in archival activities, ranging from cataloguing to digitising and scanning the collection for further use.
- A proper procedure should be followed for this purpose. For example, students applying for these positions should write a proposal to be evaluated by the host institute. Funding should be handled by a centrally authorised office. These positions can be modelled after projects are granted by the funding agencies.

Archives of Indian Institute of Astrophysics (IIA), Bangalore

While developing its archives, the IIA drafted its Collection Policy to address different preservation issues. The institute has naturally inherited the Library and Records of Madras and Kodaikanal Observatories, the forerunners of the IIA. The collections have now grown and have over 5,000 items of historical importance in various formats such as Manuscripts, Photographs, Maps, Films and Awards, framed material, hand drawn sketches, pictures and instruments that are environmentally sensitive. The oldest document dates back to 1792. Apart of a collection is also displayed aesthetically in a museum, in a room adjacent to the Library in the IIA. They have also digitised Madras MS Records dating back to 1794-1812 and 1795-1800. The collections highlight the role played by various astronomers and Directors of their parent Observatories. They are looking forward to procure trained manpower from NAI.

Banking and Corporate Archives

Central Archives of the Reserve Bank of India (RBIA)

Central Archives of the Reserve Bank of India was established in the campus of the College of Agricultural Banking in Pune on 24 August 1981. It houses the non-current permanent records of the RBI as a Central Repository of the Reserve Bank located in different parts of the country. Dr R L Sahoo is the Chief Archivist, Deputy General Manager, assisted by specialist officers, Archivists, Assistant Archivists, Chemists, Assistant Librarians and other supporting officers and staff of the Bank in general cadre. The RBIA functions under the Department of Economic and Policy Research, Central Office, RBI, Mumbai. Its functions include scientific preservation of records, photographs and paintings. It has records of historical and legal value, transferred after 12 years for scientific preservation. Besides other means for repair and preservation of brittle and fragile records, they have Vacuum Fumigation Chamber too. The Archives also maintain an archival library consisting of RBI publications, such as books, reports, journals, manuals, brochures etc. They prepare reference media of records and publications for access and retrieval. RBIA works as a nodal agency in records management in the bank, and monitors the implementation of the Archival and Records Management Policy (ARMP) in all departments and offices of the RBI. They preserve oral history recordings, organise exhibitions on the history of the bank and digitise and microfilm records. The RBIA gives access to scholars as per the RBI Historical Research Rules, 2001, to non-current records which are more than 30 years old. The RBIA also has an Archives Museum.

RBIA regularly organises workshops and training programmes for training the officers of RBI in various cadres. The objective is to create awareness about the importance of archives and records management, and to familiarise the participants with the internal guidelines on records management. It provides a platform to discuss the Archival and Records Management Policy (ARMP) of the Bank so that the records management activities are streamlined.

It also provides professional guidance to outside institutions. The RBI should develop modules for training the archival community of the banking sector to promote bank archiving and digital preservation.

Godrej Archives

Godrej Archives is under Corporate Human Resource Department of Godrej and Boyce Mfg Co Ltd, and is responsible for collecting official records besides private and corporate historical records. The Archive Collection, as on 1 April 2019, consists of over 1,500 product catalogues, 50,000 photographs, 1,500 objects, around 1,00,000 documents and over 300 oral history interviews. Their staff consists of two professionals trained in Archival Science, one in Museology and Library and Information Science, and two in Scanning and Conservation.

The institution recruits and determines the promotional criteria for archivists in consultation with the Chief Archivist on contractual basis with a salary ranging between Rs 25,000-35,000 (depending on the level of experience). Employee promotions are given as per the policy of the parent organisation. There is no separate recruitment policy for the archives. People with the minimum qualification of post-graduation, preferably in History/Library and Information Science/Museology, are eligible to work in Archives.

Godrej Archives has observed that it is difficult to find trained Archivists fit to work in corporate Archives, hence they provide training on the job. They also send some team members for training in fields, such as NAI short-term training courses in Archival Science, Conservation, and Digitisation etc. as is required. They do not prefer to hire trained archivists.

The organisation encourages training the staff since there is a dearth of adequately trained people. Training in History, Museology or Library and Information Science has proved useful for the Godrej Archives and Museum. The employees receive a foundational introduction to Archival work and its various processes on the first day of their service, following which they are trained in each function on rotation basis for few days. Induction training is given in the beginning following a formal structure. Unlike a diploma course, their training is need-based, although the staff is sent for training in areas such as Museology (locally available), and Conservation (across the country). The organisation supports the training through institution as they have sufficient funds. They also promote and support archivists without a formal degree or a certificate who wish to work for an Institution and pursue a degree or certificate course with the support of the institution through their 'leave for education' policies.

Godrej Archives and Museum requires professionals trained in Archival Management, Conservation and Digitisation. Every year funds are allotted for training in archives and the organisation supports the training as they do not hire trained archivists. They have hired professionals trained in History, Library Science, and Museology from the Universities within Maharashtra. Training in History, Museology or Library and Information Science has proved useful for their archives and museum.

DCM Shriram Archives and Heritage Gallery DCM

DCM Shriram Archives and Heritage Gallery is located in Shriram Hostel Campus, Shriram Nagar, Kota (Rajasthan), as an independent Archive. They are responsible for collecting official records besides private and corporate historical records. The total numbers of records are approximately 17,000 including Files, Published Reports and in-house publications, Industrial Drawings, Souvenir, Books, Memoirs, Biographies, Photographs, Memorabilia etc. housed in a repository covering 4000 sq ft area.

The working professionals here include one Archivist, with PG Diploma in Archives and Records management from SAS, and one Consultant (Retd Assistant Director of Archives, NAI). They have recently recruited one archivist; hence they have two regular and one professional consultant on contractual basis. As per the company policy, they have not shared any salary range. The minimum prescribed qualification is diploma in Archival Studies. However, depending upon requirement, candidates with a diploma or short-term course in Records Management, Preservation or background in Business Archives could also be considered for a position. They have hired only one person since the last five years. Archives and Records Management has adopted a systematic approach after the engagement of a professionally trained archivist from NAI, who possesses the skills required for implementing the system of records keeping and Preservation of Records on scientific lines.

Internal training programmes have been conducted for selected Archives personnels in various units of the company to familiarise them with the process of managing records. The guidelines for a systematic apprenticeship programme have been developed. The institution supports the archival profession staff in training outside the institution and offers the related facilities. Moreover, they have the funds to send new (or even experienced) employees to national professional archival meetings or training workshops sponsored by the NAI. They also invite Preservation and Conservation expert from NAI to seek guidance on preserving big industrial drawings available in the DCM Shriram Archives and Heritage Gallery.

Delhi Land and Finance Limited (DLF)

DLF Documentation Centres are located in New Delhi and Gurugram. The centre collects official records only of DLF Company. These records are Sale Agreements, Sale Deeds, and Customer Files, Accounts Ledgers, Legal Documents, Drawings, and Contract Papers kept in three places—Documentation Centre, Jhandewalan, New Delhi; Documentation Centre Gurugram; and Documentation Centre, Golf Links, Gurugram. It covers more than 10,000 sq feet area.

The centre had just one Archivist, who had joined after leaving NAI, besides a Librarian and six supporting staff. These centres are a part of company office of DLF. It has a managerial system, with staff designated as Manager, Deputy Manager, Assistant Manager and attendants; etc. Their salary range is not provided. The minimum qualification is Master's in History or Library Science. However, no proper recruitment policy has been formulated to hire Archivists. Yet, the archival training has been helpful in managing records/files at the Documentation Centre in Delhi.

Currently, there is no archival trained person except one senior trained Archivist, who also trains others. They have developed a mentoring system and formal guidelines for in-house use as the records kept in the repository are property deeds, agreements, construction drawings, and site maps, etc. There is no professional training support or opportunities as the authorities do not have any interest in training.

An archive of Reddy's Laboratories, Hyderabad, is in its nascent stage as per information provided by the Archivist of Reddy's Lab. The infrastructure for the archives has not been set up so far, and the archival policy is also yet to be implemented. This archive is in a very preliminary stage.

On the basis of field survey and the feedback received through questionnaires, it is recommended to motivate all corporate houses to encourage and promote their professional staff for training in the SAS to learn to upkeep, manage, arrange and preserve records scientifically and professionally.

There is a need to refer to a study conducted by ICA in August 2017 titled 'ICA Member Training Needs Survey conducted in August 2017- Analysis of Responses' for better understanding of Archival Science and Training. As per the report analysis, there was very low participation of members—only 7 per cent, including 2 per cent of the institutional members and 12 per cent of the individual members (142 out of 2071). 68 per cent of the respondents were members of ICA. The maximum responses were from regional branches of ICA WARBICA, SWARBICA and CARBICA. The broad parameters of the study and findings are:

- Language of preferences
- Institutional support for training
- Educational levels
- Delivery preferences
- IT Literacy and Access to Technology.
- Training Subject areas
- Partnership
- Experience of ICA Training or Development

Under language preferences, 53 per cent preferred English, 24 per cent French and 14 per cent Spanish. The highest demand was for digital-related training. Out of all the ICA branches, most of them (73 per cent) preferred training in Digital Records and Archives Management, Digitisation (43 per cent), Managing Current Records (37 per cent), Legal Issues (37 per cent), and Archival Description (33 per cent). When it came to course duration, 30 per cent respondents preferred duration of 1-3 weeks, and the institutional support was accessible to 62 per cent of the respondents. The delivery of the courses got a mixed response, 70 per cent preferred face-to-face and online delivery. Moreover, advance or expert training levels were sought by 86 per cent.

The survey also found that most of the respondents had good access to technology. 95 per cent of them have individual computers, 86 per cent have adequate bandwidth and 98 per cent had reliable internet. Regions with the least reliable connection included Central Africa Regional Branch of ICA (CENARBICA) and Southeast Asian Regional Branch of ICA (SARBICA). A higher number of respondents did not have adequate bandwidth to download or stream files. 50:50 of the respondents said that access to training on mobile devices would help 84 per cent of the respondents who were IT literate. Most of them had some IT skills across a range of areas, including knowing how to use common online accounts, forms and websites.

However, in India, there are limited opportunities for partnership. Increased investment in partnership is needed for this area to grow. As per survey, only one institution offered online or face-to-face training packages that ICA members could use or adapt. The current reach of training and development is limited as only 7 per cent of the respondents had received ICA training, with around 30 per cent of them having participated in section, branch and ICA conferences and congresses.

Regarding Institutional support for training, 62 per cent of the respondents were able to access a range of institutional support for online training. The nature of support ranged from no support to paid or unpaid leave; from 3 hours per week to 1-10 day per year; to payment of participant fees from US$ 100-200 per participant to 6,000 Euros. It also included support by way of travel expenses or participation fees. The regions where respondents had the lowest rate of institutional support were Asia, Western Africa and Europe while the regions of highest rate of institutional support were Europe, Oceania, Caribbean, North, Central and South America and North America. Around 30 percent of the respondents supported the idea of sponsorship, bursaries or scholarships (from ICA or other parties) for travel and accommodation costs. Some advised that their institutions would be much more likely to fund the fees and offer leave provided the travel and accommodation costs were covered. Some (17 per cent) even requested that training fees be kept to a minimum and mooted that longer and international events (potentially like the Congress) which are more expensive, are prohibitive for them or their institutions. Hence, it was noted that the course needs be advertised well in time to allow budget planning and funding approval processes.

Appendix–A

Survey and Field Work: A Status Report of visit to various Universities and Colleges and Upcoming Archives with Some Observations

The strategy has been to cover important universities and colleges that have university archives/cell in addition to Department of History and have facilitated Archival Science education and training. The parameters of the field work were same as those in the questionnaire for online survey. The raw data has been collected through field work and online questionnaires, based on the survey conducted during the project period (March 2018-February 2020) along the following parameters:

1. Institutional Information from those having Archives/Archival Cells
2. Hiring trained people
3. Providing training within the institution or outside
4. Post appointment training outside the institution, University/ Institutions conducting courses in Archival Science.

Basic questions included are:-

- Since when they have been offering the course on Archival Science, different areas in which these courses are being offered, duration of the course etc.
- Target group of the courses
- Whether these courses are standalone or a part of other discipline, such as history
- Whether it is a Diploma or Graduation level course and if it is recognised by the UGC
- Eligibility criteria for undertaking these courses, intake of students, etc.
- Papers offered as part of these courses
- process followed for formulating or devising the syllabus
- Procedure for evaluating the syllabus contents, and provision for practicals
- Extent of emphasis on Reprography and/or conservation of documents

5. The outreach of the course
6. Nature of the faculty—whether they are specialists, researchers, qualified Archivists or historians, regular or seasonal.
7. Their tie-up/association with any other professional archives, such as NAI, State/Provincial archives or Business Archives, students field-visits or training, Internship programme,
8. Provision for full-fledged Conservation Laboratory
9. Financial support from NAI or State/Provincial or any other Business Archives

IHRC had passed resolutions recommending establishment of archives in the universities established prior to 1900 and introducing the subject of Archival Science.[1] After the fourth and fifth five-year Plan, the UGC had been funding such proposals. They had decided to assist selected universities during the sixth Five year Plan as well, vide circular letter dt 24 September 1981, NoF22-2/81(HE-II), from Secretary, UGC, to all Heads, Department of History, and also to Registrar, Punjab University(established in 1886), Chandigarh. The Archival Cell of the University is well-established, having a good collection of rare books and manuscripts. To further develop the Archival Cell, the university had also sanctioned a budget of Rs 50 Lakhs. The Archivist in-charge, Dr Mrityanjay Jha, is a product of the SAS.

As per the UGC plan for the establishment of Archival Cells in the universities, the UGC had made a provision to provide the minimum staff of an Archivist, a Chemist and other supporting staff as part of Library Cadre, along with library equipment, and chemicals etc. Though many universities tried establishing their own archives, they could establish only archival cells like Universities of Punjab, Chandigarh and Guru Nanak Dev, Amritsar, Delhi University. During the field visits, it was found that many of them were unable to sustain or maintain University Archives Cells. The Aligarh University Archives, though not fully furnished, was functional when the author visited in 2011 for conducting the IHRC session (hosted in collaboration with the Aligarh University). This is due to lack of funds and support from within the system. Many universities in India do have archives but they do not maintain university records as such. This is true in case of all the three universities in Delhi—Delhi University, Jamia Millia Islamia and Jawaharlal Nehru University, as mentioned earlier.

1. Resolutions of Indian Historical Records Commission, Vol II, 1948–73, NAI, 1979, p 74.

A visit to Guru Nanak Dev (GNDU) and other universities had similar stories to tell. A meeting with the Chairperson, Prof Amandeep, Department of History, Guru Nanak Dev University (22-24 August 2018); and Prof Radha Sharma revealed that they are not teaching anything related to archives. GNDU also has an Archival Cell established under the UGC scheme, and looked after by the Anthropology Department. It has been renamed as Khalsa Heritage Centre. They have no university records; they only keep prospectus of all the courses conducted at the University. Currently, there is no regular archivist, and the archivist appointed long back has since retired. They don't even plan to appoint someone in the near future. Many old scientific instruments are on the display, in addition to some old archaeological findings, old fossil items and artifacts found in the region. Another gallery displays coins from the sixteenth century of Muslim Rulers including the Mughals and Maharajah Ranjit Singh, along with old utensils and some musical instruments, etc. Being a state university, GNDU's Department of History has a regular problem of funding. There has been no regular recruitment for many years. For 30 students they had faculty varying from 3-5 teachers. Only recently two faculty members have been appointed on regular basis. They are teaching the history of ancient, medieval and modern India at PG level. Some of the affiliated colleges too have PG courses in History. They have 10-12 students doing PhD. There have been discussions with the Dean (Academics) of the university regarding teaching archival science and maintaining University archives with the hope that they can convince the university authorities in this regard.

The Visit to Osmania University, Telangana State Archives and Dr Reddy's Lab Archives in Hyderabad (21-23 January 2019) was a blend of hope and despair. The hopes were revived at visiting the Osmania University and meeting Chairperson Prof (Dr) RN Giridhar, Department of Archeology and Ancient Indian History. The Department is conducting PG diploma course in Archival Science and Manuscriptology since 1975, and has customised it as per the requirement of the Telangana State Archives. There are 12 seats, 6 for private candidates and 6 for sponsored candidates from within the University, State Archives and other State Government and other offices. The syllabus includes 4 Papers:

1. Archival Science- Theory and Practice
2. Manuscriptology- Theory and Practice
3. Indian Art
4. Indian History

The Department has collaborated with Telangana State Archives for practical classes. It was noted that the syllabus is very old and does not include modern theory and practices of Archives Management like ICT and Digitisation and e-Records and their management. Course is rather customised as per their local requirements; Archival Records mostly are in Persian of Nizam Darbaar and Osmania University. University Library holding include collections of printed books and Reports of the Nizam Administration on various aspects. Discussions were held with the Director of Telangana State Archives regarding the training and the undergoing digitisation project. They are able to deploy their trained archivists within the State. A meeting was held with Director, Andhra Pradesh State Archives, who are shifting their records from Hyderabad to the new Andhra Pradesh State Archives coming up at Vijayawada.

Dr Reddy's Lab Archives is still in an infant stage. They have already appointed a trained archivist from the SAS.

Mata Sundari College for Women, Delhi University, is planning to develop their college archives as developed by Indraprastha College for Women and St Stephen's College under DU. The College has also introduced a Paper under skill enhancement course 'Archives and Museums' as part of BA (Programme) and BA (Hons) under CBCS (Choice Based Credit System) of University Education at the instance of the UGC. An interaction with the students and faculty revealed that the college students need more awareness programmes as the subject appears new to them and they are unaware of its future scope.

Department of History, Punjab Historical Studies, Punjab University, Patiala, is more a Research Centre on Studies of Punjab History and Culture (visited on 24-25 February 2019) as was revealed during discussions with the Prof and Head, Dr BK Bhatti. They have nothing in the name of archives. However, they are developing a Centre of Oral Studies, as part of the Department, and have collected data of more than 500 people, including freedom fighters, history of freedom movement in the State, Praja Mandal Movement in the princely states of undivided Punjab, victims of partition of India, national and political leaders of Punjab relating to history of Punjab and India, Sikh Gurudwaras and their history, and on many more subjects, covering the period 1973-2007. The author also checked their website for details of the courses covered but they offer nothing other than some lectures on Research Methodology and Historiography to their MPhil/PhD students and introduce them to archival sources for their historical research.

The Sushant School of Art and Architecture, Ansal University, Gurugram, was also explored as author was invited as one of the speakers for the Panel Discussion on 'The Archives Today' held on 14 February 2019. A visit to the Archives of Centre of Art and Archaeology revealed that the archives are mostly related to art and artifacts found in Museums. They have digitised their collections and are maintaining the archives and antiquities available in Indian Museums and built heritage in India.

The visit too many upcoming archives, particularly of scientific institutions in Bangalore, Department of History, Tumkur University, Regional Office Library of Indian Council of Historical Research and Karnataka State Archives was quite enlightening and informative. The Archives of NCBS has been set up as a repository, dedicated to holding institutional records and records related to the history of contemporary Biology in India. The Archives aims to be a living and breathing place to understand our intertwined histories and the moving frontiers of biology. The physical and digital archive was opened to the public in February 2019. The Archives at the NCBS also offer internship programme, seeking students as interns to work with the archiving team. Deviating from the conventional methods of archiving, they believe that to archive is to collect, sort and make sense of history. It is an opportunity for them to think about the links between journalism and storytelling using archival material, web annotations, scientific research, IT law and classification of information. This is also an opportunity to spread awareness about the archival material, through design narratives and artwork. They are not necessarily looking for students specialising in the biological sciences, but invites undergraduate and postgraduate students from all disciplines—sciences, engineering, history, sociology, art, design, law, archival/library/museum studies, and theatre. Depending on their background, the range of work also changes.

The records at NCBS are primary research material, including administrative records, annotated manuscripts, maps, architectural drawings, lab notes, photographs, negatives, slides, oral histories and other electronic audio/visual material. The student is expected to be a part of a team that is helping build a new approach to physical and digital archives in the sciences.

Their future work will include systematically collecting archival material under the archives team at NCBS in the form of both conducting interviews and sourcing primary documents from other institutions. NCBS Archives also have a conservation unit.

The State Archives of Karnataka was disappointing. The Director is not a professional archivist, but is a part of Karnataka Administrative Service. Later, the author interacted with some senior officers in the State Archives and shared their experiences and practices. The Archives is short of professional staff and no efforts are being made for upgrading their skills. Despite sharing the questionnaire, the feedback was never received.

The meeting with Ms Sowmithri Rangarajan, formerly Consultant with IISc Archives, Bangalore was very fruitful. She opined that education and training is an important element but is being neglected for the want of trained manpower.

The visit to Regional Office of ICHR and its Library on 4 April 2019 was a good experience. Meeting with the Regional Director, Dr Aruni proved to be very useful as detailed discussions were held for the status of archival education in South India and the support extended by them. It is a very well stacked library for the scholars researching on the history of South India, as the scholars working in the library claimed. It has very old and rare catalogues and books for reference and historical research. However, they hardly had any information to share with the Director about the workings of archives, archival education or training.

The visit to the Department of History, Tumkur University,

was fruitful, facilitating detailed oral interaction held with Prof (Dr) US Moorthi, Chairman and Head, Post Graduate Department of History, and Dr Priya Thakur, Asst Prof teaching the Paper on Archival Science, introduced from 2018-19 as per the UGC scheme. The university has introduced, as in some other universities, two papers on Introduction of Archival Studies and of Museology in the Master's course in History since one paper cannot make a student a professional Archivist or a Museum Curator without studying the respective subject in depth. But the initiative really needs to be appreciated seeing the seriousness of the faculty and students. The interaction with the students of MA first year focused on the scope of Archives for historical research and its future scope as a profession. They provided the curriculum they are referring to and even sent their feedback to the questionnaire, which has been duly tabulated in Appendix B.

The visit to the newly emerging QAMRA archives was a new experience altogether. The QAMRA Archives, an upcoming Queer Archive for Memory Reflection and Activism, is a gender and sexual minorities archive in India. The archive aims to be a living one, creating and furthering activism around gender and queer issues. Hopefully, this archive will serve both as a repository of collective memory and platform for collective action.

The visit to the Archives of the Indian Institute of Astrophysics, IIA and discussions with Prof Arun Mangalam, Professor and Chairperson, Bangalore were equally useful and informative. The institute had developed and drafted its Collections Policy while developing archives to address different preservation issues.

The Institute has naturally inherited the Library and Records of Madras and Kodaikanal Observatories, as old as 1786, the forerunners of the IIA. They have more than 5000 items of historical importance in various formats such as Manuscripts, Photographs,

Maps, Films, and Awards, framed material, hand drawn sketches, pictures and instruments, which are environmentally sensitive.

They have also digitised Madras MS Records. They don't have any skilled manpower for documentation and maintenance of the Archives. Prof Mangalam also referred to his discussion with the then DG, Raghewandra Rao, now CEO, Museums, and Ministry of Culture. He also expressed his concern for the education and training of archivists and demanded that NAI and the Government of India should do something.

The Project Director visited Gujarat Vidyapith on 22 July 2019. After visiting the Archives, discussions were held with the faculty. The Vidyapith Archives have private papers of Morarji Desai, it's first Vice Chancellor and collections of other VCs, Congress Kranti Samiti, Papers relating to Vidyapith, its publications, conference collections and their proceedings, periodical journals and other papers. They have a Conservation Lab and Reprography services. The Vidyapith reported that no student has joined their MPhil programme since years. They may conduct the Mphil programme again only if some students opt to enroll for the course. Also had a meeting with Prof Anamik Shah, Vice Chancellor of the Vidyapith, who supported and appreciated the project. He also advised that the University Newsletter carry information about the project to spread awareness about the subject and its importance after its completion.

Gujarat Central University in Gandhinagar (visited on 22 July) does not have Department of History right now. Hence, discussions were held with other faculty members, Professors and Assistant Professors in the office of Centre for Studies in Science, Technology and Innovation, headed by Dr Shiju Sam Vargees (Head of the Department). They were also briefed about the project and its relevance and scope. The faculty was happy to learn about the scope of the subject, which was quite new for them. They expressed their desire to teach Archival Science whenever the Department of History is established in near future. Subsequently, also met the Dean of the University, Prof Sarita Agarwal, Chairperson and Professor, Centre for Studies of Economics and Planning, School of Social Sciences. She also showed interest in the subject and requested to work on the syllabus when they have plans to start the Department of History.

The visit to Gujarat State Archives on 20-23 July was not fruitful as could not meet the officiating Director or any senior officer of the Archives. Meeting was held with some junior officers and it was informed that the archive was facing acute shortage of staff. The questionnaires were shared for submission by the State Archives, but the feedback never came.

The last stretch of field work by the Project Director was conducted in Calcutta during 11-13 February 2020. The Imperial Records Department/NAI was established in Calcutta in 1891. The Project Director visited both the Universities of Calcutta and Jadavpur. But, due to some student agitation in the university, could not meet faculty of Department of History, Calcutta University. Rather, a meeting was held with the In-charge, Museum, Presidency College (Deemed University), Kolkata, who was also working to oversee development of a Museum in the Presidency College, and are planning to introduce the subject on Archival Science from the session 2020-21.

At Jadavpur University, meetings were held with the faculty of the Department of History and the Vice Chancellor, Prof Suranjan Das, who himself is an historian. The discussion was fruitful and he assured working on the introducing and teaching Archival Science in the Department of History. The Department of History is also developing its own collection of private papers.

The School of Cultural Texts and Records (SCTR), an inter-disciplinary school in Jadavpur University, is doing innovative work in the field of digital archiving. It has two units: Text Archive and Music Archive. The archive focuses on Bengali cultural material, thus it is mainly based on private records. Fellows at SCTR are recruited purely on temporary basis as per the availability of project funds. There is no permanent archivist/staff at SCTR, works on contract basis with 20 persons. Fellowships usually begin from Rs 18, 200. The highest fellowship (based on project budget and funds) is Rs 25, 000. There is no substantive hiring.

Students who had undergone training in the Digital Humanities and Cultural Informatics (DHCI) course are also offered services by the archives to work as Fellows at the archives later on.

The DHCI course offered by the archive since 2013 provides training not only to prospective fellows but also to students in general. SCTR offers UGC approved one-year PG Diploma Course in Digital Humanities and Cultural Informatics. The DHCI course targets MPhil, PhD researchers and independent researchers. The aims of the course are as follows:

- Conceptualising humanities research in the context of new digital technology.
- Acquisition and processing of material (digitisation, metadata, tagging, mark-up).
- Organisation (system and platform architecture, information structure, systems of classification, etc.).
- Data mining and processing (creating and optimising search engines, performing programming operations, querying data, generating results).
- Communication and presentation (user/community interaction,

interface, front-end applications, standards).

- The course primarily focuses on the practical aspects of archiving and data creation.
- Students are encouraged to attend all the classes and participate in the hands-on sessions.
- Students also learn how to operate camera/scanners and other necessary equipment. Most importantly, students learn how to handle fragile documents. SCTR has a reprographic unit and a library.
- Outreach programmes are through seminars, workshops, and student projects.
- Faculty is drawn from Humanities, Computer Science/ Programmer, Social Science, Library Science and Archivists.
- Currently they have tie-ups with Victoria Memorial, Maulana Abul Kalam Azad Institute of Asian Studies, and Academic collaboration with international universities such as the University of Exeter.
- SCTR infrequently offers some job opportunities itself if projects are available.
- The course received grant from UGC initially. Now it is a self-sponsored course.

The Director, West Bengal State Archives, expressed her concern regarding lack of trained archivists during the discussions held with the Project Director and Archivists on 11 February 2020. The Director also expressed her concern for non-transfer of records from various Ministries and Departments of State Governments, and the pending enactment of the Bengal Public Records Act. The State Archives also conducts 3 months training for undergraduate students besides other short-term courses in conservation. In addition to visiting the various Divisions of the State Archives and the Digitisation Units, the

Project Director also visited their new archival building keeping records of the Intelligence Branch, Public Works Department and Chancellor's Secretariat.

All the recruitments at the State Archives of West Bengal are made through State Public Service Commission and the essential qualification for such posts is Master's Degree in History. All the incumbents have to undertake a one-year Diploma Course in Archives Keeping at NAI. Other posts up to the level of Deputy Director are filled up by promotion, the base post being that of the Assistant Archivist. In case of Tamil Nadu, Andhra Pradesh, Telangana, Punjab, HP, Mizoram, Madhya Pradesh, Manipur, Nagaland, Delhi, Haryana, Sikkim, etc. these are either IAS Officers, or officers from State Provincial Administrative Services being appointed as Head of Archives. (NAI, 1995, pp. 132-33)

The Asiatic Society of Kolkata has one of the oldest collections of manuscripts and rare books in India. They have a very good Museum and Manuscript Library with a strong Conservation and Reprographic Division and a good digitisation programme in place. They organise few conservation workshops as per their activities. It is an Institute of national importance for the Ministry of Culture, engaged in promoting ancient Indian history and culture. Despite sharing the questionnaire, the feedback has not been received.

The Project Director interacted with Dr Vijoy Kumar, Ex-Director of Bihar State Archives, now heading Archives of Board of Revenue, Government of Bihar. They have Revenue Records since the seventeenth century Mughals covering more than 5000 villages. The material is very rich and not yet much explored by the scholars. He also contributed his experience by sending the feedback on questionnaire.

There was a hopeful visit to the Department of History,

Delhi University, delivering a lecture on Archives and Archival Education on 22 April 2019. It was well attended by the faculty, Prof Amar Farukhi, Prof Mahapatra, Aparna Balachandran, Asst Professor, teaching archives in addition to a good number of students of MPhil and PhD. It was noted that Archives-related lectures are delivered for research scholars of both the programmes, but the paper on Archives and Museology at Master's level is yet to be introduced. However, the same had been introduced at undergraduate level in DU affiliated colleges as per the UGC policy.

Appendix–B

Tabulated List of Central/State Archives having responded to the Questionnaires

Sr. No.	Name of the Institution/ Govt Archives	Comments/Observations on questionnaire 1 and 2	Remarks
1.1	National Archives of India	SAS, NAI, working under Ministry of Culture, has three Record Centres and one Regional Office. NAI is the custodian of the records of government of India. All the repositories are part of NAI. The staff is recruited by the Staff Selection Commission following the recruitment rules of NAI and its defined requirements. The staff includes 350 permanent and 50 contractual/outsourced personnels. The position falls under the pay level 7 as per 7th Pay Commission. There is no special consideration for higher qualifications for higher start. 35 personnel have been hired over the last five years. The minimum qualification is MA in History with specialisation in Modern India, along with desirable qualification of One-year Diploma course in Archives and Records Management or five years' research experience in Modern India. The Archival Assistants are on contract/outsourcing basis for doing the work of professional archivists who are mainly trained from SAS. The present available trainees from SAS are well versed in archival studies which include archives administration, records management, conservation and reprography, ICT and business archives. They are also being trained on ICT to cope with the present trends in the Information Technology and deal with the e-office, electronic records and digitisation work undertaken by NAI. Training is provided within the Institution at regular intervals. The department has been organising in-service training programmes for the NAI staff to professionally familiarise them with the functioning of NAI.	No comments and observations are given on the Training Scheme of NAI as has already been discussed in detail in all the Chapters of the Project Report. Observations of other institutions are important and taken note of as reflected and highlighted in Chapter VI and VII under Findings.

		The selection of Assistant Archivists other than the trainees of SAS, are mainly on the basis of their teaching and research experiences. They are offered basic archival understanding through the orientation programmes. New archival employees receive a general introduction to archival work and the various processes within the institution. The department takes care of the post-appointment training. Sufficient funds are not available to send new (or even experienced) employees to national/international professional archival meetings, or training workshops, unless sponsored. The selection process is taken care of by the Staff Selection Commission following the recruitment rules of the department. It familiarises them about the role and functioning of archives through outreach programmes conducted through workshop, seminars, exhibitions, open house programmes, CEP, etc.	
		Q. 2. It started offering Diploma Courses from 1942. The courses offered are professional-level, one-year Diploma course in Archives and Records Management and short-term courses in Archives Management (6 weeks), Records Management (two sessions, each of 4 weeks), Reprography (Two sessions, each of 6 weeks), Care and Conservation of Books, Manuscripts and Archives (Two sessions, each of 8 weeks), and Servicing and Repair of Records (Two sessions, each of 6 weeks) at a sub-professional level. Its target groups are – MA History with 50 per cent marks, MA in other streams of social science, or MSc in Applied or physical sciences with minimum 50 per cent marks from recognised university.	
		The eligibility criterion is a university degree for all short-term, professional-level courses and 10+2 for courses at sub-professional level. These courses are of great importance for working in Archives offices, Documentation centres, various offices, library, museum and related allied institutions. It is related not only to history but also to allied sciences, ie, physical science and chemical science, and conservation and information technology. The syllabus for the diploma course includes four core papers namely, Archives Administration, Records Management, Conservation and Reprography and Information and Communication Technology (ICT), and one specialisation paper to be opted from two optional papers of Business and Private Archives and Library and Documentation, and Information Studies. A Board of Studies looks after the course content on the various papers being taught and guides in all related academic activities. The Board members are nominated after every two years. The Archival Advisory Board, a statutory body under Public Records Act, 1993, also lays down guidelines for the training of Archivists. The conventional archival documents and the current e-documents are part of the syllabus. Both are crucial aspects dealing with the paper records and e-records management created in government organisations for preservation and digitisation. The same is taught to the trainees in the short-term courses and the one-year diploma courses with all updates and utility.	

		The syllabus content is prepared by the SAS staff and is finalised by the members of the Board of Studies which meets at regular intervals. Every course has practical training as an essential component. Even Reprography and Conservation of Documents are essential components, since it is specifically mentioned in the PRA 1993 and PRR 1997. Outreach of the courses are by way of advertisements in the employment news, website of NAI, brochures of SAS, etc. Student intake in the diploma course is 35, for private candidates 25 and 10 for sponsored candidates. Similar numbers of seats are in short-term courses, 25 for private and 10 for sponsored candidates. Nature of the Faculty includes 1. Archivists, 2. Microphotographists, 3. Scientific officers, 4. Historians, 5. NIC experts. The faculty has informal tie-up with different government departments and universities as they are also invited as guest faculty. Study visits are also being conducted. Scholarships are given to the students/ trainees. The courses offered are job-oriented. They have a full-fledged Conservation Laboratory, Reprographic Unit, functional library and a Computer Lab attached with the School, to complement and supplement various vistas of archival Institutions. Though funds for the School are part of the NAI Budget Provisions being made by the Ministry of Culture, Government of India, they are not sufficient.	
1.2	National Archives of India, Record Centre Bhubaneswar	The setup functions as a Record Centre of NAI, HQ in Delhi, under Ministry of Culture. The mandate is to acquire non-current, 25 years old records of Ministries/Department/ PSUs/corporate/commissions and other autonomous bodies of Indian government located in Eastern India after their appraisal. They have approximately 1,10,000 files, registers, loose documents, palm-leaf manuscripts, and rare books, etc. They have one Asst Director and two Archivists, out of which one archivist is a diploma holder in archival studies. All three of them have PhD degree in history. Conservation staff (6) is outsourced. Controlled by NAI, they have regular staff though five posts are vacant. The staff falls under the Pay Matrix Level 7, and their minimum qualification is MA in Modern Indian History, with a desirable qualification of Diploma in Archival Studies. There has been no hiring during the last 5 years. Though more trained archivists are available now, they are less inclined to remain in this profession. Even the trained people, who come with some archival training, have inadequate skill and knowledge. Only one employee has the diploma course training. If hired, the employee should have done at least a certificate course in RM and preservation of records is required with 10+2 as a minimum qualification. Though in-house training follows a formal process, workshop or 'rotational' assignments of introduction programmes are available within the department. For a new archival employee, Though there is no such formal guideline for a new archival employee, they are trained when they are assigned any job. No such opportunity exists in the locality. The training provided by Utkal University of Culture is inadequate and outdated. Only NAI HQ provides proper professional training. There is no scope for post-appointment training, whether within the institution or outside.	Though more trained archivists are available now, they are less inclined to continue in this profession. Even the trained people, who come with some archival training, have inadequate skill and knowledge.

2.	State Archives of Assam	The Assam State Archives, located in Capital Complex, Dispur, has an independent building. Their records include both private and corporate historical records, kept in cubic feet. They have professional staff with proper education and training. The repository is a division of a larger institution. All staff positions, below an Asst. Archivist, including those with a promotional criterion, are recruited by the Director of Archives, including Ministerial and Technical. The entry-level salary of an Archivist is Rs 22,000-97,000 and the Gr Pay is Rs 11,500. Those with a higher qualification are not paid a higher salary. Promotion is done on the basis of seniority. For the post of Archivist and Asst Archivist, the minimum qualification is MA in History (preferably modern) and one-year Diploma from NAI. The existing staff has been trained at NAI. A basic knowledge of archives is given to the college and university students without certificate. The Directorate needs professional archival personnel Professional programmes shall be valuable for new employees and this is where NAI training can help our students to become more systematic in the Archival policies. New Asst Archivists are supported for training at NAI with a monthly pay during the training period. No Asst Archivist could be promoted as Archivist without professional training from NAI. The training is highly beneficial for an Archivist both in terms of the institution's promotional structure and preservation of Archives. Mid-career training is required from external groups for smooth and effective training. They have full-fledged Conservation Laboratory, Reprographic Unit, and functional Library, etc. to supplement the archival works.	The Directorate needs professional archival personnel. Professional programmes shall be valuable for new employees and this is where NAI training can help our students to become more systematic in the Archival policies. New Asst Archivists are supported for training at NAI with a monthly pay during the training period. No Asst Archivist could be promoted as Archivist without professional training from NAI. The training is highly beneficial for an Archivist both in terms of the institution's promotional structure and preservation of Archives.
3.	State Archives of Bihar Dr Vijoy Kumar, Ex Director,	Located in Patna is the repository of the State Government of Bihar, established formally in 1954. Reorganised in 1956, it has three Regional Offices in the State. It collects records from State Government offices, Civil Secretariat and Board of Revenue. The Directorate, under the Cabinet Secretariat of the Government of Bihar, has staff strength of 45. The officers are trained and have promotional avenues as per State Government recruitment rules. The hierarchy is Archivist, Assistant Director, Deputy Director, and Director (Ex-cadre post) and Principal Secretary, an IAS officer to look after the administration. The minimum qualification is MA in History (Modern India) and recruitment has been nil over the last 5 years.	Some of the officers are already trained, while others are yet to be trained at NAI. Lack of professional Head affects the professional growth, and slows down the work. People coming through University programs have turned out to be more effective and efficient at work. Leave is provided to the officials for training/education in service.

		Some of the officers are already trained, while others need to be trained at NAI. Lack of a professional Head affects the professional growth, and slows down the work. With no training facilities available in the State, personnel trained at NAI are hired. People coming through University programmes have turned out to be more effective and efficient at work. In-house training is also provided from time to time. There is no post-appointment training. The departments have funds for orientation and professional archival meetings. Leave is provided to the officials for training/education in service. They also organise week's refresher courses for the employees with external support. Archives have its own full-fledged Conservation Reprographic Unit and a functional library. Digitisation services are outsourced. The State Government generously provides funds. The archives digitised so far include Records series of Revenue, Education, Political, Fortnightly Reports District Records, Board of Revenue, etc.	
4.	State Archives of Rajasthan	The Rajasthan State Archives is located in Bikaner, with seven Regional Centres, under the government of Rajasthan. It holds official records of the State Govt and has collections of private papers. Though the archives are working with trained officials, the Director feels, no institutions in our country are able to give proper archival training. The total staff strength is 147, but more than 50 posts are yet to be filled. The salary range is Pay Band II 9,300-34,800 grade pay-4800, L-12. Five Archivists were appointed through RPSC. The minimum qualification is Master's (IInd class) in History and Political Science. They give in-house training to their employees, having developed its training capacity. There are no training institutions in the region/state. We need institutions and organisations for training Archivists. Funds availability is good as State Government provides enough to meet the requirements of the State Archives. The kind of training most needed is in Records Keeping, Preservation and Conservation, Digitisation of Records, Microfilming of Records, Well behaved staff, Publication based on Original records. Officers must be friendly with Staff. Q. 2. Since the last 50 years, they have been providing in-house training for 5 days every month to officers of Rajasthan government. It is a standalone course offering a practical hands-on training. However, it is not recognised by the UGC. The department has digitised more than 10 million historical documents of Rajputana and is available online on the website of the State Archives. The training gives due emphasis on Reprography and Conservation of Records. The usual intake of students is 15 and the faculty constitutes qualified trained Archivists, Historians and Researchers. The faculty has no tie up with any local or state institution. They conduct study visits, But there are no scholarships. It is not job-oriented as they offer in-service training. To complement the training, workshop, and seminars are also organised. The department has fully fledged Conservation Lab and Reprography Unit besides a functional library. No funds are received from NAI.	Comment: The Director feels no institutions in our country are able to give proper archival training. The minimum qualification is Master's (IInd class) in History and Political Science. They give in-house training to their employees, having developed its training capacity. There are no training institutions in the region/state. We need institutions and organisations for training of Archivists.

5.	State Archives of West Bengal	It is a Directorate under the Higher Education, Govt of West Bengal. They have the responsibility to collect official records besides private and corporate historical records. The quantum of records is not assessed accurately. Presently, there are 19 trained archivists, in addition to Binders, Menders, etc. The Archives have their own repository. Presently, there are 46 Permanent staff and other 40 DEO (Data Entry Operators) engaged through outsourcing, along with caretaking staff involved in Archival work. The scale of Pay follows Matrix system. The Director receives Rs 37,400-67,000 with a Grade Pay of Rs 9000, while other positions starting from Asst Archivist receive anything between Rs 9,000-40,500, and a Grade Pay of Rs 4,400. There has been no recruitment over the last 5 years. The Archivists also play the role of Administrator, performing various duties successfully. The archivists receive training from NAI. Untrained archivists are trained in-house through a Certificate course in Conservation and Preservation. Generally, after joining the post of Assistant Archivist, one has to take two Departmental exams before confirmation. After the confirmation the candidate has to go through one-year Diploma course in Archives and Records Management conducted by NAI, New Delhi. Seniors are always helpful to the new comers. This kind of training is not given here, only archivists are allowed to take the training in NAI with salary, Travel Allowance and Daily Allowance. The funding depends on the training programme and nature. Training in NAI is mandatory for promotion but promotion after completing the training is not certain. The training offers a very good exposure.	Generally, after joining the post of Assistant Archivist, they have to take two departmental exams before confirmation. After the confirmation the candidate has to go through one-year Diploma course in Archives and Records Management conducted by NAI, New Delhi. This kind of training is not given here, only archivists are allowed to take the training in NAI with salary, Travel Allowance and Daily Allowance. The funding depends on the training programme and its nature. Training in NAI is mandatory for promotion but promotion after completing the training is not certain. The training programme gives a very good exposure.
6.	Corps of Engineers Archives and Museum, M/ Defence CMC Archives, Pune	The Corps of Engineers Archives and Museum CME, Pune, comes under Engineers' Corps of the Indian Army. They collect records from all the Corps of Engineers in the country and private papers of senior Army officials from Corps of Engineers regarding their contributions. The total collection has amounted to approximately 25 lakhs of pages. The Army staff is there along with one or two civilian trained professionals from the respective field. It's a central Archive for the whole Corps of Engineers. The institution does not recruit archivists on permanent basis. Their total strength varies from 10-12. The trained Civilians start their salary from 15,000 under a designation other than Archivist. They have hired one Archivist and one staff specifically for Conservation Lab over the last 5 years. The minimum qualification for recruitment is not very well defined. The organisation hires already trained personnels, but not as archivist. Even the trained personnel was available initially, but not locally, with only generalised knowledge on the subject.	

		There are no arrangements for in-house training. They organised a workshop on Records Management, Conservation and Digitisation under the aegis of NAI, which was helpful. After joining the institution, the archivist is provided with technical requirements and training on a day-to-day basis. They also collaborate with local Archival institutions. They don't have the funds to send new (or even experienced) employees to national professional archival meetings, or training workshops. Till now, no archivist with a formal degree or a certificate from a formal educational programme has worked here. Hence, they only lookup to NAI for any training in future.	There are no arrangements for in-house training. The institution doesn't have the funds to send new (or even experienced) employees to national professional archival meetings, or training workshops. Till now, no archivist with a formal degree or a certificate from a formal educational programme has worked here. Hence, they only look up to NAI for any training in future.

Sr. No.	Name of Inst. / Archives of Autonomous Bodies under M/Culture other Bodies	Comments/Observations on questionnaire 1 and 2	Remarks
1.	Indira Gandhi National Centre for the Arts	1. It is an autonomous government body, funded by the government. It also gets project-based funding from NAI grant-in-aid schemes. They have over 2.5 lakh microfilmed and digitised copies of manuscripts in different languages and scripts, 25 collections of eminent persons, out of print and rare books, over 1 lakh visuals on Indian Art collected from various sources, and mask and puppet collections, looked after by trained archivists/personnel. The archives are stored in its own building divided into Kalanidhi, Janapada, Sampada, Kalakosa and Kaladarsana repositories. Besides their regular staff, they have professionals, scholars and technicians and clerical staff. They have a need-based deployment of scholars and trained professionals from national/ state level institutions for the projects from time to time, hiring not below the level of Master's degree. Besides, working in IGNCA in itself is a genuine working experience, where the archivists learn while working, Their skills are further sharpened through workshops and seminars. IGNCA also sponsors professional staff for training in India and abroad. It has helped new aspirants to get jobs in leading institutions in India.	The courses offered are duly recognised by the UGC. Working in IGNCA in itself is a genuine working experience, where the archivists learn while working, They have signed MoU with 25 leading academic and cultural institutions and universities to collaborate and share resources and expertise in various disciplines.

		Q. 2. Since 2018, IGNCA has been conducting 7 PG Diploma and Certificate Courses in Art, Culture and related subjects. 1 PG Diploma in Cultural Informatics 2. PG Diploma in Preventive Conservation. 3. PG Diploma in Buddhist Studies. 4. PG Diploma in Digital Library and Data Management. 5. PG Diploma in Manuscriptology and Paleography. 6. PG Diploma in Cultural Management 7. PG Diploma in South-East Asian Studies. The courses offered are job-oriented. Due weightage is given to the study of Reprographics, and practical based assignments are given and evaluated. In-house faculty is available in the Library Science and Information and Communication Technology. They have dedicated scholars in Conservation, Museum Experts, Photography experts, and Indology. They have signed MoU with 25 leading academic and cultural Institutions and universities to collaborate and share resources and expertise in various disciplines. They have both regular and visiting faculty. Study visits are conducted. IGNCA has the desired infrastructure including full-fledged Conservation Laboratory, Reprographic Unit, functional library, etc. to take care of archival holdings.	
2.	Vrindavan Research Institution (VRI) (Vrindavan Shodh Sansthan) Vrindavan	1. It is a non-government organisation, registered under the Societies Registration Act of 1860. The VRI preserves manuscripts, farmans and archival material besides its own official records. The Conservation staff is trained from NAI and other government institutes. It receives financial grants from Ministry of Culture, Government of India and Department of Culture, Uttar Pradesh Government. There are 29 staff recruited as per VRI Service Rules, VRI pay scales and the government of UP. The minimum qualification is Intermediate with Science. They provide in-service training and organise manuscript conservation workshops. No qualified Archivist has been employed in VRI so far but they do have the manuscript Conservator. The technical staff of conservation section is duly trained with proven efficiency. The VRI organises short-term training in Manuscript conservation. The present staff members also attend it. The Conservator is a science graduate. A foundational training of Manuscript conservation is given to new employees and is sent to NAI and NRLC in Lucknow. The institute needs archival training for their technical staff because now they have several artifacts in the Braj Culture Museum. 2. The VRI conducts only manuscript conservation workshop from time to time. Besides having their own experts, they invite experts from NAI, NRLC, and National Manuscript Mission, etc. as faculty for these workshops. The VRI is also planning to start a Diploma course in future.	The institute needs archival training for their technical staff because now they have thousands of records and several artifacts in the Braj Culture museum. The VRI is planning to start a Diploma course in future. Must develop its own Institutional Archives.

Sr. No.	Name of the Institution/ Archives of Scientific Institutions	Comments	Remarks
1.	National Centre for Biological Sciences (NCBS), Bangalore	It is a public archive of the history of contemporary Biology in India. The Archives keeps copies of official records as a secondary source. The original official records of the parent organisation, TIFR, are most likely at TIFR or the Dept of Atomic Energy. But the primary purpose of the Archives at NCBS is as a public archive (not an institutional archive) for individual scientist and engineer private manuscripts and related details. As of March 2019, they have approximately 65 linear feet of archives (~130 Hollinger-style archive boxes). They have one contract staff, and a number of project assistants/interns engaged over a year. There is no salary range for the Contract staff. There is not enough data to assess the changes over the years regarding the availability of trained archivists. About 35 student interns from 10+ disciplines have been trained in archives over the course of one year. They are not being trained to be archivists, but to be sensitive to historical context in their subject areas–from science to law to design to journalism. In the process, they are taught archiving methods, including provenance, original order, dealing with disordered manuscript collections, and development of finding aids, processes underlying accessioning, arrangement, description, preservation and access, archival description standards, compliance with ISAD (G), metadata structures, and others. Student's discipline has not mattered as much as the intent and clarity of thought regarding historical context of material. There was not enough staff to assess. However, we think that this programme, given the close relationship between records management and archival records, would benefit all staff members of any organisation, not just employees of an archive. There is an internship programme, a reading material list, on-site orientation, and specific project deliverables for training new employees. However, it is not meant to train people as professional archivists; this works well as a mentoring/apprentice programme. NCBs have collaborated with many archives in India and abroad to stay updated on archival methods and preservation/conservation practices. For instance, the British Library will be setting up a digitisation standards workshop at our archives in August (cost is borne by them). There has been conservation practices roundtable where NCBS hosted a conservator from CSMVS last year. There were online conference calls with various archives around the world for conversations on description standards and current tools.	About 35 student interns from 10+ disciplines have been trained in archives over one year. They are not being trained to be archivists, but to be sensitive to historical context in their subject areas, from science to law to design to journalism. In the process, they are taught archiving methods, including provenance, original order, dealing with disordered manuscript collections, and development of finding aids, processes underlying accessioning, arrangement, description, preservation and access, archival description standards, compliance with ISAD (G), metadata structures, and others. Developed over the course of two years, we have an internship programme, a reading material list, on-site orientation, andspecific project deliverables.This is not meant to train people as professional archivists; this works well as a mentoring/apprentice programme Suggestions: The community would greatly benefit from a sharing of resources and ideas which can be done through an archives association, common mailing groups and list serves. There are many online resources for individual queries, especially around archival arrangement, description, and conservation practices. Yet, the Indian community appears to be spread out with not enough routine interaction.

		Since it has opened recently in 2019, there is not enough data to assess future plans. The Archives would like to hire 2-3 permanent staff members though it might take time. Degree/certification will definitely be of interest. Though programmes are available through the SAA, for instance, those are more expensive. Funding is always limited, and evaluated on a case-by-case basis. The community would greatly benefit from a sharing of resources and ideas Which can be done through an archives association, common mailing groups and list serves. There are many online resources for individual queries, especially around archival arrangement, description, and conservation practices. Yet, the Indian community appears to be spread out with not enough routine interaction. They have collaborated with Foreign Agencies and got installed not only archives but part funding as well.	However, they think this programme, given the relationship between records management and archival records would benefit all staff members of any organisation (not just employees of an archive). The Indian Archival Community need to be organised, like SAA.
		Questionnaire 2, Not Applicable.	
2.	Indian Institute of Science, Bangalore	While IISc does have an active Archives and Publications Cell (APC) with a mandate to collect and catalogue all documents related to the history of the institute, there is no trained archivist on roll. All the work is collectively done by a small team at APC which is also responsible for various other things. However, the following suggestions may be of some help: - Students graduating from the National Archives, or elsewhere, should be allowed to apply to various archives across the country for short-term positions. With their training, they can help the host institution in archives-related activities ranging from cataloguing to digitising and scanning the collection for further use. - A proper procedure should be followed for this purpose. For example, students applying for these positions should write a proposal to be evaluated by the host institute. A centrally authorised office should handle the funds. These positions can be modelled after projects granted by funding agencies in the country.	- Students graduating from the National Archives, or elsewhere, should be allowed to apply to various archives across the country for short-term positions. With their training, they can help the host institution in archives-related activities ranging from cataloguing to digitising and scanning the collection for further use. - A proper procedure should be followed for this purpose. For example, students applying for these positions should write a proposal to be evaluated by the host institute. A centrally authorised office should handle the funding. These positions can be modelled after projects granted by funding agencies in the country. The Indian Archival community needs to be organised like the Society of American Archivists, SAA.

3.	Indian Institute of Astro-Physics Prof Arun Mangalam, Professor and Chair of Theoretical Astrophysics Group and Head of Archives.	An archive of the Institute of Astrophysics is located in Bangalore. While developing archives; the institute developed and drafted its Collections Policy also to address different preservation issues. The institute has naturally inherited the Library and Records of Madras and Kodaikanal Observatories, as old as 1786, the forerunners of the Indian Institute of Astrophysics. The collections have now grown and include over 5000 items of historical importance in various formats such as Manuscripts, Photographs, Maps, Films, Awards, framed material, hand drawn sketches, pictures and instruments that are environmentally sensitive. The oldest document dates back to 1792. A part of a collection is also displayed aesthetically in a separate room adjacent to the Library in IIA campus, Bangalore. They have also digitised Madras MS Records dating back to 1794-1812 and 1795-1800. The collections highlight the role played by various Astronomers and Director of their parent Observatories. But they don't have any skilled manpower for the Archives.	They don't have any skilled manpower for the Archives.

Sr. No.	Banking and Corporate Archives	Comments	Remarks
1.	Reserve Bank of India	The Central Archives of the Reserve Bank of India houses the non-current permanent records of the bank as a central repository of the Reserve Bank located in different parts of the country. Dr RL Sahoo is the Chief Archivist, Deputy General Manager, assisted by specialist officers—Archivist, Asst Archivist, Chemist, Asst Librarian and other supporting officers and staff of the Bank in general cadre. RBIA functions under the department of Economic and Policy Research, Central Office, RBI, Mumbai. Its functions include scientific preservation of records, photographs and paintings. It has records of historical and legal value, transferred after 12 years for scientific preservation. They have Vacuum Fumigation Chamber, and many other means for repair and preservation of brittle and fragile records. They maintain an archival library consisting of RBI publications such as books, reports, journals, manuals, brochures etc. They prepare reference media of records and publications for access and retrieval. They work as a nodal agency in respect of records management in the Bank and monitor the implementation of the Archival and Records Management Policy (ARMP) in all departments and offices of the bank. They preserve Oral History recordings, organise exhibitions on topical themes relating to history of the Bank and Digitisation and microfilm records. As per the RBI Historical Research Rules, 2001, they provide the scholars with access to non-current records which are more than 30 years old. The RBI Archives has an Archives Museum.	The RBI should develop modules for training the Archival Community in the banking sector to promote bank archiving and digital preservation.

		Q. 2. The RBI Archives regularly organises in-house training through workshops and training programmes for the RBI Officers in various cadres from Junior Management to Top Management. The objective is to create awareness about the importance of archives and records management, and to familiarise the participants with the internal guidelines on records management. It provides a platform for discussion on the Archival and Records Management Policy (ARMP) of the Bank so that the records management activities in the Bank are streamlined. It also provides professional guidance to outside institutions.	
2.	Godrej Archives	Godrej Archives is under Corporate Human Resource Department of Godrej and Boyce Mfg Co Ltd. They have the responsibility to collect official records and private and corporate historical records. The Archive Collection, as on 1 April 2019, consists of over 1500 product catalogues, 50,000 photographs, 1500 objects, around 1,00,000 documents and over 300 oral history interviews. They have recruited three people, two trained in Archival Science Short-Term Courses and one in Museology and Library and Information Science. Moreover, there are two people Trained in Scanning and Conservation. The institution recruits and determines the promotional criteria for Archivists in consultation with Chief Archivist. The salary depends on the level of experience. Promotions are given as per the policy of the parent organisation. The minimum qualification is post-graduation, preferably in History/Library and Information Science/Museology. It is difficult to find trained Archivists fit to work at Corporate Archives. They get trained on the job. Moreover, some team members are sent for training in fields such as Archival Science, Conservation, and Digitisation, etc. as required. They hire professionals trained in History, Library and Information Science, and Museology from the state universities. Two of them were sent for undertaking a short-term course in Archival Science from NAI. One is trained in Library and Information Science as well as Museology, while one was offered training in Conservation at INTACH. The organisation encourages training its staff as adequately trained people are not available. Training the staff in History, Museology or Library and Information Science has proved useful. Employees receive a foundational introduction to archives and its various processes; this is followed by training in each function on rotation for few days. Induction Training in the beginning follows a formal structure. The rotational training later follows a more informal approach. Unlike diploma, their training is need-based. However, they do send their staff for training in Museology (locally available), and Conservation (across the country) etc. The organisation supports the training as they have the funds. They promote and support archivists without a formal degree or a certificate from a formal educational programme. They can work toward such a degree or certificate with the institution's support under leave for education' policy.	-Since they are not hiring trained archivists, it is difficult to comment. -They hire Professionals trained in History, Library and Information Science, and Museology. They have hired professionals trained in History, Library Science and Museology from the Universities within the State of Maharashtra. -The Organisation encourages training the Staff since adequately trained people are not available. -Training the staff in History, Museology or Library and Information Science has proved useful for their archives. -The training they need the most includes Archival Management, Conservation and Digitisation. -Funds are allotted for training. Every year the organisation supports the training.

		The training they need the most includes Archival Management, Conservation and Digitisation. Funds are allotted for training every year.	
		Q. 2. Not applicable.	
3.	DCM Shri Ram	DCM Shriram Archives and Heritage Gallery is an independent archive of the DCM Shriram Limited, New Delhi. They are responsible for collecting official records besides private and corporate historical records. The total bulk of record approximately amounts to 17,000, including Files, Published Reports and In-house publications, Industrial Drawings, Souvenir, Books, Memoirs, Biographies, Photographs, Memorabilia, etc. The working professionals include one Archivist, with PG Diploma in Archives and Records Management from SAS, and one Consultant (Retd ADA, NAI). They recruited one archivist having all the promotional criteria. There are two regular and one professional Consultant on contractual basis. They can't share salary range as per the Company policy. The minimum prescribed qualification is Diploma in Archival Studies. However, depending upon the requirement, candidates who have undertaken short-term diploma courses in Records Management or Preservation, or have some background of working in Business Archives can be considered for suitable positions. Only one person has been hired over the last 5 years. For Archives and Records Management, a trained archivist has been engaged to adopt a systematic approach. The archivist, trained from NAI, possesses the basic skill relevant to the profession and is instrumental in implementing the System of Records Keeping as well as the Preservation of Records along scientific lines. Internal training programmes are conducted for the selected Archives Champions in the various Units of the Company from time to time. The training programme provides all the employees with the procedure of managing records. They have developed guidelines for a systematic apprenticeship programme. The institution supports the archival profession staff in post appointment training outside the institution and provides related facilities. The institution has the funds to send new (or even experienced) employees to national professional archival meetings, or training workshops sponsored by the NAI. They invite a Preservation and Conservation expert from NAI to seek guidance on preserving big industrial drawings available in the DCM Shriram Archives and Heritage Gallery.	The Archives and Records Management has engaged a trained archivist to adopt a systematic approach. -The archivist, trained from NAI, possesses the basic skill relevant to the Archival profession and is instrumental in implementing the System of Records keeping and Preservation of Records along scientific lines.
		Q. 2. Not Applicable.	

4.	Delhi Land and Finance Limited (DLF), Jhandewalan, New Delhi and Gurugram. Contributed by Dr Doonger Singh, Rt Archivist, NAI.	The centre collects official records only of DLF company. The records include Sale Agreements, Sale Deeds, and Customer Files, Accounts Ledgers, Legal Documents, Drawings, and Contract Papers. It covers an area equal to three big halls, totaling to more than 10,000 Sq feet area. The Centre had just one Archivist and one Librarian in the name of trained staff, along with six supporting staff. They follow a Managerial system, the staff is designated as Manager, Dy Manager, Asst Manager and attendants, etc. The salary range is not provided. The minimum qualification is Master's in History or Library Science. The archival training has been helpful in managing records/Files at the Documentation Centre in Delhi. Presently, there is no archival trained person except Dr Singh. They have developed a mentor system and formal guidelines as the records kept in the repository comprised property deeds, agreements, Construction Drawings, and site Maps, etc. There is no professional training support or opportunities available as authorities are not interested in training.	Recommendation is to motivate corporate houses to encourage and promote their professional staff for training in the upkeep of records and its arrangement, Management of Records in SAS for scientific and professional preservation of Records. There is no recruitment policy to hire Archivists. Presently, there is no archival trained person except Dr Singh.
5.	Reddy's Lab, Hyderabad	The authorities believe they are not in a position to answer the questionnaire. Their infrastructure for an archive is not fully developed and archival policy is also yet to be implemented.	

Sr. No.	**Universities/ Colleges Archives**	**Comments**	**Remarks**
1.	Daulatram College for Women, D U	Questionnaire 2 is applicable. They have been conducting a Paper on Archives and Museums since 2016. The target group is BA (Hons) and BA (Prog) SEC students. The course contents are approved by the UGC. The students should be pursuing graduation; specialisation is not important. The course has just one comprehensive paper, with contents developed in consultation with NAI. For evaluation, they have internal exams and end-semester exams, and the students write assignments on certain topics. Reprography and/or Conservation of documents is not emphasised as no facilities are available. Since it is a new discipline, it is important to be introduced to the students. They have no faculty and no tie up. However, they do have visiting faculty occasionally. Study visits to NAI are conducted at times. This course is job-oriented.	They have no faculty and no tie up. However, they do have visiting faculty occasionally. Study visits to NAI are conducted at times. This course is job-oriented and needs to be promoted.
2.	Mata Sundari College Dr Daljit Kaur, Department of History, Mata Sundari College for Women	-Presently, there is no particular course on archives. One paper titled 'Archives and Museums' is being taught in BA (Prog) and BA (Hons) under CBCS (Choice Based Credit System) of University education from 2016 onwards. It comes under Skill Enhancement Course in CBCS, where a student can choose this paper in the 2nd year (3rd semester). University of Delhi has designed the syllabus as follows:- I. Definition and history of development (with special reference to India).	The prescribed syllabus is sketchy and needs to be revised. Teaching should be introduced in Modular Form in Consultation with SAS.

2.		II. Types of archives and museums: -Understanding the traditions of preservation in India, collection policies, Ethics and procedures. -Collection: field exploration, excavation, purchase, gift and bequests, loans and deposits, exchanges treasure trove confiscations and others. -Documentation: accessioning, indexing, cataloguing, digital documentation and de-accessioning. -Preservation: curatorial care, preventive conservation, chemical preservation and restoration. III. Museum presentation and exhibition. IV. Museums, archives and society: education and communication, Outreach Activities: For outreach activities, students visit Archival repositories and undertake in-house seminars with experts on Archives and Museums.	Since more stress is given to Museums in the syllabus than Archival Studies, they need to review and give equal weightage. Needs to include subjects like Digital Archiving. Under funded institutions For College Archives it needs to adopt selective approach and consider: what needs to be preserved? Who is getting benefitted? How will you mobilise resources for college archives? And approach NAI for Grant-in-aid.
3.	Dr Santosh Kumar Rai, Asso Prof in Modern Indian History, Dept of History, Social Science Faculty (North Campus), University of Delhi, Delhi 110007.	Since 2012, we at Department of History, University of Delhi, are offering insights to archival science through MA and MPhil Courses. Target group are MA students. The basic qualification is graduation and modern Indian history is not a compulsory component. It is offered as the Archive and History. The syllabus contents are as per Delhi University rules. Evaluation is based on Internal Assessment and University Exam. No emphasis on Reprography and Conservation of documents; these are optional papers. They take 20 to 30 students per semester. Faculty consists of qualified historians, and they have no tie up or any visiting faculty.	Since 2012, the Department of History, University of Delhi, is offering insights to archival science through MA and M Phil Courses. However, there was no clarity on the subject as they consider archives as a subject more for historical research than of study.
4.	BHU, Central Library	BHU has a decentralised system for the official records. Each department in the university maintains their archives. Central Library, BHU has a dedicated section for Manuscripts and Rare Collections and is engaged in the preservation and conservation of these documents. Central Library is one of the depository libraries in the country receiving the Government and United Nations publications for free. Moreover, Central Library, BHU maintains an Institutional Repository to maintain and provide access to the knowledge produced by the University. For collections, depends upon the objectives of individual departments. The collections are maintained by regular staff of the university. It has an MoU with National Mission for Manuscripts (NMM) and the Central Library. BHU receives trained professionals from NMM who are engaged in the conservation work of the Manuscripts and Rare documents.	The Library has developed Mahamana Digital Library. They do not teach the subject. Have also developed Mahamana Archives. - BHU has recently started a two year degree course in Archival Studies at PG level.

<table>
<tr><td></td><td></td><td>Q. 2. Banaras Hindu University does not offer a course in Archival Science.</td><td></td></tr>
<tr><td>5.</td><td>Punjab University, Chandigarh</td><td>Punjab University Archival Cell is located in the premises of the University Library. It is not responsible for collecting any official records of the university. But, they have a good collection of rare Books. The cell is managed by an Assistant Archivist with a pay scale of Rs 15,600-39,100+5400, as recommended by the Govt of Punjab and is being rectified as matter referred to UGC. The cell staff is a part of the Library Staff strength. There are no promotional avenues so far. It is being proposed to the UGC to provide a separate identity to the Cell and increase its growth avenues as has been done for Teachers/Librarians. The minimum qualification is MA in Social Science and Diploma in Archives for Class A. There will be no professional growth without the development of the cell. Training is provided within the university. In February 2019, the University Cell received a grant of Rs 8 lakh, provided by the NAI and PU in the ratio of 6:2.</td><td rowspan="2">Archives Cell can develop better if separated from Library.
Currently, they are not running any course The cell has recently received a sanction of Rs 50 lakh by the Board of Finance, PU, to facilitate the Archival cell. The University Cell has taken steps in this direction and would like to develop a training Unit in the State for Northern States. They will also try to seek financial support from the ICHR/UGC.</td></tr>
<tr><td></td><td></td><td>Q.2. Currently, they are not running any academic programmes. The cell has recently received a sanction of Rs 50 lakhs from the Board of Finance, Punjab University, for setting up the Archival cell. The university cell has taken steps in this direction and would like to develop a training Unit in the State for Northern States. They will also try to seek financial support from the ICHR/UGC.</td></tr>
<tr><td>6.</td><td>Delhi University Archives, Dr Amrit Kaur Basara, Delhi University. Delhi-110007.</td><td>Q. 1. DU Archives was in a heritage building known as Viceregal Lodge. With the renovation of the Lodge, DU decided to reorganise and relocate its archival material and commemorate 150 years of Indian Revolt of 1857 in 2007. It collects official records and private papers. The collections include written and visual records on the ground and first floor of oval rooms and are in other places for display in the Viceragal Lodge. There was one Assistant Archivist, who has now retired. Record Keeping is done with the help of students. The post of Archivist is lying vacant and is presently looked after by the Dean/Registrar office. The minimum qualification is MA in History as per the GoI/ UGC Rules. A temporarily teaching faculty was entrusted by the authorities, as developed by Dr Basara and faculty and students from the Department of History. Dr Basara trained the students as interns to develop the University Archives and Museum, using both formal and informal methods. They prefer to approach NAI for training who can provide them with the funds if required.</td><td>Recommendation-Currently, they do not have any other programme. They need to develop a course curriculum at PG and post PG level. Though there are Museum courses in various universities, they need to give equal weightage to Archival Studies as well.
-History courses have academic linkage with NAI, but they need a formal linkage now. They need to formally sign a MoU with individual colleges for providing certificate courses. In case UGC provides financial support for professional courses taught under CBCS, they can tie up with NAI.</td></tr>
</table>

		Q.2. The course in Archival Studies is being taught under BA (Hons) history and BA (Program) level under CBCS. The target group is undergraduate students of BA (Hons) and BA (Program) studying history at graduation level and approved by UGC. The course is under revision as only some generic information is provided through examples. However, hands-on experience can't be provided through examples. Written tests are taken; students under take projects and present them for evaluation. They could not have Reprography or conservation units as they are not teaching it in depth. However, do emphasise on preservation. Outreach activities will be conducted once certificate courses are offered to regular students like other courses of BA (Hons) and BA (Program) with history/social science. The intake of students varies from college to college and ranges from 10 to 40. Most of the faculty is drawn from History Dept Though there is no tie up, students visit NAI and National Museums as part of their study visits/tours. There is no regular or visiting faculty. Courses are job-oriented. DU has also initiated digitising its records and made them available online using its reprographic/Computer Units. Funds were provided by DU. Currently, they have no other programme. They need to develop a course curriculum at PG and post PG level. Though there are Museum courses in various universities, they need to give equal weightage to Archival Studies as well. The course includes: Unit I-Definition of Archives and Museums; Unit II-History of Development of Archives and Museums in India with one case study each; Unit III-Collection, Documentation, preservation; Unit IV-Museum Presentation and Exhibition.	2. There is only one paper, 'Archives and Museums', to familiarise the students with the structure and functioning of Archives and Museums in India. This subject is expected to give them only basic information about archives and museums for employment opportunities in these institutions. - After the course, the students will be able to: -Examine these two repositories of history from close quarters, -Contextualise the way in which museums are organised and managed, -Examine the considerations governing the way exhibitions in Museums are organised, -Assessment will be based on assignments and projects involving visits to the archives and Museums.
7.	Tumkur University, Tumkur, Karnataka.	Q 2 At MA History level, they conduct one-year specialisation paper on introduction to Archival Studies for 2nd Semester, from Academic Year 2018-19. It includes basic Introduction of Archival Studies for one semester only. The paper includes: introduction, types of archives, Principles of Archives management, Conservation and Reprography, etc. The target students are MA. It is being treated as a part of MA course in History and Archaeology. These courses are PG level one, recognised by the State and UGC. Though no separate qualifications are mentioned for undertaking this course, history and/or archaeology is compulsory component.	Only introduced at Tumkur University out of all the universities I visited under the Project Study. Other Universities also need to introduce as they have not done yet and the UGC has to ensure the same.

		Archival Studies is a single paper in itself. The syllabus is created to suit the preliminary level of information for the students. At the base of the syllabus is the course offered by the NAI and UGC model. The paper gives an equal importance to both forms of documents—conventional and electronic records. Evaluation is based on internal assessment test, seminar presentation and assignment based on syllabus and field visits. The practicals involve only visits to archives. Reprography and Conservation are part of one Unit of the syllabus, and are taken care of. The department is still in preliminary stage of the course, but the students have shown keen interest. Since it is a specialisation paper, the MA students opt for it based on individual choice. At present, 13 students are studying this paper. Only one faculty teaches this, with experience in AIHC and Archaeology and Research, and work experience at Tamil Nadu State Archives. The faculty has tie-up with the Karnataka State Archives. Regular visits to KSA are arranged and made a mandate for all the students. The University offers regular scholarships as per the State Govt rules. The course is indeed job-oriented. The fully-fledged Conservation and Reprography labs are yet to be developed. The Karnataka State Archives has provided specific grants for organising workshop for SC/ST PhD scholars in 2017 related to Research Methodology. The Dept also organised an exhibition in 2016 in collaboration with the Karnataka State Archives in the University.	-Archival Studies is a single paper in itself. The syllabus is created to suit the preliminary level of information for the students. At the base of the syllabus is the course offered by the NAI and UGC model. -They give equal importance to both forms of documents—conventional and electronic records. -Practicals involve only visits to Archives. - Could develop their own University Archives/Cell with the support of UGC and use for practical purposes.
8.	School of Cultural Texts and Records (SCTR), Jadavpur University,	The SCTR is an interdisciplinary school in Jadavpur University. It has two units: Text Archive and Music Archive. The archive focuses on Bengali cultural material, thus it is mainly based on private records. The archive stores some primary material. However, most primary material is digitised and returned to the custodians of the material. The digital copies of the material are kept in the archive. Fellows at SCTR are recruited temporarily as per the availability of project funds. There is no permanent archivist/staff at SCTR. The total strength is 20. Fellowships usually begin from Rs 18,200. The highest fellowship (based on project budget and funds) is Rs 25,000. There is no substantive hiring; only project fellows are recruited for the duration of the project. The minimum qualification is Master's degree, and the fellows learn on the job. Also, students who undergo training in the DHCI course offered by the archive later work as fellows at the archive. Hence, there is a fairly consistent availability of trained archivists. Generally, the recruited fellows are former students of the university or the DHCI course. Some projects have provisions for training workshops at the beginning. The DHCI course offered by the archive provides training not only to prospective fellows but also to students in general. In sponsored programmes, external training is very rare. Funds are limited at SCTR; it may not be able to contribute for travel etc. SCTR offers UGC approved one-year PG diploma course in DHCI. Digital archiving is a part of the curriculum. Anyone who has completed a master's programme can join the course. However, SCTR/Jadavpur University does not provide any hostel facilities for outstation candidates. The DHCI course provides thorough training.	SCTR offers UGC approved one-year PG diploma course in DHCI. It is a new course, with Digital archiving as a major part of the curriculum. Anyone who has completed a Master's programme can join the course. However, SCTR /Jadavpur University do not provide any hostel facilities for outstation candidates. There is a need to popularise the course to widen its scope of deploying trained persons in Audio-visual/Sound archives in the country like AIR, Doordarshan and Television Archives, Multi-Media archives of various Govt and private channels, National Film Archives of India, Pune, Archives of Indian Music, (AIM) Bangalore, launched in 2013, and many more.

		Q. 2. Several workshops were held before the DHCI course started. MPhil, PhD researchers and independent researchers are the target group. It is a standalone, post Master's diploma course, approved by UGC. No particular subject/ discipline are compulsory for the course. The papers offered are: 1. Conceptualising the Digital Humanities, 2. The Photograph and its Digital Surrogates, 3. Digital Music Archiving, 4. Student Project The aims of the course are as follows: -Conceptualising humanities research in the context of new digital technology -Acquisition and processing of material (digitisation, metadata, tagging, mark-up) -Organisation (system and platform architecture, information structure, systems of classification, etc.) -Data mining and processing (creating and optimising search engines, performing programming operations, querying data, generating results) -Communication and presentation (user/community interaction, interface, front-end applications, standards).	
		Evaluation Procedures- The course focuses on the practical aspects of archiving and data creation. Students learn through hands-on assignments right from the beginning of the course. They are encouraged to attend all the classes and participate in the hands-on sessions. At the end of the course, there is an overall evaluation. They learn how to operate camera/ scanners and other necessary equipment. Most importantly, students learn how to handle fragile documents. Outreach activities include seminars, workshops, and student projects. The student intake is 25, and faculty is drawn from Humanities, Computer Science/Programming, Social Science, Library Science, and Archivists. Their current tie-ups are with Victoria Memorial, Maulana Adul Kalam Azad Institute of Asian Studies, and academic collaboration with international universities, such as the University of Exeter. SCTR has a reprographic unit and a library. Though it is self-sponsored, it initially received grant from the UGC. It' is a job-oriented course, offering opportunities if projects are available.	
9.	University Archives Gujarat Vidyapith	Established in 1920 by Mahatma Gandhi, and becoming a Deemed University in 1963, the Archives of Gujarat Vidyapith is controlled by the Department of History and Culture. Prof (Dr) Mehebubbhai Desai is the Head of the Department and Dr Binduvasini Joshi, Associate Professor and the Head of Archives, is a trained Archivist from SAS. The Archives is very rich in its collections. They hold private papers of Morarji Desai, it's first Vice Chancellor, and collections of other VCs, Congress Kranti Samiti, Papers relating to Vidyapith, its publications, conference collections and their proceedings, periodical journals and other papers. They have a Conservation Lab and Reprography services in its Library. The Vidyapith will run an MPhil Programme if some students opt to enroll for the course.	The Vidyapith will run an MPhil programme provided some students opt to enroll. There is a need to revive the course. Vidyapith needs to introduce the paper as per the UGC syllabus as they have the faculty to take care of it at MA level.

10.	Mr K Chaudhury, University of Hyderabad, Hyderabad.	University does not offer any such course. However, the University Library has fully fledged Conservation Laboratory, Reprographic Unit, functional library, etc. to meet the library requirements.	Dept of History of the Hyderabad University should initially introduce the course approved by UGC on Archival Sciences.
11.	Ms Sreeti Das, PhD Scholar, Hyderabad Central University.	University does not offer any such course. But University Library has fully fledged Conservation Laboratory, Reprographic Unit, functional library, etc. to complement its requirements in the Library.	University should introduce UGC approved courses.
12.	Ms Tibrata Sharma, D/ History, PhD Research Scholar Mizoram University	University does not offer any such course. But University Library has fully fledged Conservation Laboratory, Reprographic Unit, functional library, etc. to complement its requirements in the Library.	University should introduce UGC approved courses.

Conclusion

Findings and Recommendations

Findings Under the Project and Recommendations

Under the project study, Archival Science education denotes a formal system of education in archival science comprising teaching of both theory and practices of the subject. Training in archival and record management practices refers to short-term training courses conducted by NAI and State archives for Departmental Record Officers/Managers, and archives professionals, as mandated by Public Records Act of 1993. These courses are meant for sponsored Government officials from Ministries/Departments who are managing or working in the Departmental Record Rooms and cannot be spared for one-year diploma course in Archives and Records Management conducted by SAS, the only institution in the country conducting such a course. The course is also available to individuals willing to join short-term archival projects in Records Management, Archives Administration, Conservation, Reprography and digitalisation of records at professional level and Servicing and Repair of Records at sub-professional level, with emphasis on hands-on training.

The main objective and scope of the research project study

is to formally advocate and promote study of archival science education in schools, colleges and universities. It aims to draw the attention of the government and the universities to explore and take up archival science education that has been missing from Indian Universities and other heritage educational institutions. Hence, the study was taken up in a project mode for conducting research and the field survey. It was noted that it is still evolving in India.

With this end in view, raw data was collected to ascertain the current status of archival science education in India using Questionnaire method-online and Field Work. An analytical study has been conducted on the basis of: (1) Replies received from the archival bodies/academic institutions in response to the Questionnaires (2) reports of the field visits to various State and University Archives, Postgraduate Departments of History and personal discussions held with various archival professionals, Professors and students in addition to primary sources available in NAI. The data have been duly analysed, as presented here, drawing conclusions and making some recommendations.

Besides the field work, the questionnaire method has proved beneficial in collecting information. The institutions considered for the project study include public archival repositories of Central/State Governments, Central/State Universities, and other academic institutions both in public and private/corporate sector, as well as emerging new archives in all areas. Online survey using questionnaire mode has helped in giving the study an all India perspective, vide two sets of questionnaires circulated to the established archives in both public and private/corporate sector. The questionnaire was also sent to archives and universities imparting archival education and training, and offering some kind of archival education from under graduation, to post graduation level, offering Diploma, M Phil or PhD programme.

The broad parameters of the first Questionnaire were: location, status of the institution, clientele they cater to, the kind of records/collections they preserve, quantum, qualifications and recruitments, basic skills and training, skill enhancement programmes, facilities of training in-house or through outsourcing, pre and post appointment training, etc. The parameters for second questionnaire were: the kind of courses offered by the University/Institution, length and duration, the target group, nature of certification-Degree/Diploma, eligibility criteria, the course contents, evaluation methods, emphasis given to reprography, digitisation and conservation of both conventional and modern methods of preservation and storage, normal intake of students and nature of faculty, if outsourced by inviting experts/specialists of the subjects, historians, scholars, etc. as per the course requirements, teaching methodology, lecture/practical methods, field and project studies, available infrastructure, use of modern methods of teaching, funding, etc.

The Survey Questionnaires were sent and circulated to archival experts, Central/State University's History department, their students and professors teaching the subject, Vice Chancellors and Registrars of various universities, both Central and State/ UT's Archives, in consultation with Director General, NAI and Registrar, National Museum Institute (Deemed University), Ministry of Culture. Approximately 30 institutions responded, out of more than 300 institutions that were approached, may be due to lack of priority or awareness. Though the response has been only 10 per cent, they are from significant institutions. Hence, efforts were made to supplement the information during the field work, through personal interactions with the students and professors in the universities and officials in the State Archives.

According to the responses received, it was noted that repositories/institutions have different types of records, concerns and basic requirement, and need for expertise and skills. Many of them also commented upon the training programme of NAI, its utility, weaknesses and strengths, suitability for Business/ Corporate Archives, and if any changes need to be brought out by the universities and colleges in the teaching of the subject under the UGC scheme. The responses and observations received have been duly taken note of in the analysis and in making recommendations. The responses have been classified under 5 main categories as per the grouping of the institutions as duly elaborated in the chapter VI appendices. These categories are (1) Government Archives, (2) Banking and Corporate Archives, (3) Institutional Archives of the Universities and Colleges, (4) Archives of Defence Departments and Autonomous Bodies, (5) Archives of Scientific Institutions, besides upcoming Gender Archives, the Qamra Archives, covered during field work.[1]

Findings

Nature of all government archives and their workings is same as they have public, corporate and historical records catering to their own governments, historians, research scholars and the common people at large. Most of the archival institutions hire their archival staff with minimum qualification of Master's in

---

1. It is an upcoming Queer Archives for Memory Reflection and Activism, as the name suggests is a gender and sexual minorities archive in India. It is a physical archive, located in the southern city of Bangalore. While preserving memories through collecting and collating multimedia material, the archive aims to be a living one, creating and furthering activism around gender and queer issues. The idea of this archive emerged from the audio/video material that Miss Jayshree, In-charge Archives, had been collecting since 2001. The material in QAMRA is about the public history of the movement, but the focus is also on private lives of the individuals, of which there is very little existing documentation. Going about this task, it's hoped that this archive will serve both as a repository of collective memory and platform for collective action.

History, preferably in modern India, and the one-year diploma course in Archives and Records Management recognised by Union and State Public Service Commissions, Staff Selection Commission, University Grants Commission (UGC) and other public and private/business archives. Most of the archivists are trained at NAI or any other Archival Institution/University, or have 5 years of research experience in Modern Indian history. The target groups for the courses are students with Master's in Social Science or MSc in Applied or physical sciences from a recognised university. Though these qualifications have been duly recognised, they are yet to be implemented.

Most of the State Archives sponsor the training of their new Assistant Archivists at the School of Archival Studies (SAS), NAI, with pay during the period of training. In some of the states, like Assam, West Bengal, and Bihar, Assistant Archivists have found NAI professional training to be fruitful in their work, helping them preserve archives and climb the promotional structure in their institution. However, higher qualification does not guarantee higher salary. As per their analysis, mid-career training is also required for external groups, in the form of orientation courses, workshops and seminars.

In some of the state archives, like Kerala after recruitment through Kerala Public Service Commission, they give six months of customised training in Epigraphy before probation as they have a number of manuscripts and inscriptions in their vernacular language. Many of the state archives also provide regular in-house training in different subjects of archival science, particularly in Records Management and conservation, to equip their officers with new developments under the guidance of experts. Kerala has a 'Centre for Heritage Studies' in the State under the Cultural Affairs Department that conducts a diploma course in Archives and Manuscriptology. Even they depute their officers for training abroad in digitisation and conservation by signing MoUs.

All the Archives are found to be short of staff as recruitments are not regular either at NAI/State archives, or public/private archival institutions. A number of posts are lying vacant in many institutions. Most of the recruitments are contractual, offering no incentive for the Archival Assistants. These Archival Assistants are doing the work of professional archivists who are trained either from the SAS or any other short-term course, and are expected to be well versed in the work of professional Archivists.

Regarding the course contents, every Archivist needs to be competent in Information and Communication Technology (ICT) to cope with the present trends dealing with e-office, electronic records and digitisation work done in all the archival repositories. Though the NAI training scheme has one core paper on ICT, they need to upgrade their curriculum and start a specialisation course.

Currently, very few Indian institutions/universities offer courses in Archival Science. No university, except BHU, offers a MA course in Archival Studies and Management as a 2-year course. Osmania University, Hyderabad and Kerala Heritage Society offer 1-year diploma course in Archival Science and Manuscriptology. NAI has been conducting a PG one-year diploma course in Archives and Records Management since 1942.

In some Indian universities, PG Department of History are also teaching one or two papers on Archival Science under the UGC Scheme since 2016. The colleges affiliated to the DU also teach the paper 'Archives and Museums' in under graduate courses, BA (Hons) and BA (Program) level under CBCS (credit based), as part of the course, semester based under UGC Scheme. But, the curriculum and the teaching methodologies are not uniform everywhere. Certificate Courses of 4-8 weeks, or 3 months duration, are also being conducted by NAI, some State Archives, Institutes of Secretariat Training and Management (ISTM), and Indian Institute of Public Administration (IIPA) both in the Centre and the States. They also include short duration orientation and refresher courses conducted in-house by these institutions.

It was noted that the Archives of the NCBS, Bangalore, SCTR, Jadavpur University, IGNCA, and NAI have been experimenting with things. The system of archival education in India has to change with different patterns of new emerging archives, and the new challenges of digital archiving and online accessibility in digital environment.

Another finding is that many of the State Archives, like Tamil Nadu, Karnataka, Telangana, and Madhya Pradesh besides NAI, have non-archival, bureaucrat professionals as the Heads of Archives. This affects the professional growth of an institution and its people, and slows down the work. However, people coming through university programmes to work in archives have also turned out to be more effective and efficient.

Besides NAI, states, like Telangana and Kerala, are providing customised training through professional institutions. Archives like Rajasthan State Archives, Godrej Archives, and Archives of NCBS have developed their own capacity to give in-house training as per their needs.

Another problem for archival repositories is to sponsor archivists for training, as seen in the case of NCBS[2]. Many institutions don't have enough funds to send new or even in-service employees for professional training, archival meetings,

2. Link: archives.ncbs.res.in/

or workshops. Due to fund constraints they cannot hire trained personnel on regular basis. Funding is always limited and proposals are evaluated on case to case basis for training purposes. NCBS has adopted some innovative methods, hiring interns trained in archives over the course of one year. In the process, they learn principles of archives arrangement: provenance, original order, dealing with disordered manuscript collections, and development of finding aids, processes underlying accessioning, arrangement, preservation, access, archival description standards and compliance with ISAD (G),[3] metadata structures, and others. This internship programme has been developed by NCBS over the course of two years' time, along with a reading material list, on-site orientation, etc. These specific project deliverables are not meant to train people as professional archivists, but to be sensitive to historical context in their subject areas, from science to law, to design to journalism. It works well only as a mentoring/apprentice programme.

Though duly recognised by UGC[4], IGNCA courses are only on Archival conservation and not on archival sciences. They have signed MoU with 25 leading academic cultural Institutions and universities to collaborate, and share resources and expertise in various disciplines. It is noted that the students trained by IGNCA get preference in employment over other candidates. Besides, working in IGNCA in itself is a genuine working experience.

The Archives of Indian Institute of Science,[5] Bangalore, with no trained manpower has rightly suggested that archival repositories

3. General International Standard for Archival Description,(ISAD(G) defines the elements to be included in an archival finding aid as approved by the ICA as an international framework standard to register archival documents produced by corporations, persons and families
4. https://ignca.gov.in, https://ignca.gov.in/divisionss/pg-diploma-course-at-ignca/
5. Link: https://ooc.iisc.ac.in/archives/

should tie-up with NAI and other training institutions. Students graduating from the NAI or any other institute should be attached for short-term positions as interns or as an apprentice. With their training, they can help the host institution in various archives related activities. A proper procedure should be followed before implementing this. Funding should be handled by a centrally authorised office.

For business archives of the corporate houses and banking sector, the RBI Archives should develop modules[6] for training archival community of banking sector. They should promote business and bank archiving and professional digital preservation in the absence of a national policy on archival science education, Training or a recruitment policy for placement of trained Archivists as in other disciplines. Godrej archives have designed a customised Archives Management course to be conducted in collaboration with colleges/universities.

Government Initiatives

To strengthen the scheme of Archival Science Education and creation of Archival Cadre for India, the Archival Legislation Committee (1960)[7] had rightly recommended creation of an All India Cadre for Archivists.[8] It strongly recommended recruiting personnel of the Archival Service in the States through open competitions at a young age as a long-term plan, with the

6. RBI Archives have its own policy documents and conducts in-house training programs for its own officers/ officials.
7. To study the subject and make appropriate recommendations, the Government of India appointed an Archival Legislation Committee (ALC) by a Resolution of Ministry of Education in August 1959, under the Chairmanship of Dr. Tarachand, M.P, to examine inter alia, the condition of public records in India, problems of their ownership and custody, the need for legislation for governance, education and training, disposal and measures for protection of records of historical value in private custody.
8. Archival Legislation Committee Report, December 1960, NAI.paras 172-173(pp.101-102)

possibility of transforming the service into an All India Service. Promotion to higher positions should follow as they acquire experience.[9] The idea was to create a special archival cadre with not more than three ranks of Officers: Keeper (the Head of the Archives), Assistant Keepers (Senior), and Assistant Keepers (Junior). All recruitments to be made only at the level of Assistant Keeper (Junior). After selection, they were to be educated and trained in Archival Science at NAI for one year before getting posted in an archival repository. Regarding the question of, as recommended by the Committee, The government believed that constituting a Cadre of Archivists and Records Managers may be taken up if there is good progress in reorganising the Records Offices which was being done after Independence as an outcome of reorganisation of Provinces/States. However, the State Governments didn't support it and preferred universities for teaching archival science. Though attractive in principle, the government considered it premature and suggested re-examining after five years of successful working of records management in solving immediate problems.[10] But this never happened and the proposal got shelved.

UNESCO had conducted a global survey in 1979 on the required manpower of Archivists in different continents, particularly in the developing Third World countries including India, analysed by Dr Frank B Evans in his article, Indian Archival Training and the Archival Training Needs of Asia: Some Observations.[11] Evaluating India, he observes there is need of trained archivists in thousands, considering the factual

9. M/Edn. F. No. 6-13/59-A.10, copy of letter ref. F. No. 6-1/61-A-10. M/Edn., endorsed to Director of Archives, NAI.
10. F.No.4-4/70-C,p.45 (a-xii)
11. Indian Archives, July-December 1981, pp.4-5.

requirements in the Ministries/Departments of the Union and States Governments, their archives and other institutions, both in public and private sector and the emerging new archives.

Surprisingly, the ICA Directory of Archival Training Institutions included only three countries from Asia—Israel, China and Japan.[12] It didn't include SAS, NAI, which was reportedly meeting the archival training requirements of the Afro-Asia region at the time and was duly recognised by UNESCO in 1980. Dr Evans even records that between 1961 to 1979-80, 32 foreign students had joined SAS for training, and in 1979-80, 9 of the 21 enrolled students were foreign nationals.[13] Even they found the syllabus more comprehensive and attuned to international standards than the courses offered in many of the European countries at the time.[14] It is sad to note that Diploma of the School of Archival Studies is not being recognised by any Foreign University, like any other diploma or degree from a recognised university in India; a problem being faced by our students who join any university outside India.

Under the UNESCO Project, the NAI published 'Directory of Custodial Institutions having Records and Manuscripts in India' (1994) on guide to sources of Asian history. It helped in mapping institutions having records and manuscripts, newspapers, private papers, books, photographs and memorabilia to be scientifically preserved besides the need for trained manpower, though this has been very useful to the research scholars. However, this opportunity was not well utilised by the archival community in India to organise itself and develop a national policy focusing

---

12. https://www.ica.org, ICA Directory of Archival Education and Training, Compiled by FENG Huiling and WANG Jian, 2004.
13. Indian Archives, July-December 1981, pp.4-5.
14. The Indian Archives, Volume XXX, July-December 1981, number 2, p.6.

on standardising a policy on education and training in Archival Science, along with recruitment process and placement of trained archivists.[15]

It was noted that a major obstacles in the development of the NAI School has been the absence of an academic affiliation and accreditation for its programme with a university. The continued support was subject to fulfillment of its conditions and in particular affiliation with a University besides a full time faculty. The School reputation, the quality of its programme, and the absence of tuition fee had attracted trainees from neighbouring countries and increasingly from Africa. The UNESCO committee had observed that bodies like UPSC will not withdraw their acceptance of these qualifications in developing countries, and particularly India. An applicant should either possess an Archival Diploma or have 3-5 years of research work experience to be eligible to work as an Archivist in any public archival repository. Currently, a candidate should also possess a diploma or a certificate course in Computer Applications. Archivists coming with research experience from universities too have proved their worth without any formal professional archival training as their contribution is no less than any trained personnel. The UNESCO team had envisioned NAI Archival School to be located within the Department of Library and Information Science at the University of Delhi. However, this never materialised in spite of the best intent and efforts of the NAI.

Besides developing the infrastructure and course curriculum, a Fellowship scheme was also instituted by SAS, which worked

15. Now it has been updated by IGNCA under a UNESCO project in view of new emerging archives, 'Mapping of Libraries and Archival Institutions in India' launched in June 2023. Gaur. R.C. (Prof.) Mapping of the Archives in India, IGNCA-UNESCO publication, 2023

successfully from 1985-1991. The Fellows developed some teaching-learning material for the School, which are still used as important text books for the Courses in Conservation and Reprography, both in English and Hindi. In 2006 the curriculum was drastically revised at the instance of Board of Studies, introducing ICT (Information and Communication Technology) as a Core paper and two Specialisation papers on Business and Private archives and Library Science, Documentation and Information System. Further, a six-month Internship has also been introduced since 2010-11 session of the Diploma Course in Archives and Records Management. Full-time faculty is posted in SAS. The student intake has also been increased from 20 to 35, attracting meritorious students.

The only condition that NAI could not fulfill had been its university affiliation. In 2009, a Sub-Committee was constituted for the purpose, but the matter could not progress further due to some technical reasons[16]. The matter has been since revived by Ministry of Culture and has affiliated all the Training Institutes of Archaeology, Museums and SAS, NAI with the Indian Institute of Heritage and Conservation (a Deemed University) under the Ministry[17].

Archival science education in the universities is almost negligible in the country. There are Departments of Museology and Archaeology in many Central and State universities but there are no Department of Archival Science Education/Archival Studies. In every university's Department of History, as in Delhi University, they offer insights into archival science only through

16. F.N. 1-9/2009-SAS, Memo. Dt. 06.01.2010.

17. www.indiabudget.gov.in/doc/budget_speech.pdf.para.73.

MA and MPhil[18] courses in History. Even the faculty doesn't have any clarity regarding the subject. They view archives more as a historical research, than as an independent subject of study. Had this issue been addressed seriously even after submission of the Archival Legislation Committee Report in 1960, there would have been a well developed archival science education system, faculty, curriculum, training and future scope of employment, just like any other discipline.

The Library and Information Science courses in the universities include a component of Archival Science which only helps in understanding the basics of the subject. The Archival Science courses have emerged only from the Library Science courses, as in England. Though Libraries and Archives have some commonalities being centres of knowledge and information, facilitating research, they are two distinct institutions. Libraries are public places while archives have restricted access, despite their objectives being same. They differ in terms of their collections, arrangement methods, cataloguing, description of their collections and access. Libraries are centres of secondary published material in different formats whereas Archives are centres of primary source material.

Working in a Library or archives requires different qualifications. As per the UGC scheme, University Archives/ Archival Cells are a part of Central Library and the Archivists and their supporting staff is part of Library Cadre. Many Libraries are associated with Cultural Archives and manuscripts in the universities and other institutions with the understanding that a Librarian can handle them. However, very few Librarians have received formal training in both archival theory and practice. As per survey and personal interaction with Professors

18. Has been since discontinued by UGC.

and experts in Library and Information Science in universities, it is noted that Archivists working with such institutions are Master's in Library and Information Science or in History, with additional specialised training or a short course in Archives. This is another reason that the archives profession may at times appear wary of Librarians. As a result, Archivists may be sceptical of librarians who are in charge of managing archival collections without having proper training. The number of archivists is small in comparison to the Library professionals, leading to increased competitiveness for archives jobs as was reflected during interaction with the Archivists working in the University Archival Cell in Punjab University Chandigarh, Aligarh University, Jamia Millia Islamia, Banaras Hindu University, and Delhi University etc. Hence, there are very few good archives jobs available as no new positions are created separately. Librarians or Administrators are managing archival collections that, archivists feel, would be better managed by those trained to do so, the archivists themselves. The University Archives Cell could develop better as an independent entity, separated from Library, in collaboration with the Department of History, as Archival Cells are being overshadowed by the Library Department.

It's noted that no university made efforts to start an archival course due to lack of qualified faculty and resources helping the students wishing to opt for historical or archival research after their post-graduate studies, but attempted to introduce an optional paper on Archives Keeping at PG level in their Department of History[19] Willing to implement this, the Universities of Madras, Mysore, Osmania, and Saurashtra requested for syllabus and list

19. IHRC Proceedings, Aurangabad, January 1979, p. 106, NAI Annual Report, Feb. 1987, p. 156.

of books to consider introducing the paper.[20] The UGC has been providing financial assistance since Fourth Five Year Plan (1969-74) to all Central Universities to establish and develop their archives.[21] But these facilities had been located in the Central Library of the University and the posts sanctioned for the purpose are borne by the Library Cadre. The sanctioned staff included an Archivist, Chemist and other supporting staff besides Library equipments and chemicals. A Committee was also constituted to examine proposals received from Universities for establishing University Cell, like the few ones established subsequently as referred above.

Under the UGC scheme, a paper on Archives and Museums has been introduced since 2016 at undergraduate level and a specialisation paper on Studies of Archival Sciences at PG level in universities, as was noted in Department of History, Tumkur University, Bangalore. But the prescribed syllabus is very sketchy and needs to be revised. The only objective is to familiarise the students with the basic structure and functioning of Archives and Museums in India and inform them about these institutions to increase their employment opportunities. The syllabus emphasises more on Museums than Archives, whereas equal weightage should be given to both Museums and Archives with equal stress on theory and practicals, and Digital Archiving in the curriculum. After completing the study, it is expected that the students will be able to examine these two repositories of history from close quarters. Teaching should be introduced in modular form in consultation with SAS. Other Universities also need to introduce the subject study under UGC scheme, and

20. IHRC Proceedings Gujurat, 1982, pp. 86-88
21. NAI, File No. 22-2/1981 (H.E.-II) UGC , 1981

UGC needs to ensure that:

- Syllabus contents are upgraded,
- Equal importance is given to both Conventional and Electronic Records.
- University Archives/Cell is developed for practical purposes in modular form, collaborating with State repositories and archives like NCBS who have used innovative methods to evolve its own Archives by signing MoUs with foreign institutions to work more effectively.

SCTR, Jadavpur University, offers UGC approved 1-year PG Diploma Course in Digital Humanities and Cultural Informatics. Digital archiving is part of the curriculum. Anyone who has completed a Master's programme can join the course. They need to popularise the course to widen its scope of deployment of the trained personnel in Audio-visual/Sound archives in the country like All India Radio, Doordarshan and Television Archives, Multi-Media archives of various State Government and private channels, National Film Archives of India, Pune, Archives of Indian Music (AIM),Bangalore, and other private channels.

Some Observations and Recommendations

Having integrated courses of Libraries and Archives in such situations also needs to be considered. While teaching history at undergraduate and post-graduate level in the colleges and universities, there is already a hidden academic linkage with Archives, whereas formally they should sign MoUs with individual colleges for providing certificate courses. The UGC needs to make it mandatory to tie up with Archival repositories while providing financial support for professional courses, under CBCS (Credit based) programme. All state repositories need to follow practice of West Bengal State Archives, where they hold regular classes, teaching Archives Management for three months for all colleges in a year, along with practicals. It's noted that some foundational knowledge is being given through piecemeal courses, whereas they need to have formal integrated degree courses in Archival Science Education.

It is a well established fact that Archival Science is a technical-scientific subject of study like any other subject and is close to history, religious and family institutions, political science, business and management studies, contemporary history, international affairs, information and library science and more so scientific institutions because of emerging archives of scientific, medical institutions, corporate and business houses. The subject touches almost all the areas of education and development, including industry, labour, agriculture, applied sciences, multimedia, trade and commerce and more. It can be studied both as an independent subject of study and as an inter-disciplinary subject of study, much like the west and China in particular. In India, Jamia University in Delhi has started one-year PG Diploma in Preservation, Conservation and Digitisation in Library and Archives from academic year 2023-2024.

The concept of GLAM, (a combination of Gallery, Library, Archive and Museums) needs to be implemented with integration of resources and services of these cultural institutions to provide access to knowledge, as they collect and maintain cultural heritage materials in the public interest. Though they are four distinct cultural institutions, they are equally centres of knowledge and information. They might differ in their collections, policies, vision and mission but can work closely in common areas of preservation, conservation, and access to information through ICT. So far the concept of GLAM has been used only in providing access to information but not in terms of integrated education for the workforce required to work in these cultural institutions.

In India, the GLAM project study has been implemented in Maharashtra on mapping the digital transition in selected Galleries, Libraries, Archives and Museums (GLAM). The short study explores the possibilities and challenges for collaborations with Wikimedia projects.[22] However, the study is silent on collaboration of Education and Training among GLAM institutions.(Kulkarni, 2019-20) Hence the need to adopt a multidisciplinary integrated approach for promoting archival science education. International organisations for culture IFLA (Library), ICA (Archive), ICOM (Museums), ICOMOS (Monument and Sites) and CCAAA (archive audio-visual)—they all have a long cooperative relationship as library, archive, museum, monument, and sites have common interests and activities. But, India lacks collaboration in Education and Training in the discipline of Archival Science. (Cahyaningtyas, 2017, p. 7)

Earlier, the focus had been on taking care of archival material, but new technology have added new dimensions of digitisation and various related issues, necessitating adoption of new innovative ideas and approaches in real Archival Science Education. The future archivists need to learn digitisation and digital archiving as many of digital archival sources are to be preserved for posterity.

Archival science education needs to be popularised to increase its demand as a discipline in view of emerging new institutional archives in public, corporate and private sector. The field has enough scope for the Archivists to join as a profession, offering them a good career which is not only challenging but is equally professionally and financially rewarding nationally and internationally. Archival

---

22. http://timesofindia.indiatimes.com/articleshow/77075283.cms?utm_source=contentofinterestandutm_medium=textandutm_campaign=cppst

science education also helps in preserving and understanding the value of documentary heritage of the country as Archives are the authentic valuable source of information.

The primary task of an archivist is to understand that cataloguing and accessioning in archives require a different approach for audio-visual material, photographs, paintings, or textual and digital records than conventional. There are different ways of capturing Metadata manually. Hence, the different needs, standards for cataloguing and accessioning are to be understood by one who would like to become an Archivist.

One of the challenges of modern day is Digitisation and Digital Archiving. There are different kinds of archives in the country and most of them are in bad state. There are no properly trained archivists to look after them and there are no positions even in universities. With the existing archival education model, we are unable to produce competent and professional archivists.

A very pertinent question was raised by Godrej Archives —how the Indian Archival courses differ from those in other foreign countries. Their Archivists are successfully working in Corporate, Personal, Business or Government archives but ours are not. So what works for them but doesn't work for our courses? The reasons are not far to seek. There is no uniformity in the curriculum followed by Archival Training Schools, nor are there any degree courses. There is no uniformity in the recruitment in any archival repository with the exception of government repositories. Moreover, there is no certification/regulatory body for authorising an Archivist as in Medical and other services.

Conclusion

A fresh look is required to understand and prepare a blue print with the help of experts working and contributing in the field.

Though there are several archival groups and associations, they are scattered. They should come together and work closely through social media. Universities must promote integrated courses at undergraduate and PG level and make the profession of an Archivist more lucrative.

We need to revisit in the structure of the curriculum offered by our ongoing archival teaching institutions, including the new emerging models/modules of archival training adopted internationally. Universities, like the Universities of Dundee, offer online distance learning courses like Master's in Archives and Records Management with Digital Preservation. Archival professionals need to use ICA online courses to fulfill their education needs. Though little expensive, are very useful for those in the profession as happily some have joined. As per the findings of the ICA study to find out the Training Needs of its member countries by a Survey conducted in August 2017, it is noted that highest demand was for digital-related training, getting due emphasis in our courses. (Archives, 2017, p. 14)

These are job-oriented courses with good scope of employment. However, they are yet to be fully explored in the light of emerging new archives in all the public and private sector as it's still evolving. Another area which requires our attention is international cooperation, and the benefits that we can draw from ICA, SWARBICA and UNESCO. Things are changing for good as teaching Archival Science at undergraduate and postgraduate level has started under UGC scheme since 2016. Diploma courses at PG level have been introduced by universities of Jamia, Kurukshetra in Archives and Records Management and Conservation and digitalisation of Archival and Library material. Banaras Hindu University has already introduced a 2-year Postgraduate Degree course.

Participation of Indian Archivists in international events and activities of ICA and its regional branch SWARBICA have increased significantly during the past decade. Efforts are being made to form such community groups to promote archival programs in the country through some studies, as done recently with the financial support of ICA. Hence we can hope for a good future.

List of Appendices

ANNEXURE-1*

Schedule of Courses as Introduced in 1946

1. Archival Administration (Six Months)

(A) Principles-

- Definition of Archives- archives, documents and historical manuscripts, nomenclatures.
- Evolution of Archives- Archives originating bodies and problems relating to them.
- Classification- Public, Private and semi-public archives, Central and Local archives, Business and Institutional archives, active and dead archives, current and non-current files.
- Problems of Custody- concentration of Records and connected matters.
- The Archivist: i) his duties towards past Records a) physical defence-problem of Repositories, Filing, packing and shelving,

b) moral defence- reception, accessioning, numbering, labeling, alteration of reference, archival arrangement-principle of 'fonds',

* IHRC Proceedings, XXIII Session, Part I, p. 156, 20 December 1946, Indore, Appendix-H

'Provenance', and registry-main and subsidiary series–'ordre primitif' and *'pièces isolées'*–'generaha' and artificial collections–transcripts, misplaced and missing records–Special types of archives, weeding, cataloguing and inventory making, transcribing,

c) Servicing- the archivist and the administration–the archivist and the public–supply of requisitions–Organisation of reference service–compilation of reference mediums.

d) (A) Editing and publishing (ii) duties towards the archives of the future–archives making, filing technique–control of overproduction of documents.

(B) History of Archives Administration and archival practices in India and abroad.

(C) Practical training in archives administration and utilisation of Historical materials.

II. Preservation of Archives (Six Months)

2. Theoretical study of modern methods of storage, Repair and Preservation:-
   a) Preservation of Paper Records–materials and process of manufacture–retarding natural ageing–other causes of paper deterioration.
   b) Effects of light and dust and atmospheric impurities and record materials
   c) Good House Keeping, ie dusting, etc. and use of insect repellent in the stack areas
   d) Archives buildings, boxing, shelving and office equipment
   e) Air-conditioning of archives buildings
   f) Specifications for writing paper of maximum purity for permanent records

g) Inks- composition, etc., its effect on paper
h) Repairing of Palm leaf manuscripts
i) Repairing materials, comparative prices and costing of repair jobs
j) Photographic reproduction-1) Microfilming 2) Enlarging 3) Reading 4) Density measurements 5) Processing 6) Use of filters 7) Special techniques 8) Splicing 9) Storage 10) Editing and Indexing of Films

3. Repair of loose papers:-(1) Vacuum Fumigation (2) Air cleaning (3) Humidifying (in humidification chamber) (4) Flattening (5) Washing and Stain removal (6) Methods of reinforcing paper a) Minor Repairs b) Repairing with Japanese tissue c) Chiffoning d) Inlaying e) Mounting or full pasting f) Sizing g) Laminating, ie Repairing with transparent sheets without adhesive h) skilled Lamination i) Half-margin repairing.

4. Binding and Preservation and Repair of bindings:-1) Guarding 2) Guarding of laminated sheets 3) Gathering 4) binding-leather, paper and cloth binding 5) Application of leather preservative mixture.

5. Special Problems-1) Repair of maps and charts, 2) Charred and discolored Records, 3) Water-soaked Records, 4) Preserving seals, 5) Treatment of faded documents, a) Chemical Methods of reviving writing, b) Physical Methods, c) Examination of Documents, 6) Foxing and treatment of mildewed Records, 7)Fumigation of insect infested Records, 8) Testing of Repairing materials in the Chemical Laboratory-Testing of physical properties such as tensile strength, folding

endurance 9) Preparation of Dextrin paste.

III. Calendaring And Indexing (Three Months Each)

a) Calendaring-1. Principles- listing descriptive cataloguing, précis writing and Calendaring- different methods of Calendaring, collation and establishment of the texts, elimination of non-essential elements, identification of names, compilation of topographical biographical and historical notes, use of typographical conventions, preparation of introduction and special explanatory notes, chronology and conversion of dates ii) Practical training.

(b) Indexing- Theoretical- (i) General Principles of Indexing- Indexing of Records, arrangements- main entries and sub-entries, chronological, alphabetical and subject grouping of sub-entries, punctuation and spacing, typographical conventions, treatment personal and places names, subject Indexing, pitfalls in Indexing, editing (ii) Practical training.

IV. Librarianship (Six Months)

1. I. Classification:-
2. Theory and Rules (2) Nature and purpose of Classification (3) Principal Classification Schemes: their History (4) Critical Study Dewey Scheme of Classification (5) Colon Classification.
3. Practical Course in Classification
4. Cataloguing:-(1) Objects and purposes of Cataloguing (2) Forms and Kinds of Catalogue (3) Study of Anglo-American Rules for entries of various kinds.
5. Practical Course in Cataloguing
6. Library Organisation Administration and Routine Work :- (1) Principles of Library Planning (2) Arrangements of Furniture

(3) Fittings and Book Stock (4) Problems of Storage, etc., (5) Ordering and preparing Books for the Shelves (6) Administrative Records (7) Book Issue Methods and Restoration (8) Stock-Taking (9) Purposes and Functions of different types of Libraries (10) Office Routine.

7. Book-Selection, Bibliography and Reference Work:- (1) Theory of Book-Selection (2) Functions (3) Methods and Organisation for Book-Selection (4) Aids in Selection (5) Various forms of Bibliography (6) Examination of Books (7) Description of Books (8) Planning and Compilation of Bibliographies (9) Representative books on various subjects (10) Reference-Work (11) Lending Library Assistance (12) General Knowledge and Current Literary Information.

(Application form for admission to the Training in Archives Keeping in the Imperial Records Department)

To
The Director of Archives
Government of India,
New Delhi.

Sir,
I beg to apply for admission in the training course in Archives Keeping in the Imperial Records Department. I promise to comply with the rules and conditions in force there.

1. Name (in block letters)
2. Address (in full)
3. Educational Qualifications
4. Age
5. Profession
6. Domicile
7. Period of Training
8. Subjects
9. Recommended by
10. Signature and Date
11. Reason for exceptional case, if any

Not necessary in the cases of nominees of the provincial Governments, Indian States and Universities.

ANNEXURE-2*

An outline of Requirements for a Training School for Archivists (with Syllabus for the Course) under the British Records Association

By Hillary Jenkinson

1. **Aim–** To turn out trustworthy Archivists soundly versed in the principles of Archival Science, having reached one of certain agreed standards of proficiency in theory and practice of Archive work and with some actual experience of Archive Repositories and their Administration.
2. **Candidates–** The candidate for training should have an adequate educational background and in any case have preliminary qualifications in the appropriate subjects.
3. **Length of Training–** The course should take not less than one year, plus practical training at a Repository and in Repair

---

* IHRC Proceedings, XXIII Session, Part I, pp. 153-156, 20 December 1946, Indore, Appendix-H. The post and in that case the equivalent, e.g., two part-time Lecturers would have to be accepted. Summary of requirements for a small Experimental Repair Shop and School of Instruction. Accommodation and other details and list of items.

Work: but normally the length should be two years if Medieval Latin and French has to be learnt, plus the practical work.

4. **Syllabus of Course–** The Syllabus should include :
   - Paleography of English Archives: a) Medieval; and b) post-Medieval
   - Languages: - a) Latin (Medieval); b) French (Anglo-Norman); and c) English (16th and 17th centuries).
   - Transcription and Translation (Principles of and Practice in)
   - Outline of English Constitutional and Administrative History including local and Ecclesiastical Administration; and the Legal Basis of Records
   - Diplomatic of English Documents; including modern Documentary Form: main classes of Archives; Seals
   - Principles and Methods of Sorting, Listing and Indexing
   - Research Methods
   - Printing and Publishing of Archives; Methods of Reproduction, including Microphotography
   - Organisation and Administration of an Archive Office
   - Materials of Archives; Methods of Make up; Treatment of Mildew and Animal Pests; Storage
   - Archives of other countries, System and Organisation
   - Practical Work in a Repository: Training in Repair Work including Binding

The Course will include not only Lectures but also Visits and Demonstrations.

5. **Standards to be reached–** It is not suggested that the subjects enumerated above should necessarily be treated separately; or that the students should have detailed training in all. The extent to which they were dealt with would naturally vary and be governed by the special purposes of the course; some

requiring only a single lecture or even part of a lecture, while others would need all the time that could be given to them. To obtain a full Diploma, students should be required to show genuine proficiency in all: but a 'Pass' might be contemplated for students who displayed some knowledge of all subjects; and there would be definite provision for a Diploma (Second Class) for students who had not qualified in i. (a)and ii (a) and (b). In certain sections (notably xii) a Certificate from the Instructor or Demonstrator should replace examination.

6. **Accommodation–** It is presumed that the School would be attached to and housed in a college or university and would require in addition to the ordinary facilities open to all students, a Lecture Room, a Lecturer's Private Room and possibly accommodation for a Repair Shop.

7. **Administration–** There must be one full-time Lecturer,** who should also be a practical Archivist; and the occasional service of Special Experts would be required for the more technical subjects and possibly for those of History and Law. The special Lecturers would presumably be furnished for the most part from teaching staff of the college or university to which the School was attached. Extramural Demonstrations by members of the Public Records Office staff and other Institutions would also need to be provided. This represents what is ideally and ultimately required. But there might initially be some difficulty in filling.

8. **Scope–** The Training School Should aim to become a centre for information on all archives and Collections and Documents within its area as well as for Research in Technical questions of all kinds; and should offer opportunities for summary instruction in regard to Archives to various classes who have an incidental interest in such work- for example

the Clergy, Law Students, Clerks, Library and Museum Staff, etc. The latter object might be affected by public lectures and by allowing persons not entered for the whole (Diploma) course to attend certain parts of it.

9. **Finance**– Any School must ultimately form part of the organisation of an University or College, or be financed as such: but there are certain ways in which a special grant might be obtained to cover the initial cost of some parts of the School machinery** and give it an opportunity to demonstrate both its usefulness and its ability to be more or less self-supporting.
10. It is essential that all Plans and Procedure and should be pursued in the closest connection with the Public Records Office and the British Records Association and should conform to their standard of requirements.

** Notably those of a small Repair Centre; but other parts of the Scheme might also be covered.

ANNEXURE-3*

British Records Association

Draft Scheme for training Archivists and for an Experimental Repair Shop and School for Instruction–Introductory Note

At the Conference held in November 1941 the possibility of developing a Repair Service for English Archives was discussed and the question remitted to the Council for further consideration. There upon a Committee for this purpose was appointed and presented an Interim Report in 1942, sketching the possible lines of development as seen by the Committee. Owing to war time pre-occupation no further progress was made. In 1943 the Council of the Association decided to amalgamate certain of its Committees, including the one on a Repair Service etc. to form the Committee on Reconstruction, especially commending to it further investigations into the practical means of establishing a Repair Service.

The original Committee in its interim report had expressed the opinion that the question of facilities for Repair and Training

* IHRC Proceedings, XXIII Session, Part I, p. 156, 20 December 1946, Indore, Appendix-H.

in Repair Work could not in the long run be divorced from its proper setting in connection with Archival Science and the training of archivists, so that if the Repair Service were started first, of which it was quite in favor, it should be of flexible nature and capable of expansion to fit in with future developments in Archive training. (See Tenth Report of Council 1942, p. 5)

With this point in mind the Committee on Reconstruction made enquiries as to whether the Library Association training and that of the School of Librarianship at University College, London, were likely to be resumed and what possibilities there were of increasing the Archive side of the training in these courses. A further impetus was given when the Committee realised that it might be possible for facilities for training in Archival Science to be included in some of the post-War Plans under consideration by Universities and if such were the case some guidance from British Records Association as to what was required might be welcomed.

It was in response therefore to these promptings that the Committee felt bound to endeavor to put on paper a Scheme, however tentative, for training in Archival Science and linked with it, a Scheme for setting up an Experimental Repair Shop and School of Instruction.

The Schemes were submitted to Council with the recommendations that if the Council were able to agree in principle to the Schemes proposed, before plans were promulgated-steps should be taken to ascertain the opinion of bodies likely to be interested and in particular that of historians, and the matter then referred back to Council for further action to be taken.

ANNEXURE-4*

Schedule of Courses after Revision in 1952

I. Diploma in One Year's Course

(a) Archives Administration-4 months

(b) Preservation-4 months

(c) Calendaring and Indexing-4 months (two months each)

The major subjects under the above heads would be as under:

(a) Archives Administration

1. Accession-reception and moral defence
2. Servicing-the archivist and administration
3. Editing and Publishing
4. Duties towards the archives of the future-archives making, filing technique-control of over-production of Documents
5. Weeding of Records
6. Classification-Public, Private and semi-Public archives, Central and Local archives, Business and Institutional archives, active and dead archives, Current and non-Current Files

---

*** Ref. National Archives of India, 1948-1952, A Quinquennial Review, pp. 45-47. Schedule of Courses**

(b) Preservation

1. Methods of Repair, Rehabilitation and storage will be laid on the practical work. Mechanical processes of repair, cleaning, fumigation, and photo duplication to be touched upon in broad outlines.
2. Maintenance of Records
3. Enemies of Records-Precaution against white ants, insecticides, etc.
4. Storage

(c) Calendaring and Indexing

(1) Calendaring

(a) Principles, descriptive cataloguing, précis writing and calendaring-different methods of calendaring-collation and establishment of the texts, eliminating of non-essential elements, identification of names, compilation of topographical, biographical and historical notes, use of typographical Conventions, preparation of introduction and special explanatory notes, chronology and conversion of dates.

(2) Indexing

(a) General principles of Indexing-indexing of records, arrangements, main entries and sub-entries, chronological, alphabetical, and subject grouping of sub-entries, punctuation and spacing, typographical conventions, treatment of personal and place names, subject indexing, pitfalls in indexing, editing.

(3) Practical training.

II. Syllabus for Special Short Course for Three Months

(a) Archives Administration 1 Month

(b) Preservation of Archives 2 Months

(a) Archives Administration

(i) Theoretical

- Definition, evolution and classification of Archives
- Problems of custody and administration
- The duties of an Archivist

(ii) Practical

- Accessioning of Records
- Checking
- Listing (Lists of Records, Register of Lists)
- Arrangements (Series, Groups, etc.)
- Labeling, bundling, etc.
- Supply of requisition
- Restoration
- Reminder for outstanding papers
- Weeding

(b) Preservation of Archives

(i) Theoretical

- Causes of deterioration of records
- Maintenance of Records
- Repair of Records

(ii) Practical

- Cleaning of Records
- Stitching
- Flattening
- Minor repairs
- Repair with Japanese tissue and Chiffon
- Inlaying
- Mounting

- Repair of maps and charts
- Binding
- Application of Leather Preservative Mixture
- Preparation of dextrin paste
- Fumigation

ANNEXURE-5

The Aims and Objectives of SWARBICA as per the Constitution

1. To establish, maintain and strengthen relations between archivists of all countries in the region; and between all institutions, professional bodies and organisations which are concerned with the custody, organisation, administration or utilisation of archives, whether in public or private possessions;
2. To promote all measures for the preservation, protection and defence against all manners of hazards of the archival heritage of the region, and to further the progress of all aspects of the administration and conservation of these archives;
3. To promote and coordinate the efforts by the countries in the region with a view to completing the national archival heritage by appropriate methods;
4. To promote, organise and coordinate activities in the maintenance, utilisation and conservation of archives in the region;
5. To sponsor professional training of archivists in the region;
6. To cooperate with other organisations or institutions concerned with the use of that documentation for the benefit of mankind.

ANNEXURE-6

The Public Records Act, 1993
No 69 of 1993 (22 December 1993)

An Act to regulate the management, administration and preservation of public records of the Central Government, Union Territory Administrations, public sector undertakings, statutory bodies and corporations, commissions and committees constituted by the Central Government or a Union Territory Administration and matters connected therewith or incidental thereto. Be it enacted by Parliament in the Forty-fourth Year of the Republic of India as follows:-

1. This Act may be called the Public Records Act, 1993.
   - It shall come into force, on such date as the Central Government may, by notification in the Official Gazette, appoint

2. In this Act, unless the context otherwise requires, -
   a. 'Board' means the Archival Advisory Board constituted under sub-section (1) of section 13;
   b. 'Director General' means the Director General of Archives appointed by the Central Government and includes any

officer authorised by that Government to perform the duties of the Director General

c. 'head of the Archives' means a person holding the charge of the Archives of the Union Territory Administration;
d. 'prescribed' means prescribed by rules made under this Act;
e. 'public records' includes –
   - Any document, manuscript and file;
   - Any microfilm, microfiche and facsimile copy of a document;
   - Any reproduction of image or images embodied in such microfilm (whether enlarged or not); and
   - Any other material produced by a computer or by any other device, of any records creating agency;

f. 'records creating agency' includes, -
   - in relation to the Central Government, any ministry, department or office of that Government;
   - in relation to any statutory body or corporation wholly or substantially controlled or financed by the Central Government or commission or any committee constituted by that Government, the offices of the said body, corporation, commission or committee;
   - in relation to a Union Territory Administration, any department or office of that Administration;
   - in relation to any statutory body or corporation wholly or, substantially controlled or financed by Union Territory Administration or commission or any committee constituted by that Government, the offices of the said body, corporation, commission or committee;
g. 'records officer' means the officer nominated by the records creating agency under sub-section (1) of section 5.

3 (1) The Central Government shall have the power to coordinate, regulate and supervise the operations connected with the administration, management, preservation, selection, disposal and retirement of public records under this Act.

(2) The Central Government in relation to the public records of the records creating agencies specified in sub-clauses (i) and (ii) of clause (f) of section 2 and the Union Territory Administration in relation to the public records of the records creating agencies specified in sub-clauses (iii) and (iv) of the said clause, may, by order, authorise the Director General or the Head of the Archives, as the case may be, subject to such conditions as may be specified in the order, to carry out all or any of the following function, namely :-

a) supervision, management and control of the Archives;

b) acceptance for deposit of public records of permanent nature after such period as may be prescribed;

c) custody, use and withdrawal of public records;

d) arrangement, preservation and exhibition of public records;

e) preparation of inventories, indices, catalogues and other reference media of public records;

f) Analysing, developing, promoting and coordinating the standards, procedures and the techniques for improvement of records management system;

g) ensuring the maintenance, arrangement and security of public records in the Archives and in the offices of the records creating agency;

h) promoting utilisation of available space and maintenance of equipments for preserving public records;

i) tendering advice to records creating agencies on the compilation, classification and disposal of records and application of standards, procedures and techniques of records management;

j) survey and inspection of public records;
k) Organising training programs in various disciplines of Archives administration and records management;
l) accepting records from any private source;
m) regulating access to public records;
n) receiving records from defunct bodies and making arrangement for securing public records in the event of national emergency;
o) receiving reports on records management and disposal practices from the records officer;
(p) providing authenticated copies of, or extracts from, public records;
(q) destroying or disposal of public records;
(r) obtaining on lease or purchasing or accepting as gift any document of historical or national importance.

4. No person shall take or cause to be taken out of India any public records without the prior approval of the Central Government; provided that no such prior approval shall be required if any public records are taken or sent out of India for any official purpose.

5. (1) Every records creating agency shall nominate one of its officers as records officer to discharge the functions under this Act.

(2) Every records creating agency may set up such number of record rooms in such places as it deems fit and shall place each record room under the charge of a records officer.

6. (1) The records officer shall be responsible for –

a) proper arrangement, maintenance and preservation of public records under his charge;
b) periodical review of all public records and weeding out public records of ephemeral value;

c) appraisal of public records which are more than twenty-five years old in consultation with the National Archives of India or, as the case may be,the Archives of the Union territory with a view to retaining public records of permanent value;
d) destruction of public records in such manner and subject to such conditions as may be prescribed under sub-section (1) of section 8;
e) compilation of a schedule of retention for public records in consultation with the National Archives of India or, as the case may be, the Archives of the Union Territory;
f) periodical review for downgrading of classified public records in such manner as may be prescribed;
g) adoption of such standards, procedures and techniques as may be recommended from time to time by the National Archives of India for improvement of records management system and maintenance of security of public records;
h) compilation of annual indices of public records;
i) compilation of organisational history and annual supplement thereto;
j) assisting the National Archives of India or, as the case may be, the Archives of the Union Territory for public records management;
k) submission of annual report to the Director General or, as the case may be, head of the Archives in such manner as may be prescribed;
(l) transferring of records of any defunct body to the National Archives of India or the Archives of the Union Territory, as the case may be, for preservation.

(2) The records officer shall act under the direction of the Director General or, as the case may be, head of the Archives while discharging the responsibilities specified in sub-section (1).

7. (1) The records officer shall, in the event of any unauthorised removal, destruction, defacement or alteration of any public records under his charge, forthwith take appropriate action for the recovery or restoration of such public records.

(2) The records officer shall submit a report in writing to the Director General or, as the case may be, the head of the Archives without any delay on any information about any unauthorised removal, destruction, defacement or alteration of any public records under his charge and about the action initiated by him and shall take action as he may deem necessary subject to the directions, if any given by the Director General or, head of the Archives, as the case may be,

(3) The records officer may seek assistance from any government officer or any other person for the purpose of recovery or restoration of public records and such officer or person shall render all assistance to the records officer.

8. (1) Save as otherwise provided in any law for the time being in force, no public records shall be destroyed or otherwise disposed of excepts in such manner and subject to such conditions as may be prescribed.

(2) No record created before the year 1892 shall be destroyed except where in the opinion of the Director General or, as the case may be, the head of the Archives, it is so defaced or is in such condition that it cannot be put to any archival use.

9. Whoever contravenes any of the provisions of section 4 or section 8 shall be punishable with imprisonment for a term which may extend to five years or with fine which may extend to ten thousand rupees or with both.

10. No public records bearing security classification shall be transferred to the National Archives of India or the Archives of the Union territory.

11. (1) The National Archives of India or the Archives of the Union territory may accept any record of historical or national importance from any private source by way of gift, purchase or otherwise.

    (2) The National Archives of India or, as the case may be, the Archives of any Union Territory may, in such manner and subject to such conditions as may be prescribed, make any record referred to in sub-section (1) available to any bona fide research scholar.

12. (1) All unclassified public records as are more than thirty years old and are transferred to the National Archives of India or the Archives of the Union territory may be, subject to such exceptions and restrictions as may be prescribed made available to any bona fide research scholar.

Explanation:- For the purposes of this sub-section, the period of thirty years shall be reckoned from the year of the opening of the public record.

    (2) Any records creating agency may grant to any person access to any public record in its custody in such manner and subject to such conditions as may be prescribed.

13. (1) The Central Government may, by notification in the Official Gazette, constitute an Archival Advisory Board for the purposes of this Act.

(2) The Board shall consist of the following members, namely:-

a) Secretary to the Government of India in the Ministry of Central Government dealing with Culture

Chairman, ex-officio;

b) one officer not below the rank of Joint Secretary to the Government of India, each from the Cabinet Secretariat, Ministry of Home Affairs, Ministry of Defence, Ministry of External Affairs, Ministry of Finance and Ministry of Personnel, Public Grievances and Pension.

Members, ex-officio;

c) two representatives not below the rank of Joint Secretary in the Union Territory Administrations to be nominated by the Central Government.

Members;

d) three persons to be nominated by the Central Government for a period not exceeding three years, one being an Archivist and two being professors in the Post-graduate Department of History in any recognised University.

Members;

e) Director General of Archives.

Member- Secretary, ex-officio;

(3) The members nominated under clause (d) of sub-section (2) shall be paid such allowances as may be prescribed.

14. The Board shall perform the following functions, namely:-

(a) advise the Central Government and Union Territory

Administrations on matters concerning the administration, management, conservation and use of public records;

(b) lay down guidelines for training of Archivists;

(c) give directions for acquisition of records from private custody;

(d) deal with such other matters as may be prescribed.

15. The Director General shall have the power to lay down norms and standards for courses curricula, assessment and examinations relating to the training in archival Science and other ancillary subjects.

16. No suit, prosecution or other legal proceedings shall lie against any person in respect of anything which is in good faith done or intended to be done in pursuance of this Act or the rules made hereunder.

17. (1) The Central Government may, by notification in the Official Gazette, makes rules to carry out the provisions of this Act.

(2) In particular and without prejudice to the generality of the foregoing power, such rules may provide for all or any of the following matters, namely:-

(a) the period after which public records of permanent nature may be accepted under clause (b) of sub-section (2) of section 3;

(b) the manner in which and the conditions subject to which public records can be destroyed under clause (d) of sub-section (1) of section 6;

(c) the manner in which periodical review of classified public records for downgrading shall be undertaken under clause (f) of sub-section (1) of section 6;

(d) the manner in which the records officer will report to the

Director General or the head of the Archives under clause (k) of sub section (l) of section 6;

(e) the manner in which and the conditions subject to which public records may be destroyed or disposed of under sub-section (l) of section 8;

(f) the manner in which and the conditions subject to which records of historical or national importance may be made available to research scholars under sub-section (2) of section 11;

(g) exceptions and restrictions subject to which public records may be made available to a research scholar under sub-section (1) of section 12;

(h) the manner in which and the conditions subject to which any records creating agency may grant to any person access to public records in its custody sub-section (2) of section 12;

(i) the allowances payable to members of the Board under sub-section (3) of section 13;

(j) the matters with respect to which the Board may perform its functions under clause (d) of section 14;

(k) any other matter which is required to be, or may be, prescribed.

18. Every rule made under this Act shall be laid, as soon as may be after it is made, before each House of Parliament, while it is in session, for a total period of thirty days which may be comprised in one session or in two or more successive sessions, and if, before the expiry of the session immediately following the session or the successive sessions aforesaid, both Houses agree in making any modification in the rule or both Houses agree that the rule should not be made, the rule

shall thereafter have effect only in such modified form or be of no effect, as the case may be, so, however, that any such modification or annulment shall be without prejudice to the validity of anything previously done under that rule.

KL MOHANPURIA,
Secretary to the Government of India

ANNEXURE-7

One-Year Diploma Course in Archives and Records Management

School of Archival Studies conducts one-year Diploma Course in Archives and Records Management every year from November. Advertisements for this course are published every year in July-August. The applicants can also download the application forms from the National Archives website.

Duration: (One Year) November to October.

Objective: To train the candidates in various disciplines of Archival Studies, viz. Records Management, Conservation, Reprography and Information Sciences and to produce highly competent professionals in the field of Archives.

Eligibility: MA (History) second class with minimum 50 per cent marks in aggregate with one optional paper in Modern Indian History (post 1750 period) from a recognised University.

Or

MA in other streams of Social Sciences, such as Anthropology, Economics, Political Science, Sociology, Linguistics, etc., with minimum 50 per cent marks from a recognised University.

Or

MSc in Applied/Physical Sciences with minimum 50 per cent marks from a recognised University.

For sponsored candidates–10 seats, (from Indian State Archives and foreign countries)

For private candidates–25 Seats (from all disciplines, Out of 25 seats meant for private candidates, seats are reserved for SC/ST/OBC and especially abled candidates as per approved norms.

Medium of Instruction: English/Hindi.

Mode of Course: Regular (Full Time).

Age: Below 30 years for private candidates and below 50 years for sponsored candidates.

Selection: For 25 seats meant for Private Candidates, admission would be made through a written test followed by an interview. Admission is purely on merit basis. For sponsored candidates, there is no entrance test; they are admitted on the basis of sponsorship of the employer/department and recommendation of the Selection Committee.

Scholarship: Ten scholarships worth Rs 3000/month are awarded purely on the basis of merit. Six Stipends of Rs 1500/month are awarded to sponsored candidates.

Registration Fee: Application along with attested copies of educational qualification and registration fee of one-year diploma course is Rs 100 for Indian and SAARC countries and US$ 40 from foreign candidates (excluding SAARC countries) through crossed Indian Postal Orders/Bank Draft in favour of Administrative Officer, National Archives of India, Janpath, New Delhi-110001, be sent to the Director General of Archives, National Archives of India, Janpath, New Delhi-110001.

Sponsored candidates should apply through proper channel.

Course Fee: The course fee is Rs 1500 for both private and sponsored candidates, including SAARC countries, and US$ 4500 for foreign candidates, non-refundable, to be paid at the time of admission.

Boarding and Lodging: The School has no such facilities.

The prescribed application form may be downloaded from National Archives of India website (nationalarchives.nic.in).

How to Apply

- For admission to the different courses please write to:
- Director General of Archives
- National Archives of India (School of Archival Studies)
- Janpath, New Delhi-110001 (India)
- Phone: 091-011-23388557, 23383436
- Fax: 23384127
- Email: archives@nic.in(link sends e-mail)
  (9.30 am to 6.00 pm : Monday-Friday)

FORMAT OF APPLICATION

One-year diploma course in Archives and Records Management

1. Name of the Applicant ______________________________
2. Father's / Husband's Name ______________________________
3. Age and Date of Birth ______________________________
4. Postal address ______________________________
5. Telephone No ______________________________
6. E-Mail (Mandatory)______________________________
7. Permanent address______________________________
8. Name and address of the Sponsoring Department, if employed______________________________
9. Post held at present, if employed______________________________
10. Details of the crossed Indian Postal Order/ Demand Draft______________________________
11. Category: General/SC/ST/OBC/Person with disability (PH) ______________________________
12. Academic qualification (enclose attested copies of testimonials)

Examination Passed	Subject	Year of passing	Division	Percentage of marks	Name of University

Date------------- Signature of the Candidate

Signature and Seal of the Sponsoring Authority
Fax/Telephone No

Short-Term Courses

I. Archives Management

The course is planned to make the trainees aware of acquisition, arrangement, upkeep and retrieval of records.

Eligibility: Graduate in any discipline with minimum 50 per cent marks from a recognised university and should be below 30 years in age for private candidate, no age limit for sponsored candidate.

Duration: 6 weeks (session: February–March)

Application Fee: Rs 100 for candidates from India and SAARC countries and US$ 40.00 for other foreign trainees.

Course Fee: Rs 300 for Indian trainee and US$ 300 for foreign trainee (excluding SAARC countries)

Selection Procedure: Entirely on the basis of merit as per the above mentioned eligibility requirement.

Download Form

Will be available during active season.

II. Records Management

The course is to train the individual in creation, control and disposition of records.

Eligibility: Graduate in any discipline from a recognised university with minimum 50 per cent marks and should be below 30 years in age for private candidate, no age limit for sponsored candidate.

Duration: 4 weeks (May and September)

Application Fee: Rs 100 for Indian trainee and SAARC countries and US$ 40 for other foreign trainees.

Course Fee: Rs 200 for Indian trainees and US$ 200 for foreign trainee (excluding SAARC countries).

Selection Procedure: Entirely on the basis of merit (Marks basis) as per the above mentioned eligibility requirement.

Download Form

Will be available during active season.

III. Reprography (two sessions, each of 6 weeks duration)

The course is designed to train personnel in the process of reproduction of documents and manuscripts, in microfilming, handling of automated information storage, retrieval and dissemination.

Eligibility: Second class graduates from a recognised university, preferably in Science with minimum 50 per cent marks, and should be below 30 years in age for private candidate, no age limit for sponsored candidate.

Duration: 6 weeks (April-May and September-October)

Registration/Application Fee: Rs 100 for Indian candidate and US$ 40 for foreign candidate.

Course Fee: Rs 300 for Indian trainees and US$ 300 for foreign trainee (excluding SAARC countries)

Selection Procedure: Entirely on the basis of merit (Marks basis) as per the above mentioned eligibility requirement.

Download Form

Will be available during active season.

IV. Care and Conservation of Books, Manuscripts and Archives

The course is designed to train personnel in the scientific methods of conservation, repair, rehabilitation, storage and handling of documentary heritage.

Eligibility: Second class graduate from a recognised university with minimum 50 per cent marks, preferably in Science, and should be below 30 years in age for private candidate, no age limit for sponsored candidate.

Duration: 8 weeks (July-August and November-December)

Registration/Application Fee: Rs 100 for Indian candidate and US$ 40 for foreign candidate.

Course Fee: Rs 300 for Indian trainees and US$ 300 for foreign trainee.

Selection Procedure: Entirely on the basis of merit (Marks basis) as per the above mentioned eligibility requirement.

Download Form

Will be available during active season.

V. Servicing and Repair of Records

To train personnel in arrangement, supply, restoration and upkeep of records.

Eligibility: High School, knowledge of English/ Hindi, and should be below 50 years in age.

Duration: 6 weeks, Session: May-June and September-October.

Registration/Application Fee: - Rs 100 for Indian trainees and US$ 40 for foreign trainees (excluding SAARC countries).

Course Fee: Rs 300 for Indian trainees and US$ 300 for foreign trainees.

Selection Procedure: Entirely on the basis of merit (Marks basis) as per the above mentioned eligibility requirement.

Hostel Facilities: No hostel facility is available. The trainees are required to make their own arrangement for board and lodging. Pay and allowances of government sponsored candidates have to be borne by their own respective departments.

How to Apply: For admission to the different courses, please write to:

Director General of Archives National Archives of India (School of Archival Studies) Janpath, New Delhi-110001 (India) Phone: 091-011-23388557, 23383436

Fax: 23384127

Email: archives@nic.in(link sends e-mail)

(9.30 am to 6.00 pm : Monday-Friday)

Download Form – Will be available during active season.

ANNEXURE-8

Survey Questionnaire–I

Archival Science Education and Training in India - A Survey

Swami Vivekananda identified education as the 'manifestation of perfection already in man'. It is an essential ingredient for growth, wellbeing and continued development of any discipline and profession. So is the case of archival education and training in India like any other country—developed or developing. The aim of the present survey is to ascertain the present status of archival education and other educational training requirement of the institutions and profession in the country, based on the existing public archival repositories of Central/State Government Archives, Archives of Central/State Universities, and Institutions.

I. Institutional Information:

a. The administrative location of the archives- An independent/ autonomous organisation/Agency within the Union/State Govt, University, Institution, or part of the Library/any State historical Society.

b. Are the Archives responsible for collecting official records besides private and corporate historical records?

c. Bulk of archival records kept in the Institutions in cubic feet in addition to manuscripts and Private papers.
d. Do they have working professional archival staff/personnel with education and training having primary and other responsibilities for records, including regional record centres?
e. If the Repository is part/division of a larger institution:
    - Does the parent Institution recruit and determine the promotional criteria for archivists or are they different for Archivists with primary responsibilities?
    - The total staff strength in the Archives.

f. Salary range for entry-level professional Archivists. Do the Archivists with higher qualification get a higher start? If yes, then what is the level of difference, criteria/avenue determining further promotions, etc?
g. Number of entry-level professional archivists hired during the last five years.

II. Hiring of trained persons:

a. What are the minimum prescribed educational qualifications for recruitment in an entry-level archival position?
b. Does your organisation hire already trained personnel as archivists for professional archival positions? Are they usually able to do so?
c. What are the noticeable changes over the years regarding the availability of trained archivists? Please highlight the changes.
d. The people your organisation hires with training are generally trained: Within a University programme in the State/ Region/ University in another Region

Or

In another archival Institution or manuscripts collection in the State/Region

Or

In National/State or other Regional Archives.

e. Do these trained people, who come with some archival training, generally possess the basic skills and have proved to be effective officers in your institution with significant differences than those coming from University programs, etc. as referred above in 'd' from 1-5?

III. Providing training within your Institution:

a. To what degree has your present professional staff received their archival training within your institution? Is this in the process of changing? Did you provide such training by choice or because adequately trained people were not available or for some other reason? (For example, State personnel policies may have required you to transfer no archival State employees from other departments rather than to outsource them).

b. While hiring untrained personnel, what general backgrounds, or specific fields of training, have proved most useful or successful as preparation for archival work? Do you look for a similar background for those with professional archival training as well?

(The following questions may apply to new employees with archival training as well as to those with none.)

c. Do archival employees receive a general introduction to archival work and its various processes within your institution through a formal process, such as an internal workshop, or through some 'rotational' assignment of introduction to the several Departments? If so, does this occur at the beginning of their employment or at some other stage in their development as archivists? If not, do you believe such a programme would be valuable for new employees if it were feasible economically?

d. Do you train a new archival employee in his or her particular duties within your institution informally, usually in a kind of mentor system, or have you developed formal guidelines and policies for a more systematic 'apprenticeship' period of training?

IV. Post-appointment training outside your institution:

a. Are there local or regional professional development training opportunities available to your archival professional staff? Does your institution support such training through payment of workshop fees, professional leave, time to attend, etc? Who offers such training: a local university, a regional archival, other professional organisation, or some other institution?

b. Does your institution have the funds/wherewithal to send new (or even experienced) employees to national professional archival meetings, or training workshops sponsored by the National Archives of India, for additional training in archival work beyond that which you can provide for them?

c. Can archivists without a formal degree or a certificate from a formal educational programme work toward such a degree or certificate with the support of your institution through 'leave for education' policies, for instance? Would it be to their advantage within the wage or promotional structure of your institution to get such training?

d. What specific training/fillip do you most need from outside groups, and how successful have you been in finding such sources for training your staff?

Survey Questionnaire–II

Questions for the Universities/Institutions Conducting Courses in Archival Science–A Survey

- How long has been your institution offering courses on Archival Science?
- Since when have you started offering these courses?
- What are the different areas in which these courses are offered? What is the duration of this/these course/s?
- Who are the target groups of these courses?
- How do you treat the various Courses? Are they standalone, or are they part of any other discipline, such as History?
- Are these courses Diploma-based or Graduation-level ones? Are they recognised by the UGC?
- What are the basic qualifications needed for undertaking these courses? Is Modern Indian History a compulsory component for undertaking these courses?
- Which Papers are offered in these Courses?
- What are the syllabus contents of these Papers like? How have you formulated/devised these syllabi?
- How do you account for the conventional archival documents and the current e-documents as a part of your syllabus?
- What are the procedures for evaluating this syllabus content? Do you have any Practicals?
- Do you emphasise on Reprography and/or Conservation of documents?
- How do you account for the outreach of the Courses that you offer in your Institute?
- What is the normal intake of the students?
- What is the nature of the Faculty dealing with these Courses? Are they specialists, researchers, qualified archivists or Historians?

- Does your Faculty have any tie-up or association with other professional archives, such as the National Archives of India, State/Provincial Archives or any Business Archive?
- Do you have any regular or seasonal visiting Faculty?
- Do you conduct study visits or trainings?
- Do you provide scholarship to the students/trainees?
- Are these Courses job-oriented?
- Do you have a full-fledged Conservation Laboratory, Reprographic Unit, functional library, etc to complement and supplement various vistas of archival studies?
- Do you receive any funds from NAI or any State/Provincial Archives or any Business Archive in furtherance of your pursuit for propagating archival studies?

डॉ. प्रद्युम्न कुमार शर्मा
कुलसचिव
Dr. Praduman Kumar Sharma
Registrar
Tel: +91 11 23062795, 23011901
Fax: +91 11 23019821
E-mail: registrar.nmi@gov.in

भारत सरकार
संस्कृति मंत्रालय
राष्ट्रीय संग्रहालय संस्थान
जनपथ, नई दिल्ली – 110011, भारत

GOVERNMENT OF INDIA
MINISTRY OF CULTURE
NATIONAL MUSEUM INSTITUTE
JANPATH, NEW DELHI-110011, INDIA

F.No. ICHR -NMI/2018 1184

17th December, 2018

TO WHOM IT MAY CONCERN

It gives me a great pleasure to inform that **Dr. Meena Gautam** has got grant from the Indian Council of Historical Research, New Delhi for doing her project '***Archival Education in India – An All India Perspective***' for a period of two years with effect from March, 2018 and has been affiliated with the National Museum Institute (Deemed to be University), Ministry of Culture, Govt. of India, New Delhi.

For this project, Dr. Gautam has to visit various archives, documentation centres, universities and educational institutions to collect relevant datas and to study documentation records, etc. She has also to do surveys on the basis of questionnaires and interviews which has been prepared by her.

All concerned are kindly requested to extend all possible help and assistance to Dr.Gautam to complete her project work which is of a very prestigious nature for the country.

I wish her all the best.

17/12/2018

(Dr. Praduman Kuamr Sharma)
Registrar
Email: drpradumansharma@gmail.com
09811089042/ 011-3011901

REGISTRAR NMIHACM NEW DELHI

भारत सरकार
राष्ट्रीय अभिलेखागार
जनपथ, नई दिल्ली–110001
GOVERNMENT OF INDIA
NATIONAL ARCHIVES OF INDIA
JANPATH, NEW DELHI - 110001

DR. P.V. RAMESH, IAS
DIRECTOR GENERAL

125 वर्ष YEARS 1891-2016 राष्ट्रीय अभिलेखागार NATIONAL ARCHIVES OF INDIA

F.No.1-1/2019(Misc.)/DG Sectt. **Dated: 14th March 2019**

TO WHOM IT MAY CONCERN

This is to introduce Dr. Meena Gautam, formerly Head of the School of Archival Studies and Deputy Director of Archives and now Member of Archival Advisory Board, a statutory body of NAI. Currently she is the Project Director of the project, ***"Archival Education in India- An All India Perspective"***, a two year project, being funded by ICHR and affiliated to National Museum Institute (Deemed University), under Ministry of Culture, Government of India. National Archives of India is closely associated with the project by providing logistic support with the related research work and access to information available in reference to the project.

The objective of the project is to promote and advocate the study of Archival Science in the country as being one of the neglected areas of study. The project is an important area of study, with scope not only to promote archival education in the Universities and but also Archives as a profession in the country, keeping in view the upcoming archives both in public, private and corporate sector besides Union/States/UT Archives in the country.

Dr. Gautam, besides visiting archival institutions for collection of data, has to undertake surveys online/offline for collection of data on the basis of questionnaires and interviews as prepared by her. Besides NAI, all States/UT Archives and Universities Department of History and other educational institutions are requested to extend cooperation for the project study by actively participating in the survey and extend all help and support by providing necessary information.

I wish her all the best for the project.

Dr. P.V. Ramesh, IAS

फैक्स/FAX : 0091-11-23384127, 23383436 | ईमेल/E-mail : archives@nic.in | वेब/Website : www.nationalarchives.nic.in | पोर्टल/Portal : www.abhilekh-patal.in

Select Bibliography

Sources consulted and used: Although published documents are considered as secondary source of information but for the present study they are as good as primary sources as being selected for publications from the records by the government as a policy.

Primary Sources:

Hunter Commission Report of 1882.

ICA Guide to the Sources of Asian History, India, Vol 3.6, Directory of Custodial Institutions, compiled by NAI, Published under the auspices of UNESCO by NAI.

Indian Historical Records Commission Proceedings -1919-2013.

Indian Archives (January) 1947-2006.

Indian Historical Records Commission. A Retrospect 1919-1948, Calcutta, 1948.

National Archives of India, A Quinquennial Review, 1948-1952.

Proceedings of Board of Studies, School of Archival Studies, NAI, 1980 onwards.

Proceedings of Archival Advisory Board, a Statutory Body, constituted as per the provisions of Section 13(1) and (2) of Public Record Act of 1993. The first Board was constituted on 1st November 1995; vide notification of Gazette of India, Extraordinary, Part II,

Section 3, No 613. [No F. 16-2(a)/1994-RM].

Records of Home Dept Public Branch (1850-1920).

Records of Imperial Records Dept/NAI – 1891-1951.

Records of Departmental Record Room of NAI, 1950-2000.

Reports of Archival Legislation Committee 1960 chaired by Dr Tarachand.

Records Management Committee Report of 1975.

Report of the Secretary, Inter-University Board, 1942.

Selections from Educational Records 1840-1859 published by CBE (1922).

Secondary Sources:

Abulafia, David. *The Western Mediterranean Kingdoms: The Struggle for Dominion*. Longman, 1997.

AI-Suqri, Mohammed Nasser, Linda L Lillard, and Naifa Eid AI-Saleem. 'Information Access and Library User Needs in Developing Countries' *Oman: Sultan Qaboos University*, 2014.

Alegbeleye, Bunmi. 'The training of archivists in West Africa: history and trends' *The American Archivist* 46, no 3 (1983): 319-320.

Asongwa, B, and I Ezema. 'The challenges of preservation of archives and records in the electronic age' *PNLA Quarterly* 76, no. 3 (2012): 115-125.

Ballhatchet, K A (1962). India. National Archives: Fort William-India House correspondence and other contemporary papers relating thereto, thereto.(Indian Records Series) Vols I, II, vi, ix, XIII. Delhi: Manager of Publications, Government of India, for the National Archives of India, 1957–1960. Vol i: KK DATTA (ed.): 1748–1756. 23, xlix, 1160 pp, front, 14 plates. 1958. Rs. 32. Vol II: HN SINHA (ed): 1757–1759. Lii, 512 pp, front, 11 plates, 2 maps. 1957. Rs 19. Vol vi: BISHESHWAR PRASAD (ed): 1770–1772. lxii, 519. *Bulletin of the School of Oriental and African Studies*, 25(3), 655-656.

Basu, Aparna. 'Indian Higher Education: Colonialism and beyond' in *From dependence to autonomy*, pp 167-186. Springer, Dordrecht, 1989.

Begum, Bilkis, and Muhammad Mezbah-Ul-Islam. 'Developing a new academic discipline of archives and records management (ARM) in Bangladesh' *ATLANTI* 24, no 2 (2014): 119-128.

Bhattacharya, Sabyasachi. *Archiving the British Raj: History of the Archival Policy of the Government of India, with Selected Documents,* 1858–1947. Oxford University Press, 2018.

Bhange, Chinmayee. 'Digital libraries and digitisation issues' In *National Conference on Digitisation and Digital Preservation*, pp 45-49. 2008.

Bhargava, K D *Guide to the Records in the National Archives of India*. New Delhi: National Archives of India, 1959.

Boles, Frank, and Mark Greene. 'Et tu Schellenberg? Thoughts on the dagger of American appraisal theory' *The American Archivist* 59, no 3 (1996): 298-310.

Booms, Hans, Hermina Joldersma, and Richard Klumpenhouwer. 'Society and the formation of a documentary heritage: issues in the appraisal of archival sources' *Archivaria* (1987): 69-107.

Brewer, James C, Tracy Popp, and Joy M Perrin. 'REDDNET and digital preservation in the open cloud: research at Texas Tech University libraries on long-term archival storage' (2012).

Boles, Frank, and Mark Greene. 'Et tu Schellenberg? Thoughts on the dagger of American appraisal theory' *The American Archivist* 59, no 3 (1996): 298-310.

Burke, Frank G. 'The history of European Archives and the development of the Archival Profession in Europe' (1992).

Carbajal, Itza A, and Michelle Caswell. 'Critical Digital Archives: A Review from Archival Studies' *The American Historical Review* 126, no 3 (2021): 1102-1120.

Carmichael, Patrick. 'Research capacity building in education: The role of digital archives' *British Journal of Educational Studies* 59, no 3 (2011): 323-339.

Chavez, Robert, Anoop Kumar, and Nikolai Schwertner. 'Educational application - integration with digital repository' *In Proceedings of the 7th ACM/IEEE-CS joint conference on Digital libraries*, pp 476-476. 2007.

Crabtree, Jon, and Darrell Donakowski. *Building Relationships: a Foundation for Digital Archives*. Odom Institute, 2006.

Clough, G Wayne. *Best of both worlds: museums, libraries, and archives in the digital age*. Smithsonian Institution, 2013.

Cliggett, Lisa. 'Qualitative data archiving in the digital age: Strategies for data preservation and sharing' *The Qualitative Report* 18, no 24 (2013): 1.

Convery, Nicole. 'Information management, records management, knowledge management: The place of archives in a digital age' *The future of archives and recordkeeping: A reader. London*, 2010.

Cook, Terry. "CHR forum: The archive (s) is a foreign country: Historians, archivists, and the changing archival landscape' *Canadian Historical Review* 90, no 3 (2009): 497-534.

Cook, Terry, and Joan M Schwartz. 'Archives, records, and power: from (postmodern) theory to (archival) performance' *Archival science* 2, no 3 (2002): 171-185.

Crooks, Peter, and Timothy H Parsons, eds *Empires and bureaucracy in world history: from late antiquity to the Twentieth Century*. Cambridge University Press, 2016.

Crooks, Peter. 'Before Humpty Dumpty: the first English empire and the brittleness of bureaucracy, 1259–1453' *Empires and Bureaucracy in World History: From Late Antiquity to the Twentieth Century* (2016): 250-88.

Cox, Richard J. 'Graduate archival education in the United States; a personal reflection about its past and future' *Journal of Contemporary*

Archival Studies 2, no 1 (2015): 3.

Cox, Richard J. 'American archival history: its development, needs, and opportunities' *The American Archivist* 46, no 1 (1983): 31-41.

DeVivo, Filippo, Andrea Guidi, and Alessandro Silvestri. 'Archival transformations in early modern European history' *European History Quarterly* 46, no 3 (2016): 421-434.

De Vivo, Filippo, Andrea Guidi, and Alessandro Silvestri. 'Introduction to a course of study' *Archives and archivists in Italy between the Middle Ages and the Modern Age* (2015): 9-38.

De Vivo, Filippo. 'Ordering the archive in early modern Venice (1400–1650)' *Archival Science* 10, no 3 (2010): 231-248.

De Vivo, Filippo. 'Heart of the State, Place of Tension: The Archival Turn as seen from Venice (fifteenth-seventeenth century)' In *Annales. History, Social Sciences*, vol 68, no 3, pp 697-728. Cambridge University Press, 2013.

Dodd, Maya, and Venkat Srinivasan. 'Open access to archives, to support humanities research in India', 2021.

Dogra, R C. 'International Council of Archives: Guide to the sources of Asian history: India 3.1: National Archives, xi, 165 pp. New Delhi: National Archives of India, 1987' *Bulletin of the School of Oriental and African Studies* 54, no 1 (1991): 241-242.

Duchein, Michel. 'The history of European archives and the development of the archival profession in Europe' *The American Archivist* 55, no 1 (1992): 14-25.

Duranti, Luciana. 'Concepts and principles for the management of electronic records, or records management theory is archival diplomatics' *Records Management Journal* 9, no 3 (1999): 149-171.

Eastwood, Terry. 'Building archival knowledge and skills in the digital age' *Archival Science* 6, no 2 (2006): 163-170.

Enoch, Jessica, and Pamela Van Haitsma. 'Archival literacy: Reading the rhetoric of digital archives in the undergraduate classroom'

College Composition and Communication (2015): 216-242.

Erlandsson, Alf, and International Council on Archives. Committee on Electronic Records. *Electronic records management: a literature review.* Vol 10. Paris: International Council on Archives, 1997.

Eugenio Casanova, *Archaistic* (Siena 1928), 333–4.

Garg, Babita, and Salek Chand. 'Digital preservation', 2006.

Gautam, Meena. 'History of Archives and Archival Sciences from 1950 Onwards Based on Indian Practices' *Atlanti* 23, no 13 (2013): 135-147.

Gautam, Meena. 'Electronic records management: challenges and issues. A case study–National Archives of India' *Atlanti* 17, no 1 (2007): 63-73.

Gautam, Meena. 'University archives in India: issues, challenges and future trends, an analytical review' *Comma* 2018, no 1-2 (2018): 167-179.

Gautam, Meena. 'Source and Resources: Business Archives - Issues and problems ' *Imprese e Storia Journal*, 2010 issue. (Enterprises and History).

Gautam, Meena. 'Archival Education and Training in India - A Project Study ' *ATLANTI+Journal*, International Scientific Review for Contemporary Archival Theory and Practice, Trieste- Maribore 2020. (ISSN 2670-4560).

Gilbert, Catherine. 'Modern library technologies for data storage, retrieval and use', 2014: 67-68.

Given, Lisa M, and Lianne McTavish. 'What's old is new again: The re-convergence of libraries, archives, and museums in the digital age' *The Library Quarterly* 80, no 1 (2010): 7-32.

Ghose, Sailen. *Archives in India*: History and Assets. Firma KL Mukhopadhyay, 1963.

Ghosh, Maitrayee. 'Archives and e-Records Management in Canada: a state of the art report', 2010.

González, Pedro. 'Computerisation of the Archivo General de Indias: strategies and results, part II', 1999: 13-31.

Gupta, P R. 'The Bengal Record Manual 1943', 1943.

Habert, Benoit, and Claude Huc. 'Building together digital archives for research in social sciences and humanities' *Social science information* 49, no 3 (2010): 415-443.

Hamer, Alyssa. 'Ethics of Archival Practice: New Considerations in the Digital Age' *Archivaria* 85 (2018): 156-179.

Harriss, Gerald. 'Political Society and the growth of government in late medieval England' *Past and Present* 138 (1993): 28-57.

Hajtnik, Tatjana. 'Digital Age: Time To Transform of Public Archives' *Atlanti+* 29, no 2 (2019).

Harvey, P D A. 'Archives in Britain: Anarchy or policy?' *The American Archivist* 46, no 1 (1983): 22-30.

Head, Randolph. 'Knowing like a state: the transformation of political knowledge in Swiss archives, 1450–1770' *The Journal of Modern History* 75, no 4 (2003): 745-782.

Head, Randolph. 'Archival knowledge cultures in Europe, 1400–1900' *Archival Science* 10, no 3 (2010): 191-343.

Hedges, Mark, Tobias Blanke, Stella Fabiane, Gareth Knight, and Eric Liao. 'Sheer Curation of Experiments: Data, process, provenance' *Journal of Digital Information* 13, no 1 (2012).

Johare, Rusnah, and Hasnah Rahim. 'Preservation, access and technology challenges: Archives and records of 21st century', (2006): 522-528.

Katre, Dinesh. 'An Overview of Digital Preservation Considerations for Production of 'Preservable' e-Records: An Indian e-Government Case Study' *Preservation of Digital Objects* (2012): 134.

Katuu, Shadrack. 'Managing electronic records: an overview' *Information Development* 16, no 1 (2000): 34-36.

Kecskemeti, Charles. 'History and Archives (the Value of Primary

Sources)–Historians and Archivists (Enemies or Allies?)' *Atlanti* 19 (2009): 243-249.

Kemoni, Henry N. 'Management of electronic records: Review of empirical studies from the Eastern, Southern Africa Regional Branch of the International Council on Archives (ESARBICA) region' *Records Management Journal* (2009).

Ketelaar, Eric. 'Ten years of archival science' *Archival science* 10, no 4 (2010): 345-352.

Ketelaar, Eric. 'Archival turns and returns' *Studies of the Archive|| en Anne J Gilliland, Sue MacKemmishand Andrew Lau, Research in the archival multiverse. Australia: Monash University Publishing* (2017).

Klasinc, Peter Pavel. 'Compatibility Between Archival Processing of Born Digital Records and the Training of Archivists in the 21st Century' *Atlanti* 27, no 1 (2017): 45-49.

Kruse, Christian. 'All with one Aim in Mind: Cooperation at Federal Level in the Field of Digital Archiving' *Atlanti* 27, no 1 (2017): 125-131.

Kumar, Krishan, V Jeyaraj, and Ramesh C Gaur. 'India: libraries, archives and museums' *Encyclopedia of Library and Information Sciences. 3rd Edition. New York: Taylor and Francis* (2009): 2291-2329.

Kutay, Stephen. 'Advancing digital repository services for faculty primary research assets: An exploratory study' *The Journal of academic librarianship* 40, no 6 (2014): 642-649.

Lancaster, Joan C. 'The India Office Records and the India Office Library: the move to a new building' *Archives* 9, no 41 (1969): 2.

Lancaster, Joan C. 'The India Office Records' *Archives* 9, no 43 (1970): 130.

Lee, Alexander. 'How (and How Not) to Test Hypotheses with Archival Sources' (2015).

Lokke, Carl. 'Archives and the French Revolution' *The American Archivist* 31, no 1 (1968): 23-31.

Lytras, Miltiadis D, ed *Open Source for Knowledge and Learning*

Management: Strategies Beyond Tools: Strategies Beyond Tools. IGI Global, 2006.

Lewis, Stuart, Kim Shepherd, Yin Yin Latt, Andrea Schweer, and Adam Field. 'Repository as a Service (RaaS)' *Journal of Digital Information* 13, no 1 (2012).

Lokke, Carl. 'Archives and the French Revolution' *The American Archivist* 31, no 1 (1968): 23-31.

McCrank, Lawrence J. 'Documenting Reconquest and Reform: The Growth of Archives in the Medieval Crown of Aragon' *The American Archivist* (1993): 256-318.

McLeod, Julie. 'Electronic Records: A Workbook for Archivists. ICA Study 16. International Council on Archives' *Records Management Journal* 15, no 3 (2005).

Mikhail, Youssef, NohaAdly, and Magdy Nagi. 'Dar: A modern institutional repository with a scalability twist' *Journal of Digital Information* 13, no 1 (2012).

Mishra, J K, and Mange Ram. 'Digital Collections: Preservation and Problems', 2008.

Moideen, P S M. 'A Survey of Archives Relating to India and Located in Major Repositories in France and Great Britain', 1983.

Moss, William. 'Tibetan Archives: A Report from China' *The American Archivist* 59, no 3 (1996): 350-355.

Murphy, Hannah. 'Common Places and Private Spaces: Libraries, Record-Keeping and Orders of Information in Sixteenth-Century Medicine' *Past and Present* 230, no suppl_11 (2016): 253-268.

Mutero, Etiwel. *College and University Essays in Records and Library Management*. Booktango, 2015.

O'Toole, James M. 'Peter Burke, A Social History of Knowledge: From Gutenberg to Diderot; Daniel R Headrick, When Information Came of Age: Technologies of Knowledge in the Age of Reason and Revolution, 1700-1850' *Archival Science* 1, no 4 (2001): 387.

Ormrod, Mark. 'The English state and the Plantagenet empire, 1259-1360: A fiscal perspective' In *The Medieval State: Essays presented to James Campbell*, pp 197-214. Hambledon Press, 2000.

Pachauri, S K. 'Administration of Archives in India Down the Ages' *Indian Journal of Public Administration* 40, no 1 (1994): 63-72.

Pal, Anjana. 'Preservation and Management of Digital Resources: Strategies and Issues' *DIGITAL LIBRARIES: Reshaping Traditional Libraries into Next Generation Libraries* 1 (2014): 28.

Panitch, Judith. 'Liberty, equality, posterity? Some archival lessons from the case of the French Revolution' *The American Archivist* 59, no 1 (1996): 30-47.

Patra, Nihar K, *ed Progressive trends in electronic resource management in libraries*. IGI Global, 2013.

Patterson, Caitlin. 'Perceptions and understandings of archives in the digital age *The American Archivist* 79, no 2 (2016): 339-370.

Posner, Ernst. 'Some aspects of archival development since the French Revolution' *The American Archivist* 3, no 3 (1940): 159-172.

Povinelli, Elizabeth A. 'the woman on the other side of the wall: Archiving the otherwise in postcolonial digital archives' *differences* 22, no 1 (2011): 146-171.

Prasad, SN. 'Archives in India' *Archivaria* (1978): 52-60.

Prasad, Alok. 'Two decades of public records act (1993): A critical re-appraisal' In *Proceedings of the Indian History Congress*, vol 74, pp 1025-1033. Indian History Congress, 2013.

Prasad, Alok. Rs100 for Indian trainee and US$ 40 for foreign trainees. 'The Tarachand committee on archival legislation (1960) and its impact on archival policy in India' In *Proceedings of the Indian History Congress*, vol 75, pp 1370-1376. Indian History Congress, 2014.

Rahman, A, and S Tirmizi. 'Science and technology archives: A guide to records' *Science and Public Policy* 11, no 4 (1984): 243-245.

Ravindran, Jayaprabha. 'Liberalisation of access policy and

changing trends of research in the National Archives of India, 1947-2007' *Comma* 2013, no 2 (2013): 103-121.

Roy, S. 'The National Archives of India during 1947–1' *Historical Research* 23, no 68 (1950): 200-202.

Ryder, Arthur J. *The evolution of imperial government in Naples under Alfonso V of Aragon*, 1965.

Rybakou, Andrei. 'Management, Appraisal and Preservation of Electronic Records: the Belarusian Experience' *Atlanti* 25, no 1 (2015): 61-70.

Ruiz, Teofilo F. 'Thomas N Bisson, the Medieval Crown of Aragon: A Short History, Oxford, Oxford University Press, 1986, XII-239 p' In Annales. *History, Social Sciences*, vol 42, no 6, pp 1349-1350. Cambridge University Press, 1987.

Saha, Biswajit. 'Digital Archiving and Preservation: Present Scenario', 2006.

Sánchez-Lauro, Sixto. 'Producció científica de Jesús Lalinde Abadía: presentació sistemàtica de tota la seva *obra bibliogràfica i històrica' Revista de Dret Històric Català* (2009): 43-60.

Schwartz, Joan M, and Terry Cook. 'Archives, records, and power: The making of modern memory' *Archival science* 2, no 1 (2002): 1-19.

Seeger, Anthony, and Shubha Chaudhuri. 'Archives for the Future' *Global Perspectives on Audiovisual Archives in the 21st Century* (2004): 5.

Sewell, Claire. 'Revolutionising the development of library and information professionals: Planning for the future' *Library Management* (2015).

Seol, Moon-Won. 'Building participatory digital archives for documenting localities' *The Korean Journal of Archival Studies* 32 (2012): 3-44.

Seton, Rosemary. 'Guide to the Sources of Asian History. India 3.6: Directory of Custodial Institutions' *Archives and Records* 18, no 2 (1997): 222.

Shepard, Todd. "History Is Past Politics'? Archives, 'Tainted Evidence,' and the Return of the State' *The American Historical Review* 115, no 2 (2010): 474-483.

Singh, A R. *Information management in archives and libraries.* Aakar Books, 2001.

Singh. KP (ed) LIS Education, Pragmatic Paradigm Shift, 2022, printed and Published by Today and Tomorrow's Printers and Publishers. New Delhi.

Sinha, Tara Sharan. *Care and preservation of records in the Bihar State Archives as source materials for the study of modern Indian history.* Bihar State Archives Directorate, Cabinet Secretariat and Co-ordination Department, Government of Bihar, 1977.

Silvestri, Alessandro. 'Ruling from afar: government and information management in late medieval Sicily' *Journal of Medieval History* 42.3 (2016): 357-381.

Stacey, Robert C, John R Maddicott, and David M Palliser. 'The Medieval State: Essays Presented to James Campbell' (2000): 163-77.

Stoler, Ann Laura. *'Colonial archives and the arts of governance: on the content in the form' Refiguring the archive* (2002): 83-102.

Sundararaj, M. *A Manual of Archival systems and the World of Archives.* Siva Publications, 1999.

Tansley, Robert, Mick Bass, David Stuve, Margret Branschofsky, Daniel Chudnov, Greg McClellan, and MacKenzie Smith. 'The D Space institutional digital repository system: current functionality' In 2003 *Joint Conference on Digital Libraries, 2003. Proceedings*, pp 87-97. IEEE, 2003.

Tibbo, Helen R. 'On the nature and importance of archiving in the digital age' *Adv Comput.* 57 (2003): 1-67.

Tirmizi, Sayyid, Akbar Ali, Ibrahim Ali. *Guide to Records Relating to Science and Technology in the National Archives of India: A RAMP Study; General Information Programme and UISIST.* United Nations

Educational, Scientific and Cultural Organisation, 1982.

Tirmizi, Sayyid, Akbar Ali, Ibrahim Ali. *Indian Sources for African History: Guide to the Sources of the History of Africa and of the Indian Diaspora in the Basin of the Indian Ocean in the National Archives of India*. Vol 10. International Writers' Emporium, 1988.

Tramullas, Jesus, ed *Library Automation and OPAC 2.0: Information Access and Services in the 2.0 Landscape: Information Access and Services in the 2.0 Landscape*. IGI Global, 2012.

Tzoc, Elias. 'Document viewers for non-born-digital files in D Space' *Journal of Digital Information* 13, no 1 (2012).

Van Haitsma, Pamela. 'New Pedagogical Engagements with Archives: Student Inquiry and Composing in Digital Spaces' *College English* 78, no 1 (2015): 34-55.

Waddington, Simon, Richard Green, and Chris Awre. 'CLIF: Moving repositories upstream in the content lifecycle' *Journal of Digital Information* 13, no 1 (2012).

Walsham, Alexandra. 'The social history of the archive: record-keeping in early modern Europe' *Past and Present* 230, no suppl_11 (2016): 9-48.

Watts, John. *The making of polities: Europe, 1300–1500*. Cambridge University Press, 2009.

Wato, Richard. 'E-records readiness in the ESARBICA region: challenges and the way forward' *ESARBICA Journal* 25 (2006): 52.

Wato, Richard. 'Challenges of Archiving Electronic Records: The Imminent Danger of a Digital Dark Age' *ESARBICA Journal* 23 (2004): 82.

Wijesundara, Chiranthi, and Shigeo Sugimoto. 'Metadata model for organising digital archives of tangible and intangible cultural heritage, and linking cultural heritage information in digital space' *LIBRES: Library and Information Science Research Electronic Journal* 28, no 2 (2018): 58-80.

Wu-Wei, Chen. 'Digital heritage: Digital sculpting, cyber-archiving and education' In *SIGGRAPH ASIA 2016 Crafting Spirituality: A Pedagogic Project for Digital heritage: Digital Sculpting, Projection Mapping and Beyond*, pp 1-2. 2016.

Yeung, Timothy Chung Yin Au. 'The Gap between personal vs institutional digital archives of researchers' PhD diss., University of Calgary, 2010.

Yu, Shien-Chiang, Hsueh-hua Chen, and Huai-wen Chang. 'Building an open archive union catalog for digital archives' *The Electronic Library* (2005).

Yu, Shien-Chiang. 'The study of integrated frameworks for library and digital archives' *The Electronic Library* (2006).

Yusof, Zawiyah Mohammad. 'Managing Digital Information: The challenge with electronic records' *International Journal of Information Studies* 3, no 1 (2011): 1-8.

Zelenyj, Dan. 'Archivy Ad Portas: The Archives–Records Management Paradigm Re-visited in the Electronic Information Age' *Archivaria* (1999): 66-84.

Zhang, Jane. 'Archival Representation in the Digital Age' *Journal of Archival Organisation* 10, no 1 (2012): 45-68.

Online Sources:

https://www.statista.com- Internet penetration rate in India 2007-2021, published by Tanushree Basu Roy, June 9, 2022, site visited on 21 August, 2022.

The National Statistical Office (NSO), the Report on 'Household Social Consumption: Education' released in July 2020. Surveyed 1.13 lakh households spread across over 8,000 villages and 6,000 urban blocks between July 2017 and June 2018. The study involved 1.52 lakh students across different levels of study.

www.jmi.ac.in, Information regarding JMI Archives and Literary

Centre besides Historical profile of Jamia Millia Islamia.

www.jmi.in, Ordinances (Administrative/General), Part II, Ordinance No 36(XXXVI), for Records Management Policy of JMI and Preservation of various Records documents in the University.

www.jnu.ac.in, Annual Reports of Jawaharlal Nehru University for the years 2014-15, 2015-16, and 2016-17.